The Japanese High School

Japan's education system, like its economy, was long seen in Japan and elsewhere as the model of efficiency, discipline and high standards. In recent years, however, the model has collapsed. Classroom pressures mount, and incidents of bullying, suicide, 'dropout' and violence of one kind or another proliferate. The growing sense of educational crisis came to a head with the 1997 incident in which a child was murdered and decapitated, apparently by a fourteen-year-old student. When the child killer of Kobe claimed that he had been avenging himself against school which 'threatened his existence', many students were reported to have expressed understanding and support for his views. For large numbers of students in Japan, school has become a battlefield.

What is going on in the Japanese education system, and among its students? What does the crisis in the education system signify for the country's troubled economic and political systems? This book describes the Japanese high school as experienced by the students themselves: a perspective which has been largely ignored until now. Using comparative data from Japan and Australia, Shoko Yoneyama focuses on four main aspects of school life: student–teacher relationships, discipline and punishment, school rules and study. She discusses the relationship between these and the phenomena of *ijime* (group bullying) and *tōkōkyohi* (school phobia/refusal). *The Japanese High School* is an incisive and disturbing study which will be of great interest to those working in the fields of comparative education, Asian studies and sociology.

Shoko Yoneyama is Lecturer in Asian Studies at the University of Adelaide, Australia.

The Nissan Institute/Routledge Japanese Studies Series

Editorial Board

Other titles in the series:

Britain's Educational Reform: A Comparison with Japan
Michael Howarth

Language and the Modern State: The Reform of Written Japanese
Nanette Twine

Industrial Harmony in Modern Japan: The Intervention of a Tradition
W. Dean Kinzley

Japanese Science Fiction: A View of a Changing Society
Robert Matthew

The Japanese Numbers Game: The Use and Understanding of Numbers in Modern Japan
Thomas Crump

Ideology and Practice in Modern Japan
Edited by Roger Goodman and Kirsten Refsing

Technology and Industrial Development in Pre-war Japan
Yukiko Fukasaku

Japan's Early Parliaments 1890–1905
Andrew Fraser, R.H.P. Mason and Philip Mitchell

Japan's Foreign Aid Challenge
Alan Rix

Emperor Hirohito and Shōwa Japan
Stephen S. Large

Japan: Beyond the End of History
David Williams

Ceremony and Ritual in Japan: Religious Practices in an Industrialized Society
Edited by Jan van Bremen and D.P. Martinez

Understanding Japanese Society: Second Edition
Joy Hendry

The Fantastic in Modern Japanese Literature: The Subversion of Modernity
Susan J. Napier

Militarization and Demilitarization in Contemporary Japan
Glenn D. Hook

Growing a Japanese Science City: Communication in Scientific Research
James W. Dearing

Architecture and Authority in Japan
William H. Coaldrake

Women's *Gidayū* and the Japanese Theatre Tradition
A. Kimi Coaldrake

Democracy in Post-war Japan
Rikki Kersten

Treacherous Women of Imperial Japan
Hélène Bowen Raddeker

Japanese–German Business Relations
Akira Kudo

Japan, Race and Equality
Naoko Shimazu

Japan, Internationalism and the UN
Ronald Dore

Life in a Japanese Women's College
Brian J. McVeigh

On the Margins of Japanese Society
Carolyn S. Stevens

The Dynamics of Japan's Relations with Africa
Kweku Ampiah

The Right To Life in Japan
Noel Williams

The Nature of the Japanese State
Brian J. McVeigh

Society and the State in Inter-war Japan
Elise K. Tipton

Japanese–Soviet/Russian Relations since 1945
Kimie Hara

Green Politics in Japan
Lam Peng-Er

The Japanese High School: Silence and Resistance
Shoko Yoneyama

The Japanese High School
Silence and Resistance

Shoko Yoneyama

London and New York

First published 1999
by Routledge
11 New Fetter Lane, London EC4P 4EE

Simultaneously published in the USA and Canada
by Routledge
29 West 35th Street, New York, NY 10001

Reprinted 2001, 2002

Routledge is an imprint of the Taylor & Francis Group

Typeset in Baskerville by
J&L Composition Ltd, Filey, North Yorkshire
Printed and bound in Great Britain by
Selwood Printing Ltd, Burgess Hill, West Sussex

British Library Cataloguing in Publication Data
A catalogue record for this book is available
from the British Library

Library of Congress Cataloguing in Publication Data
Yoneyama, Shoko.
    The Japanese high school: silence and resistance/Shoko Yoneyama.
        p.   cm. – (The Nissan Institution/Routledge Japanese studies series)
    ‛ Includes bibliographical references (p.) and index.
    1. Education, Secondary – Japan.   2. Education, Secondary –
Australia.   3. High school students – Japan – Attitudes.   4. High
school students – Australia – Attitudes.   5. Teacher–student
relationships – Japan.   6. Teacher–student relationships – Australia.
7. Educational sociology – Japan.   8. Educational change – Japan.
I. Title. II. Series.
LA1316.Y67   1999
373.52–dc21   98-42020
                                                                              CIP

ISBN 0–415–15439–1 (hb)

To my parents

Contents

Figures and tables   xi
Series editor's preface   xiii
Acknowledgements   xvi
Notes on style   xviii
Abbreviations   xx

1 Japanese students in crisis   1

2 Methodology and comparative problems   18

PART I
Control: the structure of silence   59

3 Student–teacher relationships: the alienation paradigm   61

4 Discipline and punishment: dehumanisation   91

5 School rules: the web of regimentation   119

6 Achievement pressure and the meaning of study   133

PART II
Responses: conformity and resistance   155

7 *Ijime*: the price of super-conformity   157

8 *Tōkōkyohi*: burnout and resistance   186

9 Conclusion   242

Appendices   251
Glossary   261
Bibliography   264
Subject index   277
Name index   286

Figures and tables

Figures

1.1 The increasing 'problems' among students and teachers 15
2.1 Schools classified by the percentage of students wishing to go to university 34
3.1 Contrasting education paradigms of Japan and Australia 73
4.1 The number of Japanese teachers officially disciplined in relation to corporal punishment 97
8.1 The increase of *tōkōkyohi* students 187

Tables

1.1 Major events involving and affecting Japanese students 1983-98 11
2.1 The distribution of secondary students across different types of school in Japan and Australia 39
2.2 Percentages of female and male students in the sample within each type of school 40
2.3 Proportion of students' fathers with university qualifications 49
2.4 Proportion of students' fathers with lower secondary education only 50
2.5 Correlation matrix: social-class backgrounds of students and the prestige of school they attend 50
3.1 The hierarchy of teacher and student positions in Japanese schools 63
3.2 Comparative student–teacher relationships: the approachability of teachers 66
3.3 Comparative student–teacher relationships: teachers' respect, understanding, care and trust 70
3.4 Opposing paradigms of education 74

3.5 Comparative student–teacher relationships: unfair treatment by teachers   88

3.6 Comparative student–teacher relationships: derogatory treatment by teachers   89

5.1 School rules compared: 'sensible and based on good reason?'   120

5.2 School rules compared: 'rules are explained well?'   121

5.3 School rules compared: 'students participate in the making?'   126

6.1 Survey results: academic achievement pressure compared   134

6.2 Survey results: competition compared   135

6.3 Survey results: quantity of homework compared   135

6.4 Mean scores of 'academic achievement pressure' for different groups   136

6.5 Survey results: importance of tests and exams compared   137

6.6 Survey results: difficulty of school work compared   141

6.7 Survey results: relevance of school and learning compared   143

6.8 Mean scores of the 'meaninglessness of study' for different groups   152

6.9 Survey results: 'preparation for the future' compared   153

8.1 Types of discourse on *tōkōkyohi*   191

8.2 Analysis of the discourses on *tōkōkyohi*   192

8.3 The process and progression of *tōkōkyohi*   223

Series editor's preface

Japan, as the new century approaches, is going through a turbulent period in which some of her most entrenched institutions and practices are being increasingly questioned. The financial crisis which began in the latter half of 1997 – but whose origins go back several years earlier – gravely affected Japan, as well as other Asian countries. Quite apart from the economic and political implications of recession, widespread bankruptcies, increasing unemployment and a falling yen, the crisis is having a considerable impact on the psychology of ordinary Japanese people. They had been accustomed to steadily increasing prosperity and the international respect generated by the successes of their politico-economic model. Now, however, they were coming to wonder whether attitudes and ways of doing things that had been central to their lives and outlook over several decades were still appropriate to the disturbingly unstable world in which they now found themselves. One straw in the wind was a hugely popular soap opera aired on Fuji Television in the spring of 1998, entitled *Shomu 2* (General Affairs Section 2), in which a group of women office workers egotistically assert their rights as individuals and challenge time-honoured working practices. By challenging the prevailing atmosphere of inefficiency, refusal to face up to responsibilities, conformism, sexual harassment of women and mindless deference to hierarchy, this feisty group of 'office ladies' succeeds in saving the company from bankruptcy.

However much of a caricature the Fuji TV soap opera may be, it is symptomatic of a spreading sense that all is not right in what used to be seen as an unbeatable set of methods for running society. Grave though the crisis being faced by Japan was as the century approached its close, the impressive human and material resources that the country was still able to command were advantageous in the struggle to overcome the crisis. Whatever might be the outcome at the economic level, however, a troubling intellectual problem remained. Few could doubt that radical reform was needed, but if this reform was simply to be a case of conformity with the norms of an America-centred global economy (following the principles of the free market and egotistical individualism), where did that leave the status of Japanese values? History suggested that simple acceptance of foreign models was an unlikely outcome, and that ultimately a creative solution might emerge, mixing external with indigenous elements. To follow this process over the coming years should be an intriguing task.

The Nissan Institute/Routledge Japanese Studies Series seeks to foster an informed and balanced, but not uncritical, understanding of Japan. One aim of the series is to show the depth and variety of Japanese institutions, practices and ideas. Another is, by using comparisons, to see what lessons, positive or negative, may be drawn for other countries. The tendency in commentary on Japan to resort to outdated, ill-informed or sensational stereotypes still remains, and needs to be combated.

This book is a sobering account of the Japanese school system, concentrating on high schools. Dr Yoneyama makes a bleak assessment of the way the democratic ideas of education put forward in the 1940s and 1950s have been subverted through the imposition of authoritarian hierarchies and a plethora of stultifying rules and regulations. She takes issue with functionalist analyses of Japanese education that concentrate on the role the education system has played in the 'economic miracle', and advances a critique that focuses on the alienating effects of the way schools actually operate, upon the morale, intellectual development and mental health of many pupils. Given that all school systems suffer from dysfunctional characteristics to a greater or lesser degree, she introduces comparative data on educational practice in Australia, seen as typical of Western-style liberal education systems. From this she is able to highlight the apparent atypicality of much Japanese educational practice in its degree of regimentation of school-children.

In the latter part of the book she enters into a detailed analysis – citing many intriguing accounts by children themselves – of two disturbing phenomena that have occasioned great controversy in Japan in recent years: bullying and truancy. Disagreeing with some Japanese observers who are inclined to attribute these problems to bad family relationships or to the fault of the children themselves, she argues eloquently that they stem rather from the authoritarian atmosphere of many schools, where corporal punishment is routine, the workload overwhelming and petty regulations ubiquitous. She also controversially suspects that the system has now become so dysfunctional that it is facing collapse, and that the educational ideas of the immediate post-war period are ripe for revival. However this may be, Dr Yoneyama has written a book that challenges in the most forthright manner those who see in Japanese education a panacea for educational under-performance and indiscipline in other parts of the world.

J. A. A. Stockwin
Director, Nissan Institute of Japanese Studies
University of Oxford

Acknowledgements

Writing this acknowledgement marks the end of a project on which I have been engaged for a number of years. There are no words to express adequately my gratitude towards all who have helped me along the way.

My rather selective but heartfelt thanks should go first to the supervisors of my doctoral thesis, Dr Rosemarie Otto and Professor Yoshio Sugimoto, from whom I learnt a great deal about the sociological way of thinking at La Trobe University, Melbourne, during my formative years in Australia. Without their sustained support and scholarly terms, I would not have been able to formulate in sociological language, the many questions born from my experience of the Japanese education system.

Over 2,500 students in Japan and Australia responded to my survey, and a large number of teachers assisted me with the data collection, which provided the foundation for thinking about schools in Japan and Australia. Many others helped me in establishing contacts with schools, and even though I cannot thank them individually, I appreciate their help very much.

I am most grateful for the opportunity provided by the Research School of Pacific and Asian Studies, the Australian National University, Canberra, in 1997. The bulk of the writing was done while I was in Canberra, and I am thankful to the Heads of the Division of Pacific and Asian History, Professors Mark Elvin and Tessa Morris-Suzuki, for their understanding and encouragement. My special thanks to Professor Gavan McCormack for his critical comments and valuable suggestions on my manuscript. From him, I learnt a great deal about writing itself. I would like to thank other staff members and fellow researchers there for their assistance and friendliness, especially Ms Chienwei Yeh, Ms Dorothy McIntosh, Ms Marion Weeks, Ms Julie Gordon, Ms Jude Shanahan, and Ms Oanh Collins.

My sincere thanks to my colleagues at the University of Adelaide for their continuing support. Dr Hélène Bowen Raddeker patiently responded to my queries about English expressions on numerous occasions over the years. Ms Naomi Aoki and Ms Kayoko Enomoto helped me in many ways and gave me consistent moral support. Professor Martin Williams encouraged me to write this book. Professors Andrew Watson and Purnendra Jain made possible my secondment to ANU. Ms Jenny Dorsett and Ms Michelle Matthews also assisted me with all the business which needed to be done while I was away. Finally, I should acknowledge my indebtedness to the University of Adelaide for its support through research grants in 1995–6.

I would also like to express my appreciation to the editors of *Kodomotachi ga kataru tōkōkyohi* [*Tōkōkyohi* discussed by children], Dr Ishikawa Norihiko, Ms Uchida Ryōko, and Mr Yamashita Eizaburō as well as the Director of Seori shobō, Mr Itō Masanori, for giving me permission to reproduce substantial parts of the book. Naturally, to the children themselves I express by heartfelt gratitude. I also thank Ms Victoria Smith, Senior Editor of Routledge, and her anonymous specialist reader, who were so encouraging from the very early stage of this book project.

I should not forget to thank Professor Trevor Matthews of Sydney University and Professor Emeritus Kachi Keiko of Tsuda College who enabled me to begin my academic life in Australia under the Australian Government Postgraduate Scholarship for Australian Studies Program. I am most grateful for the incredible opportunity they provided me.

Cover artwork, by Sohmei Endoh, was first published in Kodoma ga abunai [children in crisis], a special edition of *Asahi Shinbun*, 1st November 1997. It is reproduced here by kind permission of *Asahi Shinbun*.

Last but not least, my sincere thanks to my family and close friends for their unfailing and loving support over the years.

Adelaide
December 1998

Notes on style

Japanese names are given in Japanese style, i.e. family name first, except for the cases where to refer to the person in English style is well established in the English-speaking world. Uncertainty may be resolved by reference to the index where all persons named in the text are listed in alphabetical order according to their family names.

School students who are referred to in the text are cited first by their name in full, and subsequently by their given name. Students who answered my survey have been referred to by fictitious names. In the case of Australian students, care has been taken to use names reflecting the diversity of ethnic background, but no necessary connection should be assumed between the name and the view quoted. In other words, the fact that a particular statement is attributed to a student whose name suggests a certain ethnic background should not be taken as implying that it represents the opinion of that particular group.

Quotations of the words of Japanese students were translated by myself. Words of Australian students were quoted directly, without changing grammatical and other errors. Only when there might be a problem of clarity due to a spelling error, the correct spelling is shown in square brackets.

On a number of occasions, the book refers to cases in which students were injured or sometimes lost their lives. With much hesitation, I decided to use the real names of such victims. This is partly because their names have already been widely reported in the Japanese media, but also because, although it might be painful to see the actual names of the victims, they should not stay anonymous. It seemed important that by referring to the name of each victim, readers see her or him as a real person, not just as 'a student'.

The book contains perhaps slightly more Japanese words than usually expected.

The word '*ijime*' has been preserved in the text because it has some specific features which distinguish it from the English word 'bullying' (see

Chapter 7). Where the context requires use of the word as a verb, however, 'bully' has been used, rather than the Japanese '*ijimeru*', in order to avoid unnecessary confusion caused by Japanese grammar. The word 'a bully/ bullies' has also been used to refer to those engaged in the act of either 'bullying' or '*ijime*'. The word '*tōkōkyohi*' has also been preserved in the text because it too has some specific features which distinguish it from the English words 'school refusal' or 'school phobia' (see Chapters 2 and 8).

Apart from these, Japanese words are either used or referred to when I regard them as key words in the Japanese discourse of education or when the Japanese expression carries a special nuance which is difficult to translate in full into English. In order to avoid flooding the text with too many Japanese words, in principle, only the English translation of the names of Japanese organisations and the titles of Japanese publications are mentioned in the text. Some are official translations but others are my own translation, in which case researchers are encouraged to check the original Japanese names and titles by referring to the Bibliography, Glossary and Index before embarking on, for instance, an Internet search. In order to allow readers to find the original Japanese words, the Glossary and Index contain some Japanese words even when only the translation appears in the text.

'High School', used as part of the name of a particular school in Japan, means Senior High School (*kōkō* or *kōtōgakkō*) unless it is written 'Junior High School' in which case the Japanese *chūgakkō* is indicated. In Australia, 'government school' means 'state school' or 'non-private school'.

Unless otherwise specified, all quotations of works published in Japanese are translated by myself.

Abbreviations

ABS	The Australian Bureau of Statistics
ACT	Australian Capital Territory
ANEN	Asahi Newspaper E(lectronic)-News
AS	*Asahi Shinbun*
CAE	College of Advanced Education
DY	*Daily Yomiuri*
ME	Ministry of Education (Science, Sports and Culture)
NSW	New South Wales
NT	Northern Territory
PE	Physical education
QLD	Queensland
SA	South Australia
TA	Tasmania
TAFE	Technical and Further Education
VIC	Victoria
WA	Western Australia

1 Japanese students in crisis

Are you not trying to erase my existence?

(School killer, Kobe, June 1997)

THE 'SCHOOL KILLER' IN KOBE

The ghastly murder by a 14-year-old 'school killer' of 11-year-old Hase Jun, whose severed head with mutilated eyelids and mouth was found at the school gate of Tomogaoka Junior High School in Kobe one morning in May 1997, shook Japanese society with a magnitude comparable, in the anxiety it caused, to the earthquake which hit the same city two years earlier. It had such an impact upon the people not only because the atrocity was perpetrated by such a young schoolboy, but also because a number of individuals, adults and children alike, found peculiar closeness between this extraordinary incident and their own lives, and thus it struck a responsive chord in their hearts. Unlike the catastrophe caused by the earthquake, there was something familiar, everyday-life like, and therefore directly threatening in this seemingly unusual murder case. It stirred general uneasiness regarding the way life is lived in school, family and society at large.

At the beginning, it was apparent that the crime was somehow connected to school. 'School killer' was the name the murderer called himself in the note stuck in the mouth of the victim, which read:

Now the game begins. Try and stop me, you thickheaded cops! I can't help but enjoy killing. I want nothing more than to see a person die. Exact the sanction of death on dirty vegetables. Shall my long-standing grudge be settled by the flow of blood [?]

(Shool [sic] killer, Sakakibara Seito: *DY* 29 June 1997)

In the letter he sent to the *Kobe Shinbun* one week later, the 'school killer' reaffirmed the connection between his crime and school. Writing that he had an 'especially strong attachment to his existence', he used the word 'existence' as many as eight times in his one-page letter (Kuroda *et al.* 1997: 19). He stated, however, that his existence had been reduced to that of an invisible being, and he held school and society responsible for his diminished state. The main purpose of the letter was to complain about the fact that his name 'Sakakibara Seito' – a fictitious compound written by combining Chinese characters meaning, 'wine', 'devil', 'rose', 'sacred', and 'fight', had been read incorrectly in the television news.[1] Part of his letter goes:

> If I were what I had been when I was born, I would not have dared to leave a severed head at the front gate of a middle school. . . . But I have dared to draw public attention because I want you to see me as a real person in your imagination, although I have been, and will remain, invisible. At the same time, I will never forget that it was the compulsory education system and the society that created that system that rendered me invisible, and I will exact revenge.
>
> (*DY* 29 June 1997)

In order to demonstrate the connection between school and his crime, he considered it essential to display the severed head at the school gate. After being arrested, he reportedly told the police that he left a mutilated body of a cat in front of the school gate several days prior to the murder of Hase Jun. The remains of the cat, however, were quickly taken away by the school authorities, causing no stir, which made him feel that 'his revenge was ignored by the school' (*AS* 2 July 1997). When he murdered the victim, therefore, the 'killer' reportedly took special care that the severed head would be discovered at the school gate *before* the rest of the body was found elsewhere. This was to ensure that the significance of the murder as revenge against school would be conveyed (*AS* 6 July 1997).[2]

At the beginning of the investigation, the 'school killer' expressed his resentment and grudge against his school and teachers (*AS* 30 June 1997), saying that he was 'hit by the teacher repeatedly without reason' (*AS* 2 July 1997) and 'told by the teacher not to come to school'. When he did go to school, he said, he was hit by the teacher at the school gate (Takahashi 1997: 14). The principal categorically denied that corporal punishment was used in school, but subsequently it was revealed that this was not true (*AS* 5 July 1997).

As the investigation proceeded, however, the focus of the case quickly shifted away from school to the suspect himself. Mention of school by the boy apparently became infrequent (*AS* 13 July 1997). The team of psychiatrists conducted numerous tests and concluded that he 'suffers from sexual sadism, a mental disorder in which an individual gains sexual arousal and gratification by hurting others' (*ANEN* 1 October 1997). The Kobe Family Court found the boy responsible not only for the murder of Hase Jun, but also for four assaults on children which had happened in the area in previous months, including the bludgeoning of a 10-year-old girl, Yamashita Ayaka, who died one week after the attack (*AS* 18 October 1997). The judge concluded that the boy 'is not mentally ill but should be treated because he still tries to justify his action' and that he 'suffers from deeply entrenched sadism related to aggressiveness and an immature sexual impulse' (*Japan Times* 20 October 1997). The 'school killer' Sakakibara was sent to a juvenile reformatory with medical facilities, where the length of the detention would be determined following on-going medical assessment (*AS* 18 October 1997).

So far as the 'school killer' is concerned, therefore, all reference to school in accounts of his crime disappeared soon after his arrest, although it had been central to his pre-arrest statements. His 'discourse' was silenced as the nonsense of a boy deeply disturbed by his 'uncontrolled sadistic urge'. The principal of the Tomogaoka Junior High School commented on the outcome that 'it was an extraordinary case. We cannot really say that school is not responsible, but we do not perceive that we provided the trigger to the crimes' (*AS* 18 October 1997).[3]

EMPATHY EXPRESSED BY STUDENTS

The sociological significance of the Kobe murder lies not so much in the case itself, but rather in the fact that many students found these 'extraordinary' crimes not so surprising. More specifically, students, especially junior high school students, expressed strong empathy with the 'school killer' on two points of his statement: 'I am an invisible existence' and 'I want to exact revenge on school and society which made me invisible' (Miyadai and Terawaki 1998; Ogi 1998; Kamata 1997; Miyadai 1997; Chikushi 1997). The 'discourse' of the 'school killer' was thus 'taken up' by his contemporaries. Many were sympathetic to him even though they found his 'solution' unacceptable. Their empathy with the killer bridged the 'ordinary' to the 'extraordinary', the 'normal' to the 'abnormal', and made it impossible to dismiss or silence the agenda declared by the 'school killer', even after his case was officially settled.

Some 14-year-olds indicated that they sensed something familiar in the letter written by the 'school killer' and during the early stages of the case, when adults did not dream of such a possibility, suspected that it might have been written by somebody of their age (Ebimura and Watanabe 1997).

Miyadai Shinji, a sociologist at Tokyo Metropolitan University, remarks that 'at the very least some one-third of junior high school students showed rather strong empathy' (Miyadai and Terawaki 1998). Ogi Naoki, an educational critic, went through hundreds of faxes sent from junior high school students on a TV station and was 'astounded by the extent of the empathy and support expressed' (Ogi 1998).

Ujioka Mayumi, the education reporter of *Asahi Shinbun* who observed a discussion on the Kobe murder held in the second-year class of Higashita Junior High School in Tokyo, writes that the 'consensus among the children seems to be that, appalling though the crimes were, it was only a matter of time before somebody committed them'. She reports that 22 out of 35 students in the class indicated that they 'understand what was going on in the suspect's mind' and were sympathetic to him. Likewise, 28 out of 35 students felt that 'school forces everybody into a mould', suggesting that they also understand the claim by the 'school killer' that he had been rendered invisible by the school (1997d).

The comments made by 14-year-olds after the arrest of Sakakibara included:

- The feeling that 'I want to take revenge on school' seems widely shared among students in my school.
- I have not gone so far as to take revenge on school or teachers but I often feel stressed with school and *hensachi* (the deviation score which shows one's academic position relative to others). I too would be shocked if I were told 'not to come to school until graduation'. I understand the boy's feeling.
- Teachers should not say something like 'do not come to school'. My homeroom teacher said 'you are all stupid' when I was a fifth or sixth grader. Teachers can change the personality of primary and junior high school students. I feel sorry for the student who got caught.
- There is a teacher who calls us 'you stupid pig' and hits us only because we chat a little in the class. It has become a habit to bully the weak in school.
- The boy called himself 'invisible existence'. I too sometimes think 'what do I live for?'

(Ebimura and Watanabe 1997)

It was not only the 'revenge on school' and the perception of the self being 'invisible' to which contemporaries of the 'school killer' could relate. The fact that he targeted only small children was something familiar to students. His crimes were an extension of the *ijime* (bullying) prevalent in Japanese schools. Cruelty to and the killing of small animals is also wide-spread among children (Miyadai and Terawaki 1998). His classmates remarked that Sakakibara 'often hit an intellectually handicapped child just for fun' (*Nihonkai shinbun* 30 June 1997), and that the victim, Hase Jun, was the target of his '*puroresu gokko*' (playing at professional wrestling) which was nothing but *ijime* (*Nihonkai shinbun* 2 July 1997). Sakakibara himself reportedly said to the police that 'anybody weak would have become the target' of his crimes (*AS* 13 July 1997). The judge said that the boy 'developed a fantasy of killing people while repeating the killing and dissecting of small animals' and that he 'created the self-righteous justification that if he is stronger than others he can control and kill them' (*AS* 18 October 1997).

While there was a general sympathy among students towards Sakakibara, he also caused anxiety among them that 'if I am not careful, I might be killed' (Ebimura and Watanabe 1997). This suggests that many students somehow perceived such a possibility as real. In the classroom discussion mentioned above, 30 out of 35 students indicated that they had at one time or another wanted to kill someone. Another 30 indicated that school is a 'tiring' place, and that the most tiring of all is relating to friends, i.e. making the necessary efforts to stay on the right side so as not to be considered weird and therefore ostracised and bullied (Ujioka 1997d). The crimes of the 'school killer' pushed the situation even closer to the edge, and made school even more tension-laden than before.

GOOD SCHOOL, GOOD FAMILY, GOOD NEIGHBOURHOOD

The murder in Kobe had a completely different meaning for adults. One of the worst aspects of the case for them was the fact that there was nothing extraordinary or problematic in the background of the young criminal. If anything his background represented everything ordinary citizens of Japan aspired to: the boy was a 'good child' from a 'good family' going to a 'good school' in a 'good neighbourhood' (Chikushi 1997).

Tomogaoka Junior High School is the 'best' of three junior high schools in that area. Teachers are so 'enthusiastic' that there are few delinquents, few with pierced ears, dyed hair, loose socks or mini-skirts, although such were part of teenage fashion culture (Sakamoto and Takahashi 1997). Tomogaoka students photographed by the media were extremely neat and uniform in appearance – same clothes, same shoes, same socks folded at the same length, same hair styles, same bags carried in the same way – all walking in a group along the road 'protected' by rows of parents standing at the side of the road. In other words, Tomogaoka is a school successful in maintaining order, where school rules are strictly observed and where instruction is carried out by 'enthusiastic' teachers.

The impression neighbours had of the 'school killer' was not bad. He was regarded as a diligent-looking boy who would greet neighbours properly (*AS* 30 June 1997). His family appeared to be an ideal, close-knit family, with father working for a big firm and mother a full-time wife and enthusiastic participant in school activities. One neighbour said that 'if that family has a problem, there would be no family which does not have a problem' (Sakamoto and Takahashi 1997).

They also live in a 'good' neighbourhood. The cohesion of the community is so emphasised that the representative of the neighbourhood self-governing body apologised to the public through the media for 'producing such a person from our neighbourhood'. In this community, a list of students with behavioural problems is made in order to caution their parents (Sakamoto and Takahashi 1997). The wall of the 'neighbourhood watch' office is covered with slogans such as 'Let's work hard with a smile' or 'Father is the support. The child who is led by a father's hand sparkles [*kagayaku*]' (*AS* 2 July 1997).

This is also the region where the stratification of middle schools is extremely advanced and academic competition especially stiff (*AS* 11 July 1997). Some of the local streets were informally known as 'Tokyo University Street' or 'Nada High Street' after the 'top' university and private high school in the country (Sakamoto and Takahashi 1997), indicating that these districts were regarded as good breeding-grounds for the educational elite of the nation. In the late afternoon, shining *juku*-buses go through the neat and clean streets of the town in which every corner is fully developed and utilised, collecting students from homes to deliver them to the after-school *juku* (cram school) (Yoshioka 1997).

In other words, the environment in which the unprecedented crimes were committed was one in which such crimes were least expected. The case happened in one of the most carefully guarded and cultured corners of Japanese society. The area represented an epitome of the control society, where school, family and neighbourhood functioned in a coordinated, orderly and watchful manner, just as they were supposed to function. It was the paradox of 'supreme order' and 'supreme normalcy' in the background that was most offensive and threatening to Japanese society as a whole about the horrific crimes committed by the young boy.

What was even more chilling about the Kobe murder, however, was the fact that the family of the 'school killer' had little idea what their child was up to, and worse still, that many students in his generation claimed that they understood his feelings. The murder in Kobe made it painfully obvious that there is a huge gap between children and parents. Numerous parents expressed their concern that their children might also become Sakakibaras. In one TV programme, more than 70 per cent of the audience expressed this concern. Many parents evidently feel that they do not understand their children at all (Ogi 1998).

The 'school killer' therefore caused grave uneasiness throughout Japanese society. It confronted the society with the realisation that their young were in serious crisis and that the nature of that crisis had not been fully understood by adults. The crisis emerged somehow from the very core of the social system which had been taken for granted, and it threatened the foundations of that very system in an unprecedented and unpredictable manner.

THE PREMONITION OF 'SAKAKIBARAS'

It is not that the Kobe murder occurred completely out of the blue and out of context. For those who were highly sensitised to the perceptions and feelings of students, it was something that might even have been predicted.

Miyagawa Toshihiko manages the Kokugo sakubun kenkyūjo (Institute for Essay Writing in Japanese) in Tokyo. He uses composition writing to analyse, educate and communicate with students. In 1987 he predicted that two types of students would emerge in the near future: the extremely docile, flexible, and sheep-like type who feels little and thinks little, on the one hand, and the extreme and aggressive type, whose profile matches almost exactly that of the 'school killer', Sakakibara Seito, on the other (Miyagawa 1995).[4]

The most outstanding characteristic of the crimes committed by Sakakibara is that they were constructed within a cosmic world which he had created in his mind. He was completely absorbed in the rituals and symbolisms of this world. He called himself, not only 'school killer' but Sakakibara Seito. His letters and notes were marked with a symbol which combined what appear to be a swastika, a teardrop and (possibly) the distinctive mark of a well-known American serial killer. He regarded his crimes as games or experiments; he mutilated the bodies of small animals and one human victim and carefully displayed them; he left crime notes to establish his imagined identity; and he called his victims 'dirty vegetables' which he was destined to 'crush'. In addition, he wrote notes spelling out plans and records of his crimes. Each entry begins with 'Dear God Bamoidooki', the godlike figure he had created in his mind.[5] The note dated 8 May 1997, 16 days prior to the murder of Hase Jun, reads:

Dear God Bamoidooki, I am now 14 years old. I think it is about time I decided to perform the 'anguri'[6] ritual to receive a holy name. I have thought about this for some time. I decided to stop attending school as the first step. But if I stopped going to school all of a sudden, people would be suspicious of me. So, I have already devised a plan to deal with such an event.

(*DY* 20 July 1997)

Miyagawa (1995) writes:

Children who have lost will power [*iyoku*] and feel emptiness within themselves will try to affirm their sense of selfhood by being absorbed in something. . . . Some of them will set out to behave in an extremely radical way and atrocious behaviour will be sure to come of this. Those who start losing their inner subjectivity rely upon their emotions even to tell right from wrong. . . . The kind of violence which will occur in future will differ in that one's selfhood will be clearly and purely defined through criminal activity. No concession will be made to the fact that the victim is also human. . . . Victims will be regarded just as objects. . . . The crimes will be highly premeditated and pure in execution. . . . There is no doubt that the age of such criminals will become younger and younger.

(Miyagawa 1995: 165–7).

He continues:

Furthermore, children will direct themselves towards something which is extraordinary so that they can lose themselves in it. . . . They will be gradually absorbed by occult and SF and will be devoted to irrational and mysterious things. . . . Furthermore, children will take up religion within themselves, not the established sorts, but those which . . . allow them to have mysterious experiences. . . . They will look for religions which will absorb their whole mind, something which will provide a place where they can feel absolutely secure and peaceful. . . . Children will be attracted to rituals. They will try to feel their own existence by becoming assimilated within some clearly defined value to the extent of losing their selfhood within it.

(Miyagawa 1995: 167–8)

The remarkable resemblance between the profile of Sakakibara Seito and the typology of Japanese children Miyagawa canvassed ten years earlier suggests that the 'school killer' was not a psychopathic minor but a child of the times, whose ferocious crimes somehow reflected the society in which he was born. Contemporaries of Sakakibara 'understood' his feelings, and they were not 'so surprised' at what he did.[7]

Miyagawa's prediction was based on numerous compositions which he read daily, and on constant conversation with his students. He quotes a 13-year-old girl who wrote:

> I do not have anything inside myself. In my heart [*kokoro*] self does not exist. I wonder where it has gone and I look for it, but I cannot find it. It is not in the dictionary, nor in the newspaper.
>
> (Miyagawa 1995: 85)

The emptiness the girl feels inside her *kokoro* is the same emptiness the 'school killer' refers to by his reference to his 'invisible existence'. Mimori Tsukuru (1997), a psychologist, maintains that a new type of human being, whom he calls '*kokoro-nai*' (not having a heart), had come into being. By this term he meant not simply cold, heartless, unfeeling, and inconsiderate, but a profound void, not even having the moral foundations from which such feelings might be generated. He believes that these new '*kokoro-nai*' type human beings will also be highly 'program-driven', the antithesis of the conventional 'mind-driven type' human beings who act on the basis of motives and intentions generated in their own mind. The 'program-driven type' personality acts on the basis of a 'program', i.e. a behavioural procedure which determines how to act at a given time in a given circumstance. Mimori remarks that it would be 'an act of ignorance' to use such methods as interviews to analyse this type of human being, because they simply choose the most 'appropriate' behavioural procedure for the specific time and place. According to Mimori, it will be impossible to penetrate to the mind of the 'program-driven' personality, since there is actually no mind accessible to others.

The 'program-driven' personality depicted by Mimori bears some resemblance to what teachers call '*shijimachi ningen*' (human beings waiting for their instructions) and might perhaps best be rendered in English as 'automaton'. The increase in numbers of these '*shijimachi ningen*' is, they say, the most notable change in the profile of students in recent years (Ashizawa 1997). '*Shijimachi ningen*' are '*botsu-shutai*' (void of subjectivity), apathetic, passive, bored, low in energy, unwilling to think or make decisions or initiate any action. But they are also capable of appropriate action when the recognised stimuli are applied. Many teachers feel that it is extremely difficult to communicate with children in this category. They feel that it is like 'talking to an alien' (*AS* 11 December 1994).

The student crisis, then, is also the crisis of teachers and adults who feel that they are no longer able to understand their children, who feel that they have no means to deal with children themselves or to comprehend the indefinable problems children seem to face. The 'school killer' Sakakibara Seito embodied the new syndrome as a changeling introduced into Japanese society by unknown alien forces and therefore immensely threatening to the paradigms recognised by adults. Adults do not know how to deal with these changelings, yet they can sense their presence everywhere. Those who on the surface seem so ordinary and problem free may be fundamentally incomprehensible and alien.

AN OVERVIEW

What are the characteristics of the Japanese education into which this generation of children were born, and what does the present moment represent in the over 50 years of postwar Japanese education? The chronicle of major events in terms of education since 1983, when the 'school killer' was born, is shown in Table 1.1. While the list is selective, each entry constituted a major news item at the time it was reported.

One is immediately struck by the large number of deaths of students and killings by students which have occurred, even though only the most conspicuous cases among dozens of similar cases are listed here. Of course, deaths and serious injuries among the young, or killings and injuries inflicted by youths, are not limited to Japanese society. What is distinctive in Japan, however, is the fact that tragedies involving students occur primarily in the school context. Japan's youth suicide rate, for instance, may not be especially high when compared with other societies, yet numerous examples suggest that suicide among Japanese youth are, by and large, closely related to problems with study and school. Likewise, an astonishing number of deaths and injuries of students occur in the context of their relationships with teachers and classmates. Even problems at home tend to happen in relation to school-related matters. The life of Japanese students is affected most not by drug problems, family breakdowns, or delinquency, but by school-related problems. The reason for this will be discussed in detail throughout the book.

The chronicle also indicates that there may be certain overall trends in Japanese education which influence the life of students. Most significant of all, we argue, is that the so-called 'hidden curriculum' has been augmented considerably in recent years, to the extent that the term 'hidden curriculum' is perhaps inappropriate. The New Course of Study (*Shin gakushū shidō yōryō*), launched in 1989 and fully enforced in 1993, means that not only academic performance but also almost *every* aspect of student life – including

Table 1.1 Major events involving and affecting Japanese students 1983–98

1983	The arrest of the principal of Totsuka Yacht School, where five students died between 1979 and 1982 due to excessive Spartan training.
1984	Ad Hoc Council on Education established under Prime Minister Nakasone.
1985	Takahashi Toshinao (16) in Gifu died from the corporal punishment administered for using a hair drier banned during his school trip.
1986	Shikagawa Hirofumi (13) in Tokyo committed suicide after being bullied extensively.
1987	Japanese junior high schools gained top score in the international test of mathematics.
1988	A 14-year-old boy in Tokyo committed a triple murder at home due to excessive work pressure.
1989	The New Course of Study was launched.
1990	Ishida Ryōko (15) in Kobe died after being crushed against a school gate closed by a teacher.
1991	16-year-old girl and 14-year-old boy in Hiroshima died of dehydration after being locked up in a railway container as punishment.
1992	Drop-outs from senior high schools reached over 120,000.
1993	The Education Minister requested schools to revise the school rule on close-cropped hair.
1994	Ohkōchi Kiyoteru (13) in Aichi committed suicide after being bullied extensively.
1995	Nikkyōso[1] reconciled with Monbushō[2] and lost its character as critic and opponent of Monbushō in the postwar period.
1996	The official number of *tōkōkyohi*[3] students at primary and junior high school levels reached over 94,000.
1997	A 14-year-old 'school killer' in Kobe murdered Hase Jun (11) and Yamashita Ayaka (10) and injured three other children.
1998	Series of knife attacks by junior school students against teachers, fellow students and others.

Notes
1 Japan Teachers' Union
2 Ministry of Education, Science, Sport and Culture
3 School phobia or refusal (an indefinite or frank refusal to go to school)

attitude and motivation to study, willingness to participate in homeroom activities, club activities, student association activities, and school events, as well as eleven aspects of behaviour such as volunteer spirit, cooperativeness, perseverance, care for others, sense of responsibility, etc. – is all assessed in numerical terms and contributes significantly to one's chance of being admitted to senior high school (Takeuchi 1993). This means that students need to perform constantly in front of teachers not only academically but in all aspects of their behaviour, and teachers need to watch students constantly in order to make such assessment. 'Good child competition' and the 'loyalty (to teachers) competition' have been added to the academic competition, in such a way that all have become inextricably intertwined (Yamauchi and Chōnabayashi 1997). Today, the web of control in Japanese schools is so systematic that it is extremely difficult for students to escape.

The New Course of Study also signified the completion of the major agenda which Monbushō (Ministry of Education, Science, Sports and Culture) had worked to achieve since the mid-1950s. Apart from the enhanced control over students' behaviour, it included the *compulsory* use of Japan's *Hinomaru* flag and *Kimigayo* song as its national flag and anthem in school ceremonies. The 1995 decision of Nikkyōso (Japan Teachers' Union) to 'reconcile' with Monbushō, i.e. that it would no longer form the opposition to Monbushō but work in cooperation with it, was the other side of the same coin. It signified the end of a fifty-year battle against Monbushō over such issues as the centralisation of education (textbook censorship and the reduction of local autonomy), the promotion of 'Japaneseness' and nationalistic education (the moral education and *Kimigayo/Hinomaru* issues), and control over teachers (curtailment of their autonomy regarding work and employment conditions). The year 1995 signifies the nadir of Nikkyōso's steadily declining political clout, which had originated in the postwar democratic education that came between militarism prior to 1945 and the high-growth, bureaucratically-controlled education which began in the mid-1950s (Horio 1994).

The year 1995 is considered by many a turning point for Japanese society. The Kobe earthquake proved to be as much a human catastrophe as a natural disaster, and large-scale urban terrorism by a religious sect, Aum Supreme Truth, which involved some of the brightest youth in the country, caused a 'growing suspicion that the priorities of the past fifty [years] might have been fundamentally ill chosen' (McCormack 1996:3). The 'school killer' himself underwent the devastation of the Kobe earthquake and had been outraged by the poor response taken by the then Prime Minister Murayama. In a composition written soon after the earthquake he wrote:

> When the earthquake happened, I worried more about my relatives and family than about myself, and it was scary. I am angry because [Prime Minister] Murayama did not act immediately when the Swiss [rescue team] arrived.[8] If all my family had died, and Murayama had

then visited my place of refuge, I do not know what I would have done, even if it meant that I would be executed.

(*AS* 30 June 1997)

Apart from the 'school killer', there is a general sense of hopelessness and distrust among the Japanese youth towards politicians. The climate of collusion and corruption in Japanese society at large, as indicated by numerous scandals exposed since the 1970s involving key figures of politics, bureaucracy and business, has clearly influenced the perception students have of politics and leadership in general. According to the 1988–90 comparative study by Benjamin Duke (1991), 77.0 per cent of 1,066 Japanese senior high school students indicated that they had 'little' confidence in government leaders, whereas in America and Britain respectively the corresponding figure was only 26.7 and 27.6 per cent. Likewise, 83.2 per cent of Japanese students disagreed with the statement that 'the political leaders of our country are trustworthy', as against 52.7 and 41.5 of the American and British students respectively. Only 2.2 per cent of Japanese students believed that the political leaders of Japan were trustworthy (Duke 1991: 58).

Aera, a weekly magazine published by the *Asahi shinbun*, issued a special issue in November 1997 under the title '*Kodomo ga abunai*' (children in crisis). In that issue, Murakami Ryū, a novelist, wrote that 'there is absolutely nothing to spark good feelings in children' (Murakami 1997). One survey conducted in Nagano in 1996 revealed that 22 per cent of junior high school students wished 'they had not been born' (Kuroiwa 1997). In a 1997 international survey of general happiness with school life, only 26.3 per cent of 10-year-olds in Japan indicated that they were 'very happy' and ranked last among six countries (*Nihon keizai shinbun* 1997). Satō Manabu, a Graduate School of Education professor at Tokyo University, commented that the most remarkable change over the last 15 years among children is that 'children's minds have become rough and scattered and their health overall seems to be on the decline. They are constantly irritated by things' (*DY* 23 June 1997). When Mizusato Seiga, educational commentator and a manager of a small alternative school, asked a junior high school class of first-year students what they wanted most, more than half of the girls said 'I just want to sleep a lot', and about one-third of the boys said 'I want to kill someone' (Mizusato 1997).

Despite the fact that all sorts of educational reforms have been talked about and conducted in recent years, there is a general perception that the basic problems facing schools are 'not only being ignored, [but] are worsening' (*DY* 22 September 1997). With the 'New Course of Study', the degree of control in Japanese schools has probably reached its maximum. Yet, there are many indications that the control-based paradigm of education is on the verge of collapse.

The problem of *ijime* (bullying, especially group bullying) has persisted and become increasingly insidious, prevalent, and life-threatening since the early 1980s (see Chapter 7). *Tōkōkyohi* (school phobia/refusal) has also increased steadily since the early 1980s, with an official figure of 9,400 being reached in 1996 for primary and junior high school students, which means that even by official statistics one in every 61 junior high school students had missed more than 30 school days due to '*tōkōkyohi*'. Moreover, sociological surveys have shown consistently that there is a large 'reserve army' of students who are not included in the official statistics. The students who are most 'at risk' are those who 'stay' in the school clinic (*hokenshitsu*) most of the day, every day, because they are unable, physically and/or psychologically, to attend normal classes. Even in the conservative estimate by Monbushō, there are over 10,000 elementary, junior and high school students who did this '*hokenshitsu tōkō*' in 1996, which is double the number reached in 1990 (*AS* 11 September 1997). The evidence suggests that *tōkōkyohi* has reached epidemic proportions, and that it is a structural problem rather than a problem of individual students (see Chapter 8). In November 1997, Monbushō planned a two-year pilot programme to tackle various problems including the so-called 'collapse of the classroom', i.e. chaotic classroom conditions where students behave wildly or are inattentive and the teacher loses control (*DY* 4 November 1997). The number of incidents of violence by students at public high schools surpassed ten thousand in 1996 (*DY* 23 December 1997). In 1998, there was a series of knife attacks by junior school students against teachers, fellow students and others (*DY* 28 January 1998, 3 February 1998, 11 March 1998). Academically, recent achievement tests conducted by Monbushō reveal that high school students lack the ability to think on their own and to express themselves (*DY* 2 October 1997).

It is not that only students are in crisis. Figure 1.1 shows (1) the proportion of teachers with psychiatric problems out of all the teachers who took sick leave, (2) the proportion of students classified as 'disliking school' (*gakkō-girai*)[9] of all the long-term absentees from school during the period of 1979–85 (Munakata 1991). It indicates that students and teachers had 'breakdowns' (in the broadest sense), in almost the same proportions, in the period when all sorts of school-related problems surfaced in Japan (Yokoyu 1996: 42). This could be partly because the student–teacher relationship itself caused these 'breakdowns', but it might also indicate some structural factor which could be causing the 'breakdown' among students and teachers alike, perhaps in respect of the way students and teachers relate to each other.

In the microcosm of a classroom, students interact only with teachers and

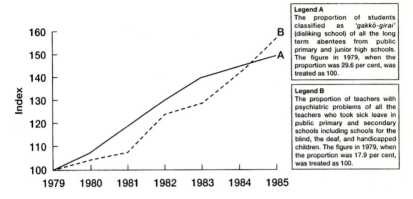

Figure 1.1 The increasing 'problems' among students and teachers
Source: Adapted from Munakata (1991: 151)

classmates. Students rarely see beyond what they encounter in their limited milieu. For students, teachers represent school most of the time. Although it is true that teachers are those who have direct control over students, it should be equally emphasised that the way teachers interact with students in itself is also largely defined by the control-laden school structure. In many ways, teachers are 'in the same boat' as students.

This needs to be emphasised because it often seems the case that popular discourse on education serves merely to deepen the antagonism between teachers and students, teachers and parents, or even students and parents, while both the origin and the solution of the problem lie in the social structure in which they live. The increase of breakdowns among students and teachers indicates that both parties are in serious crisis and that Japanese schools are 'falling apart by themselves' (Kobayashi 1998).

No matter how 'eloquent' the 'school killer' was, and no matter how widely his contemporaries sympathised with his situation, it is extremely difficult for students to explain *fully* the nature of the problem they face. Just as Sakakibara's reference to being hit by a teacher is not sufficient to explain his crimes, the various episodes other students refer to are only sufficient to suggest the deepseatedness of the problem. There is a problem, and students are in crisis, but their scattered words are difficult to synthesise and comprehend. What is lacking is a discourse on Japanese schools which focuses clearly on the *student* experience of school.

The *entirety* of school experience has to be explained, i.e. not just the phenomenon of teachers hitting students, not just school rules, not just academic pressure, not just student bullying, but the complex interrelationships of all aspects of school life in a systematic and comprehensive manner, and how it affects students as a whole. Just as it is impossible to pinpoint one cause of the crimes committed by the 'school killer', so must it be recognised that the experience of school is a 'composite' one. Student life in school is also closely linked with life at home. It is this totality which affects the overall sense of wellbeing of each individual student.

The central aim of this book is to describe Japanese high schools as they are experienced by students and to clarify the nature of the problem they face.

NOTES

1 The last character usually means 'measure', but it can also be taken as a simplified character for 'fight'. '*Seito*' (sacred fight) can also be taken as a pun on '*seito*' meaning 'student'.

2 Washida Kiyokazu, a professor in philosophy at Osaka University, visited the school gate and points out that although there is a wide road in front of the school, the slope makes it difficult to see the gate from the road; and that the other side of the road is a cliff, which suggests that the consciousness of the 'school killer' was directed only towards the school. He concludes, therefore, that the victim's head was left there clearly with the aim to show it to those in the school (Washida 1997).

3 One teacher of the school said that 'it is still a taboo' to talk about the 'school killer'. Another remarked that teachers were instructed by the Kobe Education Board to treat students with 'a counselling mind', while teachers became even busier with meetings and school events and thus had even less time to spend with students (*Nihonkai shinbun* 18 October 1997). The measures taken by Monbushō, Hyōgo Prefectural Board of Education and Kobe Municipal Board of Education were to integrate 'education for the mind' (*kokoro no kyōiku*) and 'education on death' into the curriculum (*AS* 18 October 1997).

4 The book is the reprinted version of the original which appeared in 1987.

5 The meaning of '*Ba-mo-i-do-o-ki*' is unknown, but it may be a word coined by combining sounds in two words, '*ba-i-o*' (bio-) and '*mo-do-ki*' (quasi-), alternately.

6 Unknown meaning but may be derived from the English word 'angry'.

7 The fact that the Kobe murder reflected the situation in Japanese society today is also suggested by the striking resemblance between the profile of the 'school killer' and the boy called Kaoru, who appears in the story entitled *Sinpuru raifu sindorōmu* (simple-life syndrome). This book was written and published by Araki Sumishi in January 1997. In the story, Kaoru is a 14-year-old boy and lives in a 'new town' in the West of Kobe. He cannot get used to the collectivistic atmosphere in school and worries about the lightness of his existence. He has anxiety attacks that he might 'become invisible and fade away'. He is one day attacked by a high school student and ends up killing the student in self-defence (Takahashi 1997).

8 The Swiss rescue team who flew into Japan shortly after the earthquake with

specialist skills and equipment (including rescue dogs) were held for several days at the airport for bureaucratic reasons.

9 '*Gakkō-girai*' (disliking school) is the category used to include *tōkōkyohi* students under 'long-term absentees' in the official statistics of Monbushō *School Survey* (*Gakkō kihon chōsa*). Other categories are 'illness', 'economic reasons' and 'other'.

2 Methodology and comparative problems

A CRITIQUE OF THE FUNCTIONALIST PARADIGM OF JAPANESE EDUCATION

This book adopts a focus and a problematic somewhat different from those in the dominant discourse on Japanese education in English. Japanese education has been discussed broadly within the framework of modernisation theory. For a long time, books or chapters on Japanese education have concurred in pointing out how 'successful' Japan has been in producing students equipped with a high level of academic competency, as indicated by the results of international tests, and a high level of orderliness in their personal or social behaviour (e.g. Reischauer 1977; Vogel 1979; Rohlen 1983; Duke 1986; White 1987). The 'successful modernisation of Japan' has often been attributed to the educational system, in the sense that Japanese education was able to produce a diligent and competent labour force highly cooperative to management and responsive to corporate requirements.

This fundamental view has been shared by the decision makers of Japanese education within Japan as well. Horio Teruhisa, a leading sociologist of education, remarks that there was a general expectation among parents and students that the Ad Hoc Council on Education which operated between 1984 and 1987 might be able to tackle the problems in Japanese education such as excessive academic competition, corporal punishment, *ijime* (group bullying) and *tōkōkyohi* (school phobia/refusal). The reason why this expectation was not fulfilled, according to Horio, is because the members of the Council believed that Japanese education was praiseworthy when compared to European and North American, in terms of educational opportunities as well as in terms of the results of international tests of mathematics and science; and therefore that the problems which existed in the system were peripheral compared to the core function it served, and would serve in future, for Japanese society as a whole (Horio 1996: 233).

Japanese education continues to operate on fundamentally the same principles of competition and state-control which were entrenched in the mid-1950s. Within this framework, the 'praiseworthy' aspects of Japanese education emerged: excellent results in the international tests of mathematics, a high proportion of students advancing to tertiary education, and diligent and compliant attitudes amongst students. Within this framework also emerged problems such as school violence, *ijime* and *tōkōkyohi* but these were assumed to be merely a few negatives in a generally very positive, successful system. However, as the so-called 'good' aspects and 'bad' aspects of Japanese education have intensified together over the years, we are led to consider seriously the possibility of a structural relationship between the two.

The argument that Japan's education system was the primary factor to explain its economic success was no longer able to hold much water when the Japanese economy lost its edge after the bubble-burst of 1991. Because of Japan's economic non-performance, one might have expected a different focus on education, perhaps a new and opposite one in which the 'negative' aspects would be treated as predominant. This line of argument, however, would not have been persuasive because the problem of Japanese education is precisely that it has been *unable to change*, no matter how strongly different people for different reasons have considered change necessary (Schoppa 1991).

The difference between the problematic underlying this book and the dominant view of Japanese education stems from the fundamentally interactionist approach adopted here, in opposition to the dominant view based on the functionalist approach (Okano 1993: 18). In the functionalist perspective, society is seen as a system consisting of various parts which serve to maintain the whole. While society is regarded as an entity which exists in its own right, individuals are seen only in terms of the role they play in fulfilling the 'needs' and 'purposes' of the social whole. The interactionist approach, by contrast, regards individuals as actors, each with their respective needs and with the power to change society (Giddens 1989: 700). The present study, focused on the student experience of school rather than on the socio-economic functioning of school as an institution, is based on the interactionist perspective.

Why has the functionalist tradition been so dominant in the English discourse on Japanese education?

It is firstly because the English discourse on Japanese education emerged within the framework of *Nihon(jin)ron*, i.e. Japan(ese) theory. As pointed out by Mouer and Sugimoto (1986), the main contention of the *Nihonjinron* literature has long been that 'Japanese values or thought patterns [are] the major independent variables explaining Japanese economic development' (p. 21), and this perspective was based on the holistic or functionalist view of society that:

> societies represent the major cognitive unit for analysis, that they have goals, ends and purposes which form the dominant components of the mechanism accounting for individual motivation, and that they are characterized by a high degree of consensus which means that variants in behavior may best be understood as 'deviant behavior'.
>
> (Mouer and Sugimoto 1986: 22)

In the English discourse on Japanese education, schools have been seen as *the* institution which 'makes' Japanese, i.e. socialises children into 'Japanese' by equipping them with distinctively Japanese values and norms, especially the internalisation of group values and self-discipline. To clarify the mechanism of 'making Japanese' has therefore been the central interest in the English discourse on Japanese education (e.g. Hendry 1986; Duke 1986; White 1987; Peak 1989; Lewis 1995; Beauchamp 1978). In other words, the English discourse on Japanese education has largely been a branch of *Nihonjinron*, focused on the socialisation aspect of Japanese society.

As pointed out by Befu (1990), *Nihonjinron* literature is fundamentally an ideological construct. As its sub-category, the English discourse on Japanese education also has had a strong tendency to be ideological, as suggested by such subtitles as 'Lessons for Industrial America' (Duke 1986).

Feinberg (1993) argues that the discourse on Japan is part of a larger struggle to control America's self-understanding (p. 89), and that Japanese education has been used to promote economic and cultural conservatism in America. In order to argue his point, Feinberg draws upon the example of different messages projected by Rohlen (1983) and White (1987) regarding the home desk of Japanese students – an expensive piece of furniture with a number of built-in features (such as shelves, lights, pencil sharpener, calculator, map, etc.) which Japanese parents usually purchase for their children upon entering primary school. According to Feinberg, Rohlen depicted the desk to 'illustrate the pressure that high school and university entrance examinations place on students and their families', whereas for White, the desk was 'an indication of the commitment of the entire nation to the education of its young and especially the mother's intense care and the nurturant and protected atmosphere' (p. 83). As Feinberg points out, the difference in the descriptions has little to do with the changes (or non-changes) in the desk or in the Japanese educational system (p. 84) but reflects the needs of American society perceived by individual researchers *vis-à-vis* Japanese education.[1]

Feinberg's analysis points to one indisputable fact: the English discourse on Japanese education has been heavily influenced by the eye of the beholder – the hidden agenda the researchers bring to the analysis, according to the changing tide of the time, whether it be how best to fight against Japan, to modernise Japan, to be successful like Japan, or to compete against Japan. What did not change over time was the holistic and functionalist framework within which Japan has been discussed.

This does not mean, however, that the English discourse on Japanese education has been totally mistaken. On the contrary, I argue that the functionalist view has been dominant partly because Japanese education, when viewed uncritically, *is* akin to the functionalist model of school and society. The Japanese educational system has indeed played a pivotal role in creating a society which appears, on the surface, very close to the functionalist paradise. What then is the model of education envisaged by the functionalist, and how does it relate to the Japanese education?

The functionalist perspective of education is represented by Durkheim and Parsons, and was dominant until the late 1960s in the field of sociology of education (Sarup 1978: 1; Sharp 1980: 5–7; Giroux 1983: 10).[2] The first function of school they envisaged was to provide normative consensus through socialisation, which they considered essential in order to fulfil the 'needs of society', i.e. to maintain social order, social stability and social solidarity. Durkheim writes that education 'perpetuates and reinforces the homogeneity by fixing in advance, in the mind of the child, the essential similarities that collective life presupposes' (Durkheim 1956: 92–4). Likewise, Parsons states that the function of school is the internalisation of social values, norms and morals such as 'respect for the teacher, consideration and co-operativeness in relation to fellow-pupils and good work habits' (Parsons 1956: 303).

With equal emphasis, the functionalists see selection of students for manpower allocation as the main function of school. Durkheim writes that 'education assures the persistence of [a] necessary diversity' which provides the foundation for the division of labour in society (Durkheim 1956: 92). Parsons (1956) also regarded diversification and selection of students as the major functions of school. He writes that 'the school class may be regarded as a primary agency by [which different] capacities are generated. [The school] is, from the point of view of the society, an agency of manpower allocation' (p. 298). Parsons believed that manpower allocation is based on 'a simple main axis of achievement' at school which operates on the principle of equality of opportunity (pp. 299, 308). In other words, his view on this point is little different from the notion of meritocracy.

The parallel between the functionalist theory of education and the Japanese system in practice is that socialisation and competition are commonly seen to be the main function of school. To clarify how Japanese children internalise 'Japaneseness' has been the central focus in the English discourse of Japanese education, not only because many of these studies were conducted within the framework of *Nihonjinron*, but also because the reproduction of the normative consensus, i.e. internalisation of group values and nationalistic values (*Nihonjin to shiteno jikaku*), has indeed been the focus of Japanese education in a more concentrated form than the functionalist theorists would have imagined. Similarly, the selection of students through academic competition, i.e. the notorious 'examination war', also constitutes the main feature of Japanese education to a far greater extent that it was portrayed in the functionalist theory.

Furthermore, there is a curious similarity between the nature of the functionalist theory and the nature of Japanese education: both are lacking in critical perspective.

The shortcomings of the functionalist theory of education have been thoroughly discussed since the 1970s by theorists with interactionist and Marxist perspectives. Its fundamental weakness is seen to lie in its uncritical and positivistic nature (e.g. Althusser 1971; Young 1971b; Bourdieu 1976; Sarup 1978; Giroux 1983). At the level of everyday life, however, the functionalist perspective is still embedded in the dominant view of education. This is because functionalist theory coincides with taken-for-granted notions of education and in turn it is felt to be right by many. This is the case because both functionalist theory and prevailing beliefs about education originate from the same bases, i.e. uncritical perceptions of the existing social structure and its power relationships. Functionalist theory describes society uncritically. It is inevitable that it does not greatly contradict the way it is understood by the majority of individuals whose views are also often uncritical.

The control structure integrated in Japanese education, on the other hand, is consistently oriented to suppress a critical awareness among students (see Part 1). Its composite effect is such that students' responses to it manifest themselves not as a straightforward criticism of school but in distorted and displaced forms such as *ijime* and *tōkōkyohi*. The distinctive nature of *ijime* and *tōkōkyohi* is that students themselves maintain silence in many ways, indicating, partly, a lack of clear understanding and critical awareness of the situation in which they are trapped. The dominant discourse of *ijime* and *tōkōkyohi* in Japan also works to silence students (see Part 2).

Japanese education, in other words, is like a fortress guarded by many layers of silence and with the effect of suppressing the critical awareness of students, teachers, parents and others. It is designed to prevent people from questioning taken-for-granted 'reality', and it is possible that this 'outcome' of Japanese education provides the foundation of Japanese society to which the functionalist theory is easily applied. To put it differently, Japanese education plays *the* central role in heightening the level of acceptance of the taken-for-granted 'reality' among Japanese, and this may have increased the proximity between that, on the one hand, and the functionalist perspective brought to the field by non-Japanese researchers, on the other.

This is not to say that problems in Japanese education are unseen. Whether it be stiff academic competition, corporal punishment, stringent school rules, ferocious *ijime*, or growing *tōkōkyohi*, they are too apparent to ignore. Yet, the shortcoming of the functionalist approach is that the closer the account of Japanese education gets to the functionalist theory, the more difficult it becomes to deal with these problems. Thus, flaws of Japanese education are often simply noted, acknowledged, or appended, as something which does not at all fit in the body of the main text (e.g. Rohlen 1995). On the other hand, studies which focus only on the negative aspects of Japanese education (e.g. Schoolland 1990) also present a limited account of the system. For those who actually go through the Japanese educational system, the 'successful' aspects and the 'problematic' aspects not only coexist but are intertwined. The present study aims to clarify the relationship between them.

THE APPROACH

The book is divided into two sections which are based on slightly different approaches.

Part 1, 'Control: The Structure of Silence', discusses the social structural milieu of Japanese high schools. Four key areas of the everyday life of school are examined from the viewpoint of students: student–teacher relationships, discipline and punishment, school rules and study. Since these relate directly to the nature of school as a social institution, it seemed crucial to introduce a comparative perspective, so that the characteristics of Japanese high schools could be clearly set in relief against the background of schools in other, broadly Western, liberal-democratic countries (more on this later).

My endeavour to discern the characteristics of Japanese high schools is not based on a particularistic view of Japan. The main thesis of Part 1 – that Japanese high schools represent an extreme control model of a social institution where all kinds of mechanisms operate to silence and alienate students – therefore should be understood within the conceptual spectrum of social control at school (and society in general). For instance, as will be shown in Part 1, there is some overlap in the experience of school between Japanese and Australian students. Such an overlap would be greater if

Japanese schools are compared with, say, schools in Korea. Also one can argue that Japanese high schools are akin to other social institutions such as the military and prison where regimentation constitutes the essential feature. In other words, while the Japanese high school system described here may present an extreme case, it should not be seen as a 'unique' model, but as one which has applicability in varying degrees for understanding schools and other institutions in general.

Part 2, 'Responses: Conformity and Resistance', on the other hand, focuses more narrowly on how Japanese students respond to the extremely alienating milieu of schools discussed in Part 1. It addresses two key recent issues in Japanese education, *ijime* (group bullying) and *tōkōkyohi* (school phobia/refusal). These are problems which have steadily mounted over the years, to the extent that they have become part of the everyday life of Japanese schools. There is a general perception in Japan that these problems are so deeply entwined with the nature of Japanese schools as to be virtually insurmountable. The aim of Part 2 is to demonstrate in what ways *ijime* and *tōkōkyohi* are rooted in the structure of Japanese schools, and in what ways they are by-products of the Japanese educational system. This will be done, again, by focusing primarily on the views and experiences of students themselves.

To put it differently, the backbone of Part 1 comprises the comparative data collected in Japan and Australia (see below), whereas Part 2 focuses more narrowly on the phenomena of *ijime* and *tōkōkyohi* within Japan. There are two reasons for adopting different approaches in Parts 1 and 2. One is to do with the nature, especially the causes, of such issues as bullying, school phobia, and school refusal. The second is to do with the methodological problems which arise in dealing with these issues.

Aetiological reason

Although there are various student-related problems – bullying, school nonattendance, suicide, violence – which are phenomenologically similar across different societies, this does not necessarily mean that the causes of such problems are also the same. For instance, the phenomenology of bullying seems to be remarkably similar across different cultures (apart from the fact that *ijime* in contemporary Japanese schools is always group bullying), yet one cannot assume that the reasons children and adolescents engage in bullying are more or less the same across different societies. One may argue that bullying is a manifestation of powerlessness among those who commit it, but the social-structural factors underlying powerlessness could well be different from society to society.

The same point can be made about school refusal. In terms of the phenomenology, school-phobic (or school-refusing) children and adolescents exhibit similar symptomatic and behavioural patterns. Even in terms of prevalence, so far as the official figures are concerned there is little difference between Japan and Britain, for instance: less than 1 per cent of children are affected by school refusal in Britain (Lansdown 1990: 118), as against 1.4 per cent of junior high school students and 0.2 per cent of primary school students in Japan (1995 figure). Yet this does not necessarily mean that the sociological cause of school refusal is the same in both societies; nor does it necessarily mean that the sociological and biographical significance of school refusal is the same in these two countries. The outlook of school refusal is 'optimistic' in Britain (Lansdown 1990: 118), whereas it is 'a source of acute concern' in Japan (Chiland and Young 1990: ix). In Japan, there is an extremely large pool of 'would-be school phobics' who do their best to keep going to school (see Chapter 8) and those involved (e.g. students, families, teachers) usually have great difficulties in dealing with it. But most significantly, *tōkōkyohi* is *the* mode of school nonattendance in Japan (whereas it may be truancy or dropout in other societies). As Young *et al.* remark:

> The patterns of psychopathology in school refusal vary according to the similarities or differences of the cultures compared. This mirrors a fact that is obvious, but easily forgotten: children reject school in the context of the meaning of education for them within their own society.
>
> (Young *et al.* 1990: 4)

Analysis of school nonattendance in a particular society, therefore, has to begin with the analysis of its schools and the society itself, as Lansdown says for the case of Britain:

> It is not possible to understand nonattendance at school in Britain without seeing it in the context of the educational system, and that can be understood only against the background of the country's social and political structure.
>
> (Lansdown 1990: 112)

To put it differently, to examine issues like bullying and school refusal, one has to begin with a detailed analysis within the boundary of the particular society, before introducing a comparative perspective. If a society is envisaged as a ball, schools as a social institution belong to its 'primary' sphere, i.e. close to the surface, which makes schools relatively open to comparative scrutiny. In contrast, phenomena such as bullying and school refusal belong to a more 'internal', 'secondary' sphere and, as such, they are more heavily influenced by social and cultural specificities, which in turn makes it more difficult to examine them in a comparative perspective.

The social and cultural specificity which influences the lives of Japanese youth is the fact that Japan is a 'school society'. In a 'school society', what students experience at school tends to exert greater influence over their family life than family does over their school life. In the Japanese context, the key to understanding such issues as *ijime* and *tōkōkyohi* lies in clarifying how they are related to what students experience at school. In Japan, the cause of student-related problems needs to be sought first within school walls.

Methodological reasons

The second reason for not maintaining the same level of comparative perspective in Part 2 is methodological.

While it is relatively straightforward to collect empirical data on student perceptions of institutional aspects of school (e.g. school rules and academic pressure), it is extremely difficult to collect *reliable* data, especially cross-cultural data, on bullying and school phobia/refusal.

With regard to bullying, it is universally recognised that students are generally reluctant to talk about it; otherwise, the identification of victims and bullies would not constitute an issue (e.g. Olweus 1993; Rigby 1996). In Japan in particular, where various structures to silence students are at work, the secrecy surrounding *ijime* is especially robust. As a consequence, despite the fact that it has become part of the everyday life of school, even teachers and parents are rarely aware of the *ijime* occurring in their locality, and it is very unlikely that a questionnaire survey, administered in a conventional way, would adequately capture the actual prevalence and severity of *ijime* (Fukuda 1997: 66–9). In other words, *ijime* is a topic ill-suited to investigation by conventional survey methods. Even official statistical data do not constitute exceptions. It is doubtful, therefore, how well cross-cultural comparison, which is often based on statistical data, can reflect the different realities of bullying experienced by Japanese students, on the one hand, and students in other societies on the other. In order to examine *ijime* from a comparative perspective, the first requirement is in-depth, qualitative analysis within the Japanese context (see Chapter 7).

With regard to *tōkōkyohi* (school phobia/refusal), on the other hand, the methodological difficulty lies in the confusion and inconsistency which exist in dealing with the question of school nonattendance in general (Young *et al.* 1990: 212). Specialists have yet to agree on the demarcation of such concepts as school nonattendance, truancy, school phobia, school refusal, and dropout.

The existence of Japanese terms with similar meanings (*tōkōkyohi, futōkō, gakkō-girai*, and *taigaku*) exacerbates the difficulty. Furthermore, as will be elaborated on later, the confusion over terminology in Japan reflects the existence of different discourses by different groups of adults, each equipped with a different set of (1) assumptions on human development, the relationship between the individual and society, and the role of school, (2) interpretations as to what *tōkōkyohi* is, and therefore, (3) ways of treating *tōkōkyohi*. Given this circumstance, the primary task of the present study which focuses on students is to elucidate the nature of the controversy over *tōkōkyohi vis-à-vis* the accounts given by *tōkōkyohi* students themselves, so that this complex phenomenon is examined in a new light.

The definition of 'tōkōkyohi'

Tōkōkyohi is a complex matter, and the related terminology confusing. This makes it important to clarify what the term actually denotes. Such clarification is also desirable in order to make the rich material available in Japanese accessible to those working on similar phenomena elsewhere. For that reason, I have defined this concept against the background of relevant concepts in English.

Although different people use the term '*tōkōkyohi*' in different ways, the word seems to be used most frequently to refer to a situation which might be summarised as: *school burnout which can manifest as school phobia or school refusal.*

While 'school burnout' is rarely mentioned in English literature in relation to school phobia or school refusal, it seems to constitute the common denominator of what is usually understood as *tōkōkyohi* among secondary school students in Japan. Koizumi (1990) for instance remarks that 'burnout of a good child type', together with 'separation anxiety type' and 'spoiled child type', constitute a category called 'school refusal in the narrow sense', and that 70 per cent of 9,001 school-refusing children (in a broad sense), who were consulted in prefectural and municipal 'Education Centres' in 1986, fall into this category (p. 92). Although he does not show the breakdown of the three subcategories, he does point out that 'burnout' occurs among secondary students, whereas the other two subcategories occur among younger children. It seems safe to assume therefore that 'burnout' is the main characteristic of *tōkōkyohi* among secondary students in Japan. In fact, there is abundant evidence to indicate that 'burnout' is *the* common denominator for all *tōkōkyohi* adolescents in Japan (see Chapter 8).

Apart from the fact that burnout constitutes the common denominator for *tōkōkyohi*, the phenomenology of *tōkōkyohi* seems to coincide with the concept of school phobia, the main features of which are identified by Berg *et al.* as:

1   Severe difficulty in attending school – often amounting to pro-
    longed absence.
2   Severe emotional upset – shown by such symptoms as excessive
    fearfulness, undue tempers, misery, or complaints of feeling ill . . .
    on being faced with the prospect of going to school.
3   Staying at home with the knowledge of the parents, when they
    should be at school, at some stage in the course of the disorder.
4   Absence of significant anti-social disorders such as stealing, lying,
    wandering, destructiveness and sexual misbehaviour.

(Berg *et al.* 1969: 123)

When the category of 'school phobia' is employed for the understanding of *tōkōkyohi* among secondary school students in Japan, it should be clearly differentiated from 'separation anxiety'. This is firstly because, while 'school phobia' is common among older children and adolescents, 'separation anxiety' is common among younger children (Last *et al.* 1987). Secondly, while 'school phobia' is *school-induced* anxiety which compels adolescents to run *from* school, 'separation anxiety' refers to the anxiety which urges small children to run *back* to mother. As Pilkington and Piersel (1991) argue, this conceptualisation of school phobia enables one to see it as a 'normal avoidance reaction to what appears to the child to be an unpleasant situation', and thus allows one to shift research attention from the individual child to the school environment itself (p. 300).

This conceptualisation of 'school phobia' closely overlaps with that of 'school refusal'. In fact, Hsia (1984) regards school phobia and school refusal as two ends of 'a continuum of progression from "involuntary" symptoms on one end to "wilful" refusal on the other as time elapses' (p. 361). This conceptualisation of school phobia and school refusal fits rather nicely with the accounts of *tōkōkyohi* given by Japanese students (see Chapter 8). It not only makes *tōkōkyohi* a flexible and elastic concept, but also a concept which can cover all the different stages of *tōkōkyohi*. It is with this understanding that *tōkōkyohi* is translated as school phobia/refusal throughout this book.

To ensure further clarification:

> *Tōkōkyohi* is only a subcategory of 'school nonattendance' which is a much broader concept including all sorts of modes of being absent from school, e.g. absence due to illness and injury (clearly different from school phobic syndrome), absence due to economic reasons, family reasons, or truancy.

> *Tōkōkyohi* is not truancy. There is a general agreement that school phobics are different from truants in that: (1) while truants spend

their truant time away from home, school phobics stay home in seclusion; (2) while truant children rarely exhibit somatic discomforts, school phobics typically exhibit somatic discomforts; (3) while parents of truants are unaware of their children's nonattendance at school, parents of school phobics are aware of it; (4) while truants are often engaged in antisocial or delinquent behaviour, school phobics are not (Pilkington and Piersel 1991: 291–2). These lasts two points clearly distinguish *tōkōkyohi* students from truants even when their non-attendance from school is due to 'wilful' refusal rather than just burnout or phobic syndromes.

Tōkōkyohi is not the same as 'dropout'. Although the outcome of *tōkōkyohi* could well be dropout, it differs fundamentally from dropout in that it presupposes the situation in which the possibility of returning to a school (if not the same school) is still on the cards. Because of this, *tōkōkyohi* is a 'problem' for primary and junior high school students who are completing compulsory education as well as senior high school students who are, socially and/or psychologically, bound to complete secondary school. Dropouts are called '*chūtai*' which in Japanese constitutes an entirely different category. Some 2.5 per cent of senior high school students dropped out in 1996 (*DY* 26 February 1998). The dropout rate is especially high in so-called 'rock-bottom schools' where students have difficulties in maintaining motivation to study (Kim 1991).

Having explained the broader approach adopted in this book, I would now like to move on to discussion in detail of the comparative methods used in Part 1. The detailed discussion on research methodology, however, will raise questions pertaining to the relationship between education on the one hand and the broader social structures – such as gender, social class and, in the case of Japan, the existence of 'super meritocracy' – which will also be discussed below.

THE COMPARATIVE PERSPECTIVE: AUSTRALIA AS A REFERENCE POINT

In order to discuss the characteristics of Japanese education, some compara-tive perspective is necessary. Although this is not a full-scale comparative study, Australia, which may be regarded as broadly typical of the Western, liberal-democratic education system, is used as a reference point.

The comparative data presented in this book was collected in 1984 in

Japan and Australia. Although more recent data would be desirable, trends in the Japanese and Australian education systems since then suggest that the contrast between the two systems shown by the data is likely to be greater today than in 1984. In other words, the contrast shown by the data is probably an *underestimation* of the current difference between the two systems, and therefore, it is 'safe' to use it as a reference point.

To be more specific, the Japanese data consistently indicated that school life in Japan was distinctly more 'autocratic' than that in Australia, where the pattern was, relatively speaking, more 'democratic'. As discussed earlier, the control mechanism in Japanese education has been augmented considerably in recent years. As a consequence, it may be expected that its autocratic nature has been enhanced further. Australia, on the other hand, has gone through some changes since the mid-1980s: significantly more students remain in school to complete secondary education, the proportion of students attending elite private schools has increased, the rationalisation of schools has been undertaken to reduce educational costs to state governments, and classroom discipline problems have become more serious and more common. Yet, as far as its educational paradigm is concerned, there is little indication that the democratic aspect (relative to the Japanese system) has deteriorated since the mid-1980s. If anything, the problem is that schools in Australia have not yet found ways to maintain their democratic ethos while promoting learning at school at the same time. It is expected, therefore, that the difference between Japan and Australia indicated by the 1984 data would probably have *diverged further* over the years. It is most likely that what was indicated in 1984 would offer only a conservative estimate of the current situation in Japan as contrasted with that in Australia.

The data collection

The data analysed in Chapters 3 to 6 was collected from 549 Japanese and 2,038 Australian secondary school students by using a pre-structured questionnaire. The data were designed to capture students' experiences of school, focusing on the kind of experiences students might find stressful.[3] Although there is a significant imbalance in the quantity of the data between Japan and Australia, this should not constitute a problem. The larger sample size in Australia simply means that the Australian results are more reliable than the results obtained from Japanese data, the quantity of which in itself is sufficiently large to conduct statistical analysis.

Given the limitation of a pre-structured questionnaire, in that it is not interactive, it was vital to ask questions which would capture the sort of experiences which students might find stressful. The question items were therefore compiled based on a review of literature on student stress, their complaints and dissatisfactions with school. Special care was taken to use language which would sound natural to students.

Contact with school was made by mobilising personal connections, i.e. friends, colleagues and acquaintances. None of the teachers or principals contacted declined to participate in the survey, either in Japan or Australia.

In Japan, the data were collected from nine schools, comprising four in Tokyo and five in various other cities. With the exception of two schools in regional centres, all schools were located either within or on the outskirts of the megalopolis of Tokyo or Osaka. Two were commercial high schools, and seven were academic high schools including four elite schools where over 95 per cent of students who participated in the study wished to advance to university.[4]

In Australia, data were collected from 21 schools in the metropolitan area of Melbourne, consisting of five elite private schools, nine state high schools and seven state technical schools. Melbourne, the second largest city in Australia, is the state capital of Victoria, one of the eight states and territories of Australia. About half of the schools participated in the survey were located in the inner city of Melbourne, and the other half, in the surrounding suburbs.[5]

Strictly speaking, the data collected in Melbourne alone do not constitute a representative sample of Australia. Australia, however, is one of the most urbanised societies in the world, where over 85 per cent of the population is concentrated in cities like Melbourne. Furthermore, although it would have been ideal to collect a national sample from all states, the discourse on Australian education does not usually distinguish the education system of one state from another unless it focuses specifically on differences in state policies. This suggests that differences between states would be negligible in the context of a comparative study. In the present study, therefore, the Australian data means the data collected in Melbourne unless otherwise specified.

Students who participated in the survey were in the first year of senior high school in Japan, and Year 10 in Australia, i.e. mostly 15 years of age. This year group was selected because Year 10 was the last year of compulsory schooling in Australia, where the proportion of students who complete secondary schools, i.e. Year 12, was only around 40 per cent when the survey was conducted (Lamb *et al.* 1995: 31). Although Japanese students in the same age group were already in the post-compulsory level, this did not constitute a problem, because 94 per cent of those who completed compulsory (i.e. lower middle) education progressed to senior school that year (ME 1985).[6]

Questionnaires were administered to the entire class by the teacher who agreed to participate in the survey. When it was appropriate to involve the year coordinator, the entire grade participated in the survey. Thus, there was little structural bias within each school in the selection of the group of students. In Australia, I delivered questionnaires to schools, meeting teachers and students there. For the Japanese data collection, questionnaires were mailed to the teacher who agreed to participate. Anonymity was ensured to students so that the content of their responses could in no way be used later to disadvantage them.

Because questionnaires were administered either in normal class or assembly, most of the questionnaires delivered were returned completed. Questionnaires were by and large well responded to and the overall rejection rate was negligible for both Japanese and Australian data.[7]

In order to compensate for the limitations of a quantitative approach, an open-ended question was included at the end of the questionnaire, asking students how they would like to change school if they could do so overnight. Students' responses to this question are cited in the book to supplement the quantitative results.

The research method adopted in the data collection seems to have fulfilled the intended objective of the survey for the majority of students, i.e. to collect data on students' experiences of school by asking the 'right' questions, i.e. questions to which students could relate, both in terms of content and expression. Maria Jensen attending a state technical school in Australia wrote:

> I would like to make school a much happier place instead of being depressing. I would get rid of some teachers as some don't really care about kids. I think if you're going to be a teacher you should be able to put up with kids coming to school with their problems and other things. School should be a happy place but it's hard to have a happy school because all the kids have different ideas and worries etc. I'd like to thank you for giving me the chance to say what I feel about school and home. This morning I felt really depressed as a teacher said something nasty to one of my friends and me and that made me very angry, depressed and I took all this pressure out on my friends which isn't really fair. So I thank you once again. Also, I think this has been the only survey which I have been able to relate to properly.

THE QUESTION OF COMPARABILITY

One of the most crucial methodological questions to be addressed in a crosscultural study is the comparability of data sets, e.g. whether groups of students who responded to the survey in Japan and Australia constitute counterparts which are sufficiently equivalent to make the comparison viable. There is also the question of sampling bias. In order to make a generalisation about Japanese and Australian students, it is essential to clarify where our data stand *vis-à-vis* the overall student population in each society.

These methodological questions, however, are not just demographic and technical ones. In order to address them, it is necessary to discuss broader issues of education in each society: for instance, what it means to go to a particular type of school, e.g. an elite school rather than a vocational school. What sort of options and opportunities do students attending different types of school have, or think they have? Is educational opportunity the same for girls and boys? To what extent is the type of school students attend conditioned by their socioeconomic backgrounds?

In order to answer these questions, three issues will be discussed below: typology of school, gender issues, and Japan's meritocracy. Japan's meritocracy will be discussed here because it is pertinent to the question of equality of education, i.e. the relationship between socioeconomic background and education, on which the demographic part of our data has something to show. It is included here also because it is a *distinctive* educational environment which affects all spheres of student life in Japan dealt with in the following chapters.

The characteristics of our data discussed below are as follows. When examined against the national data, both Japanese and Australian samples are over-represented by students attending elite schools as well as by those living in urban areas. This is not a serious problem, however, because the data sets share the same sampling bias, which is vitally important for the current study that aims to describe Japanese education in comparison to Australian education. Overall, the comparability of the Japanese and Australian data is adequately high.

TYPOLOGY OF SCHOOLS

There are a number of ways of classifying schools – private and government, single-sex and co-educational, academic and vocational, religious and secular, conventional and alternative, compulsory and non-compulsory, etc. Any single school is the combination of many of these categories, e.g. single-sex, private, academic school. Moreover, what each type of school represents will differ from society to society. The criterion considered most important by many, however, is where the school stands in the academic hierarchy – what sort of future it promises to students and parents. The measure frequently used to identify the academic position of a school is the proportion of students in it who advance to higher education. The first task of this study of the Japanese education system then is to create a typology which allows us to think about it in comparative terms with the Australian education system.

Figure 2.1 shows the distribution of schools which participated in the survey, ranked according to the percentage of students who wished to go to university. Although the number of schools in the sample was limited, the arbitrarily selected schools sufficiently portrayed the characteristics of the educational system of each society.

Japan

At the top of the Japanese sample come university-preparatory elite schools (*shingakkō*). In our sample, almost all students attending these schools, i.e. 95 to 100 per cent of students in each school, aspired to go to university. The distinctive feature of Japanese elite schools is that they are single-mindedly focused on academic achievement, measured by their success in placing students in famous universities. Elite private schools in particular enjoy the luxury of pursuing a single major goal of entrance to the top universities while public schools have numerous other goals and educational priorities (Rohlen 1983: 24). One of these elite schools, where *all* students who

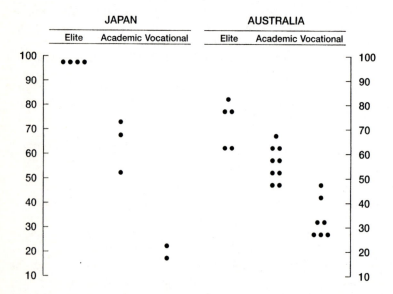

Figure 2.1 Schools classified by the percentage of students wishing to go to university
Note: Each sign (●) represents one school

participated in the survey indicated that they wished to proceed to university, is indeed one of the highest-ranked schools. In 1997, for instance, approximately half of its students gained admittance to Tokyo University and the school ranked sixth in the nation (*Sandē mainichi* 1997).

Underneath the top elite schools are general academic schools (*futsūka*). They are 'average', middle-range schools, which are predominantly public (some 75 per cent) (Hata 1983: 163). In our sample, 54 to 74 per cent of students in this category wished to advance to university. These figures are roughly consistent with the national figure: some 70 per cent of students from public academic high schools advanced to higher education in the late 1970s (Rohlen 1983: 15).[8] In fact, schools in this category constitute the backbone of Japanese secondary schools, producing most university students and catering to the needs of 'a solid middle class' of Japan (Rohlen 1983: 15–18).

At the bottom of the academic hierarchy are vocational high schools specialising in commerce, agriculture, and industry (Kim 1991: 236), and attended by more than a quarter of senior secondary school students (ME 1997). Although small numbers of students choose vocational schools (Okano 1993), the vocational specialisation means little for the majority of students – it does not reflect their interest or their desire for specialised job options in the future. Instead, the majority of students are there 'by default', having being unable to reach the entrance requirements to public academic schools and unable to afford private academic schools (Rohlen 1983: 38; Kim 1991: 238). In Rohlen's ethnographic study of five secondary schools in Japan, about one-third of the students attending a vocational school harboured the dream of advancing to university, although only 6 per cent were actually admitted to university and 10 per cent to junior college (1983: 38–9). In our sample, some 20 per cent of students attending vocational schools wished to go to university.

It is misleading, however, to position students in vocational schools only in terms of the academic hierarchy, since a disproportionately large number of students in vocational schools are from 'disadvantaged' families – families of single-parent, no-parent, ex-outcast (*buraku*) and ethnic Koreans and Chinese backgrounds (*zainichi*). In Okano's study (1993) of vocational schools, some 13 per cent of students were from single- or no-parent families in a city where only 3.7 per cent of all families with children fall into this category. In another vocational school in Osaka studied by Kim (1991), one third of students were from single-parent families, and one in four students were granted tuition exemption, which Kim notes to be common across vocational schools in general (pp. 238–9). Kim further remarks that an area where 'academic' stratification of schools is more advanced tends to have a larger number of dropouts, especially from vocational schools. This is because it is hard for students to maintain high morale in a so-called 'rock-bottom school' (p. 238). This suggests that the principle of academic competition disadvantages students from 'disadvantaged' backgrounds in two ways in Japan: first, by its general nature of converting the economic and cultural capital into academic credentials; second, by depriving them of a good educational environment through excessively sorting students into highly stratified schools (thus giving some students an irrevocable sense of failure and the incentive to leave school).[9]

In Japan, private and public schools co-exist at all levels of the academic hierarchy. Altogether, private schools account for some one third of the student population in senior secondary school (ME 1997). In our sample, two elite schools were private and two public. In clear contrast with Australia, few visible signs of prestige are displayed by Japanese elite schools, private or public. Nada, for instance, the most famous private boys' school, equivalent of 'the Etons, the Harrows, and the Grotons' in Britain and the USA, is 'neither ancient nor rich, neither aristocratic nor magnificently endowed', yet it has succeeded in placing about half of its graduates in Tokyo University and played a significant role in producing Japan's future elite (Rohlen 1983: 21).

Australia

In the Australian sample, different types of schools – non-Catholic private, state high and state technical schools – roughly constituted the academic hierarchy in that order.[10] As Table 2.1 indicates, although there is some overlap between two adjacent types of school (which may increase as more schools are included in the sample), each type of school forms a distinctive cluster.

At the top of the academic hierarchy were elite private schools where 67 to 83 per cent of students wished to advance to university. All were fee-charging, non-Catholic, single-sex schools with high prestige and top academic record, in Melbourne. They represent well the characteristics of elite private schools in general apart from the fact that there are also some co-educational private schools and a few elite Catholic schools. Being modelled after traditional grammar schools in Britain, elite private schools in Australia are almost exclusively for children from wealthy and socially established families, which can afford to pay the high tuition fees. The social status of their clientele is proudly displayed by traditional-style school uniforms, classy-looking buildings and well-kept playgrounds that occupy large plots in well-to-do suburbs. The majority of private school students in our sample spoke English at home. About half of their fathers had tertiary qualifications.[11]

Elite private schools educate around 10 per cent of secondary students in

Australia, a figure which has gradually been increasing in recent years (ABS 1996a: 10).[12] Despite this small proportion, they produce a large proportion of the doctors, lawyers and politicians in the country. Almost all students in elite private schools complete secondary education, while only four out of ten students did so in government schools in the 1980s, and less than seven in ten more recently (ABS 1996a: 67). They have constantly placed a substantial proportion of their students in universities, and those students occupy a disproportionately large place in professional faculties like medicine and law (Anderson and Vervoorn 1983). The fact that about seven out of ten students from the elite private schools in our sample wished to proceed to university reflects these realities. Clearly, elite private schools cater for the needs of the 'ruling class' of Australian society by providing an educational institution which will help them to legitimise and transmit their cultural and monetary heritage to the next generation (Connell *et al.* 1982).

Next on the academic ladder in Australia come state high schools. In our sample, 46 to 69 per cent of their students wished to advance to university. State high schools are government schools which, combined with state technical schools, educate some 70 per cent of secondary students in Australia (ABS 1984: 8; ABS 1996a: 10). Retention rates and the proportion of students proceeding to university from government schools are lower than elite private schools. Retention rates of full-time students to the final year of secondary school were 38.4 per cent for government schools and 65.3 per cent for private schools in 1984, and 65.8 per cent and 83.2 per cent in 1997.[13]

Although government statistics do not distinguish between state high and state technical schools, the two are very different, offering different curricula (academic and vocational) and serving different kinds of clientele. In our sample, state academic schools were markedly different from elite private schools as well as from state technical schools in their student diversity. They were a real 'mixed bag' in terms of ethnic and socioeconomic background. Some of the schools were located in middle-class suburbs. The majority of students spoke English at home, and the fathers' level of education was relatively high – in three out of nine state high schools, more than 25 per cent of fathers had tertiary qualifications. On the other end of the scale were inner-city schools, where over 80 per cent of students spoke either Italian or Greek at home, between a quarter and one third of the families received welfare benefits, and the great majority of fathers (around 90 per cent) had only primary or secondary education. Government academic schools thus cater for a variety of sectors of Australian society including the middle class as well as the less advantaged migrant population which tends to see education as a springboard to raise the socio-economic status of their children. In general, migrant students have higher educational aspirations than students born in Australia (Anderson and Vervoorn 1983).

The state technical school, on the other hand, sits at the bottom of the academic ladder. Only 28 to 45 per cent of their students had an ambition to go to university. Together with state high schools, they are part of the government school system, but, as the name suggests, they are vocational schools with less emphasis on the academic programme than state high schools. In terms of students' backgrounds, the profile is close to the 'traditional' working class of Australia. There is far less ethnic diversity compared to state high schools, and the majority of students (about 60 to 80 per cent) spoke English at home. The father's level of education was consistently lower compared to state high schools. Since there is no distinction between junior and senior secondary education in Australia, while the first three years of secondary school are compulsory, students can choose to go to either state high schools or state technical schools. In other words, students in technical schools in Australia are there because they want to be.

The classification of Australian schools into three groups – elite private, state academic and state technical – roughly corresponds to the typology of schools in Japan, where at the top of the academic hierarchy are university-preparatory elite schools (*shingakkō*), followed by less competitive general academic high schools (*futsūka* which are not *shingakkō*), and vocational high schools (*jitsugyōkōkō*).[14] Although there are various differences between Australian and Japanese classifications, there are fundamentally three groups of schools in both societies – elite, academic, and vocational.

Table 2.1 summarises the distribution of students in different types of school in each country as well as in our sample. The national statistics show that if ten students are chosen at random in Japan, only one would be attending an elite school, six, academic schools, and three, vocational schools. Compared to the general pattern, our Japanese sample is apparently over-represented by students who go to elite schools. Students enrolled at vocational schools seem reasonably well represented in the sample, except for the fact that schools in our Japanese data were all commercial schools. Although the breakdown of elite and academic sectors in Japan is not available, when they are put together, there has been little change in recent years in the distribution of students across different types of schools in Japan.

The same point can be made regarding the Australian data. The sample is skewed towards the elite sector. National statistics show that out of ten students selected randomly in Australia, only one would be enrolled at an elite school, seven at government schools, and two at Catholic schools. In our sample, nearly four out of ten students belong to the elite sector. This

Table 2.1 The distribution of secondary students across different types of school in Japan and Australia

Type of school	Japan			Australia		
	Sample	1984[1]	1996[2]	Sample	1984	1996
Elite	42	13[3]	} 74	39	9[4]	14[4]
Academic	33	58[5]		32	} 72[6]	66[6]
Vocational	25	29	26	29		
Catholic		–		0	19	20
Total	100	100[7]	100	100	100[8]	100

Notes:
1 Source (ME 1985: 54)
2 Source (ME 1997: 58)
3 1976 figure of schools in which over 80% of students advance to university. *Source:* Hata 1983: 163.
4 Figure for non-Catholic private (non-government) schools (i.e. the sum of 'Anglican' and 'Other'). *Source:* ABS 1984: 8, ABS 1996a: 10.
5 1984 figure for students enrolling 'futsūka' (71%) minus figure for 'elite' (13%). *Source:* ME 1984: 54.
6 Figure for government schools. *Source:* ABS 1996a: 8, ABS 1996a: 10.
7 This represents some 94% of 15-year olds in Japan. *Source:* ME 1998: 50.
8 This represents some 90% of the 15-year olds in Australia. *Source:* DEET 1988: 7.

sampling bias, however, matches rather neatly with the sampling bias in the Japanese data, resulting in two data sets quite comparable to each other.

One notable change which occurred in Australia in recent years is the expansion of students in the private sector. As the figures in the table indicate, students have been flowing out of government schools into private schools, in particular to the non-Catholic (independent) private schools.[15]

THE QUESTION OF GENDER

Japan

How about gender distribution? Table 2.2 shows the distribution of girls and boys in our data. At a glance, there appears to be a considerable over-representation of male students in the elite sector in the Japanese data. This, however, is not a sampling bias but rather a reflection of the reality. First, two out of four elite schools in our Japanese data were exclusively for boys, and the other two were co-educational. This is not accidental. In the 1980s, 14 out of the 20 highest ranked schools in Japan were exclusively for boys, and there was not a single girls' school on the list (Kariya 1995: 63).

Table 2.2 Percentages of female and male students within each type of school

	Japan			Australia		
	Female (%)	Male (%)	Total (%)	Female (%)	Male (%)	Total (%)
Elite	19	81	100	49	51	100
Academic	53	46	99	53	45	98*
Vocational	74	26	100	28	72	100

Note:

The figures for the Australian sample do not add up to 100% because some students did not specify their gender.

Moreover, the proportion of female students who advanced to university was constantly less than half that of male students in Japan until the early 1990s. For girls this figure ranged only up to 15 per cent throughout the 1980s, whereas for boys it fluctuated between the range of 35 to 40 per cent (Shimizu *et al.* 1996: 38).

This does not mean that girls are less competent academically than boys (Rohlen 1983: 308). Neither is there an inequality in the educational opportunity between boys and girls in the conventional sense – around 95 per cent of both girls and boys complete secondary education in Japan. When it comes to admission to universities, however, the difference between girls and boys is marked. Despite the ostensible equality of opportunity, university students are predominantly male (64 per cent in 1996).

This suggests that Japan's famous (or infamous) examination system is not the key factor in determining the final educational outcome of the majority of girls. Of course Japanese girls are not precluded from universities, but there are mechanisms which encourage them to divert from the mainstream career path to prepare them to follow traditional domestic roles.

Such mechanisms exists at all levels of the academic hierarchy. The lack of educational opportunity *is* indeed an issue for top female students because the majority of elite schools are exclusively for boys. It was only in the early 1990s that one school for girls emerged in the list of 'top twenty' schools of the nation. Conversely, the very fact that there are additional 'opportunities' at the tertiary level, i.e. junior colleges which are essentially for girls (over 90 per cent), provide a comfortable alternative 'receptacle' for girls in a less competitive academic and vocational environment. Junior colleges, whose courses last for only two years instead of the four years for universities, take most applicants without examination, and their curriculum is geared towards home-making and domestic science. Their primary aim is to prepare girls for future domestic roles. Furthermore, at the level of vocational schools, a tacit differentiation of gender exists. In our sample, for instance, students in vocational schools were over-represented by girls (74 per cent). This is because vocational schools participating in the survey were commercial schools. As Rohlen points out, 'commercial high schools are preferred by girls and technical ones by boys in what is in effect a voluntary sex role bifurcation' (Rohlen 1983: 38; Okano 1993: 64). In Japan, approximately two out of three students in commercial schools are girls, while the majority are boys for technical schools, e.g. agricultural and industrial schools (e.g. ME 1985: 54).

Gender then affects the educational 'opportunities' of female students in at least two ways in Japan: limiting opportunities for girls to pursue a mainstream career path at the upper level and maximising 'opportunities' to pursue conventional gender roles at the lower level. In this sense, traditional gender-specific education still exists in Japan. It happens not so much through the differentiation of curriculum between boys and girls within a school, but rather through the differentiation of schools themselves.

Underlying this is the unyielding structure of capitalism and patriarchy which dominates the spheres of work and home in Japanese society. A recent sociological study on wage differentiation in Japan revealed that (1) the male/female difference is *the most significant* determinant of wage differentials in Japan; (2) women are discriminated against, *independent of other factors* such as educational qualifications and company size; (3) sex difference in wages stems from the different treatment women get both at the point of hiring and in the process of promotion; (4) while increased age contributes to wage increase for male workers, it correlates negatively upon most female workers (Tachibanaki 1996). In other words, generally speaking, Japanese women are employed in poorer conditions than men and paid less accordingly only because they are women, and the wage they receive deteriorates as they get older while that for men improves. To put it differently, education does not pay for girls as much as it does for boys.

The patriarchal employment system of Japan is inextricably linked with the patriarchy at home. The social expectation that 'a women's place is basically in the home' is still dominant in Japanese society both among men and women. According to a survey conducted by the Ministry of Labour in 1987, 42 per cent of married women quit their job upon marriage, and a further 32 per cent upon childbirth, leaving only 26 per cent in the workforce either with or without children (quoted in Sugimoto 1997: 143). Although about one in three married women re-enter the workforce after child-rearing, they are recruited predominantly as part-timers to provide low-cost, discardable, supplementary labour for Japanese capitalism. At home too the income they provide is supplementary – which means they are locked into subordinate roles both at work and home.[16]

In this structure where capitalism and patriarchy are tightly interlocked and mutually reinforcing, the meaning of educational qualification is severely diminished for women, their social and economic power being largely determined by their gender and marital status. Unless they have some extraordinary personal solutions – such as family resources which free them from household and child-rearing duties – or choose not to get married or have children, there is not much prospect for women to utilise fully their educational qualifications in their working life. This is partly the reason why statistical equality in educational opportunity at the level of secondary education does not lead to equality in tertiary education in Japan.

However, the proportion of girls admitted to universities increased substantially between 1987 to 1994, from 13.6 to 21.0 per cent, while that of boys has not changed much since the late 1970s (Shimizu *et al.* 1996: 38). Clearly, although the Japanese education *system* is very much part of the patriarchal structure, that structure is not as robust as it is in the spheres of work and family.

In fact, as far as the everyday life of school is concerned, little difference was found in my survey between girls and boys of Japan in their experience of school. Despite the fact that educational qualification promises far less job opportunity for girls than boys, the academic achievement pressure experienced by girls was less only in elite schools. In academic and vocational schools, there was no statistically significant difference in the academic achievement pressure felt by boys and girls. Generally speaking, there were few discernible differences in the experience of school between girls and boys indicated by our Japanese data: male students found their relationship with teachers more alienating than girls did; and boys in elite and vocational schools felt more alienated from their classmates than girls did. In other areas of school life examined, however, no gender difference was found in Japan (see Appendices 3 and 4).

Australia

Compared to Japan, the educational system in Australia seems more promising in redressing gender inequality so far as educational opportunity is concerned, although this does not at all mean that it is free from perpetuating and reproducing gender inequality and gender stereotypes.[17] There seem to be three factors at work.

First is the role of elite private schools for girls. Unlike Japan, there were about equal numbers of male and female students in our Australian sample (see Table 2.2). Until recently, the main task of private girls' schools was to produce girls 'whose character was organised around sociability rather than

competition, prepared for subordination in marriage rather than dominance' (Connell *et al.* 1982: 96). Although this tradition certainly persists,
a new kind of femininity is also being formed which puts central emphasis
on the academic competitiveness necessary to prepare girls for a professional
career (Connell *et al.* 1982). One of the teachers of the elite girls' schools in
our sample was particularly proud of having produced some of the very best
students, especially in the fields of mathematics and science which were (and
still are) dominated by male students. While the construction of a new
femininity at elite private girls' schools does not solve the contradiction
built into the capitalist patriarchal order, it still presents the possibility
that 'different school policies or structures may go some way to *change* the
hierarchy of kinds of masculinity or femininity at any one time, and hence
affect the overall patterns of gender relations' (Connell *et al.* 1982: 175).

Second, the retention rates of secondary school students to Year 12 has
been consistently higher for girls than boys since the mid-1970s (ABS 1981:
7; ABS 1984: 40; ABS 1990: 56; ABS 1996a: 67), and some 60 per cent of
students who complete a bachelor degree are female students (ABS 1996b:
221). Sociologists have issued a caution regarding this data, saying that girls
still face many educational disadvantages. The argument is summarised by
Henry and others (1988: 170–2): (1) higher retention rates for girls may
reflect the greater difficulties they have in finding employment; (2) girls tend
to concentrate on the non-science and non-maths areas both in secondary
and tertiary education, which then limits their access to the highest paying
jobs; (3) girls make up less than half the tertiary students when all the post-
secondary sector (i.e. TAFE, CAEs and universities) and all students under
the age of 24 are included; and (4) women are grossly under-represented at
the higher degree level (postgraduate courses). Nonetheless, in comparison
with Japan, the data certainly indicate the first step has been taken to
correct gender inequality through education. For women to be equally or
better educated than men would certainly provide a solid ground to initiate
other changes.

The third factor which makes the educational system in Australia more
promising in redressing gender inequality than in Japan is that vocational
schools in Australia are actually technical schools (involving 'masculine'
skills), and as in Japan these tend to attract more boys than girls. In our
sample, seven out of ten students attending vocational schools were boys (see
Table 2.2). Given the fact that students in academic schools tend to have
higher educational aspirations, this sexual imbalance may become a germ to
subvert the power relations between men and women with a working-class
background, in that working-class girls, who opt to go to academic rather
than vocational schools, thereby get a higher qualification and perhaps jobs
which are securer and better-paid than their male counterparts. It has been

pointed out that the very fact of a wife's starting to earn a wage can change the power relations in a working-class family (Connell *et al.* 1982).

This rather optimistic scenario requires examination. To have work outside the home often means doubling up the total workload for most women. Moreover, as in Japan, many jobs available to women are part-time, low-cost, and dead-end (Connell *et al.* 1982: 175). In Australia as well, women tend to play subordinate roles both at home and work. There are some fundamental differences between Japan and Australia, however, in the degree of patriarchal domination. There is far more evidence of change and resistance to the patriarchal order in Australia, where gender inequality has been identified as one of the major social justice issues to be tackled in public policy. Feminism has become a legitimate social force in Australia today, either as ideas or practice or both. Education seems to have played a significant role in bringing this about.

As was the case with the Japanese students, so far as the perceptions of students are concerned, there was not much difference in the experience of school between girls and boys in Australia. With regard to the government schools, i.e. academic and vocational schools, the only area where gender difference was found at the statistically significant level was in students' relationships with classmates: male students felt more alienated from their classmates than girls. In private schools as well, boys felt far more alienated from their classmates than did girls. Gender difference was more prominent in private schools in general. The difference, however, did not suggest that private schools are merely reproducing the conventional role model for girls. Achievement pressure felt by private-school girls was higher than that felt by private-school boys. This finding coincides with the point made by Connell and others, about the formation of a 'new femininity' which puts central emphasis on academic competitiveness (Connell *et al.* 1982) (see Appendices 3 and 4).

Although to maintain the existing social order has been the function of school throughout history (Otto 1986: 1–33), Japanese schools have been especially 'successful' at it, whether it be 'Japaneseness', capitalism, or patriarchy (at the institutional level). Japan's 'success' in reproducing the existing power structure is closely linked with the perceived needs of its people to take part in education. In order to clarify this link, it is necessary to discuss the nature of Japan's super-meritocracy.

JAPAN'S SUPER-MERITOCRACY

The phenomenon of meritocracy is not unique to Japan. The idea that individuals are selected and ranked competitively according to academic merit is the fundamental principle underlying the educational system in any society today, despite its deceptive function in converting social and cultural heritage into academic heritage, and diverting attention from social inequality to an inequality in the academic ability of individuals (Bourdieu 1986).

Japan, however, 'probably approaches the ideal of meritocracy more than any other society' (Rohlen 1983: 135) as agreed by sociologists of education with comparative perspectives (Kariya and Rosenbaum 1987; Kariya 1995; Takeuchi 1995). What in fact is referred to as meritocracy in Japan is the highly developed examination system which involves almost all students. The system is admitted even officially to be the equivalent of the Japanese education system itself (*AS* 19 December 1990).[18]

Indeed, the examination system shapes a number of aspects of Japanese education – which school for a student to attend; curricula and manner of teaching; mode of assessment; behaviour and feelings of students, parents and teachers; relationship of family members to each other; and the well-being of a large number of individuals involved. Meritocracy in Japan is like climate, which determines the shape of houses, clothes to wear, the movement of people, their emotions and health, all in accordance with its seasonal changes. In order to understand the everyday life of Japanese students, which is the central aim of this book, it is crucial to understand the nature of Japanese meritocracy as *the* structure in which students live.

Meritocracy is not just an educational phenomenon. One feature of the discourse on Japanese education/meritocracy is that it is seen not just as a reflection of Japanese social order but as the very 'engine' of Japanese society – having an active rather than passive role in the making of Japanese society. Kariya Takehiko (1995), a sociologist at Tokyo University, for instance defines Japanese society itself as the 'mass-education society' – where education plays a pivotal role in the formation of the society, instead of merely functioning to maintain the status quo. His view is basically shared by Takeuchi Yō (1995), a sociologist at Kyoto University. Their view shows an interesting parallel with the fact that success at school is commonly believed to lead to success or failure in life – including the degree of future happiness (Kariya 1995). Japan may indeed be seen as a society which is centred around schools (school society) both at the level of academic discourse and popular belief.

Although emphases differ, the accounts of Japanese education and meritocracy and its relationship with Japanese society presented in recent studies by these two sociologists, Kariya and Takeuchi, are remarkably similar. Both present their arguments on the basis of an extensive review of past studies as well as empirical data. What exactly are the characteristics of Japanese education which make it particularly meritocratic and in what ways is it connected to the structure of Japanese society in general? In other words, what are the features of what Kariya calls 'the mass-education society' (1995), or what Takeuchi calls 'Japanese meritocracy' (1995)? The following are the characteristics of the 'super-meritocracy' of Japan, drawn from recent studies by these two scholars.

Kariya argues that Japan's being a 'mass-education society' (p. 12) depends on a massive number of students remaining long in formal education. In the mid-1970s, the number of students advancing to senior high schools reached 90 per cent, increasing further to around 95 per cent in the 1990s. Today, it has become 'a matter of course' for Japanese teenagers between the ages of 15 to 17 to be in senior high school. Likewise, about 30 per cent of the age cohort go to university, and another 30 per cent to other kinds of post-secondary institutions. At the age of 20, six out of ten people are still in some sort of educational institution.

However, mass education is also characterised by an 'overheat' in mass competition. As cited by Takeuchi, a survey by Monbushō revealed that the proportion of students attending after-hours coaching school (*juku*) reached 42 per cent for students in Grade 6, 53 per cent in Grade 7, and 67 per cent in Grade 9 in 1993 – a marked increase compared to the 1976 figures which were 27, 38 and 37 per cent respectively. Cramming schools are the 'strategic weapons' used in the 'examination war' (Rohlen 1980: 207). The 'examination war' has undoubtedly worsened over years driving increasingly larger numbers of people to believe that it is crucial to 'win' and survive in it. Furthermore, mass competition in the academic sphere is extended to work, involving even non-elite workers in endless competition of various sorts (Takeuchi 1995: 4).

Japan's super-meritocracy depends structurally on the ranking of all senior high schools and universities based on standard deviation scores (*hensachi*) (Takeuchi 1995). Universities are ranked nationwide and senior high schools are usually ranked regionally. Senior high schools are ranked because there is a formal entrance examination for them.[19] This means that by the time students secure admission to senior high schools, their tracking into narrow streams of academic stratification is largely complete. The track is constituted by school rather than by a separate curriculum within a school, and high school ranking largely determines the range of universities for which one can apply in three years' time. The streaming of secondary schools is so narrow that this system of selection is often referred to as 'ham-slice'. Nor is it the case that educational opportunities are totally open until the last moment before the entrance examination of a university, since actual competition occurs only among students who are ranked at a similar level.

Various measures have been taken with the aim of loosening up the academic stratification of senior high schools in Japan. Academic record in junior high schools, for instance, may be taken into consideration to give admission to a student. Academic record and examination results, however, are usually highly correlated. Even if the use of *hensachi* in the senior high schools entrance examination was officially banned in 1993, this did not help to eliminate the ranking of schools. Marks are being used instead and standard deviation scores are also made available by the gigantic examination industry, to which both students and teachers defer as the real final authority.

A glimpse of the ranking phenomena can be obtained in our data. Figure 2.1, shown at the beginning of this chapter, indicates that the Japanese schools are more widely scattered than the Australian schools – it appears as if Japanese elite schools have been 'pushed up' (to reach 100 per cent) whereas Japanese vocational schools have been 'pushed down' (to as low as 19 per cent). This suggests that the gap between different types of school in Japan in terms of placing students in universities is quite significant. It also suggests that Japanese high school students may have a more realistic view than Australian students about their chances of getting into university. In fact a comparative study of Japanese and American high school students conducted between 1982 and 1984 revealed that Japanese students are far more sober and accurate in predicting their chances of proceeding to university (Kariya and Rosenbaum 1987; Kariya 1995).

Underlying the ranking of schools and universities and the information about the relative positions of individual students is the highly developed apparatus of an examination society – its devices, services, concepts and culture. The examination industry provides all sorts of 'services' including examination-oriented study materials, classes, courses and cramming schools organised according to the specific needs of students, and nationwide examinations which produce huge data on schools; universities, cramming schools, and the performance of each individual student on the basis of standard deviation scores.

The popularisation of education, overheated competition, the ranking of schools and universities and the other apparatus of the examination society – these are all phenomenological aspects of Japan's super-meritocracy. They are relevant to what actually happens, what people can see and do. Another dimension of meritocracy is what happens in the perceptions of people, since meritocracy is also a symbolic reality which exists in the perceptions of people as a belief system and ideology. Kariya and Takeuchi agree that the most significant aspect of the super-meritocratic system of Japan is that the ethos of meritocracy has been widely internalised by the people.

For instance, drawing upon empirical data, Kariya (1995: 1–8) points out that Japanese junior high school students believe that it is important to have good marks at school even to get non-white-collar jobs such as artisan, chef, and carpenter. Even to have a happy family life in future, they thought it important to get good grades (also Kariya and Rosenbaum 1987). In another study, 80 per cent of non-university-bound students in Japan thought that they did not have the ability to go to university. In America by contrast, over 50 per cent of non-university-bound students thought that they had the ability to get university qualifications. This indicates that academic ability is considered by Japanese students as the single most important reason determining whether one goes to university or not. Similarly, Takeuchi (1995: 2–3) quotes the results of a survey conducted in Britain in 1992 as evidence that a significant number of students in comprehensive schools chose not to follow the academic path and opted for the vocational path – the kind of choice which is common in Australia and rare in Japan.

The ethos of meritocracy is prevalent at work as well. Citing the results of a survey by the Ministry of Labour, Kariya remarks that workers' perceptions and values about work and promotion are little different from those shared by the elite in Japan (p. 17). Both Kariya and Takeuchi contend that regardless of the actual effect academic credentials have upon the economic power of an individual, academic credentialism has become the dominant value system of Japanese society today, and as such it shapes the way people perceive others and themselves.

As far as the belief system is concerned, then, Kariya's depiction of Japanese society as a 'mass-education society' (*taishū kyōiku shakai*) and Takeuchi's as a 'meritocratic society' (*gakureki shakai*) are the antithesis of a class society. Both argue that, so far as values and perceptions are concerned, there is hardly any class difference in Japan. Japan is a highly stratified, seamless society where people believe that irrespective of socio-economic background there is no other means to success in life than academic credentials. People in Japan act accordingly, and the result is an epitome of the meritocratic model. Both hold that *as far as the consciousness of people are concerned*, Japan is a classless society, and that education plays the crucial role in making people see things that way.

Here their argument intersects with the proposition of Japanology (*Nihonjinron*) that Japan is an uniquely homogeneous and exceptionally egalitarian society with little class differentiation (Sugimoto 1997: 4). It also matches the results of popular opinion polls regularly released from the Prime Minister's Office to indicate consistently that the overwhelming majority of Japanese people position themselves as middle class. The 'middle classisation of a hundred million people' (*ichioku sō chūryūka*), a phrase coined to refer to this phenomenon, indeed seems firmly established in the consciousness of the Japanese.

The notion of 'classlessness' discussed by Kariya and Takeuchi, however, is a matter of perception. Neither hold that Japan is actually a classless society in economic terms. On the contrary, their arguments address the question of why people think, behave and feel in accordance with the meritocratic ideology – as if it were a fair and just system of selection, as if students were competing on an equal basis, as if their family backgrounds were irrelevant to academic outcome, as if meritocracy actually brought rewards to everyone – when empirical evidence has almost consistently indicated otherwise.

By reviewing prior studies, Kariya asserts that it is almost a 'common sense' among sociologists in Japan that socioeconomic backgrounds have a significant effect upon educational outcome (1995: 74). The student population of high ranked universities, for instance, has been consistently dominated by those from the professional, managerial and entrepreneurial classes throughout the postwar years (pp. 59–72). The educational level of parents has had a clear and consistent effect upon the academic grades of children (pp. 73–83) and their educational opportunity (pp. 85–92). Social class, which used to influence whether students advance to senior high schools or not, now influences what kind of school students go to – academic or vocational (pp. 92–7). Likewise, Takeuchi confirms the limits of academic credentialism. He points out that the virtual effect of academic qualification upon job attainment has been declining over the years (1995: 86). Moreover, academic credentials have less effect upon the economic status of an individual in Japan than in other industrialised societies, according to comparative data (Ishida 1989).

In this context, let us have a look at what our comparative data indicate. Table 2.3 shows the percentages of fathers with tertiary qualifications within each type of school. Not only in Australia but also in Japan there were striking differences in family background of students from different types of school. In both societies over half of students attending elite schools had fathers who had some tertiary education. This ratio was more than halved for students attending middle-range academic schools in both countries. Likewise, university education was low among fathers whose children attend

Table 2.3 Proportion of students' fathers with university qualifications

	Japan (%)	Australia (%)
Elite	60	51
Academic	28	16
Vocational	3	6

vocational schools in both countries. In the early 1960s when most fathers were in their late teens or early twenties, the percentages of students who went to university were still fairly small, whether in Japan or in Australia (9.7 per cent and 6.0 per cent respectively in 1960s) (Anderson and Vervoorn 1983: 20; ME 1997: 64–6). These results can be interpreted to mean that children from 'elite' families were extremely unevenly distributed across different categories of school in both countries.

Table 2.4, showing the percentages of fathers who left school without completing senior secondary education – in case of Japan after finishing junior high schools – confirms the same pattern. There is a strong relationship between family background and the type of school students attend. In the Japanese elite schools, fathers with junior high school qualifications only constitute a very small minority, whereas they constitute the majority in vocational schools.[20]

Table 2.5 shows the correlation between variables indicating socioeconomic background on the one hand and school prestige on the other, when tentative scores of 1 to 3 were assigned to vocational, academic and elite schools respectively. Although this may not be a perfect measure, it is undeniable that there is a very strong correlation between students' socioeconomic backgrounds and the type of school they attend both in Japan and Australia. Although the image people have regarding different types of schools may not be particularly class-bound in Japan, socioeconomic back-

Table 2.4 Proportion of students' fathers with lower secondary education only

	Japan (%)	Australia (%)
Elite	6	30
Academic	23	44
Vocational	50	66

Table 2.5 Correlation matrix: social-class backgrounds of students and the prestige of school they attend

	Prestige of school attended	
	Australia	Japan
Father's occupation	.53	.49
Father's education	.47	.53
Mother's education	.42	.49

ground is just as influential in students' educational opportunities as it is in Australia, where social class boundaries are much more evident.

Our own data confirm the previous studies reviewed by Kariya and Takeuchi. It shows an indisputable link between family background and educational attainment even in Japan where the meritocratic ideology prevails with such intensity. The question is how such a vast gap between the myth and the reality came to prevail in Japan without very much attention being paid to it. Several points may have contributed to this mismatch.

First, cultural differences between the working class and middle class which are often mentioned in the western context – such as language codes, values and life styles – have been less distinct and visible in Japan (Kariya 1995: 50–3; Takeuchi 1995: 229–34). There is only opaque relationship between culture and class in the Japanese context. At the same time, as absolute poverty was reduced in the process of rapid industrialisation, the difference between rich and poor became less visible (Kariya 1995: 74). Because of this, the concept of social class did not fully develop in Japan, which in turn made it difficult to see the class-based inequality in education (Kariya 1995: 29–57).

Second, egalitarianism has been the dominant tenet of discourse on education in postwar Japan. It has been a norm among educationists to give equal treatment to all students regardless of their differences, including socioeconomic differences, which might exist prior to education. It has been a 'taboo' to treat students differently, and in that sense Japanese educational philosophy was the antithesis of that underlying 'compensatory education' in Britain or 'head-start' programmes in the US. This version of egalitarianism served to promote fairness, and thus, paradoxically, diverted people's attention from the class-based inequality in education (Kariya 1995: 105–97).[21]

Third, there is a widely accepted cultural theory of learning in Japan consisting of a set of beliefs that 'people are endowed with equal ability' (Takeuchi 1995: 99), so that 'anybody can get 100 marks if one tries hard enough' (Kariya 1995: 182), and therefore that 'you have to work hard' (Takeuchi 1995: 97–8). The idea that innate ability is equal may be part of Japanese culture (Nakane 1970) or may have originated in the power struggle between the Monbushō and Nikkyōso as suggested by Kariya (1995: 182–8). The origin of this ethos of diligence needs further examination since it is hardly different from the ethos of meritocracy itself. There is even a risk of making a circular argument. Whichever is the case, however, to make a supreme effort (*ganbaru*) has been the single most important behavioural mode shared by and expected of Japanese students (Singleton 1989). The prevalence of this universal value has also served to hide the class-based inequality in education (Takeuchi 1995: 236).

Fourth, Takeuchi claims that the system of selection that is unique to Japan also serves to hide class-based inequalities. One aspect of the system is the aforementioned comprehensive ranking of schools and universities and the 'ham-slice' (i.e. narrowly tracked) mobility of students between them. These make the selection appear like a tournament game: 'when you win, you win only the right to go to the next round; when you lose, you lose forever' (Kariya and Rosenbaum 1987: 178). Takeuchi argues, however, that this system of tournament is not stringent. There are also opportunities for students who once 'lost' the game to break through the wall of the tournament (ibid.: 104–6). In that sense, Takeuchi argues, the Japanese selection system is deceptive – it is half closed and half open – and precisely because of this ambivalence, students who once lost the game cannot completely walk away from it. They are always enticed to have another game, which is perceived to be the competition between those who have higher and lower scores, rather than between those with different social backgrounds (pp. 238–42). To put it differently, Takeuchi holds that the very structure of the selection system drives Japanese students to look upward and strive endlessly and that this preoccupation itself makes it harder for them to see the pre-existing class inequality in education.

Takeuchi adds that indeed it 'makes sense' for students to strive hard in this system because, although schools and universities are ranked rigidly and accurately, they are ranked so narrowly that there is a reasonable chance for students to be 'rewarded' if they work 'a little harder'. Students are constantly encouraged to strive to reach the school or university which is one-rank higher than the one they can easily 'afford'; this causes the 'overheated' competition. In other words, Takeuchi maintains that there is a fusion between the prevalent study ethic and the particular system of selection, and that this fusion has driven students to participate further in the meritocratic competition (p. 99).

The last factor is to do with the content of education. Takeuchi points out that the school itself enhances the collective value of 'Japaneseness', which emphasises following 'common sense', being cooperative and not contradicting others or expressing disagreement, and that this provided an ideology relevant to all and thus camouflaged class division (Takeuchi 1995: 233–7). Kariya, on the other hand, argues that because class-inequality was hardly evident in schools, Japanese education produced individuals who were not divided by class antagonisms (1995: 200). Although the description of the outcome of education is the same, clearly there is disagreement over independent and dependent variables between the two.

It is also pointed out that what is required to survive in the examination war is to learn and memorise 'objective' knowledge, accessible to the masses and attainable by diligence and hard work. This seemingly class-neutral nature of knowledge and ability also serves to hide class-based inequality (Kariya 1995: 141; Takeuchi 1995: 236). At the same time, knowledge consumed in the examination war generally tends not to be highly regarded. It is widely considered that such knowledge has little cultural value and is mostly useless outside the examination system. As a consequence, Japan's elite, as the successful achiever of the meritocratic goal, is devoid of a distinct elite culture which would make them stand apart from the masses. There is hardly any cultural distinction between the elite and the non-elite of Japanese society – yet another factor serving to make class difference indiscernible (Kariya 1995: 142–3; Takeuchi 1995: 250).

Japan's meritocracy is therefore a system where a multitude of forces combine to make it hard to see the class-based inequality. The examination society is comprised of all these ideologies, educational practices, and 'media' of the examination system, as well as other social constructs peculiar to Japan such as *jukensei* (students preparing for their examinations) and *rōnin* (students preparing for examinations for the second time or more).

Takeuchi maintains that, being exposed almost a priori to this milieu of an examination society, students develop an eye to put themselves under their own surveillance, internalising the power built into the structure around them – just like prisoners in the panopticon as described by Foucault (1977). He also argues that being constantly exposed to competition and focused on winning, students tend not to hold a long-term ambition and instead develop the 'bureaucratisation of the spirit' within a 'docile body' – human beings without strong will or character, who are trained to control themselves, work diligently and cooperatively with others, perform according to external needs, able to commit themselves to a project even if they do not have much sense of purpose and meaning (pp. 249–55). The Japanese meritocracy thus produces the archetypal 'salaryman'. Kariya also shares this view, claiming that Japanese meritocracy contributed to industrialising Japan by supplying human resources who were not divided into social classes nor into elite and non-elite sectors, who are therefore able to work cooperatively either as managers or as workers (p. 200).

The outcome of the super-meritocracy, about which Kariya and Takeuchi agree, is that it has produced individuals with 'blank' characters which are suited to catering for the needs of corporate Japan. This view coincides with the image of the automaton discussed earlier, i.e. what Mimori (1997) calls the 'program-driven' personality; the new type of students discussed by Miyagawa (1995); '*shijimachi ningen*' (human being waiting for instructions) talked about by teachers; and individuals deprived of the sense of selfhood as expressed by the 'school killer' and his contemporaries (see Chapter 1). They all convey the image of individuals who are reified and alienated to the limit.

While the accounts of Japanese meritocracy given by Kariya and Takeuchi depict the broad social milieu in which students live, for the purpose of the present study, it is too structuralist. That is, the observations made remain at the structural and ideological level and convey only a superficial picture of Japanese education – superficial in that there is little analysis of conflicts and power struggles happening in the real world. For instance, although it may be true that the ideology of 'equal ability' has been strong among educationalists at the level of the educational discourse, whether or not it was in fact implemented by teachers in the classroom is a separate question. Likewise, although I agree that the hidden curriculum of schools in Japan is to enhance 'Japaneseness' among students, to present it as if it were achieved in a political vacuum is problematic. In reality, it is supported by all kinds of mechanisms of control and power and it often meets with resistance from students, parents and sometimes teachers. Similarly, it is not that the examination system alone ties school knowledge to rote learning. Careful information control in textbooks is also designed to avoid political issues as much as possible. Overall, the discourse on Japanese meritocracy tends to pay too little attention to the political aspects of Japanese education.

Contrary to the impression projected by the discourse of Japanese meritocracy, schools are full of control mechanisms, conflicts, power struggles, and resistance. Although Takeuchi's analysis that highly socialised individuals are being produced by Japan's education system may be correct, its process is not as smooth or resistance-free as is implied. The fact that student resistance no longer takes the form of an overt confrontation with the school authority does not mean that there is no resistance. Instead, student dissatisfaction with school tends to manifest in the distinctively alienated manner of group bullying and peculiar manner of nonattendance at school. As with the functionalist paradigm of education, the discourse of Japanese meritocracy has no room to deal with problematic aspects of Japanese education. Yet the fact that the meritocratic ethos is widely internalised in the minds of Japanese students does not necessarily mean that they are all totally accepting of meritocratic values. Even if they were, meritocracy alone is not able to explain why Japanese education is able to produce the kind of human being they have described – highly reified and alienated.

To put it differently, the discourse on Japanese meritocracy shares the shortcomings of the structuralist perspective in general. It is based on a passive and deterministic model of human beings trapped in a structure of power and domination that is one-sided and over-determined. Both the active nature of domination and the active nature of resistance need to be taken into consideration (Giroux 1983: 84–91).

Without this perspective, structuralist accounts tend to 'collapse into a mode of management ideology' (Giroux 1983: 90) and such theory becomes 'part of the very process of ideological reproduction' that the authors themselves are critical of (Apple 1982: 24). In other words, there is a danger that the line of argument presented by Takeuchi and Kariya might fall into the dilemma of the structuralist theory – the more logical and water-tight the thesis is, the more one-sided it becomes, until it ends up serving to reproduce the very phenomena which the theorist tries to describe critically. The more they are able to explain the all-embracing nature of meritocracy, the less room is left to explain other phenomena which are equally important to understand Japanese education – problems like *ijime* and *tōkōkyohi*.

The objective of the following section, Part 1, is to examine control mechanisms in Japanese high schools as they are experienced by Japanese students. Four aspects of school life will be discussed, i.e. student–teacher relationships, discipline and punishment, school rules, and study. It will be argued that each one of these dimensions constitutes an aspect of an integrated system of social control in Japanese schools, and that this system serves to silence and disempower students. How alienating this structure is for Japanese students will be discussed, using the case of Australia as a reference point.

NOTES

1 This book is designed to bring back, as it were, the discourse on Japanese education into the hands of the students themselves, to talk about how they themselves perceive the 'desk' they have at home, symbolically speaking.
2 The 'new' sociologists of education and Marxist writers who have emerged since the late 1960s have challenged this approach. Their criticisms have revealed various shortcomings of the functionalist theory, and it has now lost its position of dominance as a sociological theory of education.
3 The data was collected in the author's PhD project, 'Perceptions of school and school stress among secondary school students in Australia and Japan', Sociology Department, La Trobe University, Melbourne, 1993. Due to the limitation of space, only part of the data describing what sort of things students experience at school is used in this book.
4 See Appendix 1 for details.
5 See Appendix 2 for details.
6 Unless otherwise specified, all the Japanese statistics on education cited in the book are based on the Ministry of Education Statistical Summary (*Monbu tōkei yōran*) of the year.
7 For the Japanese data the rejection rate was 0.7 per cent and for the Australian data, 6.9 per cent. The rejection rate for Australia is higher only because in one particular school it was as high as 48 per cent. In that school, questionnaires were administered by a resigning teacher, who did not care to supervise students while

they were responding to the survey. A significant number of cases rejected from the analysis in Australia showed signs of resistance to do tasks prescribed by the teacher. This was ironic because the survey was designed to give students, who were generally excluded from the educational discourse, an opportunity to 'voice' their ideas. By not participating in the survey, these students 'voluntarily' marginalised themselves. The scarce information they provided – such as 'Blow up school' and 'Fuck teachers' were typically jotted down in the margins of the paper. While they conveyed their feelings well, it was insufficient to explain *why* they feel that way.

8 The national figure is higher probably because 'higher education' includes two-year junior colleges which are less prestigious and academically competitive than universities – the kind which was not included in my survey.

9 In one of the vocational schools Okano studied (1993), for instance, 17.5 per cent of students dropped out (p. 74), which is about the same dropout rate as the vocational school in Osaka mentioned by Kim (Kim 1991: 234).

10 One type of school which was not included in the Australian data was the Catholic schools. They constituted some 20 per cent of all secondary school students in Australia (19 per cent in 1984 and 21 per cent in 1996). Although some Catholic schools resemble non-Catholic, private elite schools, a large number of them cater for the working class and are closer to government schools than private schools (Henry *et al.* 1988: 122). They were excluded from the analysis because this mixed profile would make the analysis and interpretation of data extremely difficult.

11 For more details on these points, see Appendix 2.

12 Unless otherwise specified, all the Australian statistics on education cited in the book are based on 'Schools Australia' for the relevant year, published by the Australian Bureau of Statistics.

13 Since my survey was conducted in the mid-1980s, the proportion of students remaining in school to finish secondary education has increased considerably, from 45 per cent in 1984 to 71 per cent in 1996 (ABS 1984: 40; ABS 1996a: 67). While this change partly means that more people in Australia came to feel that it is necessary to get more education, it also reflects the high youth unemployment rates in Australia in recent years. That is, many opt to remain in school mainly because of the poor job prospects for school leavers. A number of teachers remarked to me that while the retention rates had increased, the sense of hopelessness among the youth that education 'does not pay' had become prevalent; and that the presence of unmotivated students had contributed considerably to classroom disruptions in recent years.

14 This classification of Japanese schools overlaps the typology of schools used in everyday life in Japan. It is also the same as the classification used by other researchers (Rohlen 1983: 11–44; Hata 1983: 163).

15 The other change is the substantial increase in the retention rate to the final year of secondary school as mentioned earlier.

16 This does not mean that women play only an insignificant role in Japan's work-force as a whole. On the contrary, more than half of all women between the age of 15 and 65 are engaged in wage labour, including 58 per cent of married women, constituting altogether over 40 per cent of the entire paid work-force in the early 1990s (Sugimoto 1997: 142).

17 There is a rich literature on the reproduction of gender identity and gender

stereotypes in Australian schools. See for instance, Davies (1996), Department of Employment, Education and Training (1993), Collins *et al.* (1996).

18 How Japan's meritocracy compares with that in Australia will be discussed in Chapter 6.

19 The exceptions are those few who go to private schools which run six-year secondary education without a break.

20 In the mid-1950s about half of Japanese students left school after finishing junior high school.

21 At the level of each individual teacher, there are exceptions like Mr Gomi in Okano's study (1993) who says that treating students with ethnic Korean and Chinese backgrounds and Japanese students in the same way does not mean treating them as 'equal' but actually disadvantages the former, so that special protection and care is needed for 'socially weak' students (pp. 104, 144).

Part I

Control: the structure of silence

3 Student–teacher relationships: the alienation paradigm

The school

The principal is the king,
The deputy is the minister,
Teachers are soldiers,
The boss in the class is the village head,
and we are commoners.
We cannot decide anything.
(Fukuhara Yōichirō, Miyazaki, Japan[1])

THE DOMINANT VIEW ON STUDENT–TEACHER RELATIONSHIPS IN JAPAN

Rohlen (1983) remarks that 'the essential point is that in average Japanese high schools the level of order is high without undue exercise of authority' (p. 18). He also writes that 'orderliness in a Japanese school does not evoke some authoritarian image in the eyes of most, but rather is pleasant evidence of benevolence, high morale, and successful instruction' (Rohlen 1983: 201). In similar vein, Merry White points out that '[c]onfrontation between teachers and students in Japan is less frequent' and that 'Japanese teachers attempt to guide and teach a teen without confrontation, [while] American teachers from the start work in the context of opposition' (White 1993: 89). Regarding primary schools, William Cummings says that Japanese teachers devote less than 20 per cent of the class time to keeping order whereas it is about 60 per cent, i.e. three times as much, in American classrooms (Cummings 1980: 111).

It is not only in the eyes of these American researchers that the Japanese classroom appears to be a model of good order. Japanese teachers who go to work in Australian schools are, conversely, often astounded by the disruptive classroom behaviour they encounter there.[2]

In fact, discipline has been a major problem facing teachers in Australia (e.g. Balson 1992).

The orderliness or disruptiveness of the classroom is often explained in terms of student–teacher relationships. In Australia, the authority of teachers is no longer readily accepted by students and each individual teacher has to establish her/his own authority over the class, by mobilising personal skills, academic, communicative or physical (Balson 1992). In Japan, on the other hand, the classroom order is maintained (according to the conventional understanding) because of the successful guidance or instruction given by teachers.

In his recent study, LeTendre (1996) elaborated on the proposition presented by Rohlen, White and Cummings. He asserts that the relationship between Japanese teachers and students is encoded by the notion and practice of 'guidance' (*shidō*). According to him, *shidō* is not restricted to the intellectual activities of teaching but includes *seikatsu shidō* (life guidance) which covers moral, emotional and physical aspects of students' lives. For instance, LeTendre explains, students in most middle schools fill out diaries, in which they write how many hours they have studied, special things they have done, and problems that are bothering them. These diaries are sub-mitted to the homeroom teacher who returns them to students with comments. In this way, he continues, the diary serves as a means of private communication between students and teachers. This allows teachers to monitor students' lives in detail, to give specific guidance to students, and to form a strong emotional connection with students (pp. 276–7).

LeTendre explains that Japanese students also form deep attachments with teachers, who supervise club activities. Clubs are the place, after the home-room, where intensive guidance is given by teachers in order to modify student behaviour – to teach students the adult norms in socially stratified situations. More specifically, this means (1) learning to endure hardships for the sake of the group, and (2) learning to obey the orders of seniors without complaining (pp. 278–81). LeTendre maintains that the relationship between teachers and students in Japanese schools signifies the relationship between seniors and juniors in general, and that the theory and practice of *shidō* is deeply incorporated in and mutually enhanced by the social hierarchy. In the case of schools this might be represented as shown in Table 3.1.

LeTendre concludes from his fieldwork that the guidance which defines the relationship between teachers (seniors) and students (juniors) in Japanese schools is based upon ideas which include:

- Teacher and learner study the same thing: i.e., there is a correct form or order to the acquisition and interpretation of knowledge – one path, one set of discoveries.

Table 3.1 The hierarchy of teacher and student positions in Japanese schools

Principal	Student body president
Vice-principal	Student body vice-president
Head of curriculum affairs division	
Head of student guidance division	
Grade committee chairs 9th	Class presidents 9th
8th	8th
7th	7th
Heads of other divisions and various committee chairs	Heads of student committees
Homeroom teachers	'In-charges'
Teachers without homeroom duties and nonteaching staff	Member of various student committees

Source: Adapted from LeTendre (1996: 286)

- The teacher is expected to have already successfully completed the path or to be more advanced than the learner.
- The learner, not knowing the path, is dependent on the teacher.
- The teacher will model the correct interpretations or correct skills, and the learner will imitate these.
- Exertion is crucial to knowing – the teacher may set the learner to strenuous and difficult tasks.
- Intense effort and a sense of appreciation of effort are necessary to successfully complete the path. But there must be balance or harmony in the learner's emotional relationship with the task at hand.

(LeTendre 1996: 287)

The student–teacher relationship in Japanese schools summarised by LeTendre is remarkably similar to the student–teacher relationship referred to by Freire as 'banking education' (1972: 46–7); by Bowles and Gintis as the 'jag and mug' approach to education (1976: 40); and by others as a 'mechanical' and 'funnelling' process of learning (Otto 1986: 25), in the field of sociology of education. All describe the same thing – the autocratic and teacher-centred approach to education. Freire calls it banking education because in this paradigm of teaching and learning, the teacher is the depositor and students the depositories. In this paradigm, their relationship is based on the following set of assumptions.

- The teacher teaches and the students are taught.
- The teacher knows everything and the students know nothing.
- The teacher thinks and the students are thought about.
- The teacher talks and the students listen – meekly.

- The teacher disciplines and the students are disciplined.
- The teacher acts and the students have the illusion of acting through the action of the teacher.
- The teacher chooses the programme content, and the students (who are not consulted) adapt to it.
- The teacher confuses the authority of knowledge with his own professional authority, which [s/he] sets in opposition to the freedom of the students.
- The teacher is the subject of the learning process, while the pupils are mere objects.

(Freire 1972: 46–7)

Freire argues that the 'more students work at storing the deposits entrusted to them, the less they develop the critical consciousness' and that the 'more completely they accept the passive role imposed on them, the more they tend simply to adapt to the world as it is' (p. 47). Freire would therefore agree with LeTendre about the expected outcome of Japanese education – that the purpose of *shidō* is to train students to accept uncritically the existing hierarchical and collective order of Japanese society.

LeTendre and Freire disagree entirely, however, regarding how students might feel about autocratic education. Freire argues that the autocratic mode of teaching and learning, which allows students to be only passive and docile recipients of a teacher's knowledge and action, is inherently oppressive and alienating. Thus he implies that the student–teacher relationship cannot possibly be satisfactory for students unless they are utterly alienated, i.e. to the extent that buds of critical awareness are stunted.

LeTendre, on the other hand, explains that the autocratic guidance given by Japanese teachers strengthens their tie with students. He argues that, instead of being alienated, Japanese students develop strong emotional connections and deep attachments to teachers through the guidance they are given. He maintains that 'life guidance', far from alienating students by extending the control by teachers in the non-academic area of the student's life, is the key to enhance the tie between students and teachers.

LeTendre is not alone in projecting this view. Other Japanologists suggest that there is something 'more' in the student–teacher relationships in Japanese schools than can be explained in western theory, something which is almost beyond the comprehension of westerners – a paternalistic relationship characterised by positive aspects such as trust, closeness, commitment, care, dedication, emotional attachment, respect, understanding, and benevolence (White 1987: 90).

Within Japan, this is precisely the line of argument which is promoted by extremely autocratic groups such as the 'Professional Teachers' Association'. A number of teachers in Aichi prefecture, where LeTendre conducted his fieldwork, would argue in the same vein (see e.g. Kato 1990) (see Chapter 4 on Aichi). A similar view would be held by the proponents of *Nihonjinron*. Nakane Chie, a leading advocate of *Nihonjinron*, comments on the relationship between the leader (senior) and the subordinate (junior) in Japanese society as follows.

> The most significant factor in the exercise of the leadership is the personal ties between the leader and his immediate subordinates. Strong, functional personal ties always derive from the informal structure. . . . The vertical personal relationship is more dynamic in character than the horizontal relationship. Protection is repaid with dependence, affection with loyalty. . . . The emotional sympathy felt by the leader towards his subordinate is expressed in the term *onjō-shugi*, or 'paternalism', and always presupposes a sympathetic appreciation of his men.
>
> (Nakane 1970: 66–8)

Although Nakane is not directly discussing student–teacher relationships in schools, she is talking about the fundamental character of human relations between seniors and juniors in Japanese society. LeTendre says that the relationship between teachers and students is not confined only to schools but is applicable to any relationship between seniors and juniors (p. 287). The student–teacher relationship we are examining in the context of the school, therefore, has a broad implication for the understanding of Japanese society in general. Although we are focusing on educational issues, there is a more fundamental underlying tension between generalist 'western-made' theories (which in this context commonly means humanist Marxist theories) and particularist views of Japanese society as a 'paternalistic dream world'. This latter view in practice is close to a structuralist-functionalist theory of society.

But theories are theories – all value laden and never free from the cultural specificity of the society from which they are born nor from the cultural expectations of researchers. Researchers, regardless of their philosophical orientation, seem to be in agreement that the student–teacher relationship in Japan is hierarchical. So if this is conceded, what still needs to be clarified is the question of whether or not Japanese students develop strong personal connections with teachers. My survey attempted to elucidate this question.

STUDENT–TEACHER RELATIONSHIPS: STUDENTS' PERCEPTIONS

I asked students whether their teachers were easy to talk to about personal problems (Table 3.2). The results obtained from Japanese students are extremely negative. The majority of Japanese students (72 per cent) indicated that it was *never* easy to discuss their personal problems with teachers. Contrary to the claim made by LeTendre, for the majority of Japanese students in our sample (93 per cent) teachers are not the kind of people with whom to discuss personal concerns. This was the case despite the fact that the students in our sample were over-represented by those attending elite schools – those who are likely to be more compliant than those belonging to the lower strata of the academic hierarchy. Furthermore, students in our sample were older than the junior high school students in LeTendre's study. According to the theory of *shidō*, older students should have been better trained to cultivate emotional and personal ties with teachers, but this does not seem to have been the case.

This result coincides with the observation made by Kohama Itsuo, an educational critic, who argues that human communication between teachers and students in Japanese schools has been broken down to the extent that the idea of teachers' listening to students' personal worries would be perceived by students as 'unreal' and almost a contradiction in terms (Kohama 1985: 108).

The prevalence of disruptive behaviour in Australian classrooms suggests that students are more rebellious and insubordinate to teachers than Japanese students and, therefore, that there might be a greater distance between students and teachers there. Australian students, however, indicated that it is easier for them to talk with teachers about their personal worries than did Japanese students. Although this does not mean that Australian students count very much on teachers to discuss personal problems, only 22 per cent of them denied the possibility entirely by

Table 3.2 Comparative student–teacher relationships: the approachability of teachers

	'Teachers are easy to talk to about personal problems'			
	Never (%)	*Sometimes* (%)	*Mostly* (%)	*Always* (%)
Japan	72	21	6	2
Australia	22	45	24	8

choosing 'never' (as against 72 per cent in Japan). For about one in three Australian students (24 plus 8 per cent) teachers were people with whom students could talk about personal matters when necessary. The result suggests that there is much more room for close communication between teachers and students in Australian schools than in Japanese schools, while for Japanese students, communication with teachers at a personal level is extremely limited.

This does not mean, however, that Japanese students do not want to have close communication with teachers. A comparative study of Japanese and American high school students found that the kind of teacher that Japanese students wished to have most was the teacher whom they could consult with ease on all sorts of things – 70 per cent of Japanese respondents wanted such a teacher if possible (Takeuchi 1983: 156).

It is not surprising to see that more than seven out of ten students in Japan categorically denied that teachers are easy to talk to about personal problems. Behind this is the reality that students are rarely listened to by teachers in Japanese schools. 'Not being listened to by teachers' is felt by many Japanese students as the key issue in their relationship with teachers, and 'to be listened to by teachers' has become such a 'big deal' to them. Okuchi Keiko, a specialist on *tōkōkyohi* students, points out that the quality of a 'good teacher' repeatedly referred to by *tōkōkyohi* students is that the teacher listens to the student (Okuchi 1992: 41). In our survey, Miyamoto Akira, who attends an elite school in Tokyo, commented that:

> Teachers should listen to students' opinions more and give lessons in which students are willing to participate. The fault is with teachers when students do not listen to them.

The dissatisfaction with their teachers of students like Akira and his class-mates, who are doing well academically, leads only to 'passive resistance' (i.e. unwillingness to participate or listen to teachers in class) – a relatively mild, though not insignificant, response. For other students who are regarded by teachers as being 'problem kids', not being listened to by teachers has far more serious implications.

One group leader of 'problem kids' in a junior high school in Chiba said that teachers had long determined that his group was bad and would not listen to them no matter how much they tried to talk. Instead, he continued, each time they tried to talk, teachers 'punished' them with violence without giving them the chance to express themselves. Only one teacher was 'kind' – each time they did something wrong, he asked them the reason (Kamata 1984: 144–5). What is striking about this episode is that this student regarded the teacher who was prepared to listen to him as being 'kind', as if to say that it is a special favour or quality for a teacher. This suggests, in turn, the barrenness and one-sidedness of the interaction between the student and other teachers.

This is a sad reality shared by many others in Japan. Hokusēyoichi is a school in Hokkaido famous for its willingness to take 'problem kids' and school drop-outs from all over Japan. Being asked the difference between this school and other schools, one student commented that 'everybody is warmer in this school – teachers, students and others around the school. *Teachers listen to students*. If teachers think that they are wrong, they apologise. This is unthinkable in other schools' (emphasis added). Likewise, in the school's speech contest another student stated that three criteria of a good teacher would be 'willingness to listen to students and not to be prejudiced against them, and the ability to apologise when in the wrong'. She had found such qualities only at Hokusēyoichi (Hirose 1989: 62).

It appears that both 'good students' and 'problem kids' in Japanese schools feel that they are not sufficiently listened to by teachers. The relationship between teachers and students is a hierarchical relationship where one-way, top-down communication is the norm, and students are not at all satisfied with this.

While I was collecting data in Japan, one teacher informed me that the principal of his school had ordered that students not be allowed to answer the open-ended question about the image of an ideal school. The reason was that 'it is an inappropriate question to ask of students at this moment'. The teacher instructed students accordingly and no students from that school answered the question. The response of the principal suggests that he had no interest in finding out what students wanted – their needs and feelings. He had no intention of 'listening' to students. His interest was rather to block any opportunity for students even to think about what they might want, and thereby to 'contain' potential discontent in their minds. Asked the same question, the principal of one private girls' school in Australia hesitated slightly but gave me permission to use the question after a direct discussion. While collecting data in Australia, I often encountered appreciation and encouragement from teachers who were genuinely interested in the result of the survey and keen to find out how their students felt about school life.[3]

What I experienced during the Japanese data collection seems to have been not atypical. Japanese schools are extremely cautious to avoid doing anything which might lead to criticism of the school by any party at all. Examples follow.

- Teachers in Hokkaido forbade senior high school students in 1983 to print a special issue of a student newspaper focusing on regimentation in schools (Fujii 1984: 281).

- Principals of a number of schools in Chiba prevented school librarians from purchasing certain books, including one entitled *Kangaeru kōkōsei* (Thinking high school students) (*Asahi jānaru* 30 November 1984).[4]
- One principal in Aichi pressured a local bookshop not to offer for sale a book entitled *Mado no nai gakkō kara* (From a school with no windows), which focuses on the regimentation in schools in Aichi (Kamata 1995: 249).
- Parents were told by the homeroom teacher to 'refrain from criticising school no matter what' on the very first day of school, in a senior high school in Nagano in 1987 (Nishizato 1989: 31).
- A citizens' group called 'The association to think about children's human rights and health in Kobe' sent letters to students' associations in the city shortly after Ishida Ryōko (15) was crushed to death against a school gate (see Chapter 4). The letters were all censored by teachers before they reached students (*AS* 16 December 1990).
- A speech which was to be delivered by a student representative in a senior high school in Nagano at a graduation ceremony of 1991 was cancelled by teachers in the name of '*shidō*' because it included a phrase: 'Do teachers really understand students?' (Higaki 1991: 232).

Teachers are also caught up in this network of censorship. One teacher in Aichi who tried to deal with such topics as peace, pollution and social welfare in the classroom newsletter was not only ordered by the principal to cancel the issue but eventually fired. This teacher had previously been criticised by the principal for listening to students too much when they broke school rules. When he was summoned by the local board of education for further 'discipline', 37 out of 40 students in his class followed him to give him moral support (Kamata 1995: 228).

There are layers of censorship in and around Japanese high schools including what students, parents, teachers, librarians and sometimes even local communities can say or do. This does not mean of course that such a system of information control is at work in every school in Japan. For many teachers, however, the greatest concern is how to prevent students from thinking critically and expressing themselves, and how to 'protect' students from being 'exposed' to 'dangerous ideas'. In this milieu of Japanese high schools in general, it would often be too much to expect teachers to listen to students or to have good communication with them.

With this milieu in mind, it is doubtful that the diary kept by students and inspected by teachers actually functions to form a strong emotional connection between a student and a teacher, as explained by LeTendre (1996). An alternative interpretation would be to say that it is a means to check and control each student individually on a daily basis and that it serves for teachers to monitor students' lives in detail and to give specific guidance to students, but not to provide any means of two-way interaction in which the teacher and the student can communicate on an equal basis.

If indeed the custom of diary inspection serves to establish a strong emotional tie between students and teachers, we cannot explain why Japanese students rarely feel that they are respected, understood, cared for and trusted by teachers. As Table 3.3 indicates, exactly half the Japanese students indicated that teachers *never* treat them with respect. More than four in ten students thought that teachers *never* really understand students. More than one in three students felt that teachers *never* care about them as persons, and that teachers *never* show that they trust students. While 'never' and 'sometimes' are put side by side, there is a qualitative difference between choosing 'never' and 'sometimes'. The former is categorical and suggests that students have no hope of seeing these characteristics in teachers, while 'sometimes' allows room for some exceptions – it indicates that there is some hope for students. Although the results obtained from

Table 3.3 Comparative student–teacher relationships: teachers' respect, understanding, care and trust

	Never (%)	*Sometimes* (%)	*Mostly* (%)	*Always* (%)
Japan				
Teachers treat me with respect	50	38	10	3
Teachers understand students	44	38	16	3
Teachers care about me as a person	39	46	12	3
Teachers show trust for students	36	39	21	4
Australia				
Teachers treat me with respect	12	49	33	6
Teachers understand students	13	60	25	3
Teachers care about me as a person	12	50	29	8
Teachers show trust for students	15	52	29	4

the Australian students are not very positive either, the proportion of students who categorically denied the possibility that teachers trust, care, understand, and respect students was far less in Australia (all below 15 per cent) than in Japan.

Nakamura Naomi (12) who has continued *tōkōkyohi* for over five years writes:

> I have a dream. It is to become a teacher. . . . Teachers tell my friends to try to understand my feelings. But it is my teacher who least under-stands my feelings. . . . I wonder if she has ever understood my feelings. That's why I want to become a teacher myself. . . . I would like to become a good teacher who would help students to have a wonderful youth – not just one filled with study.
>
> (Ishikawa *et al.* 1993: 399–400)

Similarly Shimada Erika (15) in Niigata, who has not attended school for three years, writes:

> Teachers, please look around you well. There are students who are suffering. Even students whom you think are simply noisy and cheerful may be troubled deep in their hearts. I often notice that kids who appear to be just loud and insensitive to others occasionally have an expression of sadness in their eyes. When I notice it, I call out in my heart 'teacher, please be more perceptive. . . . There are many students like this even among those whom you think are having no problems. Teacher, please notice those students, please try to see those students.
>
> (Ishikawa *et al.* 1993: 480)

Erika also wants to become a teacher in charge of the school clinic (*hoken-shitsu*) who is able to understand students well. It is precisely the quality which is lacking in their teachers for which they yearn most (Ishikawa *et al.* 1993: 482).

Japanese students tend to find it extremely difficulty to relate to teachers as humans. In the formal, authoritarian and hierarchical environment, Japanese students often crave 'warmth' and a 'human dimension' in their relationships with teachers (Fukaya 1983: 209). Among the very few comments given by the Japanese students in my survey was: 'I want teachers to be more cheerful and gentle' (Mori Miwako attending an academic high school). Sakamoto Yuri from a vocational school wanted to have a school where 'teachers and students can laugh together'. A few wrote that if they could change school over night, they would like to have a teacher like 'Kinpachi sensei' – a TV character who is a warm and open-minded

teacher, who genuinely cares about students, and who dares to contradict
fellow teachers or superiors, if necessary, on behalf of students. This TV
series, extremely popular among teenagers in the 1980s, started again in
1995 with new stories dealing with more recent school-related problems
such as *ijime* and *tōkōkyohi*.

Perceptions Japanese students have about their relationships with teachers,
as well as other evidence quoted above, indicate that student–teacher
relationships in Japan are extremely teacher-centred and autocratic. While
there are ample indications that student–teacher relationships are hierarchical, as the conventional theory of Japanese education admits, there is little
evidence that Japanese students actually develop a sense of the benefit of
receiving paternalistic 'care' and 'guidance' from their teachers. On the
contrary, Japanese students seem to feel that their relationships with
teachers are thin, impersonal and alienating. They do not feel that they
are nurtured by their supposedly close relationships with their teachers.

We have seen that Japanese students are more negative than Australian
students about the quality of their relationships with teachers. They feel less
cared about, less trusted, less understood, less respected, and less able to
discuss personal matters with teachers. This difference reflects the difference
of educational paradigm – Japanese students are more alienated in their
relationship with teachers because the educational system in Japan is more
autocratic and teacher-centred.

AUTOCRATIC PARADIGM, DEMOCRATIC PARADIGM

It is my hypothesis that Japanese education represents an autocratic
paradigm of education, while Australian education represents a combination of democratic and autocratic paradigms. This is not to say that Japanese
education is completely autocratic. There are a number of teachers who
fight against the system and try hard to establish democratic relationships
with students. Yet to do so is often a battle against the system, as it was
indicated by the example of the teacher in Aichi who was dismissed for
'being understanding to students' and for his 'political bias'. Conversely, the
Australian system is not completely democratic either. Rather, it is a system
in which both the democratic paradigm and the autocratic paradigm co-exist
with comparable strength (see the conceptual diagram shown in Figure 3.1).

In the autocratic paradigm, student–teacher relationships are hierarchical and authoritarian; teachers are respected by students and not vice versa,
whereas in the democratic paradigm, student–teacher relationships are
relatively equal, and mutual trust and respect are promoted. In the auto-

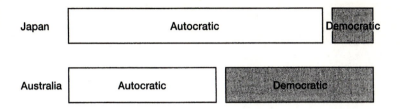

Figure 3.1 Contrasting educational paradigms of Japan and Australia

cratic paradigm, discipline is primarily a means to establish teacher control over students, and the use of corporal punishment is justified, whereas in the democratic paradigm, emphasis is on ways to persuade students and negotiate with them to maintain necessary order in school, and physical coercion is not used by teachers. In the autocratic paradigm, school rules are minute and detailed and imposed by teachers upon students, whereas in the democratic paradigm, school rules are kept to a minimum and students generally understand the necessity of such rules. In the autocratic paradigm, learning and teaching is mechanical, instrumental and competitive, and students are only the recipients of prescribed knowledge, whereas in the democratic paradigm, the learner is encouraged to interact with and relate to knowledge and there is much room for cooperation with classmates. In the autocratic paradigm, teachers are the only decision makers, whereas in the democratic paradigm, students participate in the decision making. In the autocratic paradigm, relationships between teachers are also hierarchical, whereas in the democratic paradigm there is more equality in the way teachers interact with each other. The autocratic paradigm ultimately aims to mould students into the pattern prescribed by the society, whereas the democratic paradigm aims to foster the individuality of each student. The autocratic paradigm is oriented towards uniformity, whereas the democratic paradigm promotes diversity. The autocratic paradigm is fundamentally alienating, whereas the democratic paradigm tries to achieve de-alienation (see Table 3.4).

Some Japanese students directly comment on the autocratic paradigm of education in a critical manner. Shimada Erika, I quoted above, comments on the ritual of bowing to teachers, which is one symbolic representation of the autocratic and authoritarian mode of education.

I really hated to bow to the teacher at the beginning and the end of each lesson. It really puzzles me why teachers make us bow to them, sometimes repeatedly when there are students who did not bow properly. Teachers

Table 3.4 Opposing paradigms of education

	Autocratic	*Democratic*
Student–teacher relationships	Hierarchical and authoritarian; one-way respect to teachers	Equal, based on mutual trust and respect
Discipline	Means of teachers' control over students; corporal punishment justified	Emphasis on persuasion of and negotiation with students; no corporal punishment
School rules	Minute and detailed; imposition by teachers	Minimum of basic principles; no imposition
Study	Mechanical, instrumental, competitive; learners as passive receivers of knowledge	Interactive and cooperative learning
Decision making	Teachers are in charge	Students participate
Teacher–teacher relationships	Hierarchical and authoritarian	Less hierarchical; more equality among teachers
Aims	To mould students into a prescribed pattern	To promote individuality and strength of each student
Orientation	Uniformity	Diversity
Main feature	Alienating	De-alienating

must be thinking that they are 'kindly doing us the favour of teaching'. Otherwise it does not make sense, because we have the right to be educated, teachers have the duty to teach, and without students there will be no teachers.

(Ishikawa *et al.* 1993: 479)

Similarly, Kameyama Masami (13) in Kanagawa, who is also a *tōkōkyohi* student, points out that it is the absolute power given to teachers and the total subordination expected of students that he resents most. In his words:

There are many reasons that I came to be disgusted with school but first, I *really came to be tired of taking the side of the powerful, pleasing and fawning on teachers.* The weight of teachers oppresses us tremendously. We are scolded by teachers if we say or do something which disadvantages them. In other words, we, *tōkōkyohi* people, are truly fed up with sucking up to teachers. Teachers are judgemental and get angry at us for doing things we believed right. Adults tell us to think before doing something, but as long as teachers behave this way it will be impossible to learn to think before taking an action.

(Ishikawa *et al.* 1993: 437)

It is not that students are only critical of their subordinate position in relation to teachers. A 15-year-old girl with the pen name of 'Serurian', who also did *tōkōkyohi*, comments on the way teachers interact with each other in Japanese schools.

To be frank, the junior high school is a place which is full of ideas beyond the comprehension of ordinary people. It's a kind of 'other world'. Teachers who occupy the top of this 'the other world' have no brains . . . they do not think about anything. (It seems that those who think less about things survive better in that world.) They are just well-behaved robots who simply say 'yes, yes' to their seniors. This is apparent if you speak to them only a few minutes.

(Ishikawa *et al.* 1993: 473)

In these comments, students in Japan reject hierarchical relationships in-herent in the autocratic paradigm in Japanese schools and ask fundamental questions – why should it be necessary to be forced to bow to teachers, to be submissive to teachers, to accept unjustified scolding? And why should junior teachers be so obedient to their seniors?

COMPETING PARADIGMS IN AUSTRALIAN EDUCATION

Compared to the Japanese system in which the democratic feature of education is pushed into a corner, the Australian education consists of two competing paradigms of education with comparable strength. Although there are teachers who stick with the autocratic paradigm, there is also a comparable number of teachers who practise the democratic approach.

For instance, there could be two deputy principals with very different approaches to students, as is commented on by a teacher:

Kids who perform outrageously in class, they can hurl furniture or abuse, to the *n*th degree, and if you go to the Boss [the former deputy] . . . [he] will crucify them. . . . [However, the new deputy who replaced the Boss], you'd be a fool to send anyone to him, you really would, because he sides with the kid.

(Connell 1985: 108–9)

Some teachers maintain an authoritarian approach in education and impose a 'cheerful brutality' with no reservations, including 'coming down hard in the first week; punishing a couple of kids, no matter who, for any offences, no matter how small; and then when they are under control, easing up in the following weeks' (Connell 1985: 105). Alan Watson, a teacher at a private school states, for instance:

> My general philosophy is that in First Form you terrify [students] so much that it takes them six years before they realise that you're at all human.
>
> (Connell 1985: 104)

For many teachers, to become authoritarian is a pragmatic choice. Arlette Anderson, a teacher at state high school in a working-class suburb of Sydney, admits that she had to become 'very autocratic' to control students who were 'so undisciplined, so noisy, so rude' (Connell 1985: 103).

Other teachers, however, advocate and adopt a 'progressive' or 'liberal' approach to education. Many believe that the good teacher is someone who is successful at persuasion and stimulates participation in learning, and does not rely on coercion, whether psychological or physical (Connell *et al.* 1982). One private school teacher decided not to send her child to the school she herself taught in because:

> I wouldn't like any child of mine to be spoken to in the way that the head speaks to the kids.
>
> (Connell 1985: 112)

As Sheila Goffman, a young teacher working in a state high school, puts it:

> Learning doesn't necessarily happen in a dead quiet classroom with everyone jumping when you say 'jump'.
>
> (Connell 1985: 14)

Sheila gained her strength from her immediate supervisor, the subject head of English, who not only provided 'a warm reception for her flow of bright ideas about the curriculum, but also a context of support for her student-centred practice' (Connell 1985: 18). This did not mean, however, that there was a consensus in her school that democratic education was to be promoted. Connell explains.

> The English staff as a group decided to throw open their staffroom to the kids to come in and chat, to convey the idea that they think of them

as 'people' with whom one can have a relationship outside the class-room. Other departments, Sheila notes, think they are 'crazy' to give up their privacy – and, no doubt, create unwelcome precedents. The custom in the school is that the kids stop at the door and do not come into the staffroom.

(Connell 1985: 18)

The existence of the competing educational paradigms in Australian schools means that students in Australia do not face a 'united front' of teachers such as might constitute an overwhelming power in the school as well as in the broader educational environment. This explains the less 'extreme' responses obtained from Australian students in my survey compared to those given by Japanese students. It also explains the diversity of comments given by Australian students about their relationships with teachers.

Some students expressed their discontent with formal and hierarchical relationships with teachers, by referring to 'barriers between students and teachers' which they want to 'break down'. Jane Galley, a private school student, commented that if she could change the school, she would:

> make the school a more comfortable community. Improve the rela-tionships between students and teachers. Make the atmosphere less formal, strict. A student's self-esteem is destroyed by the way teachers treat us, the way they do not respect us and the way they embarrass us in front of our peers. They are very inconsiderate of our feelings. We are *just another number in their roll books*. A more personal, closer relationship should be encouraged between students and teachers (emphasis added).

Jane refers to an element of alienation – reification, i.e. treatment of people as things. This is a source of discontent expressed also by state high school students, Tom Patterson and Angela Pavkovic.

> I would like there to be better qualified teachers who are more able to assist us both academically and personally. *Too many teachers see us as being objects* and do not care if we succeed or fail as long as it looks as if they have done their job. Many teachers are unfeeling and fail *to teach us as humans*. There are some exceptions (emphasis added).

> I think teachers should trust students more at school and treat them as adults and individuals *instead of just a robot* (emphasis added).

Jane, Tom and Angela all indicated that they did not want to be treated like things – numbers, objects and robots. As they say, the antithesis of being treated as objects is to be treated as humans. Treatment as a human would mean teachers caring about how they are doing academically, making an effort to understand their feelings, trusting them, and treating them as individuals – some of the central features of the democratic mode of student–teacher relationships (or any other human relationships).

Other students in Australia, however, express their appreciation of the democratic approach their teachers have. Ian Summerfield, a technical school student, wrote:

> This school is a school with a lot of personality. The teachers enjoy a good joke as long as it is in good taste. The rules are quite slack as we have a lot of trust put in us and that trust is respected by the students (or most of them). The more we are trusted the better things work.

Helen Erindale from a private school wrote:

> My school is very large and so I tend to feel like just one of the multitude rather than an individual person. I would like all my teachers to be modelled on my Science teacher. She is pleasant and the class is very relaxed. She is young and appreciates humour all the time. She is not only a very interesting person, she makes the lessons interesting so that we always look forward to Science. She makes us work hard but you tend not to realise it because there is no tension in class or fear of being told off.

What Helen appreciates in the relationship with her science teacher are (1) the ability to relate to students as individuals (in an informal and relaxed manner) and at the same time to have (2) the ability to teach, i.e. to make lessons interesting and get students to learn. These are the points made by Joanne, a private school girl in the study by Connell and others (1982: 101).

> *What's the science teacher like?*
> Oh, I don't like Mr Andrews much. . . . He's – boring. He cracks these smart jokes that aren't funny. And then gets annoyed when everyone doesn't laugh. . . . We've [also] got a student teacher that comes in. She teaches a lot and I like her better.
>
> *What does she do that's better?*
> She gets us to work but she doesn't sort of – I don't know – push us that much. He says 'Right you've got to do this'; and she says 'Right we'll do

this now, okay?' Everybody just says 'Oh yeah, right-oh' and they do it. But he just says 'Do it now quickly' and you just sit there going 'ooh-er'.

Mrs Brown my Maths teacher, she gets you to work . . . she forces you but she sort of does it in a nice way, in a way that you don't really mind. And if the class has a joke, well she laughs. But then we sort of get back to our work. But other teachers they don't laugh, and make you get straight back to your work, and that just annoys you, annoys me.

It is noteworthy that students repeatedly refer to whether the teacher is able to laugh with students as an indicator of a good relationship. Laughter represents the relaxed atmosphere and the teacher's ability to relate to students as human beings, rather than just 'objects' which they are obliged to teach.

GENERAL TRENDS OF EDUCATION: JAPAN AND AUSTRALIA

Japan

Students' experiences of school in Japan and Australia reflect the overall trends in the education in each society. Generally speaking, Japanese education has become increasingly autocratic and less democratic over the years, while Australian education has become more democratic as far as student–teacher relationships are concerned.

Japanese students and teachers enjoyed a brief period of democratic education in the years immediately after the war: between wartime militarism and the resurgence of bureaucratic and nationalistic education in the mid-1950s. The 1947 Fundamental Law of Education declared the principles of the new education of Japan, i.e. that education would no longer be used as the means to promote nationalism, and that it had to be recognised as a constitutionally guaranteed right of the people (Horio 1988: 255). Basic principles of democratic education spelt out in the law were academic freedom and local autonomy.

Horio (1988) demonstrates how the spirit of the new democratic education of Japan was expressed in a number of official documents created at the time. The preface to the Summary of the Draft for a Fundamental Law of Education of 1946 states:

Educators in our country have in the past been deficient in self-awareness and critical reflection. . . . Eventually all arenas of learning and teaching fell under the sway of militarism and ultranationalism. To correct this most troubling situation, education must be reformed right down to its roots. . . . Educational administrators have to respect academic freedom and educational independence.

(quoted in Horio 1988: 256)

The same spirit was apparent even in Monbushō's Draft of the Fundamental Law of Education, presented to the Diet in 1947, which reads:

Education shall not be subjected to improper political or bureaucratic control. It shall bear an independent responsibility towards the Japanese people. With this consciouness firmly implanted in their thinking, our educational administrators shall respect academic freedom, and we must endeavor to bring about the various conditions necessary for the realization of fundamentally new educational objectives.

(quoted in Horio 1988: 256)[5]

The first Course of Study of 1947 'was an unambiguous condemnation of the prewar educational formulas for imposing unified control from above' (Horio 1988: 257). It stated:

From this time forward, however, we will proceed from the bottom up, drawing upon the collective efforts of all involved . . . . The curriculum should be decided upon at each school, after careful determination of those educational objectives appropriate to the work of the school in question. This requires consideration of the realities of the community in which the school is located. Teachers should attempt to formulate the curriculum that they will teach only after engaging in this kind of critical self-reflection.

(quoted in Horio 1988: 257)

The Course of Study in 1951 further expanded the nature of curriculum as follows.

Since the construction of curricula is best accomplished when there is mutual interaction between students and teachers, the Course of Study is best understood as an aid to teachers, a set of suggestions to be used as a point of reference.

(quoted in Horio 1988: 258)

In this milieu of postwar democracy, independent teachers' organisations sprang up in many regions and were amalgamated into a national federation which later became Nikkyōso (Japan Teachers' Union). In 1947, 98 per cent of elementary school teachers of Japan belonged to the National League of Teachers' Union which was a forerunner of Nikkyōso (Marshall 1994: 152) which adopted the motto of 'Never send our students to the war'.

Horio argues that the student–teacher relationship in this democratic paradigm of education was the antithesis of what it used to be in the autocratic paradigm of the prewar years. In the prewar years, Horio remarks, the relationship was symbolised by the children's song, 'Suzume no gakkō' (sparrows' school) which goes:

Teachers in the sparrows' school chirp while brandishing a whip . . .

The student–teacher relationship in the democratic paradigm between 1945–54, on the other hand, was less hierarchical and more equal as is symbolised by another children's song, 'Medaka no gakkō',[6] which goes:

In *medaka's* school . . . who is the teacher, and who are the students?

According to Horio, there was a genuine enthusiasm among teachers who wanted to teach something to children in the poverty-stricken yet liberated social atmosphere of early postwar Japan (Horio 1994: 186).

The ruling elite of Japan, however, launched a campaign in 1951 to 'correct the excesses' of postwar democratisation (Horio 1988: 146). In the increasing confrontation between the US and Russia, the Red Purge had begun a few years earlier in Japan (Horio 1994: 211). In the mid-1950s, in conjunction with the establishment of the 1955 system,[7] a number of changes which nullified the principles of democratic education were introduced and the so-called 'reverse-course' began.[8]

In 1956, the 1948 Board of Education Law, which had guaranteed the local self-control of education and the citizen's basic educational rights was repealed by a law which provided for boards of education not elected but appointed by the governors (at the prefectural level) and mayors (at the municipal level) (Horio 1988: 142; Marshall 1994: 183).

In 1956, Monbushō made a number of substantial changes to tighten its textbook certification procedures and, after 1957, school teachers no longer had as much input in the selection of textbooks, as the new appointed board of education exercised more control over it (Marshall 1994: 185; Horio 1988: 164).

In 1957, the Teacher Evaluation System (*kinmu hyōtei*) was introduced. Principals were charged with filing an annual personal report on each teacher in their school, including an assessment of 'loyalty and love of education' (Horio 1988: 215f) and 'how sincere, reliable, and cooperative a teacher had been' (Marshall 1994: 189). The most problematic feature of this system was 'the fact that the teacher's rating remained a secret and was generally used to promote only teachers who supported the government's educational goals' (Horio 1988: 215f). It also provided the means to punish union activists and thereby undermined the union (Horio 1994: 234).

In 1958, the 1947 Course of Study, which had been serving as reference material for teachers preparing their teaching plans, became an officially prescribed curriculum, with legal binding power (Horio 1994: 221).

With these changes, the democratic principles established in the immediate postwar years were reversed. Henceforth, instead of academic freedom of teachers and autonomy of local education, nationalistic education and bureaucratic control were promoted both by the bureaucracy and the government.

These changes in educational policies were met with resistance from teachers and other citizens. The subsequent fifty years of Japanese education were filled with controversies over such issues as 'the screening and approval of textbooks, the evaluation of students and teachers, curriculum control, and the training and retraining of teachers' (Horio 1988: 171), which were fought ultimately along the lines of nationalistic state control vs democracy, mostly in the context of conflict between Monbushō and Nikkyōso, or more broadly in the context of 'educational policy' as against the 'educational movement' by the people (Satō 1996: 66–8; Horio 1994: 262–6).

Perhaps most revealing is the issue of flag and anthem – *Hinomaru* and *Kimigayo*. In 1989, Monbushō accomplished its nationalistic agenda of making it compulsory to raise the *Hinomaru* flag and sing *Kimigayo* in school ceremonies, and yet nine years on, in 1998, it is still very much on its agenda to 'complete the implementation' of this policy. Behind this is the reality that, while this policy is followed by some 80 per cent of all public schools, there are some 20 per cent which do not comply (*ANEN* 8 May 1998).

One such school is Tokorozawa High School in Saitama Prefecture. In 1990, its student association decided to oppose the imposition of *Hinomaru* and *Kimigayo*. This decision, together with the school motto, 'Let's talk about it', have been cherished by students, teachers, and parents, as part of the school 'tradition'. This liberal tradition, however, was challenged by a newly-appointed principal who, despite hours of discussion on the matter with student representatives and teachers, insisted on compliance with the Monbushō directive (*shidō*). In the end, 400 out of 420 graduating students chose to attend the 'celebration' organised by students rather than the formal graduation ceremony organised by the principal. This incident caused a sensation all around Japan (Yonezawa *et al.* 1998; Kimura 1998; Ida 1998).

Apart from the dramatic contest that occurred at Tokorozawa, the fact is that there are also many schools where, even if '*Kimigayo*' is officially sung in a school ceremony, many teachers and students either do not sing it or only pretend to sing it. In 1996, 11 teachers were officially disciplined or warned for not singing it, or not standing up for it (*ANEN* 8 May 1998). There is also the possibility that a large number of young people do not know the words of the hymn in any case (Asō 1997).

Thus, although the level of conformity to ministerial directives and policies may be relatively high, at least on the surface, there are teachers, students and parents who defy them. Nevertheless, the general trend in the last 50 years of Japanese education has been a slow but steady retreat for those with progressive ideas. The censorship of textbooks has increased over the years; as has the state control of curricula (see Chapter 6). Political control over teachers has been augmented considerably. In 1987, the probational period for newly employed teachers was extended from six months to one year, during which time teachers on probation had to attend a series of intensive training courses outside school, while in school they were placed under constant surveillance by supervisors; their evaluation rested on the subjective criterion of 'possessing comprehensive characteristics as a person' (*zen-jinkaku-teki na shishitsu*). Presumably this means obedience to seniors, uncritical thinking, and support for nationalistic practices. In this environment, there is little chance to pursue academic freedom, or even to talk to students outside of class hours (Sakamoto 1986: 208–10). The 1995 decision of Nikkyōso to 'reconcile' with Monbushō, i.e. that it would no longer form the opposition to Monbushō but work in cooperation with it, is considered by many as the epitaph of its half-century-long struggle for democratic education. There seems little doubt that the educational paradigm of Japan today is almost an antithesis to the democratic paradigm which existed in the brief ten years between 1945–54.

Australia

While non-democratic policies were implemented in Japan one after the other, Australia experienced the period of the progressive and alternative schools movement in the 1960s and 1970s, which stemmed from 'the unease that a number of teachers and parents felt about many [government] and [private] schools at that time'. That movement is summarised by the following passage.

> [T]he traditional school is still structured in basic conformity with the industrial factory of the economic system it was founded to service. Authority flows from the top down and from unknown sources. . . .

[The teachers], ultimately, are in the service of Australia Unlimited and a growth rate of 6 per cent in gross national product.

(Schoenheimer 1973, quoted in Connell 1993: 208–9)

According to Connell (1993), the period 'from about 1968 to 1978 was probably the most exciting and productive one in Australian educational history' (p. 230). During this period, a number of new subjects such as environmental education and new social science were developed. This period also saw:

> a new understanding of learning theory, the beginning of a more responsible association between school and the community and of genuine devolution of decision making to the schools, a change in teacher–pupil relationships and in methods of student assessment, and an effort, at the Federal Government level, to remodel the objectives of the school systems in the interest of greater equity, creativity, and sensitivity to social change. In short, it was a period which saw a change in the conduct, purpose, and impact of education.
>
> (Connell 1993: 230–1)

The government policy guidelines have clearly advocated and promoted a democratic style of education in the public sector in recent years, although the tradition of an autocratic style of education also persists because many teachers are familiar with it (Balson 1992). The abolition of corporal punishment in the 1980s is the most obvious example (see Chapter 4). The democratic approach to education was indicated, for instance, in the document prepared by the Working Party on the Abolition of Corporal Punishment of the Victorian Department of Education in 1983, which reads:

> Schools which are best at developing social learning environment are those which accord equal status to all members of the school community and which have effective decision-making processes based on participation, rather than authoritarian models.
>
> (cited in Balson 1992: 11)

Similarly a Ministerial Paper (1985) reads with reference to government commitment to the democratic principle in education:

> This commitment will mean that parents, teachers, students, principals, administrators, and others closely involved in the work of education will all have the right to participate in decision-making processes. They

come together as a group charged with the collective responsibility of reaching agreement or coming to a decision on issues to be resolved.

(cited in Balson 1992: 10)

Likewise, the Victorian Ministry of Education Ministerial Paper No. 4 (1985) reads:

> Students, too, must see evidence of mutual respect, and they themselves must be equally respected, if their school experience is to meet their needs and aspirations. The measure of this mutual respect and trust will be reflected in the process and quality of decision-making in the school.
>
> (quoted in Balson 1992: 9).

Balson argues that other state departments of education have also committed themselves to promote a democratic mode of education whereby values such as mutual respect between students and teachers, cooperation, self-discipline, shared responsibility and social equality are proclaimed.

This does not mean that Australian educational system is satisfactorily democratic. The economic rationalism resulted in thousands of Australian teachers being sacked in various states in the late 1980s and early 1990s, schools being closed, run down or privatised (Welch 1996: 5). Compared to the Japanese system, however, Australia can still be regarded as broadly typical of Western liberal democratic education.

SILENCE AMONG JAPANESE STUDENTS

The most pronounced difference between students in Japan and Australia was found in the responses to the open-ended question in my survey asking how they might wish to change school if they could do so. The Australian students responded extremely well and expressed eloquently their opinions on school and education. The students come to life in comments and a reader can well understand her/his ideas and feelings about school. In a sharp contrast, the Japanese students rarely responded to the question, and if they did, the comments tended to be extremely short and scarce, mostly just a phrase or itemised points. One gets little sense of the person from these responses: communication has not occurred. The open-ended question was a complete failure so far as Japanese students were concerned – at least in the sense that it did not work in the way intended.

It would be highly misleading to assume that the failure to express views on how school might be changed means that Japanese students are contented with their school life. The unresponsiveness seems to be indicative of the nature of education familiar to Japanese students. The fact that Japanese students could not say much in response to the question may be seen as perfectly 'logical'. The extremely autocratic mode of education of Japan has trained them to be receivers of the knowledge given by teachers, not to ask questions, not to contradict or criticise teachers, and ultimately not to think but just to listen and swallow what they are told. The silence among Japanese students is the other side of the coin of the communication break-down between teachers and students. Far from being connected with pater-nalistic bonds, the student–teacher relationship in Japan represents a crude form of 'banking education', where teachers do all the talking and students do all the listening. Education in Japan is geared to silent students.

Evidence of alienation among Japanese students, therefore, is more likely to appear in negative forms – as absence, silence, default. For Japanese students, to be vocal and to be able to attend school are contradictory propositions. Fukuhara Yōichirō, the *tōkōkyohi* student who wrote the poem quoted at the beginning of this chapter, says:

> School for me is a place like prison. Only teachers and the boss in the class can express their opinions and behave as they like. In other words, school is the place where students are 'forced to do things'. The only place I feel free is home. If school were a place where I could express myself clearly, I would definitely have continued to attend school.
>
> (Ishikawa *et al.* 1993: 290)

A large number of students in Japan feel that if they want to survive the education system, they must keep quiet. To say nothing is a survival skill. This is true not only of student–teacher relationships. Many students perceive that it is best not to say anything to anyone, classmates and parents as well as teachers.

In June and July 1995, *Shinken-zemi chūgaku kōza*, a magazine for corre-spondence education for junior secondary students, urged readers to break silence and speak up about *ijime*. Although two thousand letters were sent to the editor of the magazine in response, the senders were extremely secretive and did not disclose their identity. Many said that 'it is dangerous to talk to my friends about *ijime*' and 'teachers and parents would not understand' them in any case and therefore they could speak up only in letters to the editor where they could stay absolutely anonymous.

About the importance of being unidentified one student wrote: 'I felt it safe to write a letter because it then won't be possible to identify me by voice'. Another wrote: 'while I was writing this letter, I noticed that my hands were trembling. I am scared to think that the fact of my writing this letter may become known to people around me and cause me trouble.'

When the editor approached some students to get their permission to publish their letters, one student asked the editor not to phone home because she did not want her parents to know that she wrote such a letter. Another asked the editor to change the address to hide her identity. Some girls disguised their identity by using expressions commonly used by boys (Ujioka 1997c).

It seems therefore that many students in Japan feel it necessary to maintain silence not only *vis-à-vis* teachers but also with classmates and even parents. It is not just teachers who form 'a united front' against individual students. Classmates and parents are often part of the 'united front' against which students feel compelled to guard themselves by remaining silent (see Chapter 7).

It makes sense then that the most vocal of all students of Japan are those who either refuse to go to school or are unable to go to school – *tōkōkyohi* students. It is not that these students speak like political activists, but their words come usually after months or years of solitary self-reflection at home after they stopped going to school, when they experience enormous anxiety and pain (both psychological and physical). It is so traumatic that many such students try to commit suicide. This is the period when many literally 'excommunicate' themselves from society – from school, neighbourhood, and often, even from their own family. When *tōkōkyohi* students are able to express themselves, however, their voices exist as the strongest contestation against school and society by Japanese students. It is their writings, therefore, that I quote in this book to supplement the responses I could not obtain from the Japanese students in my survey.

TWO DIMENSIONS OF STUDENT–TEACHER RELATIONSHIPS

Initially, there were 14 items in my questionnaire to do with student–teacher relationships. Factor analysis, however, identified two distinct dimensions of those relationships. So far we have focused on the alienating quality of that relationship, and dealt with a relatively mild, estranging relationship which is widespread both in Japan and Australia (though to a distinctly greater degree in Japan) – teachers not treating students with respect, not caring about them, not understanding them, not trusting them. Every student experiences this aspect of the student–teacher relationship to varying degrees in school.

The other dimension of the student–teacher relationship is something which might be called 'dehumanising treatment by teachers'. It covers far more negative, harmful and humiliating experiences – being yelled at,

'picked on', or hit by teachers, etc. Generally speaking, this kind of treatment by teachers is much less prevalent, as Table 3.5 indicates. The question
was how frequently each student experienced each one of these aspects in
the past year.

Approximately one in three students in Japan had teachers who 'lose their
temper and yell' either mostly or always. This experience is shared, less
frequently, in Australia. Likewise, one in four Japanese students thought that
'teachers are unfair' either mostly or always, whereas it was the case for only
11 per cent of students in Australia. Although these are not necessarily small
numbers, compared to the results shown in Tables 3.2 and 3.3, the number
of students who have these experiences is far less in both societies.
Dehumanising treatment by teachers is not as prevalent as lack of respect,
care, trust and understanding. Even more humiliating and degrading treatment happens even less frequently, as Table 3.6 shows.

Although dehumanising treatment is not experienced by a large number
of students, it can cause greater harm to those who do directly experience
it. Danny Lee and Maria Apostolopoulos from state high schools in
Melbourne commented on how it feels. In their words:

> The teachers should treat the kids good. The kids don't like the
> teachers swearing at us, because that makes us hate more the teachers,
> and the teachers should not tell off [i.e. scold] the kids because they get
> more angry.

> Teachers, some lose their tempers too easily, and do not think
> matters out in a logical rational way. They can be prejudiced, and
> discriminate for various reasons. Teachers usually provoke difficult

Table 3.5 Comparative student–teacher relationships: unfair treatment by teachers

	Never (%)	Sometimes (%)	Mostly (%)	Always (%)
Japan				
Teachers lose their temper and yell	14	53	20	13
Teachers are unfair	25	51	14	10
Australia				
Teachers lose their temper and yell	6	70	13	11
Teachers are unfair	9	80	8	3

Table 3.6 Comparative student–teacher relationships: derogatory treatment by teachers

	Never (%)	Sometimes (%)	Mostly (%)	Always (%)
Japan				
Teachers 'pick on' me or 'put me down' in front of the class	51	39	5	5
Teachers treat me as if I am not much good at things	57	33	6	4
Australia				
Teachers 'pick on' me or 'put me down' in front of the class	51	41	4	5
Teachers treat me as if I am not much good at things	54	38	5	2

situations, and no matter what attitude the student takes to relieve themselves of this conflict, the teacher will only try to make the situation worse. . . . Teachers also are too revengeful, and can be racist just like their hypocritical favourites or students.

There is little doubt that when students have experiences like these, both teachers and students interact with each other in an emotionally charged manner. Furthermore, although dehumanising treatment by teachers is experienced by a relatively small number of students, it is in a way 'shared' by other students who are not directly involved, i.e. when the teacher yells at one particular student, the whole class is affected by it. Disciplinary measures taken in relation to a particular student are often intended to serve as a 'warning' to others as well.

Dehumanising treatment by teachers is the dimension of the student–teacher relationship best captured by qualitative rather than quantitative means. Methodologically there is a limit as to how much data one can collect regarding this aspect of the student–teacher relationship by using questionnaires. Corporal punishment, for instance, is not considered here despite the fact that the question touches the very core of the educational system of both Japan and Australia. The topic would have been too sensitive to mention in the survey, especially in Japan where the inclusion of the question could have jeopardised the feasibility of the data collection itself. Despite the confidentiality of the data collection, it also seems possible that students might not have given frank responses to a question on corporal punishment since the question might jeopardise their relationship with teachers.

Discipline and punishment constitute the subjects of the next chapter.

NOTES

1 A poem published in *Kodomotachi ga kataru tōkōkyohi* [School refusal discussed by children] (Ishikawa *et al.* 1993: 287). This book contains in its massive 1,038 pages all kinds of messages from 402 students and pupils who *suffered* from *tōkōkyohi*. It is a collection of students' own accounts of *tōkōkyohi*, expressed in the forms of drawings, poems, diaries, letters, comments, compositions, self-introductions, stories, and fantasies. The author's name is put in some cases, but other works remain anonymous. When these students' words are quoted in the present book, only the age of the author when the piece was written will be indicated. It is painful to see the word 'deceased' next to the name of the author sometimes.

2 This is based on numerous conversations with Japanese teachers in Australia.

3 In some instances, I was pressed to report the result sooner than I could, and on one occasion I was surprised to receive a box full of questionnaires sent from a school I did not approach – a teacher who heard about the survey reproduced my questionnaire, collected the data, and requested that I analyse them.

4 Other books banned by principals include the following (*Asahi jānaru* 30 January 1984: (1) Fifteen volumes of *Nihon genbaku bungaku* (Japan's atomic bomb literature), published by *Porupu shuppan*. The reason given was: 'It is ideologically biased'. (2) Yamazumi Masami's critical examination of the Imperial Rescript on Education, *Kyōiku chokugo*, published by *Asahi shinbun*. The reason was: '*Asahi shinbun* is politically biased'. (3) Honda Katsuichi's *Chūgoku no tabi* (Trip to China) published by *Asahi shinbun*. The reason was: 'The author is an anti-establishment thinker'. In one school, the librarian was advised by the principal to stop subscribing to *Asahi shinbun* and *Mainichi shinbun* in the school library (but ignored it). *Asahi* and *Mainichi* are two of the three major, respected newspapers in Japan.

5 Horio quoted this passage from *Kyōiku Gyōsei*, by Suzuki Ei'ichi, Tokyo University Press, pp. 291–4.

6 '*Medaka*' is a tiny freshwater Japanese fish.

7 The period of the one-party rule by the Liberal Democratic Party between 1955–93.

8 The term reverse-course was first used in *Yomiuri shinbun* on 2 November 1951 (Satō 1996: 114f).

4 Discipline and punishment: dehumanisation

Teachers frequently hit students,
just at the whim of the moment.
The school is a 'lawless district', you know.

(Tatara Hiroshi, Hiroshima, Japan[1])

PHYSICAL PUNISHMENT IN JAPAN

Discipline is the issue on which autocratic and democratic paradigms of education divide most clearly, and the question of punishment is at the heart of the issue of discipline. Discipline (of which punishment is a part) is the dimension of education which presents sharply the contrast between Japanese and Australian education systems. The difference is not quantitative – it is not a matter of degree; it is qualitative.

In Australia, corporal punishment has been abolished in most states since the mid-1980s. Even when it was practised (or where it is still practised), the method of application was/is highly regulated. Only school principals or his/her delegates can administer corporal punishment by using only prescribed methods.

In contrast, there have been a number of cases in Japan where students have been killed or injured by teachers in the name of 'corporal punishment'. It is not surprising that people who are familiar with the school system outside Japan are often astonished to see that Japanese teachers resort to violence towards students so easily (*AS* 20 September 1987; Satō 1989: 50–1).

Over the past two decades, there have been appalling cases of student assault by teachers. Despite the stir and sensation they caused, however, there has been little sign of steps to root out such behaviour. On the contrary, they are on the increase. This is because no matter how extraordinary they appear, each one of these cases is woven from the fabric of practice and ideas which constitutes the everyday life of schools in Japan. The threads of seemingly 'abnormal' cases are shared by 'normal' schools which have not yet experienced 'problems'. There is often only a very fine line between the school next door and the school which has become notorious through the media. They are connected by the same complex structural problems underlying the education system and society in general. Furthermore, there is a paradox that each time the nature of this structural problem manifests itself as a tragedy with individuals involved, tighter control is exercised to further strengthen the very system which caused the problem. Let us describe some of the cases which shook the nation in recent years in order to understand how these seemingly extreme cases are part of the mainstream of Japanese education.

Death over a hair drier in Gifu

In 1985, Takahashi Toshinao, a second-year student of Gifu Prefectural Giyō Senior High School, died during a school trip after being made to sit on the floor, beaten on the head and kicked in the stomach by Amamori Kazunori, a 36-year-old homeroom teacher. The assault lasted until the boy fell unconscious. Toshinao was taken to hospital but died shortly after from head and stomach injuries and the shock. The fatal 'punishment' was inflicted upon him because he brought an electric hair drier on the trip although it had been forbidden. Despite the death of Toshinao, the school trip continued as scheduled. The defence counsel later argued that Amamori was a kind teacher who had never resorted to violence before, and who had been under tremendous pressure from his colleague to discipline students. In his school, it was a custom for some twenty teachers in charge of *shidō* (guidance) to patrol the school with a whip or a bamboo sword in hand. Amamori was sentenced to three years for involuntary manslaughter (Satō 1985; Schoolland 1990: 1–7; Sakamoto 1995: 119–27).

Death at the school gate in Kobe

In 1990, Ishida Ryōko, a 15-year-old girl, died after her head was crushed against a school gate closed by Hosoi Toshihiko, the 39-year-old teacher who was in charge of 'guidance at the school gate' in the Hyōgo Prefectural Kōbe Takatsuka Senior High School. Hosoi's job was to close the gate to shut out students late for school. A passing student heard Hosoi say: 'Only 45 seconds are left. I shall close the gate today no matter what'. Another student reported, 'I was walking just in front of her. I saw the gate was completely open, so I thought it was safe, but then it began to close very fast. I got surprised and quickly jumped through the gate. When I turned around, the girl had been caught between the gate and the wall. Anybody caught like this was bound to die. Students around shouted, "Don't be crazy!", "What have you done!". The teacher shouted back at the top of his voice, "Shut up! Go away! Move!", while the girl was bleeding at each breath'. Two hours later, Ryōko, who had never been late for school, died in hospital (Hosaka 1990).

Fudōjuku case

In 1987, Tsuchida Mikinori, a 15-year-old boy, died after being beaten with a metal baseball bat for over an hour in a small private boarding school/facility in Saitama called 'Fudōjyuku'. Kagawa Rinzō, 41-year-old head of the school, had ordered all fifteen boarders to beat Mikinori ten times each. Kagawa then joined in himself. During the assault, Michinori's hands and legs were bound with vinyl tape and his mouth was stuffed with socks. He died in the room where he was confined after the beating. Half of the students in the school had had a similar experience themselves. They followed the orders of Kagawa thinking that otherwise they themselves would suffer the same fate. The boarders had been sent to the school by their parents to 'have their behaviour corrected'. Mikinori was 'punished' because he escaped from the school. He was forcibly dragged out of his apartment by Kagawa and five students who kicked and bashed him in the car on the way back to the school. Kagawa, who testified later that he did what he believed right, was sentenced to three and a half years. It is reported that the mother of the boy said later that she owed Kagawa a great deal and that he was not to blame (*AS* 11 June 1987; Schoolland 1990: 65).

Kazenoko-gakuen case

In 1991, a 16-year-old girl and a 14-year-old boy died after being locked in an old railway container by Sakai Sachio, the 67-year-old head of a small private boarding facility called 'Kazenoko-gakuen' in Hiroshima. They were confined in the container without a window in mid-summer where the temperature probably reached 60 degrees Celsius. They were imprisoned as 'punishment' for smoking, with their hands handcuffed and with only a glass of wheat tea. Checked by Sakai 44 hours later, they were already dead. They had been sent to this school by their parents 'to correct their bad behaviour' such as their habit of being late in arriving at school or of leaving it early. Parents knew that their children might be locked up or made to fast in this school. Sakai boasted that 80 per cent of *tōkōkyohi* students who were sent to his school 'got cured' thanks to his Spartan method, and he had done nothing 'beyond what was educationally necessary' even to those who were killed. The municipal officers who had met

Sakai previously thought of him as an enthusiastic educator and introduced Kazenoko-gakuen to people who made enquires about such schools (Kato 1993: 35–44).

Incredible and extraordinary as they may appear, there are apparent similarities between the Fudōjuku and Kazenoko-gakuen cases – both special boarding schools for 'problem kids' (mostly *tōkōkyohi* students) where excessively Spartan methods are used to 'straighten' their behaviour and their spirits (*konjyō*). In fact, the prototype of this kind of school can be found in the Totsuka Yacht School where five students died between 1979 and 1982.

TOTSUKA YACHT SCHOOL

Despite its name, Totsuka Yacht School is not a school of seamanship but has no purpose other than training itself, i.e. sailing is a means rather than the end. Three students died of excessive physical punishment and two disappeared (after jumping into the sea to escape from violence on board) between 1979 and 1982. Totsuka specialised in *tōkōkyohi* students, including those who had been violent towards their parents. Even during the court case which lasted between 1983 and 1992, while Totsuka and his 15 trainers were on trial, parents continued to send their children to the school. In the end, ten coaches including Totsuka were given sentences of less than three years each. All of them decided to proceed with further appeal. In his 1992 press conference, Totsuka asserted that 'corporal punishment equals education' and said that he often got irritated because he could no longer use as much corporal punishment as he wanted. This limitation slowed down the 'improvement' of students (Kato 1993: 45–68).

The father of one of the two boys who jumped into the sea wrote to Totsuka:

> The violence of our son which was diagnosed to stop when he became a senior high school student has hardly changed. As his body grows, so does the risk to us at home. . . . [I]f we keep him at home, the whole family may be ruined. The incident of the other day (where a professor emeritus of Tokyo University was stabbed to death by his grandson) comes to mind. . . . We have tried everything, but to no avail. One of our relatives recommended you. I may be asking too much, but I earnestly beg you to accept my son as soon as possible.
>
> (Kato 1993: 57)

Like this boy, many of the 'trainees' of the yacht school were *tōkōkyohi* students who were handed on from school to counselling, to the police, to hospitals (ordinary and mental) without 'success'. Many parents saw Totsuka's Spartan school as the last resort. Before jumping into the sea, one boy wrote to his father:

> This is not a place for human beings. Day after day, we get beaten up and live a life worse than that of an animal. Father, Mother, this is the only request I will ever make of you. Please do come to collect me. . . . I have a dream. I want to eat what Mother cooked as much as I want. I want to study with Father for my examination. I want to relax with my family. I want to live like a human being.
>
> (Kato 1993: 58)

The letter was confiscated by Totsuka and the boy was 'punished' so badly that he could not open his eyes because of facial bruising. The letter reached his parents after his death.

DEATHS WITHIN NORMAL PRACTICE

While these 'special schools' appear particularly appalling because of their unconstrained and unashamed use of militaristic and brutal methods, their philosophy is shared, even if implicitly, by schools like Gifu Giyō High School and Kōbe Takatsuka High School mentioned above. The tragedies that happened at Gifu Giyō and Kōbe Takatsuka were not just unfortunate accidents, but were firmly rooted in the 'normal' practice of school. Similar accidents, of students injured through being caught between the gate and the wall, were reported by students attending other schools (*Asahi jānaru* 24 August 1990: 25).

In Kōbe Takatsuka High, Hosoi was not the only teacher at the school gate. Two others were outside the gate for *shidō* (guidance), and one of them gave the students the countdown through the microphone, 'two more minutes before the gate closes', 'One more minute. Run fast!' (*AS* 10 July 1990). Students shut out of the school by being seconds late would be punished with an 800-metre run around the school grounds (*AS* 15 July 1990). Similarly, 50 students who were late for the morning assembly during the school trip were forced to do 50 'pushup-and-standups' each; a student who did not move swiftly enough at the entrance to the school building was made to sit erect on his knees (*seiza*) in the corridor; when some students were late for the class of physical education, everyone in the class was forced to run around the school for the entire class hour (*AS* 15 July 1990).

It was revealed later that another student had been caught previously between the wall and the gate closed by Hosoi, but had had the strength to push the gate back (*AS* 13 July 1990). Hosoi reportedly told the police that on the day Ishida Ryōko was killed he closed the iron gate hard, in order to prevent students from forcing themselves through it (*AS* 15 July 1990). While other teachers were aware of the danger the 6-metre-long, 230-kilogram gate could cause, they did not caution Hosoi (*AS* 7 July 1990). Hosoi, who was the supervisor-cum-coach of the baseball club at Takatsuka High and generally considered to be a 'stern and enthusiastic teacher in *shidō*', had been admonished six years earlier in another school for hitting a student and inflicting an injury that had taken two weeks to heal (*AS* 15 July 1990).

Immediately after the accident, while Ryōko was fighting for life in the hospital, the end of term examination proceeded as usual. It was the hospital, not the school, that contacted the police. When the police arrived at the gate, the blood had been washed away by the school. On the following morning, the principal summoned all students and said, 'If all of you would only come ten minutes earlier, teachers would not have to shout at you. I have no intention of shifting the responsibility onto you, but I urge you once again to revise your attitude'. Another teacher said, 'The examination is just about to begin. Let us get more marks to make up for the marks lost by Ryōko' (Hosaka 1990). Nakajima Junko (50), representative of 'Kobe kodomo no jinken to kenkō o kangaeru kai' (The association to think about human rights and health issues of children in Kobe) points out that only a few teachers felt that they had been partly responsible for the death of Ishida Ryōko, that the incident was hardly discussed seriously among teachers, that both in Kobe and in the Hyōgo Prefecture teachers did not give any chance to citizens to discuss the matter with them, and that letters the association addressed to the students' association had all been censored (*AS* 16 December 1990).

THE PREVALENCE OF PHYSICAL PUNISHMENT/VIOLENCE

Physical punishment is often used in Japanese schools. The physical violence may not be confined to slapping, hitting, bashing, and kicking, it also includes other treatment which causes physical pain such as making students 'kneel' on a hard floor or ground (*seiza*), or stand for a long time, or even not allowing students to have lunch (Sakamoto 1990: 120). Between April and October 1985 there were a staggering four thousand cases, where local educational boards and public schools at all levels investigated cases of 'physical punishment' (*taibatsu*) in response to claims made by parents (*AS* 29 April 1987). This means that, on average, there were twelve *official* investigations of physical punishment per month in every prefecture. Given the fact that parents usually do their best to avoid conflict with teachers, this figure itself probably indicates no more than the tip of the iceberg. Elsewhere, a study of 230 university students in 1983 indicated that 97 per cent of them reported that they had first-hand experience of physical punishment at some stage of their school life (Satō 1985: 19).

The prevalence of physical punishment is not surprising because a large number of parents and teachers in Japan believe it necessary and approve its use. Numerous studies conducted in the past have shown that 60 to 80 per cent of parents and over 45 per cent of teachers support the use of physical punishment (*AS* 28 November 1986; Sakamoto 1995: 149, 155–6). In a survey conducted in Fukuoka in 1987, 70 per cent of teachers of primary and junior high schools indicated that they believed that physical punishment was necessary, and 90 per cent admitted that they had administered it (*AS* 10 April 1988). The fact that the School Education Law of 1947 prohibits the use of physical punishment by teachers is almost completely disregarded in the everyday life of Japanese schools.

Moreover, physical violence to students has steadily increased in recent years. Figure 4.1 shows the number of teachers against whom disciplinary actions were taken for reasons related to 'physical punishment'. Each of these cases appears in statistics which usually mean serious injuries, intimidation and terror on the part of students. The following are a few more

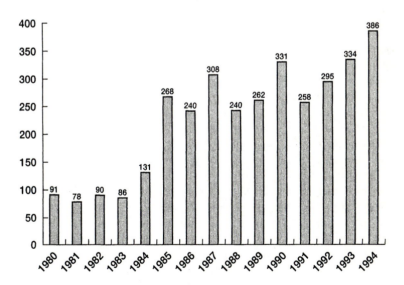

Figure 4.1 The number of Japanese teachers in primary and secondary schools officially disciplined in relation to corporal punishment
Source: Adapted from Monbushō (1995a)

examples. Dozens of similar cases can be found in a random search of the daily newspapers.

- In July 1986, a junior school student of Narashino Nanachū in Chiba was forced to kneel on the floor and kicked hard twice in the face by a teacher because he was late for school lunch. His lower lip was lacerated, two of his front teeth knocked out, and his tooth nerve became paralysed – requiring medical treatment for five months (Sakamoto 1995: 331).
- In July 1990, two students of Iki Junior High School in Fukuoka were made to sit fully dressed in holes on the beach and were buried, by seven teachers, up to their necks for twenty minutes as punishment for allegedly extorting money from the students of another school (*AS* 12 July 1990).
- In 1990, a junior high school student in Yamanashi who was watching television late at night during a school trip was kicked in the back, the stomach, and the face without warning by a 31-year-old 'enthusiastic' teacher, causing head injuries which took 39 days to heal. The boy was not even allowed to visit a doctor during the trip, despite discharges from his nose and ears. The incident was not officially recorded by the prefectural board of education (Hasegawa 1990).

From the students' point of view, the worst aspect of the 'physical punishment' meted out in Japanese schools is probably that it is administered mostly for very trivial offences in such an arbitrary, unregulated and unpredictable manner. Students do not know what kind of behaviour will be met with what sort of 'punishment'. Not wearing socks of the permitted colour can lead them to be slapped in the face by teachers (White 1993: 90). Reading a comic book can result in their being made to kneel on the playground and kicked by teachers (*AS* 22 July 1987). Using a 'sharp pencil', banned in school rules, can cause one to be slapped in the face (*AS* 20 April 1988). Not going to sleep on a school trip after lights-out can lead to bashing with a steel bat on the head (*AS* 23 August 1987). Incidents like these are countless and it is impossible to grasp the full extent of physical punishment in Japanese schools. This is particularly so because teachers often order students not to mention it to anyone. Even the deaths of students discussed earlier were caused by 'punishment' for breaching trivial rules such as being late for school or taking a hair drier on a school trip. What does this pattern of physical punishment signify in the Japanese education system?

Most apparent of is the lack of human rights of children in Japanese schools and Japanese society in general. In this context, let us consider some of the comments given by the Japanese students in our survey. Motomura Osamu, a student from an elite school wrote:

> I want to normalize teachers. Now we are threatened by teachers. Give us more human treatment.

Similarly, Usui Tadashi, Nagai Yōnosuke, and Takeuchi Ken from academic schools said that:

> I would like to have a school where the human rights of each student are protected.

> Teachers control the school too much. Let more rights at school be given to students. The students' association is too weak.

> I want to make a 'students' school' where students are not oppressed by teachers. I want them to educate us in such a way that it heightens our humanity.

Generally speaking, school as an age-specific institution defines the roles of individuals in terms of age. Whether one looks at it critically or not, schools produce 'children' by forcing the young to play the role of children; and on the basis of that, schools socialise them while teachers, as adults, provide them with 'custodial care' (Illich 1971: 32–5). Underlying this is the tacit assumption that 'human nature in its "raw", "uncivilised" state, as in children prior to appropriate socialisation, consists of "urges" and motives which would endanger social order' (Otto 1986: 25). Teachers have long been considered to act *in loco parentis* and are expected to 'subdue, restrain and control natural impulses [of children] and to instil obedience and conformity' (ibid.). In other words, education has been perceived as 'a curative for all evils' inherent in human nature (Corrigan 1979: 19). It was with this understanding that discipline has been part of schooling for many centuries. This 'traditional' paradigm of education, with its negative images of children, now seems less pronounced, at least in the West, including Australia where a more democratic mode of education has been promoted.

In Japan, this 'traditional' aspect of school seems particularly strong, if anything intensifying in recent years, contrary to the trend of the times elsewhere. Thomas Rohlen writes that '[o]ne of the most profound discoveries for me when I began visiting Japanese high schools was that teachers regularly refer to students as *kodomo*, "children"' (Rohlen 1983: 195). After pointing out that this is not the case in the US, Rohlen continues his observations of the student–teacher relationship in Japanese high schools as follows.

> Japanese high school teachers in no way encourage their students to regard themselves as adults. In fact, it is their duty to prevent them from experimenting with adult pleasures and vices. . . . No one suggests they have rights. . . . It is a teacher's job to assume a parental attitude. The ideal teacher is one who is devoted and involved but not an equal or a pal. Of the two sides to parenting, affection and discipline, it is the latter that most parents want teacher to provide. In fact, Japanese parents typically look to the teacher for the discipline that they feel their affection for their children prevents them from exercising fully. I have in my notes many instances of either parents asking a high school teacher to shape up their wayward or unmotivated child, or of teachers going to parents and telling them what must be done to bring a student back into line.
>
> (Rohlen 1983: 196–7)

Rohlen's remarks point to the fact that the most fundamental assumptions of the 'traditional' paradigm of education (as against a liberal democratic education) are preserved in Japanese high schools. Students are viewed as children who have few rights and who are in need of constant check and guidance by adults; while teachers are seen as *in loco parentis*, assigned by parents and society great power and responsibilities to regulate and discipline students. As Amano Ikuo, a sociologist of education, suggests, no educational reforms can bring fundamental change so long as the notion of teens as 'big children' rather than 'small adults' persists in the minds of educationists in Japan (Amano 1995).

A review of recent cases of student abuse, however, indicates that what has happened in Japanese schools since the early 1980s has gone beyond what can be explained by the 'traditional' model of education. In the 'traditional' model, teachers may be alienating and scary to students but they are not supposed to have the power to *abuse* students. To be authoritarian, stern, and strict does not necessarily mean life-threatening; the importance of that qualitative difference should not need to be stressed and in fact the whole subject of physical abuse by teachers warrants a study in its own right.

Teachers in Japanese schools have been given enormous power and responsibilities over students, even to the extent that they become a life-threatening force. Quite paradoxically, they have become extremely powerless in providing basic safety to students, or to protect students from potentially life-threatening *ijime* from classmates, as will be discussed in more detail in Chapter 7.

The student–teacher relationship in Japanese schools today has absolutely nothing to do with what is supposed to be the cultural ideal of the paternalistic relationship between senior and junior (or superior and subordinate), – no matter how tempting it may be to apply Confucian ideal precepts to the understanding of this hierarchical relationship. If anything, the hardship which oppresses Japanese students more resembles that of factory workers and coal miners during the industrial revolution than the hardship endured by the trainees (*deshi*) learning the skills of their masters (*shishō*) in traditional Japanese arts. Many students cease using the word '*sensei*' (an honorific expression to mean teacher) to refer to teachers, preferring instead the word '*kyōshi*' which means teacher as an occupational category with no cultural implication of honour or respect. The paternalistic model used in the educational context is merely an ideology preached by those who want to further teachers' power to control students, in the name of 'education', 'guidance' and 'love'.

But why is it necessary to control students to this extent? There would seem to be something more involved than just the deprivation of human rights of children and young people. What is the nature of this abuse of children and young people in the context of education? In order to investigate this point, let us focus on the places where corporal punishment, the form of student control at its most excessive, is most intense and rampant.

PHYSICAL EDUCATION AND ATHLETIC CLUB ACTIVITIES

It is widely known among teachers and students that teachers of physical education and coaches of athletic clubs tend to use physical punishment more than other teachers (Sakamoto 1995: 211). According to the Justice Ministry, persistent 'physical punishment' administered in anger – including not just slapping but also kicking and sometimes hitting with a bamboo sword – is on the increase, and it is particularly common among young, male teachers of physical education (PE) (*AS* 21 September 1987). In 1994 PE teachers accounted for some 40 per cent of all teachers subject to disciplinary action because of physical violence to students (Shimizu *et al.* 1996: 121). According to Monbushō, 26 per cent of the 'physical punishment' (which in the official statistics actually means physical violence) was administered in playgrounds and gymnasiums, second only to 31 per cent in the classrooms. Of PE teachers included in the survey, 67 per cent are also reported to have used corporal punishment in the previous year, as compared to 37 per cent for teachers specialising in academic subjects, 39 per cent in technical and vocational subjects, and 49 per cent for primary school teachers (where PE teachers are not specialists) (Sakamoto 1995: 221). These data consistently indicate that sport activities, especially athletic club activities, constitute a hotbed of corporal punishment and physical violence towards students. It may even be that physical violence to students increased recently because many schools opted to employ 'tough' teachers willing to use 'physical punishment' to discipline students effectively (Kohama 1985: 126; Kamata 1995: 200).

In particular athletic club activities (*bukatsu*) often constitute a harbour of physical violence in the name of 'training', 'discipline', and 'punishment'.[2] The example of Nakatsu Commercial Senior High School in Gifu, where a girl committed suicide after excessive 'training', constitutes a case in point (Sakamoto 1995: 205–23).[3] According to the court record, the coach of the club was an 'enthusiastic' teacher with a firm faith in the way he trained and guided students, which often meant he resorted to violence when there was something he did not like. He used violence not only against the members of the club but also against non-members. For instance, girls who declined to join the club were made to 'kneel' down on the floor of the PE teachers' room where they would be hit on the head with a metal stick. At the school-gate check, he hit one girl with a bamboo sword because she took a taxi to school. Another girl lost some hair because at the school-gate check he noticed her hair was curled and grabbed the hair and pulled it hard. Another girl was dragged around the gymnasium and the PE teachers' room by her hair by the same teacher. Her resultant injuries required 20 days of medical treatment.

The student who killed herself belonged to the javelin club, where this teacher was the coach. She was the best javelin thrower in the prefecture who also ranked high in the nation. The relationship between the coach and club member was that of total domination, which went well beyond the boundary of club activities. This teacher-coach made members of the club write diaries which he inspected daily, gave them rides in his car after the evening training, and made them wash his car and his training gear. Some of the 'corporal punishments' meted out to the javelin thrower and kept in the court record include:

- The teacher ignored the doctor's order that the girl should not train for two months due to a bone fracture induced by exhaustion (caused by excessive training).
- In the training camp, he got angry with the fact that girls ate only one bowl of rice each and bashed them with the bamboo sword. He bashed them so hard that the stick was smashed. Three girls had the meal crying.

- He scolded the girl for over two hours because a junior member did not turn up to the training. The girl apologised with a kowtow.
- He got furious with the fact that her record had not improved as well as the fact that the girl did not submit her diary and hit her on the face at least twice.
- He shouted at the girl and preached at her for over an hour for her mark in the end-of-the-year examination, and told her that he would not allow her to do further training or to participate in the training camp. The girl hanged herself that night.

Not all coaches of course are as violent as this teacher, and many teachers disapprove of the use of 'physical punishment'. According to Sakamoto, however, who specialises in human rights issues regarding Japanese students, this violent coach is the archetype of PE teachers (1995: 207). Furthermore, physical violence could not be used in this way if it were not approved and supported by the school authority and, in fact, the Gifu Prefectural Board of Education supported all the deeds of this coach, claiming:

- All he did was to 'lightly knock' the student (i.e. not hitting, bashing, or beating) and this was also accepted by the student.
- The diary is an important means by which a teacher maintains heart-to-heart interaction with each student and therefore it is a serious negligence on the part of the student not to submit the diary to the teacher.
- Even if the coach was indeed harsh on the student, he was merely expressing his love as a coach trying to train the student who had great potential.

The ideology of paternalism reviewed in the previous chapter is evident here: corporal punishment, diary inspection, and the ideology of love and guidance are its main ingredients. The prefectural educational board, which held the dominant power in the district, also held to the same tenets, which indicates that the case of Gifu Nakasu Commercial School is not at all an isolated incident but was a case well-entrenched in the educational system as a whole.

It is not just because of a particular educational ideology that the educational board supported this extremely violent teacher. At a deeper level is the fact that athletic club activities in general are close to the core of what many schools have become in Japan in recent years. For the Educational Board not to support the teacher would ultimately mean to contradict themselves.

Athletic clubs reveal fundamental characteristics of Japanese schools more crudely than the classroom does. First, the boundary between 'train-ing' (education) and 'discipline' (violence) is easily blurred in athletic clubs because of the very nature of the activity (i.e. sports). In this setting, students are trained to be more prepared to accept violence by their teachers and seniors. It is also the place where to be 'physical' is inherently more important than to be 'verbal' or to 'think'. The fact that PE teachers themselves tend to resort to violence is a case in point (Sakamoto 1995: 211–12). In other words, athletic clubs are rooted in the structure which silences students.

Second, in an athletic club, team unity is often essential to victory and the emphasis on group (as against individual) comes across far more strongly than in classrooms. It is customary in athletic clubs for the whole group to be punished for the deed of one member. A senior student might well be scolded because a junior student did not turn up to the training. An athletic club represents a small society which is closed off from others. Just as the school gate symbolises the school territory isolated from the outer world, so students and teachers outside a club tend not to know what is going on in the club.

Third, winning at athletic games is considered important to bring glory to the school and credit to the principal. This explains why PE teachers often make their influence felt in the school. PE teachers with a successful sporting record tend to be given advantages in getting promotion quickly, and in some regions to become the chief of the PE section guarantees a managerial career in the future (Creative21 1996: 140–1). To look at it differently, students can be put under enormous pressure to produce these results.

Fourth, athletic clubs take most of the non-class hours of the life of students and indirectly function to deprive students of any chance to 'go astray'. In the javelin club mentioned above, for instance, students had 40 minutes morning training before class, two to three hours each day after school, three hours on Saturday afternoons, and seven hours on Sunday; not to turn up to training can mean serious trouble later, as we have seen above.

Finally, athletic clubs provide the reason and opportunity to promote the unification and the group spirit of the entire school, just as on a larger framework the Olympic Games promote a sense of identity and pride in the nation. Many schools organise a special assembly attended by all students to cheer the team of athletes before they go off to games. In my school days, such assemblies I remember as the most scary and dreaded occasions. The assembly was led by the cheer group (*ōendan*) who behave like military officers in their military-style stand-up collar uniforms, white headband and white gloves. They shout at students, intimidate them with bamboo swords, while strutting up and down before the neatly lined-up students. During this exercise, just a single smile could provoke them to belt the offender with a stick. They lead students to sing, clap, and roar in unison in praise of the school and the group spirit, to the accompaniment of thunder-like drums. On such occasions, violence dominates 'legitimately' and the school has an overtly totalitarian atmosphere. Some 20 years after my own school experience, the same practice persists, although the principal may now warn the cheer group not to hit students during the assembly.[4] In such an exercise, it is not hard to see glimpses of the pre-war Japanese school, which, with the army itself, was one of the two main forces behind militarism and ultra-nationalism (Yamazumi 1986: 90).

AICHI AND CHIBA AS THE 'MECCA' OF REGIMENTATION

The prefecture where this kind of exercise is most promoted is Aichi. Particularly notorious is the 'Marutō' exercise in Tōgō Senior High School, in which all students are forced to do military-style mass exercise under the yelling and shouting of teachers for 45 minutes a week (Fujii 1983, 1984). In 1982, 15-year-old Sasaki Midori, who was dreading the exercise, leaped from the fourth floor of the school building in the middle of this exercise. Within several weeks of that incident, another girl hanged herself, a boy jumped out of the window, and a girl collapsed and died in the middle of her school's annual 30km-walk competition. All this occurred in nearby schools equally notorious for excessive regimentation (Kamata 1984: 50).

If athletic clubs are the hotbed of physical violence towards students in each school, Aichi and Chiba are the 'Mecca' or the 'advanced prefectures' of the regimentation of education, from which other regions learn (Kamata 1995: 247).[5] Just as the examination of athletic clubs sheds light on the totalitarian sentiment in Japanese schools, Aichi and Chiba help to illuminate other aspects of regimentation of education, in which physical violence is an integrated part.

The first is to do with the way teachers are recruited or promoted. However remarkable it may seem, according to Kamata, it is common sense that teachers are recruited by means of personal connections (1995: 196). He quotes the 1987 survey by Nikkyōso, in response to the question, 'Do you think that teachers are recruited based on nepotism and favouritism?', 47.6 per cent said 'yes', 6.9 per cent said 'no', and the rest, 'I do not know'. The teachers indicated that the three most commonly used connections were: (1) an introduction by a member of the Diet or prefectural assembly, (2) being the child or acquaintance of a principal, head teacher, teacher, (3) being the child or acquaintance of a head teacher or of a member of the local board of education (ibid.: 197). This nepotism is felt most strongly in such prefectures as Chiba and Aichi. In another survey conducted in Chiba, only one out of 44 new recruits denied that nepotism existed in recruiting teachers (ibid.: 199). In Aichi, it is often said that the son of a principal will himself become a principal. There are also rumours of corruption in the educational circle in Aichi such as:

- To be recruited through the 'introduction' of a politician will cost an applicant one to two million yen.
- Teachers send 'gifts' to the principal when seeking to be assigned as homeroom teacher of a desired class.
- To become the middle-management teacher (*shunin*) costs a car (in the form of a gift to the principal).
- To become a principal can cost up to twenty million yen.

(Kamata 1995: 225)

Such transactions are technically illegal. Kamata critically points out that the practices adopted in Aichi are roughly ten years more 'advanced' than those in Chiba, which itself is more 'advanced' than other prefectures.

It should be noted that the political inclination of applicants is often screened in the process of examination for teachers. For instance, questions asked can include the following:

- What do you think about *Hinomaru* and *Kimigayo*?
- When there is a disagreement between the principal and the staff, which side would you take?
- What would you do if the majority of the people had communist-like opinions?

Applicants who hesitate to comply with school authorities and the policy of Monbushō and those who show any inclination towards 'democratic' ideas are weeded out in this process (Kamata 1995: 200). As this kind of political screening has become enhanced in recent years, teachers became more and more unthinking and docile to authority, and less and less critical or politically aware.

Close cooperation between schools and the police is another feature particularly 'advanced' in Aichi and Chiba. In Nagoya, the center of Aichi, the names of 'problem kids', along with personal information such as 'having a step-mother' and 'lack of concentration', came to be passed on to the police by schools much earlier than in other regions (ibid.: 204–5). In Chiba in the early 1980s the Blue Sky Movement established a community-based comprehensive surveillance system of children and young people.

According to Kamata, these are part of the School–Police Contact Association, launched by the Liberal Democratic Party (Kamata 1984: 192–4). The list of 'problem children' usually includes *tōkōkyohi* students, who for this reason are often suspected by police for cases like robbery, murder and arson (Katō 1993: 14–22).

The strict control of students often goes hand in hand with the strict control of teachers (Kamata 1995: 194). There are even examples in schools in Aichi where teachers and students were made to 'kneel' down on the floor together to be scolded by the principal. A teacher in Aichi was ordered by his principal to have a close-crop hair-cut (ibid.: 227). In another school, teachers made a decision to use only black ink to write teachers' reports (ibid.: 235), and it is not rare for teachers to be verbally abused by the school principal (Creative21 1996: 121).

Despotic control by the principal is not compatible with a labour movement of teachers. Nikkyōso lost its clout in Aichi and Chiba long ago (Kamata 1984: 197, 1995: 222–3). At one school in Aichi, teachers have to use part of their annual leave to go out of school to collect children from the day care centre, drop them home, and return to school, in order to attend the staff meeting held after hours (Kamata 1995: 233). According to a survey, teachers in Japan actually take only an average of 7.1 out of 20 days annual leave entitlement as against an average of 9.1 days for other workers (Creative21 1996: 97). Another study revealed that the average lunch time was 8 minutes for junior high school teachers and 22 minutes for senior high school teachers, and the time for breaks was 16 and 21 minutes per day respectively (Creative21 1996: 103). 'Death by overwork' (*karōshi*) hits particularly male teachers in their thirties and forties who are heavily involved with athletic club activities (Creative21 1996: 12–20).

In fact, there seems to be a correlation between dehumanising treatment of students by teachers, on the one hand, and the lack of political power among teachers, on the other. As discussed above, both the 'hair drier incident' and the 'javelin club incident' suggest that in Gifu Prefecture teachers' use of violence is firmly supported by the local board of education. Gifu was the primary target of so-called 'normalisation' in the 1960s (Horio 1994: 235–8), which was the systematic de-unionisation movement conducted by Monbushō. It was the prefecture where a young 'crackerjack' bureaucrat from Monbushō, Takaishi Kunio, was dispatched in 1960 to fight back against Nikkyōso. Takaishi was exceptionally 'successful'. While he was posted to Gifu Prefectural Board of Education, between 1961 and 1963, the membership of Nikkyōso in Gifu declined by 64 per cent, from 9,800 to 3,500 (Shimojima 1989: 67). In that sense, Gifu represents a model Monbushō prefecture; so too do Aichi and Chiba.[6]

What are the factors which enabled Aichi and Chiba to be so 'advanced' in regimenting both students and teachers? Kamata argues that in the case of Aichi it is the domination of automobile, armament and other manufacturing industries (Kamata 1995: 247). It is well known that Toyoda city in Aichi is the prototype of the 'castle town' developed around the Toyota car manufacturing company, where the influence of the company permeates almost every sphere of everyday life (e.g. Kinoshita 1988). According to Kamata, exactly the same tactics of control are used in factories and schools – virtual domination of labour union and student association by the management and teachers, respectively; detailed and precise standardisation of factory work (in minutes and seconds) and teaching based on the teaching manual (which regulates both content and time spent for each topic down to the minute); the strict censorship of political inclinations of workers, teachers and the editors of textbooks – for the common goal of heightening conformity among them, ultimately thereby solidifying the national consensus that is deemed essential for Japanese industry to be competitive and therefore for the Japanese nation to survive (Kamata 1995: 129–54). It is not coincidence, Kamata argues, that Tōgō High School, the pinnacle of regimentation, boasts that the diligent attitude among its graduates 'to work without sparing themselves' impresses employers and that they are therefore in great demand from first-class corporations (p. 139).

While Aichi represents the extreme of parallels between school and factory (or education and industry), Chiba represents the extreme of proximity between school and bureaucracy (or education and politics). It has been pointed out that Chiba Board of Education is the place where officials from the Monbushō are sent to try out new ideas before returning to the ministry often with promotions. It is almost 'under the immediate control' of Monbushō, partly due to the physical closeness to it (Kamata 1995: 247), and perhaps partly due to the extremely conservative political climate of the region (Takabatake 1986: 77). The political inclination of the board is suggested by the fact that one of the former superintendents of the board became famous after claiming that the 'strategic command of the army' is useful for the management of schools. In fact, the model of schooling in which physical education is central was created in Chiba as early as the mid-1960s, and the All Japan Teachers League (*Zenkoku nippon kyōshokuin renmei* or *Zennikkyōren*) which strives to 'nurture the heart of beautiful Japanese' was founded in Chiba in 1983, as a rival organisation to combat Nikkyōso (Kamata 1984: 178–202).

If the structural cause of the dehumanising treatment of students is traced back, step by step, we reach the bedrock of the ruling national elite in the spheres of education: Monbushō, the LDP (especially its education clique) and economic circles (e.g. Takayama 1989; Yamazumi 1986; Kamata 1984, 1995). There is no doubt that the postwar history of Japanese education has been a history of the decline of the democratic ideals embodied in the Constitution and Fundamental Law of Education (Horio 1988). In that process, both the human rights of students and freedom of education were 'continuously eroded by the ever-increasing interference of the state's administrative machinery' (Horio 1988: 3).

Within the nationalistic and conservative camp, the most influential voice has been that of the former Prime Minister Nakasone Yasuhiro, who held office between 1982 and 1987. His creed on education is clearly expressed in his 1967 speech to the students of Takushoku University where he was then president. Referring to kamikaze pilots who died towards the end of World War Two, he said:

> Did these pilots die for the sake of self interest, or was it for the sake of vain-glory or for imperialism [sic]? Or was it not rather that they set off on their mission with their hearts filled with pure love of their father-land and their people? There is nothing more precious in any society than the voluntary abandonment of one's life for the sake of one's country and compatriots.
>
> (Yamazumi 1986: 108)

The members of the Nakasone Cabinet's Ad Hoc Council on Education included conservative nationalist bureaucratic and business leaders unified around the demand for the revision of the Fundamental Law of Education (Kamata 1995: 256). One of the major proposals put forward by the Council was that the 'eternal, unchanging traditions' of Japan be given greater emphasis, that the mythic dimensions of Japanese nationalism be restored, and that a tightly controlled form of moral education be imple-mented (Horio 1988: 366). Although it was not without conflict and dis-agreement that the educational reform agenda was discussed (Schoppa 1991), in the end, the nationalistic programme was accomplished in 1989: the order to hoist *Hinomaru* and sing *Kimigayo* at all school ceremonies. Although this had to some extent been practised previously, the 1989 policy 'guideline' was accompanied with the comment that teachers who resisted this policy would be disciplined. At the same time, the content of textbooks was revised considerably, along the lines of glorifying the nationalistic history of Japan while erasing the references to aggression of the Japanese military during World War Two, and deleting any elements of peace education from textbooks.

LEGITIMATION OF VIOLENCE AGAINST *TŌKŌKYOHI* CHILDREN AND YOUTH

The third place to be examined to understand the nature of teachers' violence toward students is the special private institution which has adopted Spartan methods to 'rehabilitate' children and teenagers who do not go to school. As we have seen, the most cruel, vicious punishments happen in these special private facilities (such as Totsuka Yacht School, Fudōjuku, and Kazenoko-gakuen) which are supposed to fulfil the 'needs' of *tōkōkyohi* students. Since we have already described the tragedies that have occurred in these places, let us now examine how *tōkōkyohi* students themselves view these 'schools'. Their insights are suggestive of the nature of these facilities and provide clues as to how such places continue to exist, even flourish, despite the repeated occurrences of abuse and the deaths of children and teenagers there.

The first point indicated by *tōkōkyohi* students is the proximity between the everyday life they lead as *tōkōkyohi* children and the horrific deaths which appear so extraordinary. The case of Kazenoko-gakuen seems to have been particularly shocking to those who live in the district. It was not the physical closeness, however, that shook them, so much as the realisation that they themselves might very well have been sent there. Tosaka Yumi, a 17-year-old *tōkōkyohi* student in Hiroshima writes:

> When I first saw the case of 'Kazenoko-gakuen' I felt so angry and scared. . . . I myself was told by the principal to go to the facility managed by Sakai [i.e. Kazenoko-gakuen] because I too refused to go to school. It gives me a chill to think that it might have been myself [who got killed in the container]. . . . I went to see Kazenoko-gakuen the other day. . . . When I saw the container where they were locked up, I got shocked beyond words. It was so vivid [*manamanashikute*] that my knees trembled with fear. In the facilities, their shoes were still there, their washing was still hanging, it was so vivid. . . . I could not bear to see them. I knew the girl who got killed at the primary school.
>
> (Ishikawa *et al.* 1993: 588)

Likewise Kanewaki Tokuji in Hiroshima writes:

> Although I refused to go to school, I went neither to counselling nor to the special institution [for *tōkōkyohi* students]. . . . I do not remember my parents reprimanding me for not going to school. Until the Kazenoko-gakuen case happened, I did not even know that I could very well be subject to that kind of home. . . . The person who was

killed in the container could have been me. . . . When I heard the news, I thought that it is like a Nazi concentration camp such as Auschwitz. . . . I went to see Kazenoko-gakuen. . . . In the tiny three-mat room, the belongings of those who got killed were left untouched. In a note by the girl, it was written in small letters 'discriminated against, scolded, hated'. It was so pitiful. What thoughts did they have when dying? All such institutions should be smashed!

(Ishikawa *et al.* 1993: 760–3)

Tatara Hiroshi, another non-attendant at school who was enraged by the Kazenoko-gakuen incident, writes that he too received a pamphlet inviting him to Kazenoko-gakuen (Ishikawa *et al.* 1993: 749). The experiences of these students indicate that once one ceases to go to school, there are all sorts of pressures to attend instead such special institutions for 'problem children'. Such pressures come from teachers and principals, parents, local educational advisers, and even through the direct mail service – suggesting that the list of students who do not attend school may be passed on to the special institutions by schools.

The testimony of these students indicates that there is a system of cooperation between public schools and special homes where the use of violence as a 'rehabilitation method' is the norm. The experiences of these students indicate that such institutions constitute a kind of substructure of the regular educational system, suggesting that they are connected to it by the same values and principles.

The series of student deaths in custody in these private institutions (Totsuka Yacht School, Fudōjuku and Kazenoko-gakuen) brought about a new development in the treatment of *tōkōkyohi*. In 1997, six years after the Kazenoko-gakuen incident, an amendment to the Child Welfare Law was passed in the Diet under which facilities for juvenile delinquents were to be opened to 'children who have committed, or are likely to commit, delinquent acts' and/or children who 'require guidance in their day-to-day lives'. In fact, part of a reformatory for boys in Kansai had already been used for about four years to confine non-delinquent *tōkōkyohi* children who were referred by the Child Consultation Centre that the Health and Welfare Ministry operates in each prefecture (*ANEN* 23 June 1997).

Noting this development, Kanewaki Tokuji, quoted above, also writes:

Many people, without questioning, agreed to the opinion: 'the poor quality of the private institutions caused the incident [of Kazenoko-gakuen]. The government, therefore, should set up public institutions [for *tōkōkyohi* children]'. . . . But what we need most is neither private nor public institutions. . . . I would like people to stop controlling children by violence when they do not follow their orders. . . . Children who do not go to school should not be cut off from their friends and the local community in closed institutions.

(Ishikawa *et al.* 1993: 769–2)

Kitani Kentarō (16), a former *tōkōkyohi* student in Hiroshima, comments:

Why do they isolate children from society as if they have a contagious disease, just because they do not go to school? And why were those children [in Kazenoko-gakuen] killed only for that same reason? In response to the question as to why confine *tōkōkyohi* children in an institution someone has said: 'It is to maintain the order in schools and to prevent delinquency'. In the mind of such a person, totalitarian ideas, fading elsewhere in the world, are still flourishing. There are even those who say that *tōkōkyohi* children are not human beings. Will everything be solved if *tōkōkyohi* children are put in institutions?

(Ishikawa *et al.* 1993: 565)

A parallel may be seen between disciplinary perceptions of *tōkōkyohi* and the thinking expressed in the Primary School Law of 1890, when the emperor had absolute power over education. Article 23 of that Law specified who should be excluded and expelled from primary schools, which were regarded as places to educate the 'emperor's people'. There were three criteria of exclusion: (1) a contagious disease, (2) delinquency, and (3) inability to perform academically. Since high schools in the Meiji era (1868–1912) were primarily to educate the elite, the reasons for exclusion from them were also (1) delinquency, (2) inability to perform academically, (3) absence from school for more than a year (with or without a good reason), and (4) absence from school for more than a month without a good reason (Sakamoto 1995: 18–19). In Japanese society today, where there is a social expectation that children and teens should be in school, the situation is different, but it is striking that students who do not go to school have come to be regarded in the same way as those who have a 'contagious disease' or as 'delinquents', and are thus treated in 'isolated institutions' – hospitals, mental hospitals (more on this later) and reformatories (which are, essentially, youth prisons). Some attitudes have changed little over 100 years.

By treating children and teenagers who do not go to school as 'abnormal', Japanese society today is medicalising and criminalising the act of not going to school. As the number of *tōkōkyohi* students increased, and the voice of those students and their supporters began to be heard, the notion of 'abnormality' was gradually revised somewhat. Yet, the idea of confining *tōkōkyohi* students to public institutions persists (see Chapter 8). The more means become available to address the 'problem' within the same paradigm, the less 'escape hatches' there will be for children and teenagers who reject it, and the greater the danger that dehumanisation of the young will become even less visible.

COERCED SILENCE

The most problematic aspect of the 'corporal punishment' administered by teachers, apart from the physical and psychological aspects of the actual deaths and injuries, is the fact that it deprives students of any opportunity to express themselves in ways contrary to the teachers' prescription – whether by words (i.e. thoughts, opinions, ideas), behaviour, or even just appearance. In Japanese schools, the biggest crime committed against teachers is the act of asking a question, presenting a counter-argument, explaining one's position or situation, all of which are taken to be 'talking back' and acts of rebellion. The surveillance file of Akasu Hironori, a senior high school student in Nagano, who was driven by teachers to quit school 'voluntarily' because of his 'delinquent' behaviour reads: 'first we have to make the student realise that he has been critical of teachers [which is unforgivable] and then encourage him to be grateful to teachers' (Higaki 1991: 227). Fujii Seiji, an educational activist, admits that he noticed himself becoming more uncritical and unthinking the more he accepted physical 'punishment' without resisting it. He also stated that teachers who resort to corporal punishment had themselves 'lost words' (i.e. the habit of communicating verbally with others) (Hirano *et al.* 1990: 88).

The examination of corporal punishment in Japanese schools suggests that corporal punishment – physical violence – by teachers is the crudest manifestation of the extremely autocratic and hierarchical nature of Japanese schools, and that it stems from the very foundation of the Japanese educational system which is deeply entrenched in the structure of nationalistic and bureaucratic control of both students and teachers.

What are the consequences of being a 'subordinate' in this autocratic system? In a survey conducted in the early 1980s, more than half of the junior high school students who participated indicated that they felt a desire to hit their teachers (Fukaya 1983: 199). In my survey, no students expressed such a desire, although there were comments which were negative and resentful, and which suggested that students wanted to be in the position of being able to oppress their teachers, instead of just being oppressed themselves.

Kondō Takashi, from an elite school wrote, for example, 'I would like the positions of students and teachers to be reversed'. In a similar vein, Nagai Sumiko, from an academic high school said, 'I want students to be like teachers and treat teachers as if they were students'. Hase Tamotsu, a vocational school student, wrote that he wanted to 'make the position of teachers and students equal, so that students can also admonish their teachers. It is unfair that only students get scolded'. While there is little doubt that these comments reflect the sense of powerlessness among Japanese students and their desire to hold more power *vis-à-vis* teachers, they also suggest that students who are so accustomed to being held down by power come to think in terms of assuming the position of the oppressor as an alternative, rather than critically looking at the structure of oppression itself.

As will be discussed in more detail in Chapter 7, a large number of students try to restore their sense of power by bullying others who are socially and physically weaker than themselves. It is important to note therefore that the hierarchical relationship between teachers and students is often replicated and extended to the relationships between students themselves.

SCHOOL AND DISCIPLINE: ANOTHER APPROACH

The manner in which 'physical punishment' is applied to students by some teachers in Japan is in clear contrast with the highly regulated and codified (and increasingly rare) way corporal punishment and discipline is administered in Australia. In the 1980s corporal punishment was abolished in most states of Australia, while guidelines and procedures for school discipline are usually stipulated in detail in public documents, and there is little room for teachers to administer arbitrary punishment to students in anger. In Victoria, where I conducted my survey, corporal punishment was banned in 1983 in all state schools. Likewise, it was abandoned in South Australia (SA) and Western Australia (WA) in 1987 and in Australian Capital Territory (ACT) in 1988. A number of schools actually ceased to use physical punishment long before it was officially abolished (Sato 1989: 50). Even in New South Wales (NSW) where the 'cane' was re-introduced in 1988, 'fewer teachers than before regard[ed] the cane as a weapon in their disciplinary armour' (Seymour 1992: 44). Unlike Japan where the ban on corporal punishment has little effect in practice, corporal punishment has been completely abandoned by schools in most states of Australia. Teachers are not allowed even to touch students – putting their hands on the shoulders of a student could be sufficient reason for a teacher to be dismissed from school.[7]

Underlying the official abolition in most states of Australia was the view that corporal punishment is 'somewhat brutal' and needs to be replaced with 'modern approaches' (Slee 1992b: 3), and that it contradicts the general trend towards social justice, and is inconsistent with the rejection of violence and the pursuit of peace. For instance, the policy document of the Education Department of South Australia stipulates (p. 2):

> Corporal punishment is incompatible with a commitment to child protection and to the reduction of domestic and social violence; it incorrectly models violence as an acceptable way of dealing with difficulties; it does not teach students alternative ways of behaving.
>
> (quoted by Johnson 1992: 81)

Likewise, the 1984 Conference Decision of the NSW Teachers Federation states:

> Federation believes the implementation of Peace Studies involves the total educational process of the day-to-day operation of every school. . . . Accordingly, it is totally inconsistent to be promoting Peace Studies and still be using corporal punishment as a discipline process. Federation is to ban the use of corporal punishment from 1986 by any Federation member.
>
> (quoted in Seymour 1992: 46–7)

There is also the view that corporal punishment is not only ineffective but that 'heavier-handed discipline [was] a recipe for more conflict' in schools (Connell *et al.* 1982: 61). This was the practical reason underlying the official abandonment of corporal punishment (Slee 1992a: 16, 1992b: 3). It is, in my experience, also a view widely shared by teachers in Australia.

And yet the discipline problem in Australian schools is real. According to a recent survey, 70 per cent of over two hundred teachers with more than five years of teaching experience felt that there had been an increase in student behavioural problems (Bor *et al.* 1992: 83). There is no single cause of student misbehaviour. It could be caused by those aspects of school which students find alienating – hierarchical relationships, irrelevant curricula and pointless routines, or it could simply be due to the fact that students increasingly remain in school simply to avoid unemployment. It might very well be that the traditional pattern of authority has crumbled in society at large and that teachers can no longer expect to be respected just because they are teachers. For some students, serious discipline problems may be 'symptomatic of wider family, personal and/or psychological problems' (Stoddart 1992: 160). The existence of conflicting paradigms among teachers (conservative vs. progressive) itself may have contributed to the problem (Connell *et al.* 1982: 109). It is interesting to note that none of the teachers who responded to the aforementioned survey attributed the increase in discipline problems to the abolition of corporal punishment. My own experience of talking with teachers in Australia on many occasions confirms this view.

Whatever the causes, the focus of the discipline issue in Australia has largely shifted from questions of punishment and control to the question of human relations (Slee 1992b: 2). The school discipline guidelines of the Ministry of Education in Western Australia reads (p. 20):

> Discipline is not just a process of responding to behaviour problems after they have occurred. The key to effective school discipline is the quality of the relationships between teachers and students.
>
> (quoted in Hyde 1992: 76)

'Interpersonal relationships' was one of the four themes of the collection of papers presented at the National Conference on Student Behaviour Problems in 1991 (Elkins and Izard 1992). This is also the area of training available to teachers (Bor *et al.* 1992: 83). The human relationship itself has become one of the foci of education in Australian schools and the issue of discipline is addressed within this new framework.

Even though there are a number of commonalities between Japanese and Australian schools, the extent to which the human rights of students are protected differs significantly between the two societies. Although a number of Australian students commented on how they thought teachers might improve their attitudes, none of them mentioned the violation of human rights as an issue. In contrast, Japanese students, although being generally reticent, did mention occasionally, the violation of human rights as an issue.

As I explained at the end of the previous chapter, corporal punishment is a qualitative matter – most teachers in Japan try not to use it, even if they believe that it is sometimes inevitable that they have to. The issue of corporal punishment is important, nonetheless, since it stems from a deep level within the fundamental structure of the Japanese educational system.

It would be wrong to assume that Japanese classrooms are just spontaneously and naturally orderly. The majority of the class in the commercial school observed by Rohlen in the late 1970s were inattentive, if not disruptive (1983: 40), as were the students in another vocational school observed by Okano in the 1980s (1993: 135). A former junior high school teacher from Japan told me that students sometimes played cards at the back of her class – a story repeated by another former teacher from Japan. When I mentioned that some students in a class I had observed in Australia did not even bring a pen to school, the latter teacher said, 'So the situation is the same in Australia then!'[8]

It is not that students are always on the receiving end of violence. Cases of student violence towards teachers are also reported (Chōnabayashi 1997). Just as students' human rights need to be taken more seriously in Japanese schools, so the human rights and labour conditions of Japanese teachers also deserve attention (Creative21 1996). It should be noted that the hierarchical structure in which students are oppressed by teachers is also the structure which oppresses teachers themselves who hold non-managerial positions (Kamata 1995).

I recently had an opportunity to meet some junior high school students from Japan who were visiting a secondary school in Australia. Being asked what was the aspect of the Australian school of which they felt most envious, all the students said, 'the school starts late and finishes early'. Precisely the same point was also made, enviously, by the Japanese teacher who was accompanying the group. The students said that not only does their school finish later than Australian schools, but they have three hours of sports club activities after school every day. Although they may enjoy this, it is simply too long for both students and teachers. The teacher said that the guidance of students and other business keeps her busy long after school hours, and even if she is in charge of club activities (which occupy her for three hours after school), the extra allowance is negligible.

This episode, together with the issue of human rights of students and teachers, makes one wonder about the nature of schools in Japan. The way they are run exhausts both students and teachers and makes them feel their human rights are being violated and/or their labour conditions need drastic reform.

Similar questions arise in relation to school rules, which may be regarded as the superstructure of school. Not only students, but also many teachers, feel that school rules have 'gone too far'. The nature of school rules in Japan is explored in the following chapter.

NOTES

1 This is part of his writing published in Ishikawa *et al.* (1993: 747).
2 Strictly speaking, the word '*bukatsu*' means club activities for both athletic and non-athletics clubs. The distinction, however, is rarely made and '*bukatsu*' in most cases refers to athletics club activities.
3 The description of this incident has been drawn from Sakamoto (1995), pp. 205–10.
4 Interview with a teacher from my own former senior high school.

5 The following discussion on education in Aichi and Chiba is adopted largely from Kamata (1995).

6 Takaishi's 'success' provided him with a stepping stone to climb up the Monbushō ladder all the way to Administrative Vice-Minister (*jimujikan*) in 1986, supported by the LDP education clique (*bunkyōzoku*). He came to play the central role in the final stage of the educational reforms initiated by the Ad Hoc Council on Education (Rinji kyōiku shingikai or Rinkyōshin), and was especially enthusiastic to implement the nationalistic 'flag and anthem' (*Hinomaru/Kimigayo*) policy. This was done just on the eve of his arrest on charges of corruption in the Recruit Scandal in 1989 (Takayama 1989; Yamazumi 1989; Schoppa 1991: 243). A similar case of suspicion of corruption, involving those with close connections with the LDP, Monbushō, and key figures in physical education circles, has been reported more recently (Kuji 1997).

7 I was rather sceptical about this and expected that there would be hidden cases of corporal punishment. But numerous conversations with students and teachers confirmed that corporal punishment is indeed not used in Australia except in a small number of private schools.

8 Interview in Canberra, on 28 August 1997, with Mr Matsushita Kazuyuki who has worked as a senior high school teacher in various schools in Tokyo for over 30 years.

5 School rules: the web of regimentation

> Although I do not believe that this is realistic,
> I really want to be free!
> Teachers make school rules too much.
>
> (Nakamori Miyoko, vocational school student, Japan)

In response to a question 'what do Japanese schools equate to', a student who returned to Japan after spending three years in Rome answered, 'rules' (Kunie 1991: 253). It is reported that 97 per cent of 1,125 public junior high schools in Japan have regulations on school uniforms – the symbol of school rules (Sakamoto 1990: 48). The ratio of prefectural senior high schools which have school uniforms is 100 per cent in many prefectures; and even in Tokyo where rules on uniforms are most relaxed, it reaches 55 per cent (Sakamoto 1990: 49).

Rohlen comments that Japanese teachers take responsibility over what in the United States would be considered private matters (Rohlen 1983: 42) and rules in Japanese schools usually cover vast areas of student lives, both during and after school hours. Similarly, White points out that there are up to 200 complicated rules in some schools (White 1993: 92), including, for example, regulations as follows.

- No one should have a permanent wave, or dye his or her hair. Girls should not wear ribbons or accessories in their hair. Hair dryers should not be used.
- Wear your school badge at all times. It should be positioned exactly.
- Going to school in the morning, wear your book bag strap on the right shoulder; in the afternoon on the way home, wear it on the left shoulder. Your book case thickness, filled and unfilled, [should be such-and-such].

- Girls should wear only regulation white underpants of 100 per cent cotton.
- When you raise your hand to be called on, your arm should extend forward and up at the angle prescribed in the handbook.
- Your own route to school is marked in your student rule handbook; observe carefully which side of each street you are to use on the way to and from school.
- After school you are to go directly home, unless your parent has written a note permitting you to go to another location. Permission will not be granted by the school unless this other location is a suitable one. You must not go to coffee shops. You must be home by ___o'clock.

(extract from White 1993: 223–5)

Not every school's regulations are as detailed as this. However, the result of my survey indicates that one cannot underestimate the prevalence of trivial and nonsensical rules. Forty-two per cent of Japanese school students in my sample indicated that their school rules were *never* sensible or based on good reasons, whereas those who chose 'never' was only 10 per cent in Australia (see Table 5.1).

Takagi Yoshinori, from an academic high school in Japan, commented:

> I want to abolish unreasonable and stupid rules. The rules we have now are meaningless and senseless. For example, why is it that our socks should not have lines or be of red colour? Why must boys' hair be short enough not to touch the ear? I do not think that there is any sense behind these rules and if they decide to have these rules, I want them to explain the reasons.

In a similar vein, Ikeda Masaki, from an elite school, wrote: 'Teachers are very strict about students' hair, but I wish I were able to perm my hair because it would not cause trouble to anybody'. Shimada Akio, also from an elite school, wrote: 'I want to check teachers' hair'.

Table 5.1 School rules compared: 'Sensible and based on good reasons?'

	'Our school rules are sensible and based on good reasons'			
	Never (%)	*Sometimes* (%)	*Mostly* (%)	*Always* (%)
Japan	42	34	19	5
Australia	10	37	41	12

In response to the statement, 'If teachers set rules they explain the reasons well', 42 per cent of the Japanese students again responded: 'never' (see Table 5.2). In other words, more than four in ten Japanese students think that school rules are 'never' sensible *and* that teachers 'never' explain the reasons for them. These findings indicate the largely non-negotiable nature of rules in Japanese schools.

The non-negotiable nature of school rules in Japan is well demonstrated by the attempt by Nakajima Ryū (14) in Kyoto who tried to open a fair discussion with teachers regarding school rules and students' rights before he began *tōkōkyohi*. He addressed four questions to his homeroom teacher in writing, for which he received verbal responses as follows.

Q: What would you think of the fact that there are a number of students who side with me [in opposing rules on school uniform and long hair]?
A: I want you to observe the rules until new rules are made.
Q: Could you please explain the difference between asserting one's rights and being selfish?
A: You want to say that they are different, don't you?
Q: Please write succinctly what human rights are.
A: You said that it is the rights each individual is born with, didn't you?
Q: How far would you think that one can assert one's rights?
A: You said one can assert one's rights so far as it does not cause trouble and inconvenience to others, didn't you?

(Ishikawa *et al.* 1993: 879)

The teacher simply repeated what Ryū said previously, because the points he tried to make were all valid, reasonable, and irrefutable. The reality is that whether teachers are able to explain the reasons behind school rules or not is not an issue for teachers. If anything, having to explain the reasons itself contradicts the very nature of school rules. This is partly reflected in the action taken by the teacher mentioned above after his 'discussion' with Ryū. He made a copy of the questions without Ryū's consent and handed it

Table 5.2 School rules compared: 'Rules are explained well?'

	'If teachers set rules, they explain the reasons well'			
	Never (%)	*Sometimes* (%)	*Mostly* (%)	*Always* (%)
Japan	42	27	22	9
Australia	20	45	26	9

to the principal, who then passed it to all staff saying, 'What extremely radical things he has written!' (Ishikawa *et al.* 1993: 879).

What precisely was so 'extremely radical' in what Ryū did in the eyes of the principal? Ryū is not a 'delinquent' in need of 'guidance' and 'rehabilitation'. The polite wording of the questions he posed to his teachers suggests this. At home, this 14-year-old boy did most of the house work (including preparing meals) and looked after his little sister while his father was in the hospital and his mother was busy caring for his father. In his diary, there is absolutely no indication of his having a 'behavioural problem' in a 'normal' sense (Ishikawa *et al.* 1993: 878). Apart from his resistance to school rules, there was no sign of 'behavioural problems' on the part of Ryū, yet in the eyes of the teachers, Ryū had caused a 'political' problem. It is by means of school rules and school rules alone that he was defined in these terms.

Whether the primary objective of school rules is to 'guide' students into 'correct behaviour' is questionable. A number of Japanese students wrote in response to my survey that they did not need school rules to behave themselves. Machida Yumi from an academic school wrote that she wanted to 'abolish school rules and to behave on the basis of what I think is right'. Elsewhere, another student commented:

> when I was at junior high school, school rules were not strict, but we had no problems, and there was a sense of trust between students and teachers. Now, everything is decided by rules in the senior high school, and I wonder if teachers trust us. . . . Some students do everything to rebel against school rules, but there would be no need to rebel if there were no rules.
>
> (Kunie 1991: 246)

It is not just students who question the meaning of having trivial and coercive school rules. Questions are sometimes raised by parents. Teachers, however, tend to maintain obstinate attitudes regarding school rules even when questions are raised by parents. A father who tried to support his son in resisting school rules realised after a strenuous attempt to negotiate with teachers that in the minds of teachers 'what was forbidden by school rules was not to be tolerated irrespective of the reason' (Nishizato 1989: 27). Another parent says that teachers put a ban on the distribution of a special issue of the PTA's newsletter focusing on school rules; and that several teachers joined the public-relations committee after the incident in order to gain control over the content of the newsletter. Most parents were shaken by this and fell silent as a result (Imahashi *et al.* 1992: 82).

These episodes, as well as the responses to my survey, make one wonder what the real aims of school rules are. Apparently, there is a considerable gap between what rules are supposed to be and how they are actually used in Japanese schools. The hidden functions of school rules seem particularly strong. What are the school rules really for?

THE FUNCTION OF SCHOOL RULES

In order to think about this question, the regulation that boys must have close-cropped hair may be considered as an example. According to Sakamoto (1990), this regulation was adopted in about one third of all public junior high schools in Japan in the 1980s (p. 47).[1] As he points out, it is impossible for students and parents to find any reason why boys should have close-cropped hair. For teachers, however, this regulation has two functions.

First, it makes 'hair style' a non-issue. If students have close-cropped hair, teachers can suppress all resistance over hair style, whether concerning length, colour, perm or the use of driers. Thus the teachers' degree of control over students is maximised. Second, this is the crudest form of deprivation of student individuality. Hair style is an important fashion point for teenagers. In fact, it ranks highest among the school regulations from which students wish to be liberated. According to a 1988 survey involving over ten thousand students, 66 per cent of junior high school students and 51 per cent of senior high school students wanted this regulation to be abolished (Sakamoto 1990: 32,43–4). Unlike school uniforms, moreover, hair style cannot be changed after school, and thus it binds students at all times.

By imposing the rule of close-cropped hair, therefore, teachers are actually forcing male students to follow an order which is almost intolerable; they thus demand absolute obedience. This explains why the act of asking questions and explanations in a civilised manner was perceived by teachers to be 'extremely radical'. It is a violation of the 'hidden' and 'real' meaning of school rules, which is perhaps worse than the simple infringement of the rule itself. The prevalence of rules on close-cropped hair in Japanese schools suggests that this hidden function of school rules is often of crucial importance.

For students, school rules, epitomised by the close-cropped hair rule, signify precisely the deprivation of individuality and the negation of oneself. Enforcement of such a rule can also be a humiliating and dehumanising experience, especially for boys who have never had their hair closely cropped before. *Tōkōkyohi* students frequently mention that the longer they stayed in school, the stronger became their sense of loss of selfhood (see Chapter 8). Japanese schools have become a place which threatens and subverts the students' sense of their existence as human beings, both physically and psychologically. It is not coincidental that 'Sakakibara', the 'school killer', was so concerned about his 'existence' and his sense of being himself (Kuroda *et al.* 1997: 20).

The other function of trivial rules is to identify non-conformists by raising the standard of conformity as high as possible. Trivial rules function like a fine-tooth comb to weed out students with the slightest tendency to resist the control of teachers. Some schools in Aichi are (in)famous for their extreme regimentation. One such school published a collection of essays written by teachers, entitled '120 Stories to Build Schools'. In the book, one teacher revealed that school rules regarding hair style, school uniforms, school bags and shoes had been tightened, based on the underlying assumption that students whose behaviour would in due course become problematic manifest themselves first through different ways of speech and difference of appearance (Kamata 1984: 19). In other words, by imposing stricter rules as a screening device, teachers think that they are able to discern the tendency towards becoming a 'problem kid'. This remark illustrates the process through which school rules function to 'criminalise' non-conformist attitudes well before students actually develop any 'delinquent' tendency (if they ever do).

AUTHORITARIANISM AND GROUPISM

At the same time, the Aichi teacher's remark is suggestive of the symbiotic relationship between authoritarianism and groupism, control and conformity. To conform means both to observe rules prescribed by teachers and to belong to the group which follows the rules. In answering the question as to why students obey rules – whether it is because they believe that it is right to do so or because everybody else obeys rules – one student answered that 'it is because everybody obeys them' (Okuchi *et al.* 1989: 68). Here we may discern the juncture between the power of teachers on the one hand and the power of the group on the other. The group becomes the device for teachers to exert their power over students, and the school rules provide the means to reinforce both conformity and groupism. The conformity and groupism thus created, in turn help to facilitate the smooth operation of school rules. Authoritarianism and groupism, control and conformity, support and enhance each other.

This means that by emphasising the importance of the 'group', teachers are actually nurturing the mechanism through which they exert their power. A student who refuses to wear a school uniform, for example, is banned from club activities for the reason that 'her wearing non-uniform clothes disrupt[s] the team work' (*AS* 16 September 1995). The student who resists school rules is punished not directly for opposing teachers but indirectly by her/his classmates – as the disrupting element which brings a disadvantage to the group. The more nonsensical and trivial the school rules are, the more effective they become for teachers to exert their power. Seen in this way, it 'makes perfect sense' for Japanese schools to be saturated with rules which do not make sense to students, however much they try to find a sound argument ('*seiron*') to justify them.

It is not, however, that the majority of students have any 'natural' tendency to obey school rules or to hold conformist attitudes. The Japanese educational system has a number of mechanisms of control in which peer management plays the central role. Children are socialised to develop the sense of 'group' in kindergartens (Peak 1989), and small-group management plays a central role in the everyday life of primary schools (Lewis 1995). In high schools, as well as in primary schools, students are given token roles to induce them into participation in decision making and in the maintenance of school rules.

Student associations, for instance, are often involved in the management of school rules, just as unions are involved in decisions regarding rationalisation in large car manufacturing companies in Japan. In introducing the standardisation of school slippers one teacher wrote: 'we have entrusted the task of standardisation of school slippers[2] to students. We thought that it would be far more effective to implement it as an activity of the Student Association rather than to impose it upon students' (Kamata 1984: 20). Although it may sound fair to let students take part in the process, in reality, everything was decided by teachers in advance and students were just used in an effort to make the operation smooth (Kamata 1984: 20). In a high school in Fukuoka, one vow in the Student Association Charter which has been in effect for twenty years reads:

> Even if we are allowed to have long hair, we will not have a hair style inappropriate for high school students [i.e. long hair]. . . . All judgements regarding hair style and long hair are entrusted to the Long Hair Committee consisting of [four student representatives and several teachers], and we, students, will not contest their decisions. . . . When a student breaches the rule, we will make him close-crop his hair, and when the general discipline becomes corrupt, we vow that we all shall have close-cropped hair.
>
> (Nagahata 1991: 215)

Students serve to police other students. Senior students are often stricter than teachers in checking on junior students (Hayashi 1994). Students are assigned to positions specialising in 'school discipline' (*fūki iin*) so that they can watch their classmates in cooperation with teachers. That students are given opportunities to make their own weekly, monthly, or term objectives is also part of the emphasis on internalisation of prescribed rules (Sugimoto 1983: 131). My survey also shows evidence of this system. Fifty-four per cent of Japanese students indicated that teachers let them have a say in making up classroom rules either 'mostly' or 'always'; whereas 55 per cent of the Australian students chose 'never' in answering the same question (see Table 5.3).

Table 5.3 School rules compared: 'Students participate in the making?'

| | 'Teachers let you have a say in making up classroom rules' | | | |
	Never (%)	*Sometimes* (%)	*Mostly* (%)	*Always* (%)
Japan	18	28	35	19
Australia	55	33	9	3

This does not mean, however, that Japanese students have genuine autonomy in making classroom rules. Decisions are made under the supervision and the guidance of the teacher, and never contradict prescribed school rules. Classroom rules are best understood as a regulatory mechanism which enhances peer management. When students are given opportunities to make rules, the results do not differ from the rules prescribed by teachers (Murakami 1990). If indeed this procedure were to lead to the adoption of student preferences on rules and regulations, it would be impossible to explain the finding that three quarters of the Japanese sample consider their school rules unreasonable.

Students are also trained constantly to internalise their teachers' values through various forms of 'self'-discipline. They have to write a 'self-discipline diary' (*shūyō nisshi*) (Ikeda *et al.* 1991: 256) or 'self-discipline composition' (*hanseibun*) (Nishizato 1989), to participate in 'self-discipline meetings' (*hanseikai*), and to think about points of self-discipline for the week, the month, or the year (Sugimoto 1983: 131).

BEHAVIOURAL CONTROL THROUGH STUDENT ASSESSMENT

There is also a more 'effective' form of student control – confidential reports written by teachers on students (*naishinsho*) to be used as part of the assessment for admission to senior high school. Although this system was developed, at least on the surface, as part of an attempt to reduce the pressure to perform at the entrance examination to senior high schools, it resulted in effect in the granting of enormous powers to teachers. Teachers can use this power to prevent a student from being admitted to senior high school (Hosaka 1992). One student says how each time she displeased teachers she was blackmailed that they had 'yet another negative remark to include in the school report' and that they would 'pay her back later' (*AS* 21 April 1988). The system has the power to shut out discontented parents as well. All teachers need to say is: 'If you say such a critical thing about school, it will go against your child's interest' (*AS* 18 April 1988). One parent, whose son was forced into quitting a senior high school, explains how resisting teachers ultimately resulted in the significant deprivation of educational opportunities and thus the curtailment of the life opportunities of his son (Nishizato 1989).

The new assessment system included in the 1989 New Course of Study which was fully implemented in 1993 in junior high schools, further enhanced this trend. It elevated the non-academic evaluation of students from the peripheral to the central part of the school report. New criteria such as enthusiasm and motivation to study, general attitudes, and participation in club and volunteer activities came to be included in the main part of the student assessment. This change drove students to compete against one another to give a 'good impression' to teachers. Students came to raise their hand in class, for instance, regardless of whether they knew the answer to the question, or to participate in volunteer activities, only to obtain a certificate. To contradict teachers came to be seen as an absolute disadvantage. One junior high school teacher says that since this policy was introduced, the majority of students came to say that 'it is selfish for a student not to observe school rules' (Yamauchi and Chōnabyashi 1997: 12). Another teacher was shocked to discover why a first-year student in his junior high school followed him around like a faithful dog – the student's explanation was that 'if I get along with you, I will get high marks, won't I?' (Yamauchi and Chōnabayashi 1997: 10).

In order to check on students, teachers carry out inspections. One report of a survey conducted in five prefectures involving 2,900 senior high school teachers revealed that a large proportion of schools have some sort of inspection. The following figures show the percentage of teachers who indicated that they conduct inspections daily, regularly, or occasionally with regard to each item (Sakamoto 1990: 32).

Dress	95 per cent
Hair	89 per cent

Lateness	75 per cent
Possessions	42 per cent
Conduct outside school	42 per cent
Greetings	33 per cent

Inspections are often conducted in the morning at the school gate by teachers in charge of 'life guidance' (*seikatsu shidō*) because it is a convenient time and place for them to check on students – their appearance, punctuality and greetings – i.e. their compliance with school rules as well as their respect for teachers. It was in Kobe in this setting that Ishida Ryōko was killed when her head was caught between the school gate and the wall in 1990. Despite this tragedy, this surveillance system continued in 80 per cent of schools in Kobe (Nagahata 1991: 211) – suggesting that it probably had even less effect upon schools in other regions. It was also in this context that the PE teacher in Nakatsu Commercial School in Gifu hit and shouted at students, behaviour which was considered normal and necessary.

For students, the school gate functions as the place for surveillance and for the demarcation of school territory: it is the symbol of their oppression. Fukuhara Yōichirō, a *tōkōkyohi* student, describes what the school gate means for students in these terms.

> Sometimes the science teacher in charge of 'life guidance' [*seikatsu shidō*] is there at the school gate in the morning glaring at students. . . . He checks whether each student is wearing the name plate and the school cap properly. He is there usually on Monday and Friday, but we never know, as it depends on his mood. He is very scary. Fortunately there is a crossing bridge in front of the school gate and our group [*han*] uses that bridge.[3] So, we can check whether the teacher is standing there or not in advance. The first person in the group who sees the teacher lets others know. If we are given the sign [that the teacher is there], my right hand checks my cap and my left hand touches my name plate reflexively. Those with no cap or name plate prepare themselves and walk towards the gate – if noticed, you get hit with a fist. . . . There is also a rule that we must bow to the gate. When the teacher is not there, we bow rather casually. When the teacher is there, we have to line up and bow properly. Bowing to school will not bring us anything good anyway, so we skip it sometimes. We feel very tense in the morning. We really do not know why we have to bow to school at all.
>
> (Ishikawa *et al.* 1993: 288)

The school gate represents school as an institution. It is the point where only students who have passed the examination can enter. It is the spot where the compliance of students to school rules is screened. It is the place where students who do not obey rules get punished. The physical force of the school gate which killed Ishida Ryōko symbolises the power under which students live. More recently, the crime committed by the Kobe 'school killer' directed people's attention yet again to the school gate, when he placed the severed head of his victim on it. It was his 'revenge' against a school which had 'erased' his existence (see Chapter 1).

COMPARATIVE ASSESSMENT

Compared to the tension surrounding school rules in Japan, the atmosphere in Australia regarding school rules is much more relaxed (see Tables 5.1 to 5.3). Nonetheless, there are many commonalities between Japan and Australia in terms of student perceptions of school rules. As in Japan, rules relating to appearance and fashion, i.e. school uniforms, school bags, name tags, and hair style, drew many comments in Australia, particularly from private school students. What Jim Hutchinson and Briony Summers wanted was:

> Less uniform rules (e.g. blazers in street)! Being able to wear PE uniform to and from school, to wear sneakers in assembly hall, and PE winter cheaters with summer uniform. Being able to wear summer or winter uniform all year round!!!

> For petty little rules that are not necessary to be abolished, e.g. not being allowed to wear studs [earrings], T-bar shoes, white ribbons, socks with our summer uniform, as well as other rules on jumpers in the street, and length of hair.

Such comments on school uniforms, however, were made mainly by private schools students where school uniforms are considered as a status symbol. For students attending government schools, there are far less restrictions on appearance, and school uniforms are hardly an issue. In Japan, on the other hand, the tendency is opposite. Generally speaking, rules regarding school uniforms are more stringent in schools where the academic standard of students is low. In such schools, uniforms are regarded as the means for containing 'behavioural problems' of students. The uniform thus becomes a label of non-achievement and low status as well as a symbol of coercion – a combination which naturally elicits student resentment and resistance.

Rules which students perceive to be nonsensical were also resented in

Australian schools. Kim Pak from a private school and Di Phillips from a technical school set out some of the changes they wanted:

> I would change the system [that if we are late we] get 'late passes', and I think there should be a different (or no) punishment for being late. I would like rules to be changed within the school.

> Not having detention when being 5 minutes late.

It is not that students are against all rules, however. Rather, as was the case in Japan, students want to have rules which are sensible. Chris Barlow from a private school and Tony Jenkins from a technical school wrote:

> If I could change things at school it would be [sic] less strict and there would be lighter punishments for petty crimes.

> If I could change school, I would be out of uniform, have less rules but proper ones, make sure the teachers are hard working, and not strict at all, so that way, make it easier for the kids.

What was clearly different in Australia compared to Japan was that some Australian students wanted to make rules stricter. Sue McEwan, a private school student, stated:

> If I could change things overnight, I would tighten up school discipline as the current school discipline is virtually nil. I would cut out the wearing of ear-rings (boys) and outlandish hairstyles and the like, I would clean up the school into a more respectful state, in the process expelling people who do not conform with school rules and the like who put down teachers and more to the point, pupils. This I would hope to do; but yet I think it will never happen!

In state high schools as well, some students thought that school rules should be stricter, as Tania Downes and Joe Schmid wrote:

> I would want school or teachers to be more strict. This, I believe, helps the student to become respectful, polite and well-mannered.

> I think high schools should be stricter . . . [especially in year] 7,8,9, because I know when I was [at that level], particular teachers could not control the class and we didn't learn a thing. This has only been [sic] a few teachers, NOT ALL.

These comments suggest that in some schools in Australia, school rules and regulations as the traditional means of controlling students have broken down, to the extent that teachers cannot 'control' the class. Whether stricter control really would enhance the teacher's ability to manage the class is a contentious point, however. One teacher, 'Jane', who teaches in an inner suburban high school in Melbourne, comments on how she can prevent stress in teaching as follows:

> I don't suffer from stress in the classroom as many other teachers do, probably because I didn't start teaching till I was in my mid-thirties and had kids of my own and therefore haven't treated kids as objects. They have always been persons to me. I've no need to be in power conflicts with them. I always trust kids. . . . I never think in terms of 'discipline' or classroom 'control'. . . . I just think, let's be considerate to one another. I negotiate anything every time I go into a new classroom. I have gone into a class which has caused three teachers nervous break-downs and discussed with them what students and teachers should do to work well together. Instead of saying: these are the rules, I will ask: 'What do you think?'. . . . I believe teachers should give kids respon-sibility. A lot of them don't. . . . If you can accept that students can make some decisions, half the problems are gone. . . . I have no need to set up any power structure.
>
> (Otto 1986: 155)

This is the view shared by Ian Summerfield, a technical school student quoted earlier, who wrote:

> This school is a school with a lot of personality. The teachers enjoy a good joke as long as it is in good taste. The rules are quite slack as we have a lot of trust put in us and that trust is respected by the students (or most of them). The more we are trusted the better things work.

Overall, there was much variation in Australian students' opinions with regard to school rules. Some were critical of the ways rules restrict their lives, others called for the introduction of stricter rules. The variation in comments from Australian students seem to suggest that schools in Australia are full of dynamic interactions. Power struggles between teachers and students do not always occur along the clear-cut lines of division between teachers who represent authoritarian traditionalist values and views and students with the urge to escape from them. Some teachers may try to introduce more liberal ways of organising school, and this may sometimes result in class disruption and student dissatisfaction at not being able to learn properly; at other times it may create a better environment for teachers and students to work. The richness of comments made by Australian students in general seems to reflect the fact that their schools are going through a lot of changes, that students are aware of the possibility of alternative ways of school organisation, and that they also recognise the need for some structure so as to be able to learn things in the classroom.

No student in Australia expressed the desperation to be freed that is relatively common among Japanese students. Not a single Japanese student wished school rules to be stricter.

Thus far, I have examined non-academic aspects of school – the student–teacher relationship, the questions of discipline and school rules, all to do with human relations and student behaviour, i.e. about socialisation in the broadest sense. In this area, as we have seen, the educational systems of Japan and Australia have been heading in opposite directions – Japan, towards an increasingly autocratic and hierarchical paradigm; Australia, towards a more democratic and egalitarian paradigm, even though there is still much overlap and commonalities between the two systems.

Whichever the paradigm being promoted, its success or failure almost always hinges on the academic dimension of school – students' perceptions of academic achievement and the meaning of study, in particular. It is difficult to imagine that the heavy-handed approach common in Japanese schools would be tolerated by students if they did not believe, as I mentioned earlier, that the academic record ultimately determines the level of happiness in life. Conversely, the democratic approach in public schools in Australia may be less inclined to give rise to 'discipline problems' if more students perceive it crucial for them to learn at school. It is also in the academic dimension where the social class factor becomes relevant. The next chapter aims to find out how the academic achievement pressure and the meaning of study are perceived by students in Japan and Australia.

NOTES

1 The situation changed significantly after the then Education Minister, Akamatsu, requested schools to review this rule in 1993.
2 In many schools, students are required to change into special school shoes (or slippers) at the entrance hall.
3 Pupils at primary school often go to school in a small group called '*han*'.

6 Achievement pressure and the meaning of study

Out of Interest

Study can be about anything.
From any one thing, questions without end arise.
Study springs from an interest in things.
Because your interest is aroused, you doubt,
And then, you investigate.
Investigating such doubts, your study goes deeper and deeper.
This is what I see as real study.

(Shimane Jun, 12-year old, Kanagawa)[1]

ACADEMIC ACHIEVEMENT PRESSURE

The hegemony of meritocracy in Japan was discussed in the first chapter – the ideological and structural features of the 'mass-education society': how Japanese people are driven by the belief that one's academic achievement has a crucial impact upon almost all spheres of life, regardless of social class or vocational aspiration.

If almost every corner of Japanese society is saturated with the meritocratic creed, there should be little difference in academic achievement pressure, for instance, felt by students attending different types of schools, i.e. elite, academic and vocational. The result presented in Table 6.1 indicates that that is indeed the case.[2]

There is little difference in the perceived level of academic achievement pressure among Japanese students, whether they attended elite schools where literally all students intended to advance to university, or vocational schools where only one in five students intended to do so. This was the case in spite of the fact that (1) our sample included one of the most elite senior high schools in the nation from which a large number of students were regularly admitted to Tokyo University, and (2) a considerable discrepancy

Table 6.1 Survey results: academic achievement pressure compared

	'This school pushes you to achieve academic results'			
	Never (%)	*Sometimes* (%)	*Mostly* (%)	*Always* (%)
Japan				
Elite	30	38	20	12
Academic	20	42	26	13
Vocational	25	41	17	17
Australia				
Elite	4	24	36	36
Academic	17	37	33	14
Vocational	19	47	25	10

presumably existed between those vocational school students who 'intended' to go to university and those who were actually admitted to one. Given the wide spectrum of student population covered by the sample, the uniformity observed in Japan is striking.

The peculiarity of this phenomenon is further accentuated when it is compared with the result obtained in Australia. In clear contrast with the Japanese situation, there is a vast difference in the intensity of achievement pressure experienced by students attending different types of schools in Australia. This pressure is greatest in elite private schools, followed by state (academic) high schools, and then state technical (vocational) schools. As shown in Tables 6.2 and 6.3, the same contrast between Japan and Australia may be observed in two other aspects related to achievement pressure.

Quite unexpectedly, the results also show that academic achievement pressure was less prevalent in the minds of Japanese students than in their Australian counterparts. In fact, the majority of Japanese students chose either 'never' or 'sometimes' (as against 'mostly' and 'always') for all these statements. Over 60 per cent of them thought that school pushed them to achieve academic results either 'never' or only 'sometimes'. Over 70 per cent of them felt that school was a competitive place either 'never' or only 'sometimes'. Over 80 per cent of them responded that there was a lot of homework either 'never' or only 'sometimes'.

The paradoxical reality of super-meritocratic Japan is suggested by these two findings: (1) there are few inter-school differences in the perceived level of academic achievement pressure in Japan despite the fact that schools are thoroughly stratified and ranked; and (2) the perceived level of academic achievement pressure is lower in Japan than Australia.

Table 6.2 Survey results: competition compared

	'School is a competitive place'			
	Never (%)	Sometimes (%)	Mostly (%)	Always (%)
Japan				
Elite	45	34	15	7
Academic	37	38	18	7
Vocational	37	36	20	7
Australia				
Elite	3	36	38	23
Academic	14	47	26	14
Vocational	16	46	25	13

Table 6.3 Survey results: quantity of homework compared

	'You must do a lot of homework at this school'			
	Never (%)	Sometimes (%)	Mostly (%)	Always (%)
Japan				
Elite	38	44	11	8
Academic	37	45	12	6
Vocational	40	42	12	6
Australia				
Elite	3	24	47	26
Academic	3	45	38	13
Vocational	17	54	22	7

The findings as to the first item (i.e. achievement pressure from school), seem to suggest two things. One is that in a society where the achievement of high marks has become a fundamental value, schools do not need to exert much pressure on students because academic achievement pressure has been highly internalised in the minds of students as the 'task' and 'problem' of each individual. Teachers 'push' their students when advising them on the university to which they should apply, saying 'if you try a little harder, you can apply for a university which is one rank higher'. This is closer to 'advice' than 'pressure'. At the same time, the fact that senior high schools are finely ranked and stratified makes it unnecessary for teachers to push students much, since the ranking of the school more or less determines the level of academic ability of new entrants, which in turn more or less predetermines the ranking of the school to be aimed at three years later.

This is particularly obvious in the case of elite schools in Japan. As we have seen already (Figure 2.1), in elite schools where literally nobody thinks twice about applying for highest-ranking universities, students have already been selected to meet high academic standards and would work hard with or without external pressure. In Australia, on the other hand, students in elite (private) schools are a mixture of students with varied academic abilities and aspirations (as suggested by Figure 2.1). They have been selected primarily in terms of the economic power of their parents, which is yet to be translated into academic ability. With extremely high tuition fees, this is precisely what is expected of elite private schools in Australia. They are accountable to parents for the academic achievement of their students. It is *the* task of elite private schools to exert pressure on students.

A similar point can also be made about competition. Two explanations as to why it is felt less in Japan are possible. First, in the massive, nationwide 'competition' for university admission, competition becomes abstract, impersonal and individualistic. There is no overt, face-to-face competition with one's peers in class, in school, or even in the region. Often students are competing against numerous strangers in other cities and districts. Second, because schools are being 'ham-sliced' and because teachers often give each individual student sober and well-founded advice as to which university or senior high school to approach, the actual competition rate for a particular institution is not high (Amano 1995: 81–3). Homework also becomes a 'non-issue' in a society where students study a lot in any case, either at home or at *juku* after school. Interpreted in this way, the findings reflect, somewhat paradoxically, the all-encompassing nature of meritocracy in Japan.

Table 6.4 presents the same results by using a different statistical measure. Figures under the 'types of school' employ a scale score called 'achievement pressure' which was created by combining answers to the questions regarding academic achievement pressure, competitiveness,

Table 6.4 Mean scores of 'academic achievement pressure' for different groups

	Mean	Standard deviation	Elite	Academic	Vocational	ANOVA (F =)
Japan	6.5	(2.7)	6.5	6.5	6.6	1.1
Australia	8.2	(2.5)	9.4	7.9	6.8	183.2*

* Statistically significant differences at $p < .001$ or better.

homework, tests and exams, and the difficulty of work (see Appendix 4 for the scale reliability). The score ranges from 0 to 15 – the higher the score, the higher the pressure felt by students. Figures in the far right column indicate whether the differences among different types of school are statistically significant or not.

The results confirm our previous findings. The level of academic pressure felt by Japanese students were more-or-less the same regardless of the kind of school attended. This is shown by the scale scores ranging narrowly between 6.5 and 6.6, as well as by the *F*-value of 1.1 (insignificant). For better or worse, there is an 'equality' or 'uniformity' in the achievement pressure felt by Japanese students. In Australia, on the other hand, the F-value of 183.2 indicates that the inter-group difference was enormous across different types of schools. As we observed earlier, students attending private schools were under far greater pressure than those attending state high schools, who in turn were under more pressure than students attending state technical schools.[3]

The contrast between Japan and Australia was less prominent with regard to the question on 'tests and exams', however. As Table 6.5 shows, the majority of students in both societies indicated that they had to think about tests and exams either mostly or always. The finding suggests that formal assessment procedure is the aspect of student life which weighs on students almost universally.

On this point, elite private school student Rebecca Lilley wrote:

> I like school as it is, but I get very worried about the fact that I want to do medicine, and there is a chance I won't get in to Monash or

Table 6.5 Survey results: importance of tests and exams compared

	'You have to think about tests and exams'			
	Never *(%)*	*Sometimes* *(%)*	*Mostly* *(%)*	*Always* *(%)*
Japan				
Elite	7	34	36	23
Academic	6	30	52	12
Vocational	6	26	40	28
Australia				
Elite	1	16	35	48
Academic	1	19	30	50
Vocational	4	31	31	34

Melbourne University because of the shortage of vacancies. I do not do a group 1 maths and the maths I do (and will do in HSC – Maths at work – group 2 subject) is not recognised by universities. I do not do a language either, so I could not get into a science course with that. I very strongly wish to be a psychiatrist, but I will have to get excellent marks in HSC to get into medicine. I know I have the ability, and I should have no trouble at all, but if I don't get accepted I don't know what I will do, because other medical fields, such as physiotherapy, nursing etc. do not really interest me.

Although comments on achievement pressure were not found in Japan in the responses to the open-ended question (excepting four short responses which read 'to abolish tests and exams'), there is no question that students in Japan are also under immense pressure before the entrance examination of universities. The pressure is particularly fierce for *rōnin* (students preparing for the examination for the second time or more) and *yobikō* (special educational institute for *rōnin*) students who spend an additional year studying, after unsuccessful attempts in the first round. Each year, one quarter to one third of all applicants to universities are *rōnin* students (ME 1997: 67). One such student says:

These days I can't study at all. When I am studying mathematics, I start worrying about English, and when I study English I start being concerned about social sciences. And when I am playing, I start worrying about studying. Whatever I do, I tend to scatter my concentration over different things.

(Tsukada 1991: 62)

What we did find in the questionnaire returned from Japanese students were expressions of craving for 'some time off' (*asobitai*). Thus Ishigaki Jirō from an elite school and Kobayashi Kayoko from a vocational school wrote:

[If I could change school overnight] I would make a school which has nothing to do with study or preparation for the entrance examination for universities. [I would turn a school into] a paradise on a sandy beach with clean water where I can eat delicious food as much as I want.

[The school I dream of is the place where] there are no classes. We would clean the school first thing in the morning, allow students from other schools to come to our school freely and have fun by showing them films and opening our pool. We would have no club activities in the afternoon. We would be able to go out for lunch freely. We would receive pocket money from school and go shopping in town, and thus the day finishes.

These 'wishes' convey the atmosphere of schools which do not allow students to relax. One indication of how pressed Japanese students are is the length of time they spend studying. In the early 1980s, Rohlen calculated that Japanese students received schooling equivalent to three months each year more than American students, which amounted to a staggering four extra years by the end of secondary school (1983: 160). The gradual reduction in the length of the school week which started in 1992 (when, for one week a month, students attended for five days a week rather than five-and-a-half) may appear to have changed the situation but, even in the year 2000 when the five-day week will be fully implemented, it will reduce the class hours by only 140 hours per year – the same amount of reduction already introduced by Monbushō in the name of '*yutori no jikan*' (Takeuchi 1993: 137).[4] Under this scheme, the English lessons at the junior high school, for instance, were reduced from five to three hours a week. This has been done, however, without changing the curriculum. The pace of teaching and learning, fast even before the change, was further quickened. In order to digest the substantial curriculum in a shorter time, it became necessary for many students to supplement the day-time schooling with private after-hours schooling. The so-called 'double-school' phenomenon became more widespread (Takeuchi 1993: 134–5). As mentioned earlier, as many as 67 per cent of Grade 9 (14-year-old) students attended *juku* in 1993. These *juku* usually finish around 9 or 9.30 in the evening (Miyagawa 1995: 18). In some cases there are even primary school children who return home from *juku* at around 11 p.m. during the New Year period – the most important festive season in Japan (Kamata 1995: 253).

Why do students work so hard in Japan? Even granting the dominance of meritocratic ideology, it is hard not to wonder why 67 per cent of 14 year olds attend cram schools when less than half of them apply for tertiary education (universities and junior colleges) and less than 40 per cent to universities?[5] One reason for it, already discussed, is so as not to 'fall behind' or 'drop out'. Some other explanations were given in Chapter 2 (see the discussion on meritocracy). Most important of all, however, is the close relationship between academic hierarchy and employment hierarchy.

As Rohlen succinctly summarises, 'the precise and elaborate ranking of universities by the measure of exam competitiveness correlates with the ranking of jobs to be gained four years later' (1983: 87). In other words, the name of the university from which one has graduated has a direct and singular bearing upon one's employment. Large corporations designate only a few universities from which to take their new recruits. Close to 80 per cent of large corporations surveyed in one study (with over five thousand employees) answered that they take first-ranking universities either 'most seriously' or 'very seriously' (*Sekai*, January 1988: 135). Tokyo University, which stands at the top of the pyramid, 'can claim one-third of all large company presidents' (Rohlen 1983: 88). This tendency is even more striking in government. Of all higher rank section chiefs and bureaucrats in the Ministry of Finance, the Foreign Ministry, the National Land Agency and the Ministry of Transport, between two thirds and 90 per cent are Tokyo University graduates (van Wolferen 1989: 111).

The significance of the educational hierarchy extends to non-elite jobs. As Rohlen points out, '[e]mployment prospects are allocated by school rank down through the entire spectrum of middle-class positions. All companies, even modest ones, rank universities and high schools when hiring new employees' (1983: 90). It is hard for students to disregard study altogether because the correspondence between education and employment (in terms of the composite effects of the size of the company, occupation, and income) exists throughout the society.

Okano's ethnographic study of vocational school students (1993), for instance, describes how academic performance is often the first criterion considered in the internal selection process, whereby it is determined which students to recommend to which employer. Even though other factors (e.g. health, school attendance, personality, sports club and student council involvement, motivation, personal connections and family background) are also taken into consideration, the perception that the emphasis is on academic mark seems particularly strong among students. Kieko, one of the students Okano interviewed, for example, explains the process of consultation with the teacher as follows:

> [The teacher and I] looked at the academic marks of last year's recruits at Saki Steel: it was 4.2. My mark was not that high at that stage. I also noticed that many other classmates were thinking of Saki Steel as one of their first five companies. Mr Kodama said to me, 'It may be a bit difficult for you'.
>
> (Okano 1993: 171)

Yoshie, whose company preference also coincided with others', remarks:

> Yayoi [who wanted to go to the same company] would win the game. She had better marks. . . . More important, she was thought more reliable since she was an elected member of the student council.
>
> (Okano 1993: 172)

Natsumi, who was in a similar situation, talked about her classmate Oriko:

> Oriko did not make the final decision until much later. That annoyed us. You see, until the top student decided, [the rest of us] couldn't make our own decisions.
>
> (Okano 1993: 173)

Their words illustrate how academic marks play the central role in determining the future employment of students who do not advance to either universities or colleges. They also explain how Japan's meritocratic ideology is supported by the overall proximity between education and employment – the fact that the educational hierarchy based on academic credentials is matched at all levels with a corresponding occupational and vocational hierarchy.

Closely linked with the demand to study hard and for long hours in Japanese schools is the fact that the content of study is quite difficult. As Table 6.6 shows, over 60 per cent of Japanese students answered that 'school work is difficult' either 'mostly' or 'always', whereas only up to 23 per cent did so in Australia. It is reported elsewhere that 50 per cent of junior high school students and 70 per cent of senior high school students in Japan cannot keep up with the learning pace (van Wolferen 1989: 90).

School work *is* actually difficult in Japan, especially mathematics. Over and over again, I have heard Japanese youth studying in Australia say how easy mathematics is in Australian schools. It is widely known that Japanese excel in international tests, which are usually mathematics. According to Stevenson (1989), one of the main reasons for this is that the mathematics

Table 6.6 Survey results: difficulty of school work compared

	'School work is difficult'			
	Never *(%)*	*Sometimes* *(%)*	*Mostly* *(%)*	*Always* *(%)*
Japan				
Elite	3	31	40	25
Academic	6	33	42	20
Vocational	8	34	44	14
Australia				
Elite	2	75	20	3
Academic	4	77	17	2
Vocational	7	78	14	2

curriculum in Japan is much more difficult than in other countries (i.e. America, China, Taiwan). His research revealed that Japan was first (of four countries examined) in introducing 68 per cent of the common topic in mathematics textbooks in primary schools, and that Japanese students felt that the subject was more difficult than did students in other countries (ibid.: 92). On the other hand, I know few people who remember anything substantial about mathematics taught at the upper secondary level (because it is simply too complicated to *remember*). Why is the content of study so difficult and why is there just so much to learn in Japanese schools? In order to answer these questions, we need to look into the nature of school knowledge in the Japanese education system.

THE MEANING OF STUDY

Koike Hiroshi, an academic school student, wrote:

> If I have to go to school anyway, I want them to teach us something useful. Frankly, the sort of study we do at school has no meaning. It is only to prepare us to pass university entrance examinations.

Hiroshi's perception that school work is 'useless' and 'meaningless' (and therefore most likely uninteresting) is widely shared by a large number of Japanese students. Table 6.7 indicates that as many as 35 per cent of Japanese students felt that they could 'never' learn things that interest them; and 41 per cent, that the school 'never' taught them things that were immediately useful. Close to half of them (46 per cent) indicated that they could 'never' have a say in what they wanted to learn at school.

This is no surprise. It is widely known that the exam-oriented study in Japan is based largely on rote learning, which is inherently uninteresting. It is not simply due to the examination system, however, that so much emphasis has been put on the sort of study which relies on memorisation. It is rather the consequence of several factors which combine to reinforce the mechanical nature of learning (and teaching) in the Japanese education system.

First, the nature of school knowledge is linked closely to the nature of pedagogy. As discussed in previous chapters, traditional, teacher-centred pedagogy still prevails in Japan. In the field of sociology of education, it has long been pointed out that this mode of teaching and learning goes hand in hand with the objectivistic (or positivistic) view of knowledge – the understanding that knowledge is 'out there', as external and unquestionable reality to the individual, an entity completely detached from human

Table 6.7 Survey results: relevance of school and learning compared

	Never (%)	Sometimes (%)	Mostly (%)	Always (%)
Japan				
'At this school I can learn things that interest me'	35	55	9	2
'School teaches me things that are useful in my life right now'	41	46	11	2
'I can have a say about what I want to learn at school'	46	28	20	6
Australia				
'At this school I can learn things that interest me'	2	43	44	12
'School teaches me things that are useful in my life right now'	8	59	27	6
'I can have a say about what I want to learn at school'	9	37	38	17

subjectivity. As Esland (1971) points out, such a view 'implicitly presents [the individual] as a passive receiver, as the pliable, socialised embodiment of external facticities' (p. 75) – which explains why objectivist knowledge is an integral part of traditional, teacher-centred pedagogy.

Just as conventional pedagogy is alienating for students, so objectivist knowledge is alienating in that it leaves little room for them to interact with the knowledge. Just as students are not supposed to question the authority of teachers, so objectivist knowledge does not allow students to question its validity. Both are based on a philosophy which presupposes for students only the passive and limited role of learner.

In Japanese schools where teacher-centred pedagogy is dominant, the student is discouraged from relating knowledge to individual experience – as someone who has her/his 'own' views, ideas, needs, emotions, and experiences, and mobilises these resources to interpret, modify, analyse, create, and play with the knowledge. The dominance of the teacher-centred approach in Japanese schools does not encourage students to have a meaningful relationship with school knowledge. This mode of pedagogy and school knowledge has 'silencing effects' upon students in Japanese schools.

Secondly, the examination system has played a critical role in 'modernising' the traditional paradigm of education, of which positivistic knowledge is a part. In the traditional paradigm, what is allowed for students is to memorise the prescribed knowledge and to use it to answer questions given by teachers. This is precisely what happens in the modern examination system. The system enhances it, by *rewarding* students for giving 'correct' answers, by memorising the prescribed knowledge as 'facts' and 'truth'. With the over-developed examination system, objectivist knowledge came to dominate Japanese education well beyond what would have been imagined by Esland, Young and others (the 'new sociologists of education') when they critically examined the nature of school knowledge (see Young 1971b).

In fact, school knowledge in Japan has been reduced to 'examination knowledge' over the last 40 years. We are not simply talking about the universal complaint of students that academic subjects are rarely relevant to their everyday life. We are talking about the fact that 'examination knowledge' in Japan has become so specialised that people are generally cynical about its absurdity (e.g. Kariya 1995: 142). One case in point is that of native speakers of English, sent to Japanese schools as teaching assistants, who are often marginalised so that they least disturb students' learning exam-oriented skills of English. What is expected in English examinations is not English language ability. The comments made by two *yobikō* students clarify this point.

> Mr. C's class 'English Grammar' has 120 per cent student attendance. Learning English grammar increases test scores in English easily. He is popular because he relates everything useful to the entrance examination and teaches it to us.
>
> (Tsukada 1991: 28)

> [Mr. F.] tried to make us memorize mathematics in the form of 'patterns' and he regards it as a subject to be memorised. It is very much to the point for us to master it since we have been preparing for 'Mathematics for the Entrance Examination.' He is one of the most popular teachers in the *yobikō*. In addition, he prepares his unique 'secret techniques for the entrance examination' xeroxes and these xeroxes won a reputation among us.
>
> (Tsukada 1991: 29)

These students experience the reality that 'English for the entrance exam-ination' and 'Mathematics for the entrance examination' exist as separate bodies of knowledge from 'English' and 'mathematics'. '*Such-and-such* for entrance examination' exists virtually for all academic subjects. Shimizu Yoshinori's novel *Gendai kokugo hisshō hō* (A sure way to pass the contempor-ary Japanese language examination) is a cutting parody illustrating the absurd and nonsensical characteristics often found in the examination of contemporary Japanese language (Shimizu 1990). It deals with the story of a 17 year old, Asaka Ichirō, who cannot make head nor tail of passages which appear in examinations of contemporary Japanese. He can read it through with no problem, i.e. he 'knows' the vocabulary and the grammar, but has little clue as to what it is about. Nor can he make any sense of the questions. Driven by the need to improve his marks, he finds himself a private tutor, who teaches him all the skills to *guess* the right answers – which has absolutely nothing to do with the comprehension of the passage (supposing that the passage is, after all, comprehensible).

In mainstream and cram schools alike, it would not be too much to say that school knowledge in Japan has been superseded by examination know-ledge. Although it is true that *juku* and *yobikō* are more sharply focused on 'examination knowledge', so far as the content of the academic subjects is concerned, mainstream and cram schools do not greatly differ. As Rohlen puts it, even in mainstream schools, 'most teachers design their lectures with only entrance examinations in mind' (Rohlen 1983: 243). Thus, hours allocated for moral education by Monbushō, for instance, are often diverted to the study of subjects more directly relevant to the examination (Watanabe 1994: 37).[6] In the pursuit of the most effective knowledge to pass the entrance examination, school knowledge has become standardised, driven by the needs of students, and its instrumental nature has become exagger-ated almost to infinity in Japan's education system.

School/examination knowledge has also become a commodity in Japan – to be sold, bought, and marketed in the gigantic examination industry (Horio 1994: 343–4). In this system, students are consumers who purchase it when it appears to 'work'. As the *yobikō* students indicated above, the market value of the teacher goes up when the teacher is able to provide students with a skill immediately useful in examinations. The teacher's class becomes popular, and the business of the *juku* and *yobikō* as a whole flourishes. The same principle applies in the mainstream schools, where students are obliged to participate. The difference is that, in the day schools, students' assessment of the 'commercial value' of the lesson is reflected by the level of attention paid.

One of the most vivid memories of my senior high school days is the sight of some 40 students in a class of 43 having a complete 50 minutes nap, resting their heads down on the desk, while a teacher carried on the class in 'politics and economics'. It was close to the end of the year and the class comprised students in 'the top science stream for national universities' mostly boys applying for medicine and dentistry in high-ranking universities. Most students knew that their universities did not have any examination in this subject and decided to catch up on sleep. The teacher, knowing the students' situation (sleep deprivation) very well, and perhaps respecting their academic ability, hardly looked upset about losing most of his class in this way. For me, this so-neglected subject was the one I enjoyed most.

What this example suggests is that, although teacher-centred pedagogy and positivistic knowledge are philosophically connected, this does not mean that Japanese schools are somehow theoretically coherent. As discussed in previous chapters, the learning environment is more alienating for students in Japan than it is in Australia. The nature of school knowledge also seems more alienating in Japan, so that Japanese students are surrounded by the dual features of alienation – two 'minuses'. What ties Japanese students to these over-developed structures of alienation is the belief in meritocracy – or simply the notion that there is no alternative if one does not want to lose in the competition. What persuades students to accept, tolerate and endure alienating features of school is their utilitarianism and pragmatism.

When students can find pragmatic 'value' in a class, it is most efficient for them to accept the whole package – not to question either the authority of the teacher or the validity of the knowledge. In order to do well in the examination system, Japanese students have a vested interest in being obedient and uncritical. Students comply with orders when they believe that 'it pays' to do so in order to survive in the competition. As long as teachers play a useful role in it, 'it pays' to suppress one's questioning mind. To alienate oneself becomes *the* hidden curriculum of the Japanese education system.

Conversely, the utilitarian and pragmatic thinking of students as 'consumers' can very well jeopardise the whole system. When students do not find much value in the content of the class, they cease to participate, even passively, in the teacher-centred mode of teaching. When this happens, the authority and the existence of the teacher is ignored, defied or resisted. The whole structure collapses. The linchpin which holds together the alienating structures of the Japanese education system is the pursuit of individual interest by each student, trying to survive in a super-advanced capitalist society. The greater role cram schools play in the 'double-school' phenomenon, however, the weaker the holding power of the 'linchpin' becomes. Although day schools are still the main place for learning, they are becoming steadily less absolute. The less absolute they become, the less reason students have to put up with their other alienating features – whether authoritarian teachers or the nationalistic agenda of *Monbushō*.

Before elaborating on this point, however, let us point out that the characteristics of school knowledge we have discussed so far: (1) the equivalence of school knowledge and examination knowledge; (2) the specialisation, standardisation, and commodification of school (examination) knowledge, and (3) the consumer character of students – are the 'end product' of a policy adopted more than 40 years ago. Let us see next what this policy was and how it has affected the nature of school knowledge.

As Horio (1988) maintains, the basic framework of the present mode of education was established around four decades ago, both by the government and the business world, as an integral part of the comprehensive programme for high-speed economic growth. More specifically, the main role of education advocated by the policy makers was 'manpower development' – especially, to classify and sort out young people on a single criterion of 'ability' (p. 337). This enabled large corporations to absorb a small number of elite students for their professional, white-collar work, while at the same time taking advantage of the inexpensive labour force of those who left school earlier. From the policy maker's point of view, therefore, school knowledge became the instrument, the 'tool' to discriminate between 'more able' and 'less able' students.

It is not surprising, therefore, that after this policy of 'education' for competition was implemented in the early 1960s, the curriculum was expanded and the number of students who could not keep up with their classes increased substantially (Sanuki 1996). Competition-oriented education contributed to making the content of study more difficult. Perhaps it had to be this way, if education was to function as the sorting machine for the more than one and half million students who graduated from junior high schools every year. For the same reason, it also became necessary for school knowledge to be highly standardised. Standardisation made it possible to screen out students uniformly. The selection-oriented, competition-based education system virtually killed self-expression, individuality, creativity and critical thinking.

This suggests that, as long as the examination system remains the main feature of the Japanese education system, the nature of school knowledge will also remain the same, as will the role of students as passive learners of prescribed knowledge. In other words, even if students become less exclusively tied to day schools, because of the availability of examination knowledge in cram schools, their relationship with teachers at cram schools is not necessarily based on a different paradigm of teaching and learning; it is likely to remain the same teacher-centred approach. What is different in cram schools is the fact that they are nothing but a commercial enterprise – with no responsibility for the socialisation of students, for the pursuit of the nationalistic agenda promoted by Monbushō.

Along with mass popular consumerism and the economic rationalism of large corporations, Monbushō contributed to the standardisation and unification of school knowledge in Japan. It did so partly by cooperating with the business sector in promoting examination-based, manpower-oriented education. It did so also by intervening and controlling the content of education. Knowledge is socially constructed, reflecting the power relationships within the society (Young 1971a), and Japan is not alone in this respect. In the past four decades, however, state intervention in things to do with the content of education (among other things) became incomparably coercive in Japan, generating much controversy. The most controversial of all is the textbook dispute, known, after its central figure, Professor Ienaga Saburō, as the Ienaga Cases, which began in 1965 and concluded, 32 years later, in 1997. The Ienaga Cases illustrates how the rights of free expression and academic freedom guaranteed by the constitution have been increasingly eroded by the intensive state screening of textbooks (see for details Horio 1988: 171–212).

Although the Ienaga Cases focused upon the censorship of history textbooks written by Professor Ienaga, according to Horio (1988, 1992, 1994) the textbook issue is broader than often understood. He argues that the significance of the textbook issue is not confined to history, but extends to a broad process of thought control by the state. This occurs at three levels.

One is the control of the content of knowledge as was problematised in the Ienaga Cases – whether to include or exclude from the textbook, reference to things like wartime atrocities, whether to take the position of the elite historian or the social historian, what expressions to use for what ideological effects (e.g. whether to use 'invasion' or 'advance' to describe Japanese expansion in Asia during World War II), etc.

More fundamentally, however, textbook censorship implants in the minds of students a positivistic way of thinking – the readiness to accept whatever the content of prescribed knowledge might be. It is not only that the positivistic way of thinking is promoted by means of a hidden curriculum. According to Horio (1988), critical thinking itself has been the target of the state censorship. He refers to the case when Monbushō refused to certify a textbook which was designed for the very purpose of breaking out of the positivistic mode of thinking – the case of a physics textbook written by Nobel Prize winner Tomonaga Shin'ichirō. Horio's explanation follows.

> In writing his textbook Tomonaga attempted to develop a new style for getting students to think about physics. But in response to this the textbook inspectors in Monbushō declared that his book was not a

textbook. To be a text appropriate for use in schools, they asserted, a book must be written in a form in which correct knowledge is presented in a predetermined and exact style. Any work which does not adopt this approach or conform to its underlying view of education cannot, in other words, be considered for approval as a textbook regardless of the pedagogic aims of its author. As it was precisely Tomonaga's desire to develop more thought-provoking teaching materials, in the end he had no choice but to abandon his attempt to creatively reform the composition of science textbooks.

(Horio 1988: 174)

Horio maintains, further, that through the textbook screening system thought control also penetrates into the arena of students' sensitivity. Monbushō, for instance, replaced an onomatopoeic play on the sounds of a river expressed by a poet – 'sarasaruru piruporu doburu ponpochan' – with a singular adverb '*sarasara*', an officially preferred expression describing the running water of a river. Horio argues that this is an attempt of Monbushō to prescribe how students should see and feel things, while at the same time claiming the 'ownership' of the national language – that national language is not something belonging to the children, but something whose use is controlled by the state for the children (Horio 1988: 174). By mentioning two other examples where original, creative and intriguing expressions were replaced with moralistic, standardised and boring expressions in the officially approved textbooks, Horio explains how teaching materials left little room to help heighten students' sensitivity to language, emotions, people and various other matters in life (Horio 1992: 13–6).

With these characteristics, Horio concludes, the textbook in Japan 'seeks to instill in [children] an allegiance to a single, systematized body of knowledge about the world', rather than 'exposing [them] to the play of different constructions of knowledge and allowing them to work out the conflicts and disparities on the basis of their own comprehension of the world' (Horio 1988: 176). The censorship of textbooks is a coordinated attempt on the part of the state to standardise the entire thought process of its people. It is an attempt to diminish people's power to think, analyse and reflect upon things on their own accord. Positivistic knowledge has been a 'must' in this political scheme. For many years now the textbook screening system has been an insidious structure working in the name of education to silence Japanese nationals.

Considering the textbook screening system against the background of the political economy of postwar Japan, Horio points out that the present orientation of the system emerged in the post-Korean War era out of the government's intention to rearm. Accordingly, the main thrust of the textbook certification was (1) to suppress peace education and promote patriotic and nationalistic sentiment in children, and (2) to suppress democratic ways of thinking and behaving in general (Horio 1994: 215–17).

Horio's analysis has not lost its relevance towards understanding the Japanese education system today. The handing down of the most recent judgments on the conclusion of the Ienaga Cases does not signify the end of the textbook issue after 32 years either. The trajectory of Japanese education since the mid-1950s is often referred to as 'reverse course', a term suggestive of an analogy with the switch in economic policy by the American Occupation in early postwar Japan. The nationalistic and anti-democratic tendencies seem to have grown steadily stronger.

The New Course of Study of 1989 firmly entrenched these policies for the post-Showa era. The most telling example is the introduction of the *compulsory* raising of the national flag and the *compulsory* singing of the national anthem in school ceremonies. This was coupled with the upgrading of moral education, returning to the prewar tradition of patriotic education (*shūshin*). The 1989 revision also brought about the abolition of social studies (*shakaika*) which, in a limited way, had retained the spirit of 'education for human rights and critical thinking' (Ichikawa 1989). Instead, the history component was upgraded with the official 'suggestion' of 42 figures to be mentioned in the textbook, including nationalistic figures such as Admiral Tōgō Heihachirō, the militaristic 'hero' who contributed to the expansion of Imperial Japan. Concomitantly, the system of textbook screening became even more intensified and less democratic than before – the procedure which once enabled authors and publishers to negotiate with Monbushō was drastically simplified, increasing the likelihood of the publishers not getting approval at all (Horio 1992: 45; Tokutake 1995: 230–5). Takayama Yōji (1989) refers to this trend in Japanese education as 'war education', in contrast to 'peace education'. It is a startling declaration, but one which is nonetheless hard to dismiss.

The overview of Japanese education from the standpoint of the sociology of knowledge indicates that the alienating nature of school knowledge is supported by three major components of Japanese society – consumerism (of people), corporatism (of large firms), and nationalism (of the state). Although each group has different expectations of education, they combine to reinforce the objectivistic nature of school knowledge. For differing reasons, they all foster the standardisation and unification of knowledge, while implicitly and explicitly depreciating and suppressing the importance of critical thinking. The memorisation-oriented teaching and learning prevalent in Japanese schools is the compound result of these structural factors.

Is it any wonder, then, that a lack of creativity and individuality has been the sore point of the Japanese education system? It is true that in response to these criticisms, various measures have recently been taken, but as long as the structural causes remain untouched, there is little prospect for real change. Moreover, there seems to be a pattern in the recent history of Japanese education by which various changes supposedly adopted to remedy the situation actually worsen it. It is often hard to tell whether the 'failure' of such remedies was actually a failure in the mind of policy makers, or whether they may have been meant to 'fail' – that 'failure' was the intended outcome of reforms designed to function only as rhetoric. The highly political nature of educational reforms which are literally imposed upon teachers, students and parents by Monbushō in 'top-down' style makes it extremely difficult for ordinary people to comprehend what is really going on, until they actually have to live through it, either as teacher, parent or student.

The New View of Ability (*Shin-gakuryoku-kan*), part of the 1989 reform, is one such recent change whose objectives and implications are unclear. The reform is claimed to be designed to grapple with this very weakness of the Japanese education system, i.e. to equip children with the quality and ability to think, behave and express themselves as individuals. In reality, however, it was implemented by means of a new point-evaluation system (*kantenbetsu hyōka*) which requires teachers to assess not only the level of understanding of each subject but also to include in the academic assessment such aspects as the level of interest and the attitude and willingness to learn. This has become a nightmare for teachers. One teacher explained to me that in order to pose a fair assessment, she is now obliged to pose separate questions in the test to measure each aspect of 'ability'.

On the part of students, this system means that it is no longer good enough to be a 'no-problem' student. They now feel that it is necessary to 'perform' in front of teachers in such a way as to be seen as 'better' than others. It is perceived to be important, for instance, to raise a hand to indicate that you are keen to answer questions in class, even when you actually do not know the answer. Just being seen to be enthusiastic is important. Students are now involved not only in academic competition, but also in 'good-child competition' or 'loyalty competition' to get a good mark (Yamauchi *et al.* 1997). Quite contrary to its ostensible aim, the New View of Ability has actually functioned to standardise student behaviour by integrating it as part of 'academic' assessment. Freedom of action was taken away from students, and they are pressured into hiding their true feelings (Miyadai 1998).

It appears that the hidden function of the new assessment system is artificially to boost the *raison d'être* of schools. As discussed earlier, the tripod of Japanese education – consumerism, corporatism, and nationalism – has had the effect of standardising school knowledge and the modes of transmitting it in Japan. However, these are not static and stable forces, and are not necessarily always bound by common interest. On the contrary, there has been a constant tension between these parties, which partly explains the perpetual deadlock situation in Japanese education over the years. One such tension is between consumerism and nationalism – the potential disintegration of the school system due to the diminishing role schools play as the place of learning. The reforms in the assessment system seem to have functioned to bridge these two – to artificially tighten and hold in place the 'linchpin', thus preventing the disintegration of the Japanese school, and preserving its institutional function as the place to indoctrinate children and adolescents with a mode of thinking and behaving which makes it easy for the state to pursue nationalistic goals.

School knowledge in Japan is like a dying tree taken over by three kinds of parasite – consumerism, capitalism, and nationalism. Students are enveloped in all-embracing consumerism, corporations are obsessed with competition, and the state exacts conformity. Although the 'consumer needs' of students themselves contribute to make school knowledge alienating, this would not ease the insipidness of having to deal with something so mechanical and so demanding day-in and day-out. What are the other implications of this reality for students, the would be 'flowers' of this diseased and dying tree?

The corollary of the two conflicting realities in Japan – that schools are ranked on the basis of academic 'ability', and yet students are under the same level of pressure – is that the alienation from study is particularly strong among students attending less prestigious schools. Table 6.8 shows the mean of scale scores for 'meaninglessness of study', which was created by combining the results on the following statements. The scale score ranges from 0 to 15 – the higher the score, the higher the pressure felt by students.

- At this school I *cannot* learn things that interest me
- School *does not* teach me things that are useful in my life right now

Table 6.8 Mean scores of 'meaninglessness of study' for different groups

	Mean	Standard deviation	Elite	Academic	Vocational	ANOVA (F =)
Japan	9.7	(2.5)	9.1	10.3	10.1	10.4*
Australia	7.3	(2.3)	7.2	7.5	7.2	4.5 (n.s.)

* Statistically significant differences at $p < .001$ or better.

- School *does not* prepare me well for the future
- I *cannot* have a say about what I WANT to learn at school
- Teachers *do not* make their lessons interesting[7]

These figures show that study is more alienating or makes 'less sense' for students attending academic and vocational schools than for students in elite schools, and that the difference across different types of schools is statistically significant.

No matter how alienating and meaningless it may be, study is something that students generally perceive to be necessary for their future. As Table 6.9 indicates, however, this notion is not particularly strong in the super-meritocratic Japan. Being asked whether school prepares them well for the future, 62 per cent of the Japanese students and 71 per cent of the Australian students responded with either 'mostly' or 'always'. Students do not think much about the meaning of study. One survey on student perceptions of school revealed that nearly 40 per cent of students had not thought about the purpose of study (Hirose 1989: 142–3). Study is something that students take for granted as part of their life. The 'goodness of education' (Corrigan 1979) is rarely questioned either in Japan or in Australia. Children are bound to school by unquestioned assumptions about education, school, and study.

Table 6.9 Survey results: 'preparation for the future' compared

| | 'School prepares you well for the future' | | | |
	Never (%)	Sometimes (%)	Mostly (%)	Always (%)
Japan	11	28	45	17
Australia	3	26	48	23

I have so far analysed aspects of Japanese schools which can be alienating for students, using Australia as a reference point. I have shown that the entire paradigm of Japanese education, which is autocratic and non-democratic, is geared to control and silence students in a number of ways, including authoritarianism in student–teacher relationships, de-humanising treatment of students in the name of discipline, regimentation through excessive school rules, and academic competition and the meaning-lessness of study which stem from the super-meritocracy of Japanese society. All these aspects are linked to the education policy of Japan since the mid-1950s, which in turn is connected to the super-capitalistic pursuit of growth by Japanese society in the last fifty years.

I would now like to discuss what composite effects this system of super-alienation has upon the lives of students, by examining two major social issues related to students in contemporary Japan – *ijime* and *tōkōkyohi*. The former concerns relationships among students, whereas the latter is to do with individual students' sense of selfhood in relation to school, family and society in general.

NOTES

1 Source: Ishikawa *et al.* 1993: 164.
2 These results are suggestive of the trend among those who attend full-time, day-time senior secondary schools. A separate study will be necessary focusing upon the small yet increasing number of young people who are outside of this system.
3 In Japan, a difference between schools was found only in relation to the meaning of study, and teacher–student relationships (excluding dehumanising treatment by teachers) (see Appendix 5). In Australia it was found only in relation to academic achievement pressure and school rules (see Appendix 6).
4 Although '*yutori no jikan*' literally means 'time for leisure', it did not actually create leisure time because the same curriculum was simply compressed into a shorter time.
5 *Juku* participation is a 1993 figure, others are 1996 figures.
6 The achievement of Monbushō's objective of promoting nationalist education has been put at only 50 per cent in the past 25 years (Watanabe 1994b: 37).
7 In the questionnaire, affirmative statements were given, e.g. 'At this school I *can* learn things that interest me', instead of 'At this school I *cannot* learn things that interest me' so that the naturalness of the statement is maintained. In order to increase the scale of '*meaninglessness* of study' as a potentially stress-inducing condition, the responses to the questions were coded in reverse. The reliability for this scale was .65.

Part II

Responses: conformity and resistance

7 *Ijime*: the price of super-conformity

> Friends are nice. People in the class are caring. I want to go to a good high school, a good university and a good company. It is important to study.
>
> (Ohkōchi Kiyoteru, a victim of *ijime*[1])

IJIME SUICIDE OF SHIKAGAWA HIROFUMI IN 1986

In February 1986, Shikagawa Hirofumi, a 13-year-old student of Nakono Fujimi Junior High School in Tokyo, killed himself by hanging from the coat hook on a toilet door of Morioka railway station.[2] His suicide note read: 'I don't yet want to die, but it's like living in hell to go on like this'. In the note, he referred to his experiences of *ijime* and disclosed the names of two leaders of an *ijime* group consisting of several boys (*AS* 3 February 1986).

Hirofumi was so-called '*tsukaippa*' (*ijime* jargon for '*tsukai bashiri*') – the group member who is forced to run errands for the group (e.g. doing shopping and carrying bags for others) because of his/her 'weakness' (*AS* 24 February 1986). It was found later that he had been the target of *ijime* for months, and that a mock funeral had been held for him a few months before his actual death, arranged by the group leaders and participated in by most of the class. One day, when Hirofumi came to school, he found his desk put in front of the class, decorated with a large condolence card, a photo of himself, flowers, sweets, and burning incense. The card had been signed by 41 students, mostly his classmates, as well as four teachers including his homeroom teacher (*AS* 6 February 1986, 22 December 1986). *Ijime* escalated especially after Hirofumi tried to leave the group. He was beaten up, coerced to do humiliating things in front of others, and received a life-threatening telephone call at home (*AS* 24 February 1986). His father contacted the homeroom teacher, police and the parents of the bully only to be advised to change schools (*AS* 4 February 1986). Changing to another school in the neighbourhood, however, would not have been either an easy option or solution. New students are a easy targets of *ijime*, and Hirofumi already had trouble with some students of the neighbouring school. He had once been sent there by his group as a messenger and on this occasion had been kicked and beaten up badly by students (*AS* 19 February 1986).

The suicide of Shikagawa Hirofumi was by no means the first case of suicide driven by *ijime*. By the mid-1980s, *ijime* had already become a major social problem in Japan, and a major cause of a number of suicides. The case of Shikagawa, however, revealed the complexity of *ijime*, especially in terms of the involvement of teachers. The 57-year-old homeroom teacher, who signed the condolence card for the mock funeral, was dismissed, the principal and two teachers who had also signed the condolence card were forced to resign, and two others were ordered to take teacher training (*kenshū*) for one year. It was the first time disciplinary measures were taken against teachers in relation to *ijime* (*AS* 21 March 1986). At the same time, the files on 16 students were sent to the district attorney's office (*AS* 4 February 1986). Monbushō called a meeting for the first time to discuss emergency measures against *ijime*. The Education Minister, the head of the local board of education and the principal all proclaimed that *ijime* must be overcome by the united response of school and community (*AS* 11 March 1986). As a result, various changes were introduced. Teachers and dozens of parents in the region began standing at the school gate to greet students in the morning, and the student associations adopted slogans about eradicating *ijime* as well (*AS* 6 March 1986).

Despite all the discipline and counter-*ijime* measures, however, Monbushō had to call a second emergency meeting eight years later, after the *ijime* suicide of Ohkōchi Kiyoteru. This, among numerous other *ijime* suicides, attracted wide media attention because his parents disclosed his suicide note in protest against his school (Toyoda 1995).

IJIME SUICIDE OF OHKŌCHI KIYOTERU IN 1994

Ohkōchi Kiyoteru, a 13-year-old student of Nishio Municipal Tōbu Junior High School in Aichi, hanged himself at home in December 1994. Notes he left behind gave a brief account of his suffering from *ijime*, four names of bullies, together with a detailed record of the amount of money extorted from him by the group. The record, which he kept secretly as an 'acknowledgment of debts to Mother' amounted to over 1.1 million yen. He explained in the note that he had been almost drowned in the river by the group and that the experience made him compliant thereafter with their demands (*AS* 3–4 December 1994). Like Hirofumi, Kiyoteru too was the '*tsukaippa*', forced to run errands for the more powerful members of the group (Toyoda 1995).

The police investigation revealed that some 15 boys were involved in the bullying, and that the extorted money was distributed according to the position of each member in the group hierarchy (*AS* 7 December 1995). It was also found that Kiyoteru had become the target of *ijime* after defending another victim who had been severely injured (*AS* 4 December 1994). One of the students who came to apologise to the family after being named in the suicide note shocked Hirofumi's father by saying that 'it was fun' to bully Hirofumi (*AS* 3 December).

The principal of Tōbu Junior High admitted that teachers had noted on various occasions signs of *ijime* against Kiyoteru (e.g. facial bruises, his being without his trousers in the gymnasium, his bicycle being destroyed) (*AS* 6 December 1994). According to the report the school subsequently released to the media, the school's nurse-teacher had noticed Kiyoteru's unfocused eyes and shaking body and conducted a psychological test on him. Kiyoteru, however, merely gave a model answer to her that: 'My friends are all nice. People in the class are caring. I want to go to a good senior high school, a good university, and a good company. It is important to study' (*AS* 9 December 1994).

In the end, the school authorities failed to register Kiyoteru's case as *ijime*, partly because he was regarded as one of the 'problem kids', and partly because, according to the principal, 'as long as the student does not report himself that he [was] bullied, [the school] cannot be certain about it' (*AS* 9 December 1994). The 26-year-old homeroom teacher wrote a note to *Asahi shinbun* to express her deep sense of powerlessness in not having been able to prevent the tragedy (*AS* 14 December 1994).

The 1995 suicide of Ohkōchi Kiyoteru confronted the nation with the sober reality that the scale of *ijime* had scarcely improved in eight years despite all the 'uprooting *ijime*' measures taken. If anything, the situation had got worse. The intervening decade had been one of steady intensification of control over students and teachers by Monbushō (as discussed in previous chapters). Anti-*ijime* measures, which took place within this framework, were often in practice little more than 'beefing up' the regimentation in school and the surveillance system involving the community. The school and social environment became more stifling for students and *ijime* became ever more intense, widespread, insidious, unpredictable and inescapable.

THE PREVALENCE OF *IJIME*

The *ijime* suicides of Shikagawa Hirofumi and Ohkōchi Kiyoteru gathered extremely wide attention because the victims' parents released the suicide notes to the public, so that schools, local boards of education, and Monbushō were obliged to respond in public in one way or another. More important, however, these cases caused a public outcry because they represented common features of *ijime* prevalent in Japanese schools – their cases were by no means isolated and extreme incidents.

The cases of Shikagawa and Ohkōchi represent a tiny tip of a huge iceberg. A number of other *ijime* suicides received far less media attention. In 1986 alone, the year Shikagawa Hirofumi died, for instance, at least eight other students killed themselves for reasons clearly related to *ijime*. Likewise in 1994, when Ohkōchi Kiyoteru died, there were seven other known cases of *ijime* suicide (Toyoda 1995). In other years it appears that there were some ten cases of *ijime* suicide each year reported in the newspapers. Unless victims have clearly stated, however, that their suicides are directly linked to *ijime*, it is almost impossible to define a suicide as *ijime* suicide. Thus, there are numerous cases which are suspected to be *ijime* suicide but not officially recognised as such. Moreover, there are also numerous attempted, i.e. 'unsuccessful' suicides. And the *ijime*-related suicide itself – including suspicious cases and attempts – is like an iceberg floating in the vast sea of *ijime* in the everyday life of Japanese students.

One indication of the prevalence of *ijime* in Japanese schools today is the emergence and prevalence of *ijime* jargon used widely among students. Some expressions describe violent physical assault, which are more common among boys but are used against girls as well. '*Bokoboko*' (derived from '*bokoboko naguru*') and '*fukuro*' (derived from '*fukuro-dataki ni suru*') mean collective violence against a victim including bashing, hitting, and kicking. '*Erubō*' (elbow) is to hit the victim with the elbow – one of the tactics used in such assaults. Often physical violence is exerted in a form of 'play' such as '*puroresu gokko*' (mock pro-wrestling) and '*kagome rinchi*' (lynch), where a victim is made to kneel on the floor (*seiza*) to be hit and kicked by bullies who circle around the victim as they sing a children's play song '*kagome kagome*'.[3] '*Konjōyaki*' means to put a burning cigarette onto the skin of the victim.

Other expressions describe the coercion exerted upon the victim. '*Pashiri*' (derived from '*tsukai-bashiri*') means to make the victim run errands such as going to buy snacks for others during the recess without being giving enough money. The victim in this role is called '*tsukaippa*' – as was the case for Shikagawa Hirofumi and Ohkōchi Kiyoteru. '*Katsuage*' (derived from '*kyōkatsu*' and '*makiageru*') means to extort money from the victim.

The most commonly used method of *ijime* is '*shikato*' – to ignore the victim completely, which often escalates to '*zen'in shikato*', for the whole class to behave as if the victim does not exist. '*Chikuru*', on the other hand, means to tell the teacher about *ijime* in order to stop it, and '*mukatsuku*' (irritating, annoying) is used to describe the victim, often giving an entirely subjective and unjustifiable 'reason' for bullying the victim.

There are all sorts of other forms of *ijime* which do not have special terminology. There is less violent physical harassment such as tripping up the victim, throwing things upon the victim from the top of the stairs, putting stick pins in the shoes or on the chair of the victim, stabbing the victim with a pencil with full force (usually from behind), etc. In the verbal intimidation and abuse, such words as '*kusai*' (stink), '*kitanai*' (dirty), '*baikin*' (germ), '*gomi*' (trash), '*shine*' (die) are used. Non-physical and non-verbal harassment includes hiding, damaging or throwing away the victim's possessions (often into the toilet). *Ijime* often involves sexual harassment as well, including stripping the victim in front of others, reporting aloud the activities of the victim in the toilet by watching over the wall of the toilet, tying a female victim's skirt over the top of her head, and various other acts of sexual violence and assault.

Many of these methods of *ijime* seen in Japan, however, are also found in other societies (e.g. Olweus 1993, Rigby 1996). It is necessary, therefore, to examine Japanese *ijime* from a comparative perspective.

IJIME FROM A COMPARATIVE PERSPECTIVE

Monbushō held an international symposium on bullying in 1996 to which it invited experts on the subject from all around the world (*AS* 25 June 1996). Studies conducted outside Japan indicate that there are indeed many common features in bullying across different societies including Japan (e.g. Besag 1989; Olweus 1993; Rigby 1996). Just as it is true that bullying has existed in Japanese society throughout its history, it is undeniable that it exists in every other society. However, this recognition does not imply any diminution in the seriousness of *ijime* as a major social issue in contemporary Japan.

The question is whether or not bullying is a structural problem in each society – accountable for in terms of both quantity (to what extent) and quality (in what ways) – and if so, what aspect of that society is most directly related to the problem of bullying within it (i.e. bullying could be a common manifestation of different social problems). When considering the *ijime* problem in Japan from a comparative perspective, we need to ask the following questions. In what society, apart from Japan, are so many students so exposed to the fear that they might become the target of collective bullying? In what society apart from Japan, is there a prevailing sense of being trapped and stuck with the problem of bullying as a major social issue? In what society apart from Japan, are both teachers and students largely convinced and resigned to the fact that it is almost impossible to do anything about it? Kawai Hayao, a psychiatrist with a broad comparative perspective who also counsels students, asserts that, although bullying is definitely universal, it is by far the severest in contemporary Japanese schools, worse now than ever before, and more severe than in any other society in terms of its frequency, cruelty and insidiousness (Kawai 1996: 103).

One of the difficulties we face when trying to grasp the problem of bullying is that the questionnaire survey methods, widely used to study bullying outside Japan, would mean little in the Japanese context. It would be almost impossible to capture the reality of *ijime* in Japan by using this method, comparatively or not, because, as will be discussed below, the most distinctive characteristic of *ijime* is that it stems from the very structure of schools in Japan, and that all parties concerned apart from the victim, students, teachers, and parents, have a vested interest in maintaining the silence (e.g. Fukuda and Arimoto 1997). This is well illustrated by the experience of Fukuda Hiroyuki, a teacher at Higashita Junior High School in Tokyo who tried to crack down on *ijime* in his class for over two years. His experience describes the nature of *ijime* most tellingly. The following is a summary of his experience as it was reported by Ujioka (1997a, 1997b).

Fukuda ventured into tackling the problem after being informed by a parent that there was *ijime* in his class. In order to avoid retaliating repercussions aimed at the victim, Fukuda adopted an educational method (instead of a heavy-handed approach), attempting to extract information from students through essay writing, which he fed back to the class for discussion. In the end, students wrote 12 essays each, and as many as 30 hours were spent in one year on what turned out to be an 'anti-*ijime* course'.

Fukuda started his venture at a very general level, by setting the first assignment topic as simply 'problems in the classroom'. Not a single student mentioned *ijime* despite the fact that they all wrote the essay anonymously. In the second essay, Fukuda gently introduced the topic of *ijime* by asking students to write their view of the suicide note of Ohkōchi Kiyoteru. Even then, students' responses were detached and impersonal. One student wrote that 'in this school there are neither bullies nor victims' (Ujioka 1997a). The third topic, along similar lines, produced similar results, but in the fourth essay students finally began to talk about their first-hand experiences of *ijime*, as bully, as victim, as witness. These included:

> There was this girl the rest of us avoided. If she spoke we all ignored her. This girl, I really hated her. She was everything I wasn't: smart, athletic, cute . . .

They stuck my hat on dog turds, called me bad, said my breath stank, told me to move my desk away . . .

Mornings I would scream and cry that I didn't want to go to school . . .

I was afraid, so I went along. Just like a dog . . .

(Ujioka 1997a)

As Ujioka writes, 'it was evident that bullying was in the very air these students breathed' (1997a), quite contrary to the impression they gave initially. Even with this method, it took three weeks for students to admit that there was *ijime* in their school. For the fifth essay, Fukuda put together some excerpts from students' essays, handed them out to the class without disclosing the writers' names, and asked students to write their observations. After reading this collection, one student commented:

Every laughing face looked fake . . . . Inside, I thought, they're crying.

(Ujioka 1997a)

Two months into the course, a survey was conducted which revealed that out of 95 students who participated in the programme:

- 51 per cent had the experience of being bullied at one time or another;
- 56 per cent had bullied others;
- 75 per cent had witnessed bullying.

Fukuda then asked students whether bullying could be eliminated – expecting an affirmative answer from students. The reality was that 'for every student who thought it could be rooted out, two said it couldn't' (Ujioka 1997a). One student stated:

[*Ijime*] arises because each person is different; you can't stamp it out as long as everybody's not the same.

(Ujioka 1997a)

Nobody in the class refuted this view. It was disturbing to Fukuda because it implied that: 'students basically feel that human differences justify bullying' and that 'teachers themselves deserve some of the blame, for treating all students as identical in deference to "school rules" while only paying lip service to the need to respect individual differences' (Ujioka 1997a).

A survey conducted two months later showed some improvement. Two thirds of the students who participated in the programme thought that *ijime* could be eliminated from their school. The rest of the students, however, did not think that it would be eradicated even after this intensive analysis and soul searching. This seems to suggest that students knew from experience (if not consciously) that *ijime* derived from the fundamental structure of their school. And in fact it persisted, although the next victim got support from a number of classmates, a major breakthrough in the context of contemporary *ijime* in Japan (Ujioka 1997a).

Fukuda's anti-*ijime* course was an extraordinary attempt not only in terms of the approach he adopted but in the sheer amount of time committed to the programme (Ujioka 1997b). This was made possible in a fairly liberal school environment presided over by a principal who gave considerable autonomy to teachers (Fukuda 1997). Although Fukuda's attempt was exceptional, however, his students' experience of *ijime* was not. His story depicts the deeply structural and remarkably hidden nature of *ijime* in Japan today. Given this clandestine nature of *ijime*, the problem of understanding and analysing it has to be faced. The questionnaire survey method is obviously ill-suited to capturing its reality, whether it be employed in a comparative study or not.

How does Japanese *ijime* differ from bullying in other societies, what exactly is the structural cause of *ijime* in Japan, and how do we know about it?

THE IDIOSYNCRATIC NATURE OF JAPANESE *IJIME*

Ijime *as collective bullying*

There are a number of features of bullying which are remarkably similar across different societies: what bullies actually do to the victim, the victim's reluctance to seek help from others, the fact that intervention from teachers and parents is often insufficient, the fact that the victimisation of a particular child can last for months or years. Japanese *ijime* distinctively differs from bullying in other societies, however, in that it is *always* collective bullying. This is not to say that group bullying does not occur in other societies. It does. It sometimes involves active bullies and the victim, and at other times they are 'joined' by passive bullies, followers or henchmen (Olweus 1993: 34), as is usually the case in Japan. Yet there are also substantial cases outside Japan, where victims are bullied primarily by a single student. A Scandinavian study found that some 35 to 40 per cent of bullying was committed by a single bully (Olweus 1993: 9). An Australian study of secondary students found that 61 per cent of bullying against a male victim and 44 per cent of bullying against a female victim were committed singly (Rigby 1996: 39).

In clear contrast, contemporary *ijime* in Japan occurs as the victimisation of a single individual by a group (often extended to the whole class or beyond). According to Kobayashi Tsuyoshi, an educationist, for each case of *ijime* there are some 3 to 10 active bullies, with about half of the rest of the class as spectators who approve it and enjoy it, and another half as bystanders who are present without intervening or participating (1985: 5–8). It is also reported that the tendency to overlook *ijime* increases as the grade year of students gets higher (*AS* 23 December 1986).

Ishikawa Norihiko, a psychiatrist at Tokyo University specialising in children, compiled two huge volumes containing the voices of *tōkōkyohi* children (Ishikawa *et al.* 1993) and their parents (Ishikawa *et al.* 1995). He points out that *ijime* in Japanese schools today is closer to '*shigoki*' rather than what used to be meant by '*ijime*' in Japan. *Shigoki* was most typically practised in the Japanese military to 'make a man'[4] out of the 'weak' who might otherwise jeopardise the collective order, spirit, cohesion and conformity of the military. The similarity between contemporary *ijime* and *shigoki* in the prewar Japanese military has been pointed out by others (e.g. Kawai 1996: 103), and so has the similarity between contemporary Japanese schools and prewar Japanese militarism (e.g. Azuma *et al.* 1986: 57).

Ishikawa argues that although both *shigoki* and *ijime* refer to harassment and torment of the less powerful by the more powerful, *shigoki* occurs only in closed group situations, often in a closed, hierarchical structure. This differs from the traditional type of *ijime* which does not presuppose the existence of a group. Furthermore, *shigoki* occurs in a group which does not actually possess much power of its own, and which itself is often under the power of other superior forces. In such a situation, Ishikawa explains, members of the group often do not clearly understand why they practise *shigoki*, why it escalates as the regimentation of the group is tightened, the hierarchy among the members or groups becomes more clearly defined, and the situation confronted by the group more difficult. He therefore asserts that contemporary *ijime* (which resembles *shigoki*) can only be worsened as a more concerted effort is made by external groups (teachers, parents, local boards of education, Monbushō, etc.) to eradicate it, without liberating each individual student from the framework of the group itself (Ishikawa 1986).

The distinction Ishikawa makes between '*shigoki*' and '*ijime*' (in the traditional sense) in Japanese language seems to correspond to the difference between '*ijime*' as it is used in Japan today and 'bullying' in English. In either case, the key factor which distinguishes the two is the presence (or absence) of group domination. In order to capture this idiosyncratic feature of the *ijime* phenomenon in contemporary Japan, '*ijime*' and 'bullying' are used separately in this book.

The lack of recognition among most adults, of the difference between contemporary and traditional *ijime* in Japan, often causes frustration and outrage among students. One student remarks:

> Adults cannot actually see *ijime* happening [because it is well hidden] and yet say things 'from above' which are quite irresponsible. If you just put up with the violence of *ijime* today, you can be killed. These days, *ijime* is never as soft as it used to be known to the adults. Definitely not.
> (Tsuchiya *et al.* 1995: 40)

Ijime *as over-conformity*

There is another crucial difference between *ijime* and bullying. Despite the unsocial nature of the act itself, *ijime* arises from over-socialisation – it is an act of *over-conformity*, and therefore opposite to social maladjustment as bullying is generally perceived outside Japan.

To put it differently, *ijime* is an evil consequence stemming from the very characteristics of Japanese education. There is nothing new in this view. There is a general consensus in Japan that *ijime* arises from various 'oppressive' aspects of contemporary Japanese schools and Japanese society at large – regimentation, academic pressure, stress, excessive pressure to conform, the collapse of social norms, etc. Few dispute this. Yet on the other hand, anti-*ijime* measures are directed only at students, as if to say that *ijime* has little to do with any of these structures. This was the case even with Fukuda who devoted himself to the anti-*ijime* course – the teacher who really cared about students. In other words, although people are aware of the link between the social environment of students and their 'pathological' responses, and although they can see various fragmented linkages, *how exactly* and *how systematically* they are linked is rarely understood.

My hypothesis is that this may occur because the voices of students themselves have largely been absent from the discourse on *ijime*. Given the clandestine nature of *ijime*, this is a serious void. Even in the attempt by Fukuda, it was the remarks made by students which enabled him to see that what teachers do to students may be both directly and indirectly linked with what students do in *ijime*. The 'powerlessness' felt by the homeroom teachers of Shikagawa Hirofumi and Ohkōchi Kiyoteru ultimately derives from this fact.

Assuming that *ijime* is an act of over-conformity to school, what exactly is it that students try to conform to? What are the indicators of their over-conformity?

There is ample evidence which indicates that by engaging in *ijime* students conform, consciously or not, to what teachers do to them and what teachers tell them to do. The most interesting perception a number of students have about *ijime* is that they were 'bullied' by teachers. Students seem to have no problem in applying the word '*ijime*' to what teachers do to them. This is in clear contrast with adults' perception that *ijime* is exclusively children's business. Even after the incident of the mock funeral where teachers *did* participate in *ijime* (though passively), it was not publicly recognised as such. Instead, it was registered as a 'mistake', something which should not have happened. Indeed it should not have happened, but by registering the fact that teachers did participate in *ijime* merely as 'mistake', adult discourse on *ijime* which excludes teachers is kept intact. The student perception of being bullied by teachers implicitly challenges this and suggests that in fact there is no a priori demarcation between what teachers do and what students do.

Shortly after the suicide of Ohkōchi Kiyoteru, *Shōnen Jump*, an extremely popular comic magazine for youth, urged its readers to speak up about *ijime*. They received some 1,800 letters from young people, many of which were compiled into a special issue, *Jump Ijime Report* (Tsuchiya *et al.* 1995). There are numerous claims in the report that students were 'bullied' by their teachers. One was bullied by her homeroom teacher badly when she was only 7. According to her, the teacher ordered pupils in the class to hit her with desks and chairs, gave her (who had been abandoned as a baby) a nickname of 'cyborg', told her that she was ugly and deserved to be abandoned, and told the class that she (the teacher) wished her (the student) dead (pp. 138–9). One girl wrote that she too was picked on and bullied by her homeroom teacher constantly when she was a second grader – being hit by teaching instruments, grabbed by her hair to be dragged to the corridor only for looking out of the window, and hit in the face for not cleaning the classroom when nobody else was (p. 144). Another girl wrote that she was bullied when she was a fifth grader also by her homeroom teacher, who shouted at her because the teacher spotted a hair in the place she had just cleaned. She was made to sing a song in front of the class, just one among numerous incidents of her being picked on by the teacher (p. 145). A boy wrote that his homeroom teacher drew a picture of a toad on the black-board with his (the student's) name on it when he was a first grader, and that he ended up being bullied by his classmates for the next six years with the nickname of 'toad' (p. 164). An 11 year old pointedly said that there are 'successful' teachers and 'disqualified' teachers and that there is no *ijime* in the class of a 'successful' teacher (p. 226).

As Rigby, an Australian expert on bullying, points out, there are teachers also outside Japan who 'deliberately lead children into bullying others'. Moreover, 'the use of sarcasm and subtle form of ridicule by teachers is not uncommon' and they too 'can contribute substantially to classroom bullying'. He goes on to say, however, that there are also 'many teachers [in Australia] who effectively model a democratic style of interacting with others' (Rigby 1996: 84), suggesting that behaviour of teachers which can lead to bullying among students derives from a non-democratic style of human interaction.

To translate this to the Japanese context, it would mean that students' experiences of *ijime* by teachers are founded upon the authoritarian mode of human interaction which is dominant in Japanese schools (see Chapters 3 to 5), and that these experiences can contribute substantially to classroom bullying among students themselves. Asō Nobuko, an ex-junior high school teacher in Fukuoka, admits that teachers 'hit only students who appear physically weaker than themselves. When a student appears to be strong, more than two teachers get together to hit the student' (Murakami 1990). When a teacher is surprised to find that 'the words the students used when they were bullying someone were the same ones she was using to scold a child' (Azuma *et al.* 1986: 58), she is actually witnessing the transmission of bullying behaviour from teachers to students, which occurs in a school environment dominated by the principle of non-democracy and domination by the powerful.

The disconcerting fact is that *ijime* is far less mysterious if it is understood basically as 'copycat' behaviour in which Japanese students model them-selves on their teachers. This sounds terrible because there are numerous, truly caring, good-hearted teachers in Japan (as elsewhere), who work hard to help their students, often to the extent that it jeopardises their health. The point is that those teachers work in a structure which leaves little room for autonomy (often with the consequence that their role becomes merely that of 'regimentation enforcement agents'). Moreover, as we briefly touched upon earlier, in recent years Monbushō's control has been tigh-tened not only against students but equally against teachers – with the effect that both teachers and students have neither the will nor the time to interact with each other.

One of the most unfortunate consequences of the suicide of Shikagawa Hirofumi in 1986 is that the disciplinary measures taken against the teachers (including the dismissal of the homeroom teacher) made schools even more closed and impenetrable than before. By making scapegoats out of these teachers and by creating the precedent that teachers are punishable for their involvement in *ijime*, the question of responsibility became the focus of the discourse of *ijime* – driving all parties concerned (teachers, students and parents) into blaming and antagonising each other, while leaving the structural cause of *ijime* largely intact and unattended.

Juxtaposing and analysing the fundamental similarities between what teachers do and what students do, therefore, should not be taken as a 'culprit finding' exercise. Instead, it aims to find the hidden social function of *ijime* with reference to the role teachers play (intentionally or not) in

Japanese schools. It aims to point out that the hidden function of *ijime* is fundamentally the same as the hidden function of schools which are (in the eyes of students) operated by teachers and nobody else. This analysis is mandatory to understanding the nature of *ijime*.

THE HIDDEN FUNCTION OF *IJIME* 1

Policing non-conformity and stamping out individuality

The first hidden function of *ijime* is to enforce the uniformity of the group by stamping out individuality. A 16 year old wrote to *Shōnen Jump* that 'these days, if you cannot think and behave in the same way as others, you are most definitely bullied' (Tsuchiya *et al.* 1995: 131). This is the same point made by a student in Fukuda's anti-*ijime* class: *ijime* arises because each person is different; so long as people are not the same, you will never be able to stamp it out (Ujioka 1997a). As a 17 year old who returned from overseas commented, 'it is very bad to be different from others' in Japanese schools (*AS* 9 August 1987).

In *Shōnen Jump* there are many examples of victims being bullied because they were different from others in one way or another. For some students the difference was physical handicap (pp. 90, 125, 173, 205), while for others it was to be new to the school (pp. 150, 155, 174, 213) or simply being 'poor' (pp. 130, 158, 173, 175). The bullied can also be students who cannot do things as well as others – who are either slow, timid, or 'sissy' (*AS* 23 June 1987) or who can do things *too* well (*AS* 30 May 1987); or who prefer to be left alone rather than mix with others (Murakami 1984). According to one study, two thirds of 50 returnee children (*kikokushijo*) who responded to a survey indicated that they had been bullied because of their overseas experience – because of their English ability, lack of competence in Japanese, different manners, attitudes and ways of thinking (Miyachi 1990).

With the drive to extinguish difference, *ijime* often serves as an illegitimate, 'school-floor', peer-surveillance system, which helps to perfect the enforcement of school rules. For instance, one student who refused to follow the school rule of close-cropped hair was severely victimised by other boys who observed the rule (Murakami 1984). A girl who lost everything in a house fire became the target of *ijime* because she had to use a bag different from the one prescribed by school (Tsuchiya *et al.* 1995: 173). A girl was bullied by senior students (*senpai*) of the club (*bukatsu*), who checked whether she observed the dress code (in even more detail than teachers do) and whether she greeted them properly or not (Tsuchiya *et al.* 1995: 171). Peer pressure to conform became ferocious in the early 1980s as students were put under military-like measures, introduced to suppress so-called '*kōnaibōryoku*' (violence against teachers and school premises) (Murakami 1984).[5]

One of the reasons frequently mentioned by aggressors is that the victims were bullied because they were selfish, egotistical, self-centred ('*wagamama*', '*jibun katte*' or '*migatte*') (Tsuchiya *et al.* 1995: 193, 196). These are the key criteria on which Japanese students are customarily judged, scolded, and labelled by adults, especially teachers. They are now adopted by students themselves to 'punish' their classmates. Although '*wagamama*' is now used with a negative connotation, the original word is 'waga-mama' – literally to be oneself. Even if the positive meaning of the word is now lost, the fact is that it is the self or the individuality of the victim which students on the bullying side find irritating and annoying (*mukatsuku*).

I discussed previously how petty rules are used by teachers to weed out students who appear 'different and therefore problematic'. I also described the ways peer-management is tacitly used to ensure the smooth operation of school rules. I explained how various mechanisms to promote 'self'-management' are at work in Japanese schools. There is an irrefutable similarity between the hidden function of *ijime* (i.e. students' stamping out meticulously any element of difference), on the one hand, and the hidden function of school as discussed earlier, on the other. This analysis of *ijime* suggests that in effect it functions to penalise those who disturb the conformism which is systematically fostered in Japanese schools. *Ijime* may be understood as collective violence to extinguish any buds of non-conformity. Within school territory, this means the enforcement of conformity to the standards set by teachers.

It is probably not the case, however, that students try consciously or intentionally to maintain group solidarity – let alone to cherish the value of collectivism. If anything, conformism is a 'by-product' of *ijime* which takes place in a social environment where to be different stands out and to be non-conformist is seen as weakness. The question of power and power-lessness among Japanese students therefore seem to be crucial to understanding *ijime*.

HIDDEN FUNCTION OF *IJIME* 2

Legitimating the power-dominant society and creating the power-docile mind

Although some victims of *ijime* know why they were bullied, most victims have little idea why they became the target of *ijime*. Most of the 117 letters from victims contained in *Shōnen Jump* include some sort of reflection and interpretation as to why they were bullied. Even if they could not think of any, the desperate search for the reason often continues because it may provide the key to escape from the *ijime*. For the aggressors, however, the reason is often not only vague, but simply non-existent. It is enough that the victim was somehow '*mukatsuku*' (annoying). It is quite possible, in other words, that even the 'difference' which victims themselves identified as the reasons for *ijime* is not as clearly registered in the minds of bullies.

On this point, Inaizumi Ren, a former *tōkōkyohi* student in Kanagawa, explains as follows.

> There are no reasons behind *ijime* these days. Bullies are not even aware that they have malice. This makes *ijime* even more fearful. . . . The group is in need of *ijime* and it needs a victim. If it loses a victim, it needs another one. It is just like animal instinct, and the target of *ijime* is decided in a matter of seconds.
>
> (quoted in Inaizumi 1997: 289)

When students say 'there is no reason behind *ijime*', it means that there is no good reason or justifiable reason behind *ijime*. What do the bullies themselves say on this point? According to one 13-year-old girl:

> There is no particular reason, but I am bullying a girl. *Ijime* gives me the best pleasure. It probably releases stress, I feel refreshed. . . . I hesitate to say this myself, but I am like the boss of the class. So, when I bully this girl, other girls follow. As a result, the girl is bullied by almost every girl in the class.
>
> (Tsuchiya *et al.* 1995: 198)

In other words, *ijime* provides her with a sense of power which helps her to release stress. Similarly, a male student explains that *ijime* is all about power:

> *Ijime* occurs in a world of the survival of the fittest. As you go up the hierarchical ladder of a group, you get urged to bully someone. If the powerful do not bully, the less powerful do not follow him.
>
> (Ujioka 1997c)

Kubota Gen, a 17-year-old student of Surugadai High School, Tokyo, expressed a similar view in the memorial service for his friend, who died in an *ijime* suicide.

> In an imperfect world, children have to be given a poison vaccine in order to survive. We're told, 'Let's make this a world in which the weak

can survive' – but that's whitewash. When a child who's been fooled by the whitewash sees how things really are, he thinks to himself, 'The world is evil, I can't live in it.' Children need to be taught early that equality is a lie. They have to be immunized to some extent against the harshness of reality.

(Ujioka 1997d)

Another 13-year-old girl expressed her disgust in finding someone timid:

First, victims always look so timid, they look at people with upturned eyes. To see such a look makes me feel utterly *mukatsuku* (sick)! It makes me feel 'Let's give her a blow of *ijime*'.

(Tsuchiya *et al.* 1995: 201)

These accounts indicate that in a classroom power operates as the most fundamental ruling principle of human relations. If you have power, you are admired. If you do not, you are despised, hated, and bullied. The irony is that, in schools where so much emphasis is put on 'being the same as others', the 'power' of the 'powerful' is not much different from that of the others. The group becomes important, in this context, as the only certain source of quasi-absolute power. Only when one 'belongs' to the group – the side where everybody else is but a victim – is one's security ensured (albeit just for the time being).

The more standardised students are, the more chance there is that today's 'boss' becomes tomorrow's victim (although in a class where a group of 'problem kids' exists, the hierarchy may tend to be more stable). A student says:

The difference between the bully and the victim is not even as much as the thickness of a sheet of paper. It can also depend on the mood of each individual for the day. It is extremely simple, yet extremely complex.

(Ujioka 1997c)

In such an environment, it becomes important to demonstrate the power you have by being aggressive, violent, nasty and cruel – by arousing fear in others. This explains the observation made by a student: 'the more audience there is, the more ferocious *ijime* becomes' (Toyoda 1995).

A number of students actually say that they feel 'safe' while seeing someone else being bullied or while engaging in the act of bullying. Inaizumi Ren writes:

Naturally, there was something like *ijime* [in my senior high school]. Yet, I was used to seeing *ijime* in the junior high school and sometimes I even participated in it. It was best to do so in order not to be ridiculed or bullied myself, and even if I try to stop *ijime*, it would not mean that it is eliminated. . . . [I really dreaded going to school but] I worried that if I failed to go to school, my classmates might alienate me immediately and look down upon me increasingly. I could not bear to think about it. With such a state of mind, to see others being bullied did not cause me anger. While others are bullied, I felt safe and at ease.

(Inaizumi 1997: 270–1)

In order not to be alienated by classmates, Ren 'had light conversation with friends and made every effort to tune in to what others had to say in order not to be regarded as strange' (p. 270). Another student says:

once I enter the school gate, the 'performance' begins. With 'Get set!' and 'Go!' [in my mind] I change my expression and make a face for school.

(Ujioka 1997c)

The need to perform at school is mentioned by a number of students. Ishiwari Minako, a 16-year-old *tōkōkyohi* student, remarks that she used to wear her 'school smile' in school (Ishikawa *et al.* 1993: 307). Another high-school girl wrote that 'Everyday is a strain. To live is to perform, isn't it?' (Miyagawa 1995: 132). Because of the need to be cheerful and to perform, the expression 'the face gets weary' (*kao ga tsukareru*) has become a common expression even among students of primary and junior high schools (Miyagawa 1995: 90). A 9-year-old girl jumped from the top of the school building after leaving a note which says '*oshibai* [acting], *oshibai, bye-bye, oshibai*' (Miyagawa 1995: 132).

The mask that students feel compelled to wear in school is not only worn to protect themselves from classmates but also to conceal themselves from teachers. Whether it is for teachers or classmates does not matter, however, in an environment where classmates can play ultimately the same (or often an even more fundamental) role as teachers. Many students perceive that 'school is a battle ground' (Ishikawa *et al.* 1993: 381; Ujioka 1997c). What is referred to is not just the examination war but the tension and anxiety they feel at school, where students are constantly compelled to be vigilant and psychologically ready for the unpredictable 'attack' by teachers and classmates in a society which operates on the principle of power (and conformity).

There is little question that the foundation of a power-dominant environment in the classroom is mapped out by teachers, intentionally or not.

Olweus, a Norwegian psychologist working on bullying, remarks that the level of aggression of children is raised when parents use power-assertive child-rearing methods, such as physical punishment and violent emotional outbursts (Olweus 1993: 40). In the Japanese context, where power-assertive methods are still dominant in child-rearing, there is a parallel in the pattern of aggression exhibited by students and teachers.

Undoubtedly, there are similarities in the manner power is used by bullies and teachers. The fact that students actually use the expression of '*ijime*' to refer to what teachers do to them, as discussed earlier, indicates the likeness between the two. The group 'lynch' where the victim is made to 'kneel' on the floor to be hit and kicked by others, for instance, is chillingly similar to the cases where a teacher assaulted a student who was made to 'kneel' on the floor. Just as teachers have power over students in Japanese schools, the bullying group also has overwhelming power over its victim. The arbitrary way that power is exerted in *ijime* also resembles the unpredictable manner in which corporal punishment is used by teachers (i.e. a student is 'picked on' in both cases). The fact that *ijime* is often targeted against the socially weak is also the same in both cases. The way violence is used in an emotional manner (i.e. *mukatsuku*) also reminds us of the way some teachers resort to corporal punishment (see Chapter 4).

The Human Rights Protection Bureau of the Justice Ministry clearly sees corporal punishment as the fundamental cause of *ijime* – and this view is supported by many in Japan (Teshigahara 1986: 61). According to Kobayashi, as many as 58 per cent of junior high school bullies in his data, but only 28 per cent of non-bullies, had been recipients of corporal punishment (Kobayashi 1995). Kobayashi also points out that a teacher, who was proud of his 'ideal class', which he maintained by applying corporal punishment almost daily, failed to see *ijime*, while another teacher with a less heavy-handed approach spotted it almost immediately when he took over the class (Kobayashi 1985: 97–9). Kawai Hidekazu (15), who was a representative at a student association of a junior high school in Kanagawa, remarked that *ijime* increased after the adoption of totalitarian measures, such as the attribution of responsibility to the whole class when one of its members did something wrong (*AS* 6 March 1985).

Hirayama Katsumi, an educational critic, points out that excessive regimentation was indeed the problem of the Aichi school attended by Ohkōchi Kiyoteru. Immediately after the death of Kiyoteru, Hirayama visited the school and heard a teacher, presumably the principal, shouting at students in the assembly. Under the circumstances he found this most inappropriate and insensitive (Hirayama 1995). Another student of the same school was also reported to have killed himself six years prior to the death of Kiyoteru under conditions suspected to amount to *ijime* suicide (*AS* 3 December 1994).

Although Monbushō does not release the data which shows the breakdown of suicides by prefectures, four out of 19 suicides (i.e. 21 per cent) reported in newspapers that year occurred in Aichi, which is notorious for excessive regimentation (Oride 1996: 132–3) (see Chapter 4).

The root of the problem, however, is perhaps deeper than just corporal punishment or regimentation. The incidence of *ijime* is unlikely to be reduced until Japanese students are freed from these oppressive classroom practices. What *ijime* represents, though, is not just the problem of corporal punishment or excessive regimentation, displaced from the student–teacher to student–student relationship. It represents the authoritarian, non-democratic, power-dominant human relationship that is so pervasive in schools and the educational system in Japan in general (including teachers, local boards of education, and Monbushō). Corporal punishment and regimentation are the most salient manifestations of the alienating human relationships promoted in the system.

As long as teachers remain the key players in this non-democratic system in the everyday life of Japanese schools, they remain largely powerless and have little chance of resolving *ijime* problems. Irrespective of the creed and educational philosophy of each individual teacher, they are, by definition in this particular system, obliged to control or manage students from above. Is it any wonder then that teachers often 'side with' the bullying group, unwilling to do anything, or much about *ijime*. One high school teacher admits that:

> This is something that I should not admit, but for the management of a class, it is easier to stand on the side of bullies and force the victim to put up with it (*gamansuru*).
>
> (*AS* 27 December 1994)

In fact, it is a common experience of victims, even when they gathered up the courage to ask help of a teacher, to be told only to '*ganbaru*' (hold on) or '*gamansuru*' (endure) (Tsuchiya *et al.* 1995: 107, 147, 162). Both *ganbaru* and *gamansuru* mean nothing but to accept being bullied – they are equivalent to being told that 'it is your problem'.

Azuma *et al.* observe that:

> The reason bullying grows serious is that the teachers are psychologically aligned with the bullies. When the teacher feels that bullying a particular child is only natural because the child is an oddball, the bullying can become very severe.
>
> (Azuma *et al.* 1986: 58)

Some victims were saved by the intervention of a teacher after appealing for help (Tsuchiya *et al.* 1995: 129, 146, 152), and numerous teachers have seriously tackled the problem as we have seen in the example of Fukuda (see also Tsuchiya *et al.* 1995: 211, 235–6). Yet according to a telephone counselling service for victims of *ijime*, some 30 per cent of students and parents who called for help complained that the teachers whom they had contacted did nothing (Ayukyō 1995).

Criticism of teachers' inaction has been expressed by numerous parents of victims, including the parents of Shikagawa Hirofumi and Ohkōchi Kiyoteru (Ishikawa *et al.* 1995). The mother of a 13-year-old girl who committed *ijime* suicide revealed that she had alerted both the principal and the homeroom teacher, only to receive unconcerned and non-committal responses. The principal said that he would let the homeroom teacher know, while the homeroom teacher simply said that he knew about it but did nothing. The school did not contact the mother even once despite her repeated expressions of concern (*AS* 23 January 1985). The father of another *ijime* victim was arrested after hitting two bullies. He stated that he lost his temper when he found his son being called 'Ohkōchi', with the implication that he was to commit *ijime* suicide. Like Ohkōchi Kiyoteru, his son had been bullied relentlessly for over a year. When he heard the homeroom teacher say that he knew nothing about *ijime* in his class, he felt that school was unreliable and undependable (*Nihonkai shinbun* 20 March 1995).

What we are observing here is the grey area where the structural cause of the problem merges with the individual motive of the parties concerned. In fact, in order to fully understand why the problem of *ijime* has persisted for so long without much prospect of a 'solution', it is essential to examine it from two perspectives. One is the structural perspective – that *ijime* is a product of the very system promoted in school – a system of control by the powerful of the less powerful, or powerless, in which conformity plays a key role. The other is a perspective which looks into how each individual acts when confronted with *ijime*. In reality both are entwined and inseparable. In order to explain why cases of *ijime* suicide, like Shikagawa and Ohkōchi, are repeated year after year, it seems necessary to clarify how the structural aspect is entwined with (and supported by) the motives and actions of individuals and parties involved.

The inability of teachers to resolve *ijime*, for instance, partly stems from the structural cause that teachers themselves are the promoters of the very structure of school which cultivates *ijime*. Their inability is the inability of those who are themselves caught in the structural contradiction. To punish a teacher who could not stop *ijime*, therefore, simply means scapegoating. The inability of teachers, however, could also reflect unwillingness to do anything about *ijime*, outright negligence or even false denial. There is a vast difference between being caught in a structural dilemma and exploiting the problem to further one's interest. The same argument can be made of other parties concerned.

The reason that we have seen little improvement in the *ijime* situation in Japan is not only because it is a structural problem, but because it is surrounded by layers of silence by all parties concerned. We have discussed in the previous chapters the way that the mechanism of control in Japanese schools is ultimately the structure of silence – which makes it extremely difficult for students (and teachers for that matter) to speak their mind. The silence surrounding the *ijime* phenomenon is more problematic in that it does not necessarily reflect a coerced silence, for that silence may be deliberately chosen to protect one's interest. It is this aspect of *ijime* which makes the phenomenon doubly difficult to solve. Let us re-examine the *ijime* phenomenon from this perspective.

THE STRUCTURE OF SILENCE SURROUNDING *IJIME*

In the extremely tense and highly sensitive environment of Nakano Fujimi Junior High School shortly after the death of Shikagawa Hirofumi, there was a small incident which provided an extraordinary opportunity for those outside school to observe in microcosm the *ijime* world. The following is the account of the incident based on the newspaper reportage (*AS* 13–18 February 1986).

Eleven days after the death of Shikagawa Hirofumi, one of the teachers who signed the mock-condolence card addressed his class at the beginning of his lesson to talk about the need to 'tackle seriously the problem of *ijime* to eradicate it'.

Some minutes into the class, the teacher spotted a student playing with a small bottle of eau de Cologne and confiscated it. The student got upset by this and started hitting the student sitting in front of him quite hard (with some 70 per cent of full force). The bully hit the victim 50 to 60 times in total, while saying, 'What the teacher says sounds real cool, but we'll see if he means it. If he cautions me, I'll stop bullying you. You are a second Shikagawa. Kill yourself as Shikagawa did. Come and fight with me'.

The bully and the victim were sitting in the second and the third rows, i.e. fairly close to the teacher, and the victim repeatedly pleaded with the teacher '*Sensei*, help me!' during the assault which lasted for some 20 minutes. Several students told the press later that 'the hitting was rather hard, and the victim's pleading must have reached the teacher'. The teacher, however, pretended that he did not notice, and kept writing on the blackboard. Shortly after the hitting began, one of the other students said, '*Sensei, ijime* has started. Please stop it', but the teacher did nothing. Another student said to the victim, 'You are deserted by the teacher, too'.

After enduring the assault for some 20 minutes the victim finally stood up and hit back in desperation at his predator, realising that no one, including the teacher, would intervene. A fight began between the two. It was then that the teacher intervened. Instead of scolding the bully, however, he told the victim to stop it. Being outraged, the victim rushed out of the class, saying 'The teacher is too unfair. I'll kill [the bully] and kill myself. I'll go get a knife'. The teacher was alerted and chased after him all the way to the hardware shop in the neighbourhood, where they had an argument. The incident was disclosed because their argument was spotted by a policeman. The bully said later that 'My violence escalated as I got more and more angry with the teacher who ignored my bullying [the victim]'.

The bully was later arrested. The teacher was ordered to take teacher training (*kenshū*) for one year. The principal told the press that he thought that the teacher had 'a good trusting relationship with students'. A parents' meeting was held to discuss the *ijime* issue, but few were prepared to speak up because 'if you criticise teachers, it may rebound negatively upon the teacher's report (*naishin*) on your child' and 'if you say too much, that will spread among students and it may trigger *ijime* against your child'.

This small incident illustrates the crude reality of *ijime*, its naked power dynamics, the depth and the complexity of the problem. It shows the phenomena of (on the part of the teacher) lip service, unwillingness to notice *ijime*, alignment with the bully, and taking action only when there is a danger of its leaking outside the class, and (on the part of the bully) ill-directed aggression, and (on the part of the victim) complete isolation and being attacked with no reason, and (on the part of other students) their detached attitudes, their disillusionment with teachers, the sense of resignation and helplessness. It is also significant that the incident was disclosed to the public almost by chance, that the principal issued a superficial and irresponsible statement, that parents feared retaliation from both teachers and students. It is not surprising that the measures taken were inadequate. As a student points out, one of the problems of *ijime* is that:

Adults, teachers and children – look out first for their own interests.

(Ujioka 1997c)

What the episode above suggests is that every party and every single individual present at the scene of *ijime* is inclined to keep silence or maintain non-involvement, in the pursuit of their own individual interests – except for the victim who in the end broke his silence in desperation, after being cornered and driven to desperate steps.

As we have already discussed, among students the *ijime* phenomenon is deeply clandestine. Given that informing teachers about *ijime* ('*chikuru*') is the most serious crime punishable by *ijime*, students try to be silent as much as possible. Students who are not the victim also have a 'vested interest' in keeping silent, because victimisation of somebody else may ensure one's own safety.

Like Ohkōchi Kiyoteru, victims themselves are largely secretive about their being bullied. They dread the revenge that would follow their informing teachers about *ijime*. And they themselves are sceptical that talking to teachers would resolve the problem in any case. One survey revealed that only 15 per cent had consulted teachers, and most felt that the only thing they could do was to 'endure and persevere' (Kobayashi 1985: 48–9).

There is also a deep-seated perception among students (both bullies and victims) that teachers will be able to do little about *ijime* in any case. This is understandable if we recall the fact that 72 per cent of the Japanese students in my survey indicated that their teachers are *never* easy to talk to when they have a personal problem; 44 per cent thought that teachers *never* really understand students; 39 per cent, that teachers never care about them as people. These findings demonstrate that students have little confidence in teachers; that the student–teacher relationship is rather distant and remote; and that there is little foundation in student–teacher relationships to enable students to feel comfortable in seeking help. In any similar survey in Japan, the proportion of students who approach teachers to discuss their worries and problems is no more than 7 per cent (Kobayashi 1985: 3). It is no wonder, then, that many victims of *ijime* perceive that seeking help from teachers can only make things worse rather than better.

Teachers also have a 'vested interest' in not being committed to resolve *ijime* if they are keen to 'manage' the class. *Ijime* becomes threatening to them when a situation arises where teachers' negligence may be questioned – the case of serious injuries inflicted by *ijime* or *ijime* suicide. It is 'best' for them not to know about it or deny it as much as possible. The clandestine nature of *ijime* 'helps' in this regard, as it was apparent in the words of the principal of Ohkōchi Kiyoteru's school, i.e. as long as the victim himself does not claim that he was bullied, the school authority cannot be sure about it.

Monbushō is not an exception in this 'pact of silence' surrounding *ijime*. As the single most powerful policy maker in the educational system Monbushō is in a self-contradictory position (even more so than teachers) *vis-à-vis* the *ijime* phenomenon. Its responses reflect its fundamental way of thinking, and the current educational system of Japan is founded on that way of thinking.

It is the Monbushō system which cultivates the *ijime* phenomenon. The basic stance taken by Monbushō manifests itself most conspicuously in the way it collects the national data on *ijime*. Monbushō conducted the national survey of *ijime* in 1985 after being pressured by the then Ad Hoc Council on Education, and publicised the result of the data only after being urged by the press after the death of Shikagawa Hirofumi (*AS* 22 February 1986).

The definition of *ijime* on the basis of which the data was collected through schools and prefectural boards of education is very problematic. Between 1985 and 1993, *ijime* was defined not only as 'one-sided, continuous attacks' that accompany 'a serious sense of pain' on the part of the victim but also as attacks which 'had been confirmed by schools' (*ANEN* 18 December 1995). In other words, as long as the school authority did not acknowledge (for whatever the reason) an incident as *ijime*, it was not officially recognised. By 1994, however, Monbushō had 'eliminated the definition and instructed school officials to make their judgments of whether an act constituted bullying in terms of how it was seen by the victim' (*ANEN* 18 December 1995). While the definition itself was thus improved, Monbushō then used this to underestimate the *ijime* phenomenon – it attributed the increase in *ijime* which appeared in the statistics in 1994 to the change in the definition.

Even with the new definition, however, the 'spirit' of bureaucratic defensiveness in this exercise of data collection seems to have trickled down to the school authorities and the local board of education. In Yachiyo-city in Chiba, for instance, despite the repeated submission of complaints (five times over two years) by a victim and his parents, the case was judged by the local board of education not to constitute *ijime* and their complaints were never filed. The reason was that they did not satisfy Monbushō's 'official definition of *ijime*, which states that the torment must be "of a continuous nature" in order to qualify' (Hirai 1997).

The occurrence of *ijime* in the official statistics (1985–96) was the highest in 1985 when national data was collected for the first time. Even in 1985, however, the gap between prefectures with similar attributes was such that Monbushō itself was deeply sceptical of the reliability of the data – one prefecture reported that *ijime* occurred in 12 per cent of schools, whereas another prefecture with similar attributes reported that it occurs in 83 per cent of schools (*AS* 22 February 1986). Endō Toyokichi comments that the 1985 official statistics are so distorted as to be 'laughable'. He points out that *ijime* occurs in almost all schools (*AS* 22 February 1986).

Educational critics in Japan are in agreement that *ijime* is so grossly underestimated in the official statistics that they hardly mean anything (Imahashi 1995). An investigation by the Osaka Board of Education, for instance, revealed that there had been some seven times as many cases of *ijime* (about which school authorities were aware) as were officially reported (Imahashi 1995). Actual cases of *ijime*, including the ones which do not come to the attention of the school authorities, are thought to be on an enormous scale. According to a survey conducted by Imahashi regarding experience of *ijime* by university students in their school days, some 60 per cent of the respondents who were at secondary schools between 1988 to 1993 reported that they witnessed 'excessive *ijime*' and some 17 per cent had themselves experienced being the victim of 'excessive *ijime*' (Imahashi 1995).

The reason that the *ijime* phenomenon persists, therefore, is not just structural but also because the many parties to it maintain silence about it for many reasons. This 'wall' of collective silence, including that of victims themselves, corners victims into the situation in which they feel so powerless and hopeless that they can think of no other solution but to kill themselves.

IJIME AS A STRESS-COPING MODE AND A MANIFESTATION OF POWERLESSNESS

Analysis of the *ijime* phenomenon allows us to shed light on various aspects of everyday life in Japanese schools which are not readily visible from outside school walls. Having examined it from various perspectives, let us return to the most fundamental question of the present chapter. What sort of place is school for students and why does *ijime* occur so intensively and extensively in Japan?

Kanbe Tomoko, 14-year-old *tōkōkyohi* student remarks pointedly that:

> What is it that I learnt at school? It is to study what is in the textbook and to learn that it is necessary to do the same thing as others.
>
> (Ishikawa *et al.* 1993: 442)

We now understand the full weight of Tomoko's statement – 'to study what is in the textbook' refers to the restrictive mode of teaching and learning we have discussed earlier (Chapter 6), as well as the excessive pressure to study in order to survive in a society which revolves around meritocratic ideology (see Chapter 1). We also understand what she means by the necessity 'to do the same thing as others'. The pressure to conform is not just coercion from above but the fierce pressure from below (from classmates), which makes it impossible so long as one stays within the school walls to avoid being 'the same as others' or to resist being '*futsū* (ordinary)'.

We need to understand that students are exposed to these pressures – to study and to conform – in the space called the 'homeroom' where they are confined almost all day and every school day of the year. In Japanese schools where students do not move from one classroom to another to study different subjects, the sense of spatial constraint and permanence can be enormous. Kurita Takako, 18-year-old *tōkōkyohi* student writes:

> In that square space called a classroom [i.e. homeroom], I have to spend most of the day, with other people who are put together in the name of a 'class', with whom I share only being of the same age. . . . Once I enter that square space, I am not allowed to be myself. I have to assimilate with others as a member of the class. We sit in the same direction, we study the same thing, we wear the same school uniform whether it suits us or not, and we also have to learn the ability to 'tune in and get along with others well' without causing trouble.
>
> (Ishikawa *et al.* 1993: 609)

Classroom is a space where students are put under enormous pressure to perform both socially and academically. It constitutes almost the entire space and time available to them as students. *Ijime* is a phenomenon which occurs when excessive pressure to conform socially and excessive pressure to perform academically fuse in a closed, prison-like space.

Another 13-year-old explains:

> And also, we are under so much stress from study and exam. But there is no place we can release this stress, there is no method to release it. *Ijime* is an easy way to release our stress. As long as such an environment lasts, *ijime* will never go away. It will surely continue.
>
> (Tsuchiya *et al.* 1995: 201)

A most commonly heard 'explanation' given by students is that *ijime* is simply 'fun'. The boy who told Kiyoteru Ohkōchi's father that it was fun to bully Kiyoteru was not a psychopath. A girl confesses that *ijime* was the only fun she had at school, even though she knew that it cornered the victim into an attempted suicide (Tsuchiya *et al.* 1995: 195).

Another wrote:

> I am a 14-year-old girl, and so-called 'bully'. I am bullying a girl with several others in the class. We do things like pasting together the pages of her science notebook and putting pins in her shoes, etc. We repeat things like this. Reason? The girl is irritating [*mukatsuku*]. Our teacher found out about our *ijime* and asked 'why do you do such a thing?'. We just answered 'because she is *mukatsuku*'. There is no other reason. The teacher says, 'Even if she is *mukatsuku*, it does not give you a reason to bully her!' He is right. But we don't feel better or refreshed, until we do

something nasty to someone who is *mukatsuku*. The more we do something which annoys her, the more we feel cleansed in our hearts [*kokoro*].
Whatever people say, this is our real motive.

(Tsuchiya *et al.* 1995: 190)

She points out that *ijime* is the only stress-coping mode readily available to
students in this limited space of the classroom. Why is it though that
bullying someone helps to release stress? Ohtorii Yūko, a 16-year-old
tōkōkyohi student explains:

I have bullied someone. . . . I did not enjoy bullying. I just felt relieved
by watching someone being bullied and suffering. My action elicits a
response – this is such a matter of course. Yet I could confirm it only by
bullying someone and by watching the victim suffer. In the place called
school which is set in a rigid framework, *ijime* might have been the only
thing we could create.

(Ohtorii 1995)

What she suggests here is that *ijime*, and only *ijime*, can provide the sense of
power in the limited space of the classroom – that it is the only way to
counteract the sense of powerlessness.

Once the lessons for the day are over, most students of junior high schools
participate in club activities which often have their own human relationships
where power and hierarchy may count even more than in the classroom.

Once outside the school walls, students have 'no place to go' (Nishiyama
1997). Spaces outside the school boundary open to students are extremely
limited, confined mostly to commercialised spaces – game centres, karaoke
boxes, eating places, etc. – and they require money. Extortion as a form of
ijime is linked to this reality of the outside school world. With this reality
many students adhere to the understanding that money provides happiness
– which in turn binds students to school even more – to education as the
prerequisite of a stable income in the future.

IJIME AS '*KO-KESHI*' BY STUDENTS

Kawai Hayao asserts that the biggest problem in Japanese education today is
that of the 'individuality' (*kosei*) of students (Kawai 1997: 56). In the educational discourse of Japan, which is often reduced to ideological debate or to
simplistic search for a party to blame, this insight provides a profoundly
important basis for understanding. As Kawai points out, the two most
serious problems in Japanese schools today – *ijime* and *tōkōkyohi* – ultimately

are questions of the individuality of each student. They do not manifest themselves as abstract questions, but they deeply touch the question of life or death, revealing how the very existence of each individual student is threatened by others or by themselves (or both).

Ijime and *tōkōkyohi*, however, have diametrically opposite orientations. *Ijime* is an act of over-conformity: a group of students attack a victim ultimately to 'erase' her/his individuality (which is regarded as an obstacle to maintain conformity), and by doing so, bullies (active or passive) obtain an ephemeral sense of security and a heightened sense of cohesion. Miyagawa Toshihiko points out that '*keshi gomu*' (eraser/rubber) has become a key word in the thinking pattern of Japanese children (Miyagawa 1995: 40). '*Kiero*' (an imperative form of '*kieru*' meaning 'to erase oneself') has become a common *ijime* jargon expression used in verbal harassment. In the *Jump Ijime Report*, two girls report that they received anonymous letters containing 'Erase yourself immediately' and 'Kill yourself. Erase yourself' (pp. 183–4). The verbs meaning 'to erase' (whether the transitive '*kesu*' or intransitive '*kieru*') had not been used towards people in everyday life before (except in the specific context of assassination or murder by a professional killer). The implication these verbs carry, that people can be erased just like objects, fits nicely with what students are so used to doing – erasing 'errors' by an eraser. *Ijime* in Japanese schools today is the act of '*ko-keshi*' – erasing a child or child's individuality by children themselves ('*ko*' meaning both 'child' and 'individuality' and '*keshi*' meaning 'erasing').

In contrast, *tōkōkyohi* is an act of non-conformity, which may work in such a way as to restore a student's individuality and subjectivity. Sometimes it is an active refusal and conscious refusal to conform, while at other times it manifests itself more passively in somatic symptoms which eventually inhibit the ability of the student to conform. In this latter case, the student becomes unable to attend school, despite strongly wishing to do so. Either way, the outcome of *tōkōkyohi* is movement away from conformity.

When Ohkochi Kiyoteru committed suicide, many regretted the fact that he had continued going to school, believing that if he had joined the ranks of the *tōkōkyohi*, he would not have died. However, this would not have been easy because the long-term implications of *ijime* (over-conformity) and *tōkōkyohi* (resistance to conformity) are totally different, not only sociologically but also in the life of the individual student. *Ijime* victims endure their ill-treatment even if it pushes them to the edge of suicide. They are likely to fear that 'if I become a *tōkōkyohi* student, that is the end of my life' (Fukuda 1997: 204). For this reason, despite everything, *ijime* victims still 'hang on' to the cliff of conformity.

Yet, quite paradoxically, it is also *ijime* which works as the trigger and immediate cause of *tōkōkyohi* for some 70 per cent of *tōkōkyohi* students (Satō *et al.* 1987). It is to the examination of *tōkōkyohi* that I turn in the following chapter.

NOTES

1 A statement Kiyoteru made in response to the psychology test given by the school's nurse-teacher (*AS* 9 December 1994).
2 He apparently visited his grandmother in Morioka to no avail (*AS* 3 February 1986).
3 The Japanese word '*rinchi*', which is derived from the English word 'lynch', means group violence targeted at one person.
4 In Japanese, *konjyō* (or *seishin*) *o kitaeru* (or *tatakinaosu*).
5 Tawara Moeko, an educational critic, points out the double standard of violence used by teachers and students – teachers' violence is *taibatsu* (corporal punishment) and *ai no muchi* (whip of love) and students' violence is *kōnaibōryoku* (school violence). She also remarks that teachers' violence toward students came to be known to the public in the course of making enquires about *kōnaibōryoku* – it was revealed that students came to use violence against teachers because they had been hit by teachers frequently (Imahashi *et al.* 1986: 83–4). There would be a number of teachers who were hit by students without hitting them first, especially once student violence toward teachers became widespread (the late 1970s to early 1980s). Nonetheless, this is an important point in discussing the general trend, since *kōnaibōryoku* has often been used as *the* reason to intensify regimentation in schools.

8 *Tōkōkyohi*: Burnout and Resistance

> I cannot go to school. If I try, nausea, dizziness, and stomach-ache follow.
> . . . I want to go to school. This makes the situation even more difficult. . . .
> Many times I have thought of suicide. I am in a panic. In my depression,
> everyday I cry.
>
> (Ishiwari Minako, a *tōkōkyohi* student[1])

THE MASS EXODUS FROM SCHOOLS

In recent years, Japanese society has been profoundly shaken by the *tōkōkyohi* phenomenon. It is an exceptionally complex phenomenon and presents extremely difficult problems for students and parents. A highly controversial issue, different views have been expressed about it by different people, with different ideological and practical implications. Irrespective of the disagreements, however, one point has been remarkably clear. *Tōkōkyohi* is causing a mass exodus of students from schools, and a legitimation crisis for the Japanese education system.

Tōkōkyohi generally refers to a situation in which students do not or cannot go to school over a long time. Whether an intentional refusal to go to school or not, *tōkōkyohi* students often show signs of excessive fatigue and exhaustion, which may be accompanied by other somatic symptoms such as stomach-ache, headache, nausea, breathing difficulty, dizziness, etc. Although there is no official, academic, or lay agreement as to what exactly constitutes *tōkōkyohi*, it often excludes '*hikō*', i.e. delinquent behaviour. In this book, too, *hikō* is differentiated, for two reasons. First, *tōkōkyohi* begins with a complete withdrawal from society when students usually stay home without seeing anyone, whereas 'delinquent' students tend to have strong peer support for not going to school and a capacity to engage in some form of collective action outside the school. Second, *tōkōkyohi* occurs in a state of energy depletion, whereas 'delinquent' students tend to exert a great deal of energy in acting out their frustration in social contexts (see pp. 27–9 in Chapter 2).[2]

The number of *tōkōkyohi* students appearing in the official statistics has increased steadily and substantially since the mid-1970s (see Figure 8.1). Although the word '*tōkōkyohi*' is not used in Monbushō's Basic School Survey, the official figure for *tōkōkyohi* is drawn from the statistics listed under the category of 'long-term absence from school' due to disliking school (*gakkō-girai*).[3] The benchmark of 'long term absence' was over 50 days in a school year before 1991, and was then changed to 30 days per annum.

The number of *tōkōkyohi* students increases in accordance with the grade in compulsory education, and is most prevalent among third year students from junior high school. In 1989, the official number of *tōkōkyohi* students from junior high schools reached over 40,000. In 1993, even using the stringent official criterion of 50 days of absence from school, it reached 1 per cent of all junior high school students.

As *tōkōkyohi* became more prevalent, Monbushō proclaimed in 1990 that it 'can happen to anyone' (*AS* 7 December 1990). Previously it had attributed *tōkōkyohi* to the personal attributes of students, i.e. flaws in character or problems at home. The change of its position meant that *tōkōkyohi* was officially recognised as a structural problem rather than a problem stemming from idiosyncratic characteristics of each individual student

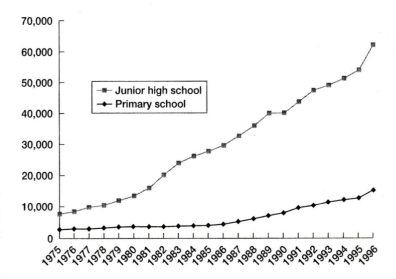

Figure 8.1 The increase in *tōkōkyohi* students
Source: Adapted from Monbushō chōgakkō-ka (1991), Monbushō (1992–7)

(although this change is not necessarily reflected in the way students are treated by teachers).

Statistics for 1996 indicate that there were 74,757 'long-term absentees' (i.e. absent for over 30 days) due to 'disliking school' at the junior high school level in that year. Of these, 62,148 (83 per cent) were absent for over 50 days (ME 1997a). In other words, one in 61 students in the lower middle school were officially recognised as *tōkōkyohi*, absent for at least 30 days from school.[4] When combined with the primary school absentees, there were some 94,000 *tōkōkyohi* students who missed more than 30 school days during the school year of 1996 (ME 1997a).

THE 'RESERVE ARMY' OF *TŌKŌKYOHI*

Okuchi Keiko – a leading consultant on *tōkōkyohi* and the founder of *Tokyo Shure*, the first alternative school designed to accommodate *tōkōkyohi* students – points out that official statistics represent only a small segment of the reality. She remarks that the official data exclude students who attend such facilities as Child Consultation Centres, Education Centres, school clinics, the principal's office, or special classes for *tōkōkyohi* or handicapped children. They go to these places instead of normal classes, which they are unable to attend. In some cases, she continues, 'putting a foot inside the rail of the school gate' is regarded by teachers as 'having attended the school for the day' in order to minimise the number of 'long-term absentees' reported to Monbushō (1992: 29).

Okuchi refers to the quantification of *tōkōkyohi* in a survey by Morita (1991) which coincides with her own estimate (Okuchi 1992: 32). In a 1988 study of 5,193 junior high school students, Morita found that one in four students have had *futōkō* (school nonattendance) of varying degrees due to being 'fed up with school', and that close to 70 per cent of students had either practised *futōkō* at varying degrees or had *futōkō* sentiment. He argues that *futōkō* is no longer a phenomenon which occurs only a minority of students but constitutes part of the everyday life of the majority of junior high school students (Morita 1991: 23–33).[5]

More specifically, Morita identified four groups of students who showed *futōkō* tendency in varying degrees.[6]

- Group 1: *Futōkō* over 50 days. At the top of the scale, there were 46 students (0.9 per cent of the sample) who would be officially classified as '*futōkō*' (i.e. those who were recognised by teachers as being absent for over 50 days). Of these, 22 were unable to participate in the survey for various reasons.

- Group 2: *Futōkō* 1 to 49 days. There were 840 students (16.2 per cent of the sample) who were absent from school 1 to 49 days in the previous year because they 'got fed up with school' (based on the report by students themselves).
- Group 3: *Futōkō* by lateness. There were 414 students (8.0 per cent of the sample) who had the experience of coming to school late or leaving school earlier than usual because they 'got fed up with school', even though they did not miss a single school day for this reason.
- Group 4: *Futōkō* sentiment only. There were 2,182 students (42 per cent of the sample) who 'got fed up with school' at some point, but 'forced themselves to go to school', even without coming late for school or leaving school early (pp. 23–33).

Morita's study demonstrates the magnitude of the *futōkō/tōkōkyohi* phenomenon hidden below the pre-1991 official demarcation of 50 days of absence a year. Clearly there is a huge 'reserve army' of students who are on the brink of the official statistics. Similar results have been obtained from other studies. Ikeda and others (1986) found that 39 per cent of 6,609 junior school students in the Tokyo region had the wish not to go to school either 'always' or 'sometimes' (as opposed to 'not at all') (Ikeda *et al.* 1986). Another survey of 1,352 Year 9 students by the Japan Parents and Teachers Association National Conference, conducted in 1988, revealed that 40 per cent felt that they did not want to go to school either 'often' or 'sometimes' (as against 'a few times' and 'never') (quoted in Inamura 1994: 187). Yet another study by the National Centre for Neuropsychiatry found that about half of junior high school students have *futōkō* sentiment and various neurotic symptoms, and reported this to the Ministry of Health (quoted in Yokoyu 1992: 15). These studies consistently suggest that 'desertion of school' by students is likely to increase in the future, as is predicted by many people (e.g. Okuchi 1992: 22–34).

The study by Morita also clarifies the relationship between *tōkōkyohi*, as captured by official statistics, and behaviour and sentiment of *futōkō/tōkōkyohi* which does not appear in the official data. In his study, he puts students in groups 1 to 3 '*futōkō* students' (who not only have *futōkō* sentiments but have actualised it in their behaviour). Such students constitute 25.1 per cent of the entire sample. The official definition would have captured only 5.2 per cent of these (Morita 1991: 29).

It should be noted, however, that Morita's study is based on a definition of '*futōkō*' which is especially broad (*Shin-shakaigaku jiten*, quoted in Asakura 1995: 220). Generally speaking, the term '*futōkō*' (school nonattendance) came to be used widely since the early 1990s instead of '*tōkōkyohi*' (which literally means 'school refusal'). Although the terms are often used loosely and interchangeably, those who use '*futōkō*' often do so because the term '*tōkōkyohi*' carries the connotation of anti-school sentiment and values held by students, whereas a large number of so-called '*tōkōkyohi* students' actually want to go to school even while they experience all sorts of physical and psychological difficulties which prevent them from doing so (e.g. Morita 1991: 4–5; Miike and Tomoda 1994: 6–7). Those who use '*tōkōkyohi*' on the other hand prefer it to '*futōkō*' because '*futōkō*' can include 'truancy', a phenomenon which they consider to be of quite a different character from '*tōkōkyohi*' (Asakura 1995: 22).[7]

The question of the definition and categorisation of *tōkōkyohi*, however, is never clear-cut. There is no consensus about it (e.g. Inamura 1994: 1–56). Even the general distinction between *futōkō* and *tōkōkyohi*, for instance, raises fundamental questions. What does the discrepancy between the consciousness on the one hand and physical conditions students experience on the other signify? If students want to go to school, why do they have anxiety panic and somatic symptoms primarily associated with the intensification of pressure to go to school? What is 'truancy'? Are students who stay home with no specific symptoms other than tiredness playing truant? Is there more to it than just idleness?

The question of the definition and categorisation of *tōkōkyohi* cannot be discussed fully without analysing the discourse about it. Apart from '*futōkō*', *tōkōkyohi* has been called by numerous other names such as '*gakkō-kyōfu*' (school phobia), '*tōkōkyohi-shō*' (school refusal syndrome), '*gakkō-girai*' (disliking school), '*taigaku*' (truancy) and '*zuru-yasumi*' (bunking off/wagging). Each term is used with differing connotations and is based on various ideological assumptions about school and children (or more broadly, society and individuals). To understand the *tōkōkyohi* phenomenon, it is essential to scrutinise competing discourses, and to measure that discourse against the words of students themselves who actually live with *tōkōkyohi*.

ADULT DISCOURSE ON *TŌKŌKYOHI*

'*Tōkōkyohi*' has been vigorously discussed in Japan. By 1993 over two hundred books had been published on this topic (Ishikawa *et al.* 1993: ii). Whatever the views projected, their advocates have almost always been adults – doctors, psychiatrists, counsellors, psychologists, academics, educationists, teachers, administrators, government officials, educational critics, journalists and parents. The adult discourse on '*tōkōkyohi*' has become so diverse as well as politically and ideologically charged that it now appears to constitute an entity quite independent and abstracted from the '*tōkōkyohi*' experienced by students. The adult discourse is important, however, since it has direct bearing upon the lives of students, affecting how they are seen and treated by people who have considerable power over their lives (Asakura 1995: 81).

In the adult discourse on '*tōkōkyohi*' there are two contentious points. One is whether to regard *tōkōkyohi* as illness or not. The other is whether to regard it as a personal problem of adjustment arising from the specific characteristics of individual students (or the families of the students), or as a structural problem stemming from the social organisation of the school (and of the society of which school is a part). The adult discourse on *tōkōkyohi* can be classified into four types on the basis of these questions (see Tables 8.1 and 8.2). They are:

1 Psychiatric discourse: *tōkōkyohi* as mental illness
2 Behavioural discourse: *tōkōkyohi* as laziness
3 Citizens' discourse: *tōkōkyohi* as resistance to school
4 Socio-medical discourse: *tōkōkyohi* as school burnout

The typology of the causes of *tōkōkyohi* by Monbushō below provides a reference point to indicate, roughly, what proportion of junior high school students may be classified into the types of *tōkōkyohi* as described in the adult discourse.

1	Experiences at school (the relationship with classmates and teachers)	9.1 per cent
2	Apathy (no particular reason)	25.8 per cent
3	Anxiety and emotional confusion (including somatic symptoms)	24.5 per cent
4	Deliberately willed abstention from school	4.7 per cent
5	Delinquent behaviour	14.0 per cent
6	Combination of all types	18.8 per cent
7	Other	3.1 per cent

(ME 1995b)

Table 8.1 Types of discourse on *tōkōkyohi*

Tōkōkyohi is:	Illness	Not illness
Personal problem of adjustment	[1] Psychiatric discourse	[2] Behavioural discourse
Structural problem caused by school	[4] Socio-medical discourse	[3] Citizens' discourse

Table 8.2 Analysis of the discourses on *tōkōkyohi*

	[1] The Psychiatric Discourse	[2] The Behavioural Discourse	[3] Citizens' Discourse	[4] Socio-Medical Discourse
Leading advocate	Inamura Hiroshi Okonogi Keigo	Monbushō (especially prior to 1990) Large number of teachers	Okuchi Keiko (*Tōkyo Shure*) Watanabe Takashi (Psychiatrist) *Tōkōkyohi o kangaeru kai*	Miike Teruhisa and Tomoda Akemi
General support	Psychiatrists and other medical practitioners	Teachers and other educationists	Some parents and psychiatrists	Small number of doctors
Tōkōkyohi as:	Mental illness	Laziness	Normal response of normal students 'Schools are sick. Students are not sick'	Structural chronic fatigue (*karō*)
Labelling	'*Tōkōkyohi* syndrome' (*tōkōkyohi-shō*), 'Apathy syndrome' (*mukiryoku-shō*)	'*Taigaku*' (nonattendance due to laziness) '*Gakkō girai*' (disliking school)	None	None
What to do	Medical treatment Medical confinement	Discipline and punishment	Sufficient rest Total acceptance by others Support network	Good rest Some medication if required
Place to go/be	Mental hospital	Special training schools Reformatory	Home Alternative school (if so wished)	Home General hospital if required

THE PSYCHIATRIC DISCOURSE:
TŌKŌKYOHI AS MENTAL ILLNESS

In what may be called a psychiatric discourse on *tōkōkyohi*, *tōkōkyohi* has been called school phobia (*gakkō-kyōfu-shō*), school refusal (*tōkōkyohi-shō*) and apathy syndrome (*mukiryoku-shō*) by psychiatrists, psychologists, counsellors and paediatricians (Kikuchi 1989: 40). The suffix '*shō*' means syndrome, indicating that *tōkōkyohi* is an illness to be treated by experts. The psychiatric discourse has the longest record among the various kinds of all types of discourse on *tōkōkyohi* in Japan. It emerged in the 1950s when students who did not go to school were treated by medical professionals as suffering from 'school phobia', a phobic syndrome originating from the 'separation anxiety' from the mother. Later it was widely felt that 'school phobia' was too narrow a concept to grasp the problem, and broader categories of '*tōkōkyohi/futōkō*' which allow more insight into school-related factors came to be used (Inamura 1994: 4, 16).

Although the strongest dissent from the psychiatric discourse has been registered by medical experts themselves (more on this later), the psychiatric discourse on *tōkōkyohi* was quite influential, at least until the end of the 1980s. Its leading advocate is Inamura Hiroshi, former professor at Hitotsubashi University, who has written widely on *tōkōkyohi* and other 'adjustment problems' among Japanese youth. He was one of the advisers for Monbushō when it compiled the 'Handbook for the Guidance of *Tōkōkyohi*' for teachers in the mid-1980s (*Kangaerukai* 1989: 21). He is also the vice-president of the Youth Health Centre, which has ten clinics and counselling places around Tokyo employing one hundred psychiatrists, psychologists, academics, and volunteers, to treat over 400 regular consultees (*AS* 16 September 1988, Inamura 1988: 182).

Inamura is representative of the psychiatric discourse on *tōkōkyohi*. In the psychiatric paradigm, *tōkōkyohi* is seen fundamentally as a matter of the individual's maladjustment and maladaptation to society. The aim of the 'treatment' of *tōkōkyohi* therefore is to change the individual shortcomings, leaving the school environment intact. Inamura writes:

In short, *tōkōkyohi* is mostly a kind of social maladjustment which includes a specific pathology (*byōri*). Because it starts around adolescence when individuals are at school, they first fail to go to school. If it is left without appropriate treatment, or if it is aggravated, the state of maladjustment continues into their twenties and thirties. In order to overcome this, their foundation as human beings must be rebuilt, so that they learn to adjust to society. Otherwise, it is possible that they may ruin their whole life, doing nothing and in a state of autism (*jihei*).

(Inamura 1988: ii)

School is seen merely as the social environment which *happens to be* the one to which the adolescent is expected to adjust when the problem of social maladjustment manifests itself. The school environment itself is fundamentally excluded from the analysis. Although the experience of school by each student is mentioned, the underlying perspective is that of how the student has 'failed' (*tsumazuita*) in school, be it at the beginning of a new term, in a new school, in study, in examination, in friendship, in athletic club activities, in school events, etc. (pp. 117–24).

The cause of the problem is sought primarily in the personality traits of the individual student. According to Inamura, the five most common personality traits of *tōkōkyohi* students are that they are:

- oversensitive and anxious (23.9 per cent);
- perfectionist and methodical (17.1 per cent);
- self-centred and *wagamama* (selfish) (15.1 per cent);
- timid (13.1 per cent);
- unsociable (12.8 per cent).

Other characteristics which constitute the rest (18 per cent) include: lack of perseverance, hyperactivity, dependence, stubbornness and obsessiveness (Inamura 1988: 51–2).[8] This is in accordance with the observation of the psychiatric paradigm of *tōkōkyohi* made by Lock, who points out (1986) that the following personality is considered to lead to *tōkōkyohi*, i.e. the child who 'is anxious, unadaptive, does not fit well into groups, cannot make decisions, is inflexible, takes things too seriously, is socially and/or emotionally immature, is high-strung (*shinkei shitsu*) and is nervous about grades, [and] his or her health' (p. 105).

The 'family factor' is assigned high priority in the psychiatric discourse. Inquiry focuses in particular on the attitude of parents regarding child rearing. According to Inamura, the two most common attitudes among mothers of *tōkōkyohi* children are 'over-interference' (39.5 per cent) and 'over-protection and excessive love' (28.7 per cent). For fathers, they are 'non-interference and escapism' (32.6 per cent) and 'over-protection and excessive love' (18.4 per cent) (Inamura 1988: 55).[9]

In addition to these, among many other family related factors, the father's lack of a 'father-image', and the mother's anxiety and lack of self-confidence in dealing with their children are also often seen to be responsible for *tōkōkyohi* (Lock 1986: 105). Mothers in particular have often been the target of criticism (Ishikawa *et al.* 1993: iii–iv), and Lock writes of 'the child and his mother . . . cajoled and coerced into accepting their inadequacies as social and moral beings' (Lock 1986: 107). In fact, out of 441 consultees of 'K clinic' (which is the central facility of the Youth Health Centre),[10] 145 were parents who visited the clinic without accompanying their *tōkōkyohi* children, and they were mostly mothers (Inamura 1988: 182–4).

Underlying such analyses of personality is an implied criticism of the individual. Inamura writes:

> It has been over 20 years since I became a clinician, and of late I am deeply moved by the fact that there are so many children who manifest problems so easily.
>
> (Inamura 1988: 58)

What Inamura means by the ability 'to adjust to society' is the ability to 'correct the problems of self-formation (*jiga-keisei*), such as the lack of perseverance, excessive sensitivity, vulnerability, perfectionism, etc. (p. 72). The treatment Inamura and his group offer in the Youth Health Centre therefore puts a lot of emphasis upon behavioural training in which pre-scribed routine and group activities play the pivotal role (pp. 178–250). These are set up ultimately on the same principle as school itself – precisely the paradigm that *tōkōkyohi* students are trying to dissociate themselves from.

An example

The problem of the psychiatric paradigm of *tōkōkyohi* is well described by the following example, one of seven cases which appeared in *Jirei ni manabu shinri ryōhō* [Psychotherapy learnt through case studies] (Kawai 1990: 1–23). Each case study consists of a report written by a counsellor, followed by comments by other experts. There are considerable variations in the cases presented as well as in the views expressed by commentators. Among them, the comment made by Okonogi Keigo – an eminent psychiatrist and professor at Keiō University who is also one of the founding members of the Youth Health Centre – concerning a case entitled 'school phobia' presents a good exam-ple of the psychiatric discourse.

The report is about a 9-year-old boy named 'M'. The report begins with a brief introduction under the sub-headings of 'main complaints and initial contact', 'family constitution', and 'life history'. In the 'main complaints' the counsellor, Akita Sumiko, writes:

> he began to be absent from school from the second term of Grade 3, and in the third term he attended school only for about 10 days. In

Grade 4, he attended the opening ceremony of the year but has been absent since. When pressed to go to school, he clings to the pillar of his home. He refuses to get up and sleeps without breakfast and lunch until after 4 pm when his brother comes home. He avoids his mother and will not talk to her. The troubled mother consulted the school principal, who subsequently contacted me.

(Akita 1990: 1)

In the 'life history' Mr 'Y', the homeroom teacher at the time 'M' started his 'school phobia', is described as a:

very enthusiastic and strict teacher, and ['M'] often got scolded by him. His friend who happened to accompany ['M'] to my counselling room one day said that 'M is the first to be scolded'. There was even such discrimination against [M] that [the teacher] did not give [M] his test paper. [M] was also made to write a special diary, and the teacher checked the spelling and the content in detail. This seems to have been painful to 'M'. He often told the teacher that he had forgotten this diary and [from around that time] he gradually came to be absent from school.

(Akita 1990: 2)

The report on the sixth visit to the counsellor reads:

'M' told his mother that he would go to school from the following Monday. 'M' then heard from his friend that Mr 'Y' [who had been hospitalised due to illness] had been discharged and would return to work. 'M' then stopped saying that he would go to school. Mr 'Y' is the teacher whose use of corporal punishment has been causing problems. When his mother said that she did not know about it, 'M' told his mother that 'I got hit over my mouth. You remember when my lips got swollen, don't you? I also came home another time with a bump [on the head after being hit by Mr 'Y'].

(Akita 1990: 10)

In the end, the counsellor who showed strong empathy to 'M' succeeded in helping him to return to school. His homeroom teacher at that time was Miss 'K', a newly-appointed 20 year old, whom 'M' thought 'pretty', i.e. the antithesis of the authoritarian 'Y' (p. 4).

Although the counsellor used quasi-medical terms such as 'treatment' and 'school phobia', what she actually did was to listen to the boy, play games with him and accompany him to school when opportunities arose.

She did not judge 'M' in any way, nor push 'M' to return to school. The comment made by Okonogi, a psychiatrist, on the counsellor's report, however, presents a different sort of interpretation (Okonogi 1990).

Okonogi remarks first that this case may be explained by 'adjustment failure' caused by 'socio-psychological stress' induced by various events including what the boy experienced at school. His analysis of the school environment, however, does not go further than this. His comment actually serves to divert attention further and further from the 'socio-psychological stress' and to shift the emphasis increasingly to what he regards as the idiosyncratic characteristics of the boy himself. Okonogi writes:

> It seems that the strict teacher, Mr 'Y', and the father, of whom 'M' is afraid, overlap in the boy's mind. He also has something which might be called 'the complex of a stupid young brother towards a wise old brother'. Thus there is a frustration [*zasetsu*] in establishing a dependable relationship with his elder brother. My diagnosis is that this case represents adjustment failure combined with neurotic conflict [*shinkeishō-teki kattō*], and that the prolongation of these two situations has developed into *tōkōkyohi*.
>
> (Okonogi 1990: 14)

Okonogi continues:

> I suspect, however, that the various life events which are regarded [above] as the cause of socio-psychological stress are in fact induced by the immature and hampered development of personality [of the boy]. It appears that his ability to adjust to the group is immature for a primary school pupil, and he does not seem to have a stable friendship with his classmates. . . . The image of father which might provide an ideal for the boy's self is poor. . . . It seems that M has not yet found a model on the basis of which he can realise his social self as a man. This is all the more reason why he exhibits weakness and reverts easily to the infantile expectation of being taken care of in all respects by his mother.
>
> (Okonogi 1990: 14)

The relevance of such an analysis might certainly depend on the individual case. What is problematic, however, is the fact that the focus of the analysis is given *a priori* to the individuals themselves or to their families, when the action taken by the boy suggests that there is a strong relationship between his *tōkōkyohi* and his experience of teacher 'Y'. The analysis is especially problematic when M's experience is shared by numerous other children all around the country who say more or less the same thing about their experiences of school. It suggests that *tōkōkyohi* is more than can be explained in terms of 'adjustment problems' and 'nervous conflict' within the mind of each individual child. Without being able to take external factors sufficiently into consideration, the psychiatric discourse about *tōkōkyohi* can easily turn to a victim-blaming and family-blaming ideology, such as Lock (1986) maintains to be especially strong in Japanese society (p. 100).

The impact of psychiatric discourse and practice upon the lives of children

How does such psychiatric discourse affect the lives of *tōkōkyohi* students? Students attending *Tokyo Shure*, a leading alternative school for *tōkōkyohi* children, conducted a survey of students attending similar schools all around Japan (*Kodomotachi* 1991: 200–40). Even though the data were collected from alternative schools, the clientele of which are expected to be relatively open-minded and understanding toward *tōkōkyohi*, this survey showed that out of 265 children of all ages, 24 per cent had previously visited mental clinics (p. 217). In fact, 62 per cent of the respondents indicated that their family 'accepted' their not going to school (p. 212–13). That one in four of these children had actually visited a mental clinic therefore probably indicates conservatively the broader social tendency to attribute *tōkōkyohi* to psychological maladjustment problems.

In *Kodomotachi ga kataru tōkōkyohi* (*Tōkōkyohi* as discussed by children), a collection of 402 accounts by *tōkōkyohi* children, it is frequently mentioned that they had either been urged to go to a mental hospital or had actually visited one. Honma Tami, a 14-year-old girl writes:

> My father died and I was in a state of shock . . . and did not go to school [for some time]. . . . One day, when I went to school, my teacher shouted at me . . . 'If you do *tōkōkyohi* because your father died, your father would feel sad'. I went home crying. . . . I stopped going to school then. . . . The teacher would visit me at home to bring exercise sheets and tests. . . . He said that if I did not do them, it would affect my teacher's report [*naishinsho*] and I would fall behind with my study. When I had an argument with him over the phone, he said 'Go to a mental hospital'. I told my mother about this and she took me to a hospital. When I got agitated they gave me medicine to take. When the medicine did not work, I was taken to another hospital. This was repeated about three times. In the hospital, they did various psychological tests and gave me lots of medicine to take. . . .

Tami continues that:

> [At the end of the year the teacher visited me again to say] 'Please write
> your memoir of the school to put in the graduation album'. . . . I wrote
> about my father's death, the fact that I was urged to go to a mental
> hospital by my teacher, *ijime* by my friends. . . . The teacher read it and
> said, 'Is this all? . . . Why do you have to write that I told you to go to a
> mental hospital'. I said, 'because I really hated it'. . . . When I went to
> school to attend the graduation ceremony, the graduation album con-
> taining compositions was handed to everyone. . . . But my composition
> was not included.
>
> (Ishikawa *et al.* 1993: 451)

The important parts of Tami's experience – the harassment by the teacher,
the mentioning of mental hospital, being taken to hospital, the visit to one
hospital after another and being given medicines,[11] the exclusion of the
student's composition from the album – are by no means isolated incidents
but shared widely with a number of students.

Muta Takeo, who has managed an alternative school for *tōkōkyohi* children
since the mid-1980s, points out that about 10 per cent of the children who
attend his school have experienced being hospitalised in mental institutions.
He remarks that parents often take their children to a mental hospital when
they get violent at home or when they stop eating meals, and that most
psychiatrists advise parents to leave the children in hospital (Kikuchi
1989: 38).

Satō Taizō, Deputy Director of Tokyo Metropolitan Umegaoka Hospital,
remarked that in 1985 one in eight in-patients were *tōkōkyohi* children
(Kikuchi 1989: 38). The 18-year-old 'E' was one of them. He was taken
to Umegaoka Hospital thinking that his eyes needed medical treatment. His
parents, troubled by his violence at home, left him there without letting him
know their intention. 'E' said:

> I would like people to stop putting dubious medical names to *tōkōkyohi*
> in order to send students to mental hospitals. I did *tōkōkyohi* because I
> did not like school because it gave me little freedom. I was put into a
> medical prison which allowed me even less freedom. There, you get
> locked up for 24 hours [in a tiny three-and-a-half-mat solitary confine-
> ment with tiny window with lattice and unbreakable plastic glass] and
> are constantly watched by tough, male nurses. . . . In that hospital,
> rules are everything. If you obey the rules, you are good, and if not,
> bad. If you resist nurses, they give your face a good slapping. . . . I
> could bear it [for three months] because my senses were numb due to

the medication they gave me four times a day. But if I had stayed there longer, I would have become like other people there, who were all so apathetic. . . . If I had not escaped,[12] I might be still there. . . . I want people to stop sending children to mental hospitals just because they stop going to school. . . . In such a place, even a healthy person will get sick due to the excessive stress.

(Kikuchi 1989: 36)

His experience indicates that some mental hospitals in Japan function almost as a sub-system of school, as an institution whose primary objective is to correct the behaviour of children with problems of 'adjustment' to society/school. The difference from school is that it is all medicalised – it is done in the name of 'treatment', using medication given by medical professionals within the framework of medical ideology.

A 19-year-old boy 'I' was also put in the same hospital in a similar situation – in his case with the understanding that he needed treatment for his legs. He was kept in hospital for seven months. He states that he came to feel more cornered and distressed after the 'treatment' than before. He says:

After being discharged from the hospital, I felt so inferior that I could not face my friends in the neighbourhood. Even if I meet someone new, I dread the possibility of their finding out that I was in a mental hospital. I have become far more isolated than before.

(Kikuchi 1989: 37)

The experiences of these students indicate that the psychiatric discourse on *tōkōkyohi* involves not just abstract views and ideas but also a concrete practice, involving specific medical examinations, medications, treatment including hospitalisation, which exerts enormous power over the lives of *tōkōkyohi* students. It is a social process in which students are first 'informally' labelled by lay people such as teachers and parents, then 'formally and institutionally' by medical professionals, as they receive more and more 'treatment'. As the words of 'K' and 'I' suggest, it is a social process which deprives them of the power to live for themselves.

It is not surprising that some psychiatrists are very critical of 'treatment' based on such psychiatric discourse. One child psychiatrist, Kado Shin'ichirō, remarks that so-called 'apathy syndrome' (*mukiryoku-shō*) is more likely to be caused by the labelling of 'being mentally sick' and 'being in the mental hospital' (Kikuchi 1989: 40). Likewise, Uchida Ryōko, a counsellor at Kōsei Hospital, maintains that it is the 'treatment' itself given in this paradigm which might be causing what Inamura and others call 'apathy syndrome' (*Kangaerukai* 1989: 14). Psychiatrists who are critical of this 'psychiatric paradigm' have 'treated' *tōkōkyohi* students in an entirely different way, i.e. by offering the kind of 'hospitals' in which *tōkōkyohi* children love to stay.

THE BEHAVIOURAL DISCOURSE: *TŌKŌKYOHI* AS LAZINESS

Second, there is what might be called the behavioural discourse on *tōkōkyohi*. Although *tōkōkyohi* is not regarded as an illness in this paradigm, the assumptions underlying it are shared with the psychiatric discourse in the sense that *tōkōkyohi* is regarded as the fault of student, stemming from laziness, idleness, selfishness (*wagamama*) or lack of discipline. Together with the psychiatric discourse, this constitutes the view of *tōkōkyohi* widely held by those who are not directly involved in it. This kind of thinking is reflected in terms such as '*taigaku*' (truancy) and '*zuru yasumi*' (bunking off/wagging), and '*gakkō-girai*' (disliking school) under which *tōkōkyohi* is classified in Monbushō statistics. Such labels indicate the way the majority of teachers see *tōkōkyohi*. A survey conducted by Monbushō in 1989 revealed that most teachers thought that the most common type of *tōkōkyohi* was '*taigaku*', i.e. illegitimate nonattendance at school due to laziness (ME 1989).

The corollary of this notion of *tōkōkyohi* is that its 'solution' lies in increased discipline, training, guidance and punishment. Until recently, many private facilities were designed as retraining centres for 'problem children' and operated on the principle of 'the tougher the training the better it serves to correct the behaviour and spirit of *tōkōkyohi* students'. Places like 'Totsuka Yacht School', 'Kazenoko-gakuen', and 'Fudōjuku', in which a number of students have died, were all based on this way of thinking and practice. These 'schools' functioned as a subsystem of formal education, often endorsed and recommended by the local school authorities. The aim of these 'schools' was to put the students back to 'normal' by resorting to a degree of violence which would be impossible in the framework of formal education (see Chapter 4).

Although Monbushō guidelines for the conduct of special schools of this sort became stricter after the Kazenoko-gakuen incident, a new possibility that *tōkōkyohi* students might be sent to reformatories (or detention homes) emerged (Fujita 1997; Akuzawa *et al.* 1997). Underlying this is the deep-seated notion that *tōkōkyohi* is problematic and socially deviant behaviour undistinguishable from other forms of antisocial, delinquent behaviour.

In the case of the murder and robbery of a mother and her 7-year-old son in Tokyo in 1988, three *tōkōkyohi* boys were arrested, based on a list of *tōkōkyohi* students handed to police by the school authorities. Out of 18 students who were absent from junior high schools in the neighbourhood on the day the murder happened, only these three boys did not have clear alibis. They were arrested without evidence, kept in custody for 22 days, during which time they were put under enormous pressure to confess, until they were released because the alibi of one of them was proved (Katō 1993: 14–21). A similar case occurred in Akita, where *tōkōkyohi* students were suspected of arson (Katō 1993: 21–3).

Because both psychiatric and behavioural discourses are founded upon the same assumption that *tōkōkyohi* is socially deviant behaviour stemming from some idiosyncratic problem on the part of each individual student, the methods adopted in institutions, whether mental hospitals or *tōkōkyohi* wards in the reformatory, tend to be remarkably similar. In both institutions, enormous emphasis is put upon the importance of locking-up the students, minute-by-minute routine, extremely detailed rules, water-tight surveillance, medication, and the use of violence as punishment for disobedience. Whether as 'treatment' or 'training', both institutions 'produce' almost exactly the same type of human beings – the kind of students who are prone to be apathetic and passive.

An even more fundamental assumption underlying both psychiatric and behavioural discourses, is 'school absolutism', the creed that it is absolutely necessary for children to go to school no matter what (Okuchi 1992: 35–7). It certainly is the most fundamental premise of the society described as the 'mass-education society' (Kariya 1995) (see Chapter 2) or 'schooling society' (*gakkō-ka shakai*) in which the whole society becomes like a school, and the school becomes a model for society as a whole (Horio 1994: 370). In such a society it is taken for granted that children are at school most of the day, and it is 'abnormal' and 'wrong' if they are not. In such a milieu, not going to school tends to be seen as 'shameful'. *Tōkōkyohi* is thus stigmatised and *tōkōkyohi* children (and their parents) exposed to the critical 'glance' of neighbours and friends. A teacher with a *tōkōkyohi* son writes that, when she wanted to show the report she had written about her son to her colleague, she was advised that she 'shouldn't show such a thing' but 'should conceal' her son's *tōkōkyohi* (Ishikawa *et al.* 1995: 85). Furukawa Akika (11) wrote a poem entitled 'Correspondence finished' regarding her experience of being cut off from her pen friend, which goes:

'I heard that you are
a *tōkōkyohi* bad child
different from myself'.
With this letter
our correspondence is finished. . . .

It is a small world.
A friend of my classmate's mother
is the friend of a friend of my pen pal's mother.
Thus she came to know about.
Tōkōkyohi
Who decides it is bad?

(Ishikawa et al. 1993: 151)

Tōkōkyohi *as laziness: the parents' view*

The prevalence and persistence of the behavioural discourse on *tōkōkyohi* is not unrelated to the fact that *tōkōkyohi* students often face tremendous difficulty in getting up in the morning, and the way they spend their time at home *does appear* to be idle and indolent. They often sleep very long hours (most of the day time), watch television, play computer games, read books and comics, often without talking much to family members or anybody else. When students do not have somatic symptoms, this kind of behavioural pattern looks bad in the eyes of parents and teachers.

The consequence is that parents often pressure and coerce students to go to school, and are likely to persist in such pressure until they are suddenly confronted with the chilling recognition that their children are genuinely in need of rest and that persisting in forcing them to go to school might actually drive the children to their deaths. The moment parents awake to this realisation is perhaps the most crucial point determining the course of *tōkōkyohi* experience of their children. It is also the most telling moment which provides the key to understanding the *tōkōkyohi* phenomenon. Several recollections of this awakening by parents are quoted at some length below, since nothing else conveys as vividly as their own words the tension and difficulty both parents and children experience in *tōkōkyohi*.

Story 1

The 14-year-old daughter of Hisatomi Masako came to miss school from time to time because of headaches. This escalated in the following year, and the doctor who examined her diagnosed that she was suffering from low blood pressure, orthostatic ataxia (*kiritsusei shicchōshō*), and depression. The mother writes:

> I did not try to understand the feelings of my daughter and thought of school as a place everyone has to go to . . . . In the morning, I would tell her to 'get up and go to school', lecture her about having to go to school, ask her questions as to why she would not go to school, and take

her *futon* away by force. She would creep under the *futon* or escape into the closet. Every day was like this, and I dreaded each morning. . . . But one day, when I tried to rip the *futon* off as usual, she glared at me with the most terrible look that I had ever seen. It was then that I saw how much I had pushed her up against the wall . . . I really felt sorry for what I had done . . . . Around that time I heard of the Parents' Association. . . . When I started to change after learning [about *tōkōkyohi* in that group], my daughter began to open her heart little by little. When I grew out of my 'faith in school' (*gakkō shinkō*), my daughter came to be able to stay home in peace.

(Ishikawa *et al.* 1995: 439)

Story 2

'Y.K.', mother of a then 14-year-old boy writes:

My son's homeroom teacher and the teacher in charge of 'life guidance' [*seikatsu shidō*] insisted: 'Even if it costs your life ['*shindemo*' which literally means 'even if you die'], you must come to school. We'll make a man out of you. It is the fault of your parents. . . . One day my son begged me to let him sleep in peace. So I contacted the school to notify it of his absence. Then the 'life guidance' teacher came to the house, entered the room where my son was resting, woke him up, made him put on the school uniform and berated him saying, 'What are you going to do about your future? What are you living for? I did not think that you were of such a pathetically rotten disposition [*konjyō no kusatta yatsu*]'. . . . Some hours later, the *fusuma* [papered sliding door] of the house was smashed to pieces. . . . On the following day, I took my son to Dr 'Y', who said to me helplessly, 'You should not corner him'. On the way back home, my son said, 'Please be careful, Mother. All I can manage is to stop myself from committing suicide; and I cannot trust myself to hold a carving knife. If I did I might hurt you'. I could not believe my ears because he said it so calmly. . . . Some days later he said, 'I will not go to high school. I don't care if I do not graduate from junior high school'. I said instinctively, 'That's all right'.

(Ishikawa *et al.* 1995: 642)

Story 3

Okuchi Shigeo in Tokyo talks about how he and his wife (Okuchi Keiko, the leading advocate of *tōkōkyohi* children) struggled to push their son back to primary school in the first two years of his *tōkōkyohi*. He says:

We were convinced that 'school is a place to go to', without thinking about what was actually happening there. I sometimes hit and kicked my son when he refused to go to school. I would take him to school on my bicycle and not let him in the house if he came back.

(Okuchi 1990: 100)

Okuchi Keiko continues about her son who by then had attended school only intermittently for some two years:

When he was Grade 5 he really pushed himself to prepare for the athletics day. He survived the day all right, but after that he became like a person whose energy had been completely drained. He developed anorexia and became unable either to digest food or to stand up and walk by himself.

Whilst they were in a state of confusion, they were introduced to Watanabe Takashi, the Head of the Department of Child Psychiatry at the National Kōnodai Hospital in Tokyo, whom they visited. On their visit, Okuchi writes:

My son saw Dr Watanabe only once. But in that single session which lasted for nearly two hours, the doctor listened to my son carefully and deeply empathised with him. [When the session was over], my son said, 'Mother, I feel so good. It's like having wings [to fly]' . . . and that was the end of his anorexia. My husband and I felt suddenly awakened by looking at our [cheerful] son and realised that we had failed to see all the signs our son was sending to us even to the extent of risking his life.

(Ishikawa *et al.* 1995: 117–8)

Story 4

Ishii Izuko, a mother of a then 11-year-old boy who had been bullied at school, writes:

My son said one day, 'Devils are living in the school, and I don't want to go where devils are'. . . . At that time, however, I thought that if my son stopped going to school his whole life would be destroyed. . . . I could not think of his future outside of the framework of schools. . . . One day, however, he looked so distressed that I said to him, 'Ken, you can let the frustration about school out to me. You can do anything. I will never get angry'. He asked me many times 'Can I really do anything? Who knows what I might do? Is it really OK? You'll never get angry?'

He then started violently to throw away everything related to school – textbooks neatly displayed on his shelf, notebooks, materials for calligraphy, music, art – smashing the window and stamping on the school bag, shouting and crying loudly and violently. When I saw this, I thought what a stupid parent I had been, forcing him to go to school while he was suffering so much. . . . I cried with him. . . .

Even after this incident, however, her son kept attending the school for some more days until he was struck with a severe headache. She continues:

I immediately took him to hospital . . . where CT scan found an abnormality with brain cerebrosinal fluid [*nōzui-eki*] [which required hospitalisation and operation]. When the doctor told me that 'this is a stress related condition', I felt as if I had been hit on the head by a hammer. . . . I had been so stupid, when school has no value at all compared to the life of my son.

(Ishikawa *et al.* 1995: 56–9)

Story 5

The 17-year-old son of Kobi Yoshie stopped going to school because he could not get up in the morning. His homeroom teacher visited him to give him a warning that failing to attend school further would mean failing the year. Under pressure, he agreed to go to school. Yoshie recalls what actually happened on the following morning:

My son came out of his room in school uniform but he could not then move from the sofa. He writhed in agony with nausea and numbness . . . and showed us a bottle of analgesics and said 'I took them'. . . . The ambulance came and took my son who could no longer stand. . . . It was a cold morning and I thought of him swallowing capsules one by one at four o'clock in the morning, in the dark before dawn, and imagined how much he had suffered. . . . At that time stories of suicide by students of junior high, senior high, and even primary school, were in the paper almost daily . . . . [My husband later said] 'Facing that sort of situation, you can see life stripped bare of all inessentials, and you can directly touch the very essence of life. Academic qualifications, occupation and social status, are all like clothing for the society. . . . But the important thing is just to live a life. . . . I suddenly gained a calmness in the conviction that it is all right just to be able to support oneself by doing something one likes'. For me too, this was a big turning point of my life.

(Ishikawa *et al.* 1995: 170–2)

Story 6

Baba Sumiko, mother of a 16-year-old *tōkōkyohi* student, writes:

> Although I was not an 'education mother' [*kyōiku mama*], I was deeply saturated with the belief that you cannot be happy unless you go to a good school and get a good academic result. So when my son started to miss school, I got terribly depressed. . . . But one day, I heard him say, 'I want to die' . . . I suddenly awoke to the realisation that we had been insensitive to the feelings of our son. . . . One day I returned home from work and could not find the kitchen knife. I rushed into his room trembling and put my hand upon the mouth of my (sleeping) son. I thought then from the bottom of my heart that 'All I need is that Kōta is alive and smiling', and that 'School does not matter at all'. It was a turning point in my life.
>
> (Ishikawa *et al.* 1995: 421)

These stories explain how the 'faith in school' and the notion of '*tōkōkyohi* as idleness' are entwined, and how difficult it is for parents, even when they are genuinely concerned about the future of their children, to break free from such beliefs. The change in the view of parents as well as in the way they relate to their children come with enormous difficulty often after sensing that their child's life is threatened. It is difficult for parents to accept *tōkōkyohi* children, if only because it ultimately challenges the very foundation of their own life, i.e. the belief system as to what constitutes 'happiness' and how to achieve it. It shakes the basis of their life, their life style, work, and family relationships, etc. By being reluctant to accept their *tōkōkyohi* children, parents are often defending values they have taken for granted. The difficulty they face is that they are required to shift the paradigm of their own lives, from the familiar to one which allows their children (literally) to live (Asakura 1995: 206–7). This is not an easy thing to achieve, and precisely because of that, the dominant behavioural discourse about *tōkōkyohi*, which demands that children change, remains prevalent, deep-seated and hard to eliminate in the 'mass-education society' saturated with 'faith in school'. The behavioural discourse serves to secure the dominant belief system of Japanese society.

Tōkōkyohi *as laziness: the students' view*

Given the nature of the behavioural discourse, it is understandable that the strongest contestation to the notion of *tōkōkyohi* as truancy has been presented by *tōkōkyohi* students themselves. Suzuki Akira (aged 16), who now attends *Tokyo Shure*, comments on the Monbushō survey which indicated that the majority of teachers regarded *tōkōkyohi* as a manifestation of laziness.

> I thought this was absolutely wrong. First of all, there is no truth in it because the questions [in the survey] were directed to teachers and not to *tōkōkyohi* students themselves. It is hard to imagine that teachers would give answers which might be inconvenient to themselves (i.e. schools). Furthermore, if indeed *tōkōkyohi* were a manifestation of laziness, it would be inconceivable that *tōkōkyohi* students could worry and suffer to such an extent that they commit suicide.
>
> (*Kodomotachi* 1991: 166–7)

With other students of *Tokyo Shure* who were also deeply disconcerted with the implications of the Monbushō survey, Akira formed an 'executive committee' to design their own survey and collect data from *tōkōkyohi* students themselves. They gathered data in 1989 from 265 students attending alternative schools for *tōkōkyohi* students all around the country (*Kodomotachi* 1991: 200–40). With regard to the results, Akira remarked:

> We found through the survey that *tōkōkyohi* is never the manifestation of laziness. On the contrary, our survey indicated that *tōkōkyohi* is a really painful experience. . . . 'To commit suicide' was the most frequently mentioned response chosen by 108 out of 265 students as the 'thought they had during the time of *tōkōkyohi*'. There were also a large number of students who indicated that they thought of 'leaving home' or 'killing someone'. If one lives a normal life, such thoughts would never come to one's mind. . . . [Moreover, the most frequently mentioned] 'things experienced during the time of *tōkōkyohi*' were headache, stomachache, fever, dizziness, etc. With these results, nobody can say that *tōkōkyohi* is an act of laziness, as Monbushō does.
>
> (*Kodomotachi* 1991: 167–8)

It should be noted, however, that the conviction that *tōkōkyohi* is not a manifestation of laziness, does not come easily even to *tōkōkyohi* students themselves. Akira himself points out that he used to think of *tōkōkyohi* students as 'the scum of the earth', and that even after he became *tōkōkyohi* himself, he suspected for about a year that it might be selfishness (*wagamama*) on his part not to go to school. He stopped going to school because of teachers who used violence and because of *ijime* among students. Although at first he pretended to be sick in order to avoid school, he soon developed real headaches and stomach-aches. Sometimes he vomited all night and in due course he was diagnosed as autonomic dystonia (*jiritsu-shinkei-shicchō-shō*) (*Kodomotachi* 1991: 160–4).

The notion that it is 'bad' not to go to school is shared widely not only by teachers and parents but also by students, and *tōkōkyohi* students often feel guilty and tormented by the thought that they are doing something wrong. This is especially the case for those *who do not have* somatic symptoms. Paradoxically the stigma of 'being absent from school' often makes it more difficult for students to resume going to school. Tsuneno Yūjirō (13) explains:

> If you miss school for no good reason [*zuru yasumi*] (?!), you are asked later 'why didn't you come to school yesterday?' So, you cannot just miss one day. Unless you miss a few days, you fall under suspicion. But this is the trap. If you miss school three days, you want to miss it another day. If you miss it four days, you want to miss it yet another day. In this way, you become more and more loath to go to school. . . . When I missed school for about a month, I began to feel guilty. I understood then that to be absent from school without having caught a cold was nothing but '*zuru yasumi*' [truancy], and that I thought that '*zuru yasumi*' is something the meanest kinds of human beings do. I often thought about returning to school, but when I began to wonder how I could explain my absence for one month, I could not bring myself to go. I felt that I reached the point of no return.
>
> (*Kodomotachi* 1991: 103–4)

The only way not to be labelled 'lazy' is to pretend to be sick (as both Akira and Yūjirō suggested above) and this adds another layer of guilt over not being truthful. Toyosato Tetsu (17), who declares himself to be a 'staunch lazy bones' writes:

> I felt shamed and disgraced for lying to my parents, missing schools for laziness . . . and, despite doing such wrong things, enjoying television. . . . I was trapped in the situation where I could not go to school because I worried about the way my teachers and friends looked at me. . . . I had reached the point of no return. I thought that I had to keep telling a lie all my life. . . . I sometimes thought about how I might kill myself.
>
> (*Kodomotachi* 1991: 111)

Both Yūjirō and Tetsu write about the realisation that they had 'reached the point of no return', a sense of hopelessness about the future as well as about themselves. This suggests that those who do not have clear somatic symptoms which legitimise their absence from school may experience greater inner conflict. Even though they do not have somatic symptoms, however, they seek the help of medical professionals. Yūjirō writes that he was so worried, 'all day and every day', about 'ending up as a beggar', that he went to see a child psychiatrist regularly to get medication, which did not work (*Kodomotachi* 1991: 104). Tetsu too visited hospitals regularly, first general hospital, and then psychiatric hospital. He writes that he himself 'had almost forgotten that he was not really sick . . . and did not have much difficulty in visiting a mental hospital' (*Kodomotachi* 1991: 109–10).

Miyamoto Akiko, mother of a then 16-year-old girl, describes how her daughter, Sakura, behaved on the way home from the hospital.

> While we were waiting for a bus, she spotted her classmates. She took out the bag of medicine from her bag and carried it in such a way that it was clearly visible to her classmates. She said, 'Today, I am fine because I got medicine'. I thought then that it was just as I expected. If she takes or carries medicine, both she and her classmates understand that she is sick.
>
> (Ishikawa *et al.* 1995: 603)

These episodes indicate that regardless of the physical condition of each *tōkōkyohi* student, the fear of being labelled as 'lazy' is strong, and the anticipation of the stigma can stain self-esteem more seriously than being labelled 'sick'. Students such as Yūjirō and Tetsu who stop going to school without legitimate reason present the most difficult case of *tōkōkyohi*, both for themselves and for those who try to understand them.

The words of Yūjirō and Tetsu also raise an important issue about the classification of *tōkōkyohi*. The realisation that 'they have reached a point of no return' indicates that there is a qualitative difference between long-term absence from school on the one hand and students who are loath to go to school but are still somehow continuing to go. While the study by Morita (1991) on *futōkō* showed the quantitative spectrum of various levels of *futōkō*, it should be noted that each individual student may cross a point somewhere in that continuum when they feel that they can no longer return to school. The accounts given by Yūjirō and Tetsu also suggest that even those who felt relatively relaxed about missing school at an early stage can feel deeply troubled as they realise how difficult it has become for them to return to school. Although Morita argues that many students have little hesitancy or feelings of guilt in missing school (pp. 5, 126–7), this perception may well change as it becomes more difficult over time for students to return to school.

At the same time, accounts of *tōkōkyohi* given by students and their parents consistently indicate that it is unlikely that students have clear anti-school sentiment or values at the beginning of their *tōkōkyohi*. The inner conflict they show suggests that their nonattendance at school arises from factors other than anti-school values that compel them not to attend school. The experience of all kinds of difficulties revealed by the survey conducted by the children of *Tokyo Shure* suggests the same, and so do the words and deeds of Tsuneno Yūjirō, Toyosato Tetsu and Miyamoto Sakura, quoted above.

It appears that *tōkōkyohi* is neither a manifestation of idleness nor the reflection of clearly defined anti-school values and sentiments. Instead, it appears that at the beginning of the *tōkōkyohi*, students may be confused, bewildered, and troubled, but not necessarily completely without a critical awareness of school. But, as they come to terms with their own *tōkōkyohi*, they gradually develop a clear understanding of their experience of school, which usually involves profound criticism of and/or detachment from the school they know. This often appears to be the case even if they none-theless decide to return to school. In the citizens' discourse, in which *tōkōkyohi* is seen as student resistance to school this is the aspect particularly emphasised.

CITIZENS' DISCOURSE: *TŌKŌKYOHI* AS RESISTANCE

A coordinated contestation of the major discourses of *tōkōkyohi*, especially psychiatric discourse, was launched in 1988 in a symposium organised by a group called '*Tōkōkyohi o kangaeru kinkyū shūkai jikkō ūnkai*' ('Executive com-mittee to call for an urgent meeting to think about *tōkōkyohi*', abbreviated as '*Kangaerukai*' in this book). This group, consisting of concerned parents, psychiatrists, paediatricians, counsellors, lawyers, teachers, and students, was formed primarily to protest against the theory and practice of Inamura Hiroshi, the leading advocate of the psychiatric discourse, that *tōkōkyohi* is an illness which can jeopardise the life of the child well into adult life. Inamura's view had been under banner headlines in the evening edition of *Asahi shinbun* on 16 September 1988. In the symposium attended by some 800 people, including representatives of 27 small alternative schools and citizens' groups supporting *tōkōkyohi* students and parents from all over the country, all sorts of distrust and misgivings about the psychiatric (and behavioural) discourse was expressed from both lay and professional people (*Kangaerukai* 1989).

The point most forcefully argued by this group is that *tōkōkyohi* is not an illness. Underlying this is the view that the problem is not one of maladjustment to school nor is it a fault to be attributed to the individual student, as tended to be the case with the labelling with negative connotations within the framework of the victim-blaming ideology (*Kangaerukai* 1989: 99). Instead, their criticism of the dominant discourse was based on the notion that 'it is school which is sick and not children' and therefore that the 'cure' of *tōkōkyohi* will not be found within the individual, but that the 'solution' should be sought in changing the schools, and the society of which school is a part (Ishikawa *et al.* 1993: ii). The insistence that '*tōkōkyohi* is not an illness' is coupled with the critique of the education system as the structural cause of *tōkōkyohi*. Okuchi Keiko, the leading advocate of '*Kangaerukai*' writes:

> Why did children begin to turn their back on school? The reasons include *ijime*, corporal punishment, Spartan training in *bukatsu*, regimentation through minute school rules, academic competition, education which is standardised, ignores individuality and destroys friendship, which inevitably induces fear, distrust, alienation, and exhaustion on the part of students. Related to this is the problem of home, which has become like school, as well as the problem of a society which overemphasises academic qualifications. School is no longer a place where each individual child can grow while feeling secure, and it therefore becomes necessary for children to distance themselves from school. . . . *Tōkōkyohi* is a response of trying to protect oneself from self-destruction. It is their challenge to the educational environment of today.
>
> (*Kangaerukai* 1989: 99)

While such a view has strong political implications, it is noteworthy that it has primarily emerged from the practical search of parents and medical professionals for a way actually to help *tōkōkyohi* children. The symposium proceedings contain doubts expressed about the psychiatric paradigm by those familiar with its practice (*Kangaerukai* 1989).

Uchida Ryōko, a counsellor at Kōsei Hospital, points out that sometimes students who missed school for several days were hospitalised in a mental institution, without being examined, and after consultation with the parents alone. Once hospitalised, they were often locked up for about two weeks without visitors under heavy medication, and released only on condition of return to school (ibid.: 14). Wakabayashi Minoru, a paediatrician, points out that the medicine prescribed for *tōkōkyohi* is mostly anti-depressant but on occasion the medication for epilepsy may also be used. Parkingson's disease medication may also be used to suppress the side-effects of taking other medication over a long time (ibid.: 22). The editor of a journal called *Psychiatric Medicine* remarked that schools, counsellors and psychiatrists often recommend *tōkōkyohi* children be committed to mental hospitals designed for adults and therefore utterly unsuitable for children (ibid.: 58). One mother with a *tōkōkyohi* child said that her son was happy not to go to school, but she got worried after reading Inamura's book which contends that *tōkōkyohi* should be treated at an early stage. She subsequently contacted Tsukuba University (where Professor Inamura was then located) which advised that her son be hospitalised immediately in Urawa Nervous Sanatrium, a facility with locked-up wards. Alerted by this, their son was persuaded to return to school, only to resume *tōkōkyohi* shortly after (ibid.: 60).

Just as the dominant discourses have their respective institutional foundation (i.e. mental hospitals and Spartan schools), so the citizens' discourse is also supported by two kinds of facilities. One is the numerous small, alternative schools and other facilities established by citizens' groups for *tōkōkyohi* children. These were founded partly due to the critique of mainstream education, but also because there was a pressing need in each locality to create a place where children could spend their time with some human company instead of staying at home for months or years.

Tokyo Shure, which was established in 1985 by Okuchi Keiko, a former teacher and the mother of *tōkōkyohi* children, was the precursor of some 150 small, alternative schools and parents' associations for *tōkōkyohi* children scattered all over Japan (Ishikawa *et al.* 1993: 15–26). *Shure* operates on the basis of the principles of 'freedom', 'self-governing by children' and 'emphasis on the individuality of each child'. These principles were gradually developed through the interaction between staff (rather than 'teachers') and children (rather than 'students'), relating with each other in an egalitarian and non-hierarchical atmosphere. The school is also open to society in that all kinds of people are invited to give all sorts of talks, varying from a talk by a homeless man about his life to one by a leading astronomer giving a series of science lectures and demonstrating experiments. Students, on the other hand, are encouraged to go out of the school for various activities, including the questionnaire survey of *tōkōkyohi* children mentioned above and various other kinds of field work (Okuchi 1992).

This citizens' discourse is also supported by medical professionals, especially psychiatrists who oppose the psychiatric discourse on *tōkōkyohi*. Watanabe Takashi, the former Head of the Department of Child Psychiatry at the National Kōnodai Hospital in Tokyo, has worked for the *tōkōkyohi* children and parents for over 40 years. He maintains that the cause of *tōkōkyohi* lies in the fundamental nature of Japanese education, and that children as living creatures have a sense of incongruity with school, subconsciously and instinctively (Watanabe 1992: 151–2). He holds that *tōkōkyohi* is the 'SOS' children send to society warning that 'their very existence and subjectivity are threatened' (p. 102). Children, however, he continues, are often either too young to express themselves, or subject to pressure so great that they are unable to express themselves (i.e. they are silenced) (p. 94). He therefore sees the child psychiatrist as 'the media for children' who:

> sees and listens to, from the perspective of biology and physiology, the message sent by the bodies [of children], translates it into words the patient can understand . . . and then translates it into words adults can understand.
>
> (Watanabe 1992: 93–4)

He writes:

> Not to attend school because of *tōkōkyohi* is like having nausea and diarrhoea caused by unknowingly eating rotten food. Nausea and diarrhoea which occur when poison enters the body are an instinctive defence mechanism to avoid dangerous things which might threaten the life and existence of the individual. The response is neither pathological nor abnormal. Rather, it is a healthy response which protects the individual.
>
> (Watanabe 1992: 84)

He continues that children:

> feel threatened when rules and other frameworks are imposed which go beyond what a living creature can take. Although there are individual differences, the defence mechanism to preserve the self inevitably sets in. Even if children persuade themselves to go to school, their sensitivities put on the brakes subconsciously and *tōkōkyohi* as a defence mechanism begins.
>
> (Watanabe 1992: 85)

Watanabe holds that in order to save *tōkōkyohi* children, it is vital to change the perception of parents who are often too involved with school and believe teachers rather than their own children. Such parents, he says, are unable to see or feel the pain, worry, and suffering of their children. Children who come to his hospital are therefore often totally isolated (pp. 105–6). On the basis of this understanding, he established the Association of Hope to help both *tōkōkyohi* children and parents, and the same principle was later adopted by Okuchi Keiko in *Tokyo Shure* (pp. 106–13).

Especially after the symposium of 1988, '*Kangaerukai*' operated as a powerful grassroots group to protect the interests of *tōkōkyohi* students and their parents. It functioned to remedy the general stigma attached to *tōkōkyohi*. With *tōkōkyohi* continuing to be its central theme, it has developed ultimately into one of the most powerful social movements in contemporary Japan, where children and parents are bound together not so much by ideology as by the sheer need to survive.

SOCIO-MEDICAL DISCOURSE: *TŌKŌKYOHI* AS SCHOOL BURNOUT

The last adult discourse about *tōkōkyohi* is what may be called the 'socio-medical', a relatively new position represented by the work of Miike and Tomoda (1994), doctors at the Medical School of Kumamoto University. As with citizens' discourse, these doctors maintain that the cause of *tōkōkyohi* lies in the social structure of school, not in the personality or other qualities of the individual student. However, they disagree with the citizens' discourse, in that they consider that *tōkōkyohi* students do suffer from a physical disorder which resembles chronic fatigue syndrome. They argue that the students have real health problems, but they regard the state of ill-health as the natural outcome of the social environment of school. In other words, they hold that *tōkōkyohi* is a social illness. They write:

> When students stop going to school it is undeniable that they have health problems. Why should *futōkō* not be an illness? . . . Would it not be problematic to say 'you are not ill' to people who are actually suffering from an illness?
>
> (p. 8)

> It appears that some students are 'pretending not to be sick' because of adults who claim that 'they are not sick'.
>
> (p. 104)[13]

> Individual qualities do not cause this 'illness'. Rather, it is 'school society' that can make students seriously sick.
>
> (Miike and Tomoda 1994: 107)[14]

Miike and Tomoda focus on the fact that *tōkōkyohi* students have common complaints such as: stomach-ache, headache, nausea, fever, diarrhoea, constipation, pains and aches of lymph nodes, joints and muscles, inability to get up in the morning, excessive sleepiness, insomnia, combination of daytime sleepiness and night-time insomnia, excessive feelings of fatigue, lack of concentration, diminished ability to think or remember, sorrowful feelings, auditory and visual hallucinations, death wishes, and negation of the self. They are critical, however, of summing up these symptoms merely as 'psychosomatic', remarking that the word 'psychosomatic' implies that symptoms can be controlled mentally and thus open the way to an ideology which blames the victims (p. 10).

Instead, based on detailed examination of *tōkōkyohi* students, they argue that the root cause is a systematic disorder, similar to the one found in the cases of '*karōshi*' ('death by chronic fatigue from overwork') among adults. More specifically, they hold that the symptoms common to the students are caused by disruptions to the biological rhythm, including abnormal functioning in (1) the autonomous nervous system, (2) internal secretions and body clock (circadian rhythm), (3) internal temperature (and sleep/awake rhythm, (4) the amount of blood influx to the brain. They argue that these are induced fundamentally by the fatigue of the brain especially in the areas of neocortex association area and diencephalic-pituitary system (pp. 11–12), which is caused, ultimately, by the excessive, school-associated demand to process all sorts of information (i.e. study, human relations with classmates and teachers, behavioural expectations, etc) (p. 62). With regard to the exhaustion of the brain function (which is central to their argument) Miike and Tomoda present two explanations, one concerning memory function, the other panic response.

Overfatigue of the memory function

Miike and Tomoda (1994) point out that some 40 per cent of *tōkōkyohi* children have a reduced level of influx of blood to that area of the brain which includes the hippocampus that plays a central role in memory function. They explain that the excessive amount of information to which students are exposed through intensive, examination-oriented study causes a state of 'bankruptcy' in the memory functioning of the brain (p. 66), i.e. a drastic excess of demand over supply.

Miike and Tomoda (ibid.) also explain that the hippocampus plays the pivotal role in emotion. They maintain that students who are generally sensitive, therefore, are more prone to experience a state of exhaustion in this part of the brain. The load to this part of the brain further increases when students become sceptical about school, when they feel anxious about their ability to keep up with study, or when *ijime* and other experiences increase the amount of emotional information to be processed. Such emotional stimuli contribute to push this part of the brain to exhaustion, causing further decline of the memory function. Miike and Tomoda hold:

> The decline of the memory function drastically impairs the ability of students to maintain life as students. They inevitably become sceptical of their ability to learn, and this induces a panic. Emotional panic also causes panic in the memory function, which accelerates further the deterioration of memory. It may be inferred that the memory channel of *futōkō* students becomes exhausted to the point of inaccessibility. . . . It is understandable that they become unable to study for months on end.
>
> (Miike and Tomoda 1994: 66)

When academic marks start to decline, therefore, Miike and Tomoda argue that it is crucial to have a good rest, instead of trying to work even harder to maintain academic performance. They are highly critical of the ideology of '*ganbaru*' (to persevere, hold on and work hard) dominant in Japanese schools and society which does not allow people to have a good rest when they need it (p. 103).

Accounts given by some students vividly describe the condition explained by Miike and Tomoda. Miura Tomoko (19) in Akita writes about the signal her body gave in relation to study:

> When I extend my arm to get the pencil, another 'I' (*mōhitori no watashi*) would tell me, 'Don't get it'. But if I just have to get the pencil, I must get it no matter what. Sometimes my arm trembled or ached, and because I experienced such conflict even over trivia, I got so tired and could not think about school.
>
> (Ishikawa *et al.* 1993: 667)

It appears that Tomoko's body was trying to prevent her from studying in order to reduce the amount of information to be processed in the brain, by preventing her from getting hold of an instrument of study (the pencil).

The account given by Echizen Takehisa in Kanagawa regarding the onset of his anxiety attack (which subsequently lead him to *tōkōkyohi*) also points to the link between study and anxiety discussed by Miike and Tomoda:

> One day in the middle of the class, I was attacked by a strange feeling. I suddenly felt extremely anxious. My palms gave off a cold sweat and I felt as if something terrible was going to happen to me. I could barely remain seated, and I felt that I was about to go mad. This strange feeling lasted for days, and I came to worry before going to school that

'I might feel unwell again'. Quite mysteriously, however, in the afternoon this strange feeling would go.

(Ishikawa *et al.* 1993: 708)

The case of a triple murder committed by a 14-year-old boy may also be explained in terms of the theory of Miike and Tomoda. In July 1988, a 14-year-old boy living in Meguro, Tokyo, killed his father (44), mother (40), and grandmother (70) by stabbing them with a kitchen knife several-dozen times each (*AS* 9 July 1988). The case was extraordinary in several respects – i.e. the brutality, the multiple homicide by a family member, and the young age of the murderer – but it stunned the nation because the crime was committed by a 'model student' who attended one of the most prestigious public schools in a wealthy suburb of Tokyo, and the boy had showed absolutely no signs of being likely to commit such an atrocity (*AS* 15 July 1988). He was a 'good boy' in every sense of the word (*AS* 9 July 1988), if anything, 'over-adjusted' to school (Murakami 1988).

The boy confessed later that he 'got really fed up with study and wanted to die' a few months earlier when he saw the new textbooks distributed at the beginning of the school year (*AS* 29 July 1988). Since around the mid-term test in May, he felt that he 'could not keep up with study and got fed up with life' (*AS* 17 July 1988), while his parents pressured him to be admitted to a prestigious private high school (*AS* 15 July 1988). After the poor results of the mid-term test, his father punched him on the head twice and said, 'I will kick you out of the house if your results are still bad in the end-of-term test. If you can only get into a mediocre senior high school, you might as well not go to one at all' (*AS* 30 July 1988). His mother also expected him to be 'in the first 99 of 268 students in his grade' (*AS* 12 July 1988). This self-professed 'intense study hater' 'thought about committing suicide' but he 'hated the parents who cornered [him] so much' that he decided to kill them before killing himself (*AS* 30 July 1988). The murder happened on the day after he got the results of his end-of-term tests; his marks were below average for all the major subjects (*AS* 15 July 1988).

What might appear to be an over-simplistic and childish solution (i.e. to kill his parents because they put him under too much pressure to study) may be somewhat more comprehensible if it is speculated that the boy's brain may have been in a state of total exhaustion due to the excessive efforts he had made over previous years to fulfil the high expectations of his parents, so that by the time his performance started to decline, it was desperately in need of a good rest. The high expectations of his parents did not allow him such rest; conversely they intensified the pressure on him even though he was no longer performing at all well academically. With pressure on his brain intensifying, while its capacity was declining, he was 'cornered', as he described himself, and could not think of any other solution but to kill them all.

The wounding and the killing of parents by children, and vice versa, are not at all rare in Japan. Often this is directly related to the fact that children fail to fulfil the academic expectations of their parents. In the same month as this multiple murder, at least one other similar case was reported. A 14-year-old girl stabbed her mother with a kitchen knife (with the intention of killing herself later) because she too was under pressure to study harder (*AS* 18,19 July 1988). The detailed accounts of *tōkōkyohi* provided by children and parents quoted earlier suggest that there is only a very fine line between these 'extraordinary' cases and the everyday life of a large number of students and parents who live in very ordinary homes and school environments.

The Miike and Tomoda theory on the relationship between academic pressure and brain fatigue coincides with the results of a factor analysis by Morita (1991). Morita reports that three aspects of student life: 'feeling sleepy and tired', 'lack of will to study' and 'inability to understand the lesson' highly correlate with each other and constitute a factor which explains 12.7 per cent of students' 'getting fed up with going to school' (p. 169,172–3). Morita calls this factor the 'apathy and weariness factor', and it is one of the two major factors found in his analysis.[15]

With regard to the causal relationships between these experiences, however, there is some disagreement. Morita *suggests* that the range of experience begins with 'not being able to understand the class', followed by 'the loss of will to study', leading to 'apathy' and then 'weariness' (p. 173).[16] Miike and Tomoda, on the other hand, argue that exhaustion of the brain, due to overwork, comes first, and that this then disrupts the biological rhythm, which subsequently induces a sense of tiredness.

While nothing decisive or general can be said about the causal relationship itself, the implication of this disagreement is quite significant. Morita believes that weariness derives from the difficulty of study, which *can* imply that the student who experiences weariness may be lacking in ability and/or perseverance at study. For him, 'apathy' and 'weariness' among children does not simply originate from their attitude, their lack of persistence, but it is also a manifestation of the erosion of the value that school is absolutely important in life (p. 176). This careful explanation, however, still bears the implication that it is possible for students to avoid their 'weariness' (and *futōkō* sentiment) if they take school more seriously and study harder. The view presented by Miike and Tomoda, on the other hand, denies outright the possibility that *tōkōkyohi* students might be lazy. According to their theory, it is impossible for the brain to become over-exhausted without hard work. Indeed, they are critical of the view that *tōkōkyohi* has anything at all to do with idleness on the part of students (pp. 22, 24).[17]

Panic and avoidance response

Miike and Tomoda also argue that the school environment is full of factors which stimulate anticipatory anxiety among students, and that repeated exposure to such an environment over-stimulates and develops subconscious phobic and avoidance responses within the brain. Students who are physically unable to go to school or to enter the classroom are experiencing a 'panic syndrome' which is beyond their consciousness or control. It is, according to Miike and Tomoda, a manifestation of an instinctive self-defence mechanism triggered by the anticipation of 'going to school' which has subconsciously been learned as a life-threatening experience (p. 64).

This explanation too is consistent with the result of the factor analysis conducted by Morita (1991), who found that the most significant factor explaining students' 'being fed up with going to school' is what he calls 'friendship-anxiety factor' (which explains 18.8 per cent of it). This consists of three elements: 'being bullied by friends', 'being subjected to mental shock', and 'being scared and anxious of school' (pp. 168–172). 'Mental shock' can be caused by things which happen to students in their relation with teachers.

The following story by Kurita Takako (18) in Kanagawa well illustrates the panic response. She writes:

> I throw my body on a *futon* which is left spread on the floor. Because I am still wearing school uniform, the pleated skirt gets wrinkled. I want it to be messier, because I simply will not and cannot go to school. . . . I have the intention to go to school. Yet, when I stand at the front door of the house, my legs start to shake, my arms feel weak, and I feel dizzy. Today, I could not even go to the front door because I was afraid of such a physical reaction.
>
> (Ishikawa *et al.* 1993: 608)

A 14-year-old boy who had been the target of *ijime* talked to his class about his phobic reaction to school:

> It was in the third term of the second year of junior high school that my *tōkōkyohi* began in earnest. I thought that I would get better in a week or two. . . . But contrary to my will, somewhere in my heart, another voice said 'You don't want to go to school. Don't go. If you go, the same thing will happen'. . . . In March I became unable to walk and I really

understood that my body was saying 'no' to school. . . . I also became unable to eat. . . . The only thing I remember about that time was I could eat 'only one slice of bread'. . . . I thought, 'Is this *tōkōkyohi?*' I knew about it but did not think that I would become *tōkōkyohi.* . . . I really was on the borderline between life and death for a while.

(Ishikawa *et al.* 1993: 296–9)

When he attended the opening ceremony for the new school year he seriously thought that he might be killed; and when he managed to come to the class some months later, his trembling body was supported by the teacher (Ishikawa *et al.* 1993: 300). The boy's experience well illustrates how subconscious self-defence mechanisms function, as explained by Miike and Tomoda, in what he perceived to be a life-threatening environment.

In addition, Miike and Tomoda assert that somatic disorders exist even when students still manage to go to school by exerting a great effort (*gamanshite*) (p. 10). They argue that the state of over-exhaustion reaches its peak and the physical conditions of *tōkōkyohi* are fulfilled when students feel that they can no longer go to school (p. 27–8). This happens, Miike and Tomoda argue, because the central nervous system 'detects' that it is dangerous to keep working (i.e. studying) further, even if students are not consciously aware of it. They point out that students who are considered to be 'just lazy' include those who are actually suffering from chronic fatigue syndrome (p. 24).

The aim of the treatment of *tōkōkyohi* envisaged by Miike and Tomoda, therefore, is to achieve recuperation of the over-exhausted and panic-stricken state of the central nervous system (p. 91). The most important thing, they assert, is to get plenty of rest both physically and psychologically, i.e. to sleep a lot and play a lot, and for people around the student to understand that the student needs a good rest. They say that when academic marks start to go down, it is time to rest, not to push oneself further (*ganbaru*) (p. 93). It is not, however, that they dismiss the use of medication altogether. When the student suffers from severe depression, anxiety and disorders of the autonomic nervous system, it is helpful, they write, to use medication for a limited period in order to make it possible to rest (p. 98).

Hayashida Akane (15) depicts how it feels to be well rested after going through the stage of overuse of the brain.

It is almost one year since I stopped going to school. Lately, I feel so very happy. It is because I came to be able to think about things deeply. I think that it is probably because my body and mind have really been calmed down. When I was still attending school, my opinions could not be conveyed clearly, and few teachers understood me anyway. Above all, we were far too busy at school. Different things I need to think about came to my brain too quickly one after the other. There was simply too much to do!

(Ishikawa *et al.* 1993: 512)

Although there is disagreement between the citizens' discourse and the socio-medical discourse represented by Miike and Tomoda as to whether *tōkōkyohi* is an illness or not, both agree that the ultimate solution of *tōkōkyohi* should be found in changing the educational system and society of which the school is a part. The proposals by Miike and Tomoda for the prevention of *tōkōkyohi* can be summarised under three points. The first involves critical assessment of the social norm of emphasis on '*ganbaru*' and creation of an environment in school and society in which people can rest free from social pressure. The second is to bring about a fundamental change of the education system which is presently based on the mechanical memorisation of excessive amounts of information and knowledge. The third is to ratify a treaty for the rights of children and for adults to learn about the rights of children (p. 103).

TŌKŌKYOHI: THE STUDENTS' VIEW

While the adult discourse about *tōkōkyohi* (by psychiatrists, teachers, citizens and other physicians) explains the social and discursive environment in which *tōkōkyohi* children live, it is ultimately a discourse by observers and saturated with all kinds of ideologies. While carefully considering it, however, it is at least as important to focus also on the accounts of *tōkōkyohi* given by students themselves. The present study examines the Japanese education system from the perspective of students.

Compared to the abundance of literature on *tōkōkyohi* by adults, accounts by students themselves have been extremely limited. In 1991 '*Tokyo Shure no kodomotachi*' ('Children of *Tokyo Shure*', abbreviated as '*Kodomotachi*' in this book) published *Gakkō ni ikanai boku kara gakkō ni ikanai kimi e* (From me who doesn't go to school to you who don't go to school). This was followed by *Kodomotachi ga kataru tōkōkyohi* (*Tōkōkyohi* as discussed by children) by Ishikawa *et al.* which contains the accounts of 402 *tōkōkyohi* students.

Although each case of *tōkōkyohi* is unique, numerous accounts given by students suggest that their experience can be conceptually organised around two questions: their physical condition, whether they experience somatic symptoms or not; and their consciousness, whether they want to go to school or not. With these two questions as axes, the *tōkōkyohi* experience may be classified into four categories, as shown in Table 8.3.

The accounts of *tōkōkyohi* given by students also suggest that it is not a static experience but a *process* which involves, among other things, changes in physical condition and perceptions of the self and the school, roughly corresponding to (1) to (4) in Table 8.3, although of course, not all students follow this passage. Some students, for instance, are suddenly prevented from going to school due to severe somatic symptoms and thus skip stage (1), while others return to school when they feel fit enough to do so and thus experience only up to stage (2), yet others may jump from stage (1) to (3) without having clear somatic symptoms at all. Nor is the distinction between any two stages as clear as is conceptualised by this table. Students may go to and fro between any two stages for a substantial length of time, and it is usually only in retrospect that they can see the change within themselves over the long run.

Monbushō's typology of *tōkōkyohi* is based on what it describes as the 'causes', including, experiences at school, apathy, anxiety and emotional confusion, deliberately willed abstention from school (ME 1995b). Nonetheless, the notion of 'process' seems crucial. Monbushō's categorisation is too rigid to capture the dynamic and transformative nature of the phenomenon. Accounts given by students suggest the strong possibility that these subcategories are not distinct phenomena but different stages of the *tōkōkyohi* process. What might be first seen as 'apathy' can develop into severe anxiety, accompanied by somatic symptoms triggered by additional pressure or negative experiences at school, while deliberate *tōkōkyohi* usually comes

Table 8.3 The process and progression of *tōkōkyohi*

Conciousness	Symptoms (visible)	
	Not present	*Present*
Wanting to go to school	(1) I just cannot go. (Lassitude)	(2) I want to go but cannot. (Physical symptoms)
Not wanting to go to school	(4) I will not go. (Refusal/empowerment)	(3) I do not go. (Critical awareness)

Pre-*tōkōkyohi*:	Unquestioning school attender
Process of *tōkōkyohi*:	1. Lassitude and burnout
	2. Physical symptoms
	3. Critical awareness
	4. Refusal/empowerment
Post-*tōkōkyohi*:	Reintegrated subjectivity

much later, if it comes at all. To put it differently, it is probable that the 'typology' merely indicates the entering point to *tōkōkyohi* of each individual.

The fact that there is a process of *tōkōkyohi* has been recognised elsewhere. Monbushō's *Seito shidō shiryō* (Student guidance booklet) states that there are three stages based on the progression of the symptoms: 1) the period when students get reluctant to go to school because of experience of somatic symptoms, etc.; 2) the period when students have severe anxiety and/or may become violent; 3) the period when the behavioural patterns of day and night are reversed and students retreat to their inner world (ME 1983).

While student accounts of *tōkōkyohi* roughly coincide with this period-isation, their primary concern is fundamentally different. The description by Monbushō is limited to the behavioural aspects of each stage. In the student discourse, the process revolves around the two questions mentioned above – whether they have somatic symptoms or not, and whether they want to go to school or not.

At the same time, in the student discourse, the question of 'self' consti-tutes the underlying thread which runs throughout all phases of the experi-ence. The words of the students suggest that they were confronted above all with the question of self. In this they are heavily influenced both by adult discourse and by their particular psychological and somatic symptoms. Yet by going through different stages of *tōkōkyohi*, many students undergo a transformation in their subjectivity, as described below.

Stage 1: 'I just cannot go' (Nantonaku ikenai)

Although the account of the beginning phase differs from person to person, common to all is the complaint of excessive tiredness and plain inability to go to school. Feeling 'tired' is such a weak and illegitimate reason in the context of Japanese society and many students can only say that they stopped going to school '*nantonaku*' (for no specific reason) or '*dōshite ka wakaranai keredo*' (without knowing why).

'Being sleepy and feeling tired' is the reason most frequently cited by students in general with the *tōkōkyohi/futōkō* wish in various studies. In the study by Morita (1991) it was selected by 73.4 per cent of students with *futōkō* tendency (p. 151).[18] According to another survey, 'no clear or specific reason' (over 30 per cent) was the most frequently quoted 'reason' for junior high school students not wanting to go to school (Nihon PTA Zenkoku Kyōgikai 1988). Likewise, the survey of 1,556 high school students by NHK (Japan Broadcasting Corporation) found that 30 to 40 per cent of students who often do not feel like going to school frequently have complaints such as 'insomnia', 'fatigue', 'lack of appetite', 'stiff shoulders', 'dizziness', 'listless-ness', whereas such experiences are less common among others who rarely dread to go to school (NHK yoron chōsa bu 1991). It is quite possible, as Miike and Tomoda point out (1994), that some invisible disorder exists well before a student stops going to school completely (p. 10).

This stage of extreme fatigue or lassitude signifies the stage often referred to as *tōkōkyohi* apathy or laziness. This is also the phase when students are more likely to be pushed to attend school. A 14-year-old boy who calls himself 'Adams' writes:

> I cannot believe that I cannot go to school. Although I was not good at study, I went to school up to the first year of junior high school. . . . [But now], I cannot go to school even if I wanted to.
>
> (Ishikawa *et al.* 1993: 533)

His mother explains in more detail:

> My son used to have two days off school saying, 'There are six classes today. It's so tiring'. . . . He said apathetically that he feels tired and exhausted if he goes to school. . . . I said, 'Well, but you don't have either *juku* or *bukatsu* . . . and you are not pressed to study either by me or by your father. . . . Why do you get so tired?'. He said, 'Who knows. School is just so uninteresting and just so tiring. I get physically exhausted when there are as many as six classes'. He told me that he would not go to school until his physical strength recovered. . . . We sometimes had arguments but whenever I heard him say 'It is not that I don't want to go', my anger subsided. . . . His academic record was not particularly good, but he has never been lazy.
>
> (Ishikawa *et al.* 1993: 534–5)

The story conveys the indefinable and overwhelming sense of tiredness Adams experienced at school, from which he had to have a break even though he did not want to. While Adams does not say much about why he felt so tired at school, others elucidate the point more clearly. Sezoko Masatomo, a 13-old-boy writes:

> It is because I did not like study. I did nothing but study at school and wanted to escape from it. There was little time to take a break, there was too much home work, and I could not think of anything else but study. I got more and more tired and I got fed up with school.
>
> (Ishikawa *et al.* 1993: 429)

It is not that Masatomo does not like to study in general. He is now a student of *Tokyo Shure*, and intends to study more and go on to senior high school (p. 430).

In the case of Kanbe Tomoko (14), it was the pressure to be constantly 'good' in relation to others which made her exhausted both at school and home. She writes:

> I myself do not know why I stopped going to school. When I was still going to school, I was a so-called 'good student'. I could follow the class, I had many friends, and it seemed that I had no complaints about my school life. . . . But I was extremely nervous. . . . I always felt tired after talking to someone. . . . I was a good docile child both at home and outside home. Unable to be myself anywhere, it made me feel very tired. My parents did not tell me to be good, but I thought that I had to be good. I did not say any '*wagamama*' [selfish things], I did not cry, I did not get irritated. It is not that I did not have these feelings, but I thought that I should not express them and kept them to myself. It might be more accurate to say that I killed all my thoughts, feelings, and emotions.
>
> (Ishikawa *et al.* 1993: 441)

Tomoko's *tōkōkyohi* was triggered by *ijime*. She explains:

> When every day I felt so tired, my classmates began to bully me a little. Although it was an insignificant *ijime*, it gave me a great shock, and I stopped going to school the very next day. I felt as if everything suppressed inside me was unleashed. My parents seemed very surprised. First, I thought that my *tōkōkyohi* was caused by *ijime*, but in retrospect, it was just triggered by it.
>
> (Ishikawa *et al.* 1993: 441)

Whether it be the pressure to study or pressure to behave in certain ways that makes students feel so tired, there is no question that many students feel that their energy is almost completely depleted by the time they reach the point of being actually unable to go to school. Before students realise that school attendance is no longer possible, there is usually a long 'grey' stage when they hang on to go to school on and off (as often referred to as '*samidare tōkō*', which means 'going to school like the intermittent rain of May').

During this stage, many try to keep going to school, as shown in the phenomenon called '*hokenshitsu tōkō*'. *Hokenshitsu* is the room in school where a nurse-teacher takes care of students who feel unwell. It is a kind of 'air pocket' in the school, where students are left free of pressure from either teachers or peer students. Nakajima Katsuyo, a nurse-teacher, writes:

At first, my job was not well understood by other staff members. For me simply to accept students as they were conflicted with the view of students held by other teachers, so there were criticisms such as 'we are having difficulties because our students are being spoilt in *hokenshitsu*' or 'is it all right for *hokenshitsu* to enjoy extraterritoriality?'.

(Nakajima 1995: 70)

Students who have difficulty in coming to school are often allowed by the principal to go to *hokenshitsu* instead, even for ten minutes or one hour a day (Ishikawa *et al.* 1993: 472). The number of students who 'attend' *hokenshitsu* instead of normal class doubled between 1990 and 1996 to reach an estimated number of some 10,000 students in primary and junior secondary schools (*AS* 11 September 1997). Furukawa Akika (11) wrote about her *hokenshitsu* experience in a poem entitled 'Hokenshitsu':

I do not study
I do not do anything
For how many days have I been like this?
From the playground
I can hear the happy voices of children
What am I doing here?

I went to school
I did nothing
What is it for
Going to school?
I feel sad

(Ishikawa *et al.* 1993: 161)

The proportion of students who 'get tired easily' has increased considerably since the early 1980s, and by 1996 some three-quarters of students of all ages complain that they tire very easily (Saijō 1996). It is also pointed out that 'busy', 'tired' and 'sleepy' are the key words children were using most frequently in the late 1990s and that even 10-year-olds carry diaries filled with study schedules, and a beeper which hurries them off to the next study appointment, while regularly consuming 'energy drinks' designed for businessmen (Arita and Yamaoka 1992).

Stage 2: *'I want to go but cannot'*

The progression from stage (1) to (2) (see Table 8.3) where clear somatic symptoms manifest themselves is often triggered by additional pressure upon students or sometimes by incidents which serve to separate students from school almost completely.

The transition between stage (1) and (2) is illustrated by the following story told by a 14-year-old girl. Regarding the onset of her *tōkōkyohi* which appears to fall within stage (1) she writes:

> I suddenly stopped going to school when I was in Grade 4. There was no specific reason for it. I had not been bullied. There was no reason I could think of. I did not understand why, and of course my parents did not know why. At any rate, I could not go to school. I stayed home alone all day every day, and sometimes I did not want to see anyone.
>
> (Ishikawa *et al.* 1993: 459)

Although at first she did not understand why she suddenly failed to go to school first, clear physical problems set in after she was exposed to intense external pressure to attend school, which seem to represent stage (2). She continues:

> My family all thought of various methods to try to make me go to school. I really hated it. Teachers, friends, and nurse-teacher also proposed various ways. I really hated this, too. Although they tried this and that, nothing worked. . . . And gradually, the condition of my health deteriorated. My whole body became numb. I had headaches and was constantly in a dopey state.
>
> (Ishikawa *et al.* 1993: 459)

T.I. (15) writes about the relationship between his class and his excruciating stomach-ache.

> When I reached the second year of junior high school, my stomach-ache became worse. . . . I felt excruciating pain, like being cut up by a knife, for hours at a time. This lasted for about two weeks. It was strange because the pain would begin as the lesson started and stop when the lesson stopped. So, I would go to *hokenshitsu* at the beginning of each class. My classmates asked, 'Why do you just get sick in class time?' 'He is just pretending!'. Teachers also seemed to be wondering what was happening. My stomach-ache just got worse and it became more and more difficult for me to go to school.
>
> (Ishikawa *et al.* 1993: 486)

Ishiwari Minako (16) was an outstanding student, who used to work to her limit without external pressure until gradually she developed, towards the end of junior high school, severe nausea and dizziness which in the end prevented her from going to school. She writes:

> I was always wearing the mask of a 'steady and reliable child'. . . . but there was no limit in the stress that built up in me. I was wearing that mask even at home. I used to come home exhausted after *bukatsu* and the student association, eat dinner alone, and immediately head for the *juku*. . . . When I was in the third year of junior high school, the study at the *juku* became very intensive (sometimes the class finished at 11:30 at night). . . . I really did not have time to catch my breath. . . . Symptoms of nausea began soon after I passed all the entrance examinations for senior high school including one for one of the very best public schools in the prefecture.

After entering this new school:

> I could no longer go to school because of terrible nausea, dizziness and stomach-ache. I could not get out of the bathroom in the morning. I had the will to go to school, but this made the situation even worse. I could not go out at all – had a phobia about going out, a phobia of people – I thought about suicide many times. I was in a state of panic. In my depression, I cried every day.
>
> (Ishikawa *et al.* 1993: 302–5)

According to the survey conducted by the students of *Tokyo Shure*, the somatic symptoms experienced by 265 *tōkōkyohi* students included:

Stomach-ache	39.2%
Headache	23.2%
Nausea	27.9%
Breathlessness	16.6%
Dizziness	16.2%
Other	26.0%

(*Kodomotachi* 1991: 232)

As discussed earlier, students in this stage are often undergoing tremendous pain, both physically and psychologically, and are desperately in need of rest. Regarding the importance of having a really good rest, Kusachi Yukiya (15) writes:

> Children have energy. . . and the time when they remain in their room or in their house is the time when they recharge themselves. If you take

off the battery from the recharger when the energy level is still low, children cannot use their power well. Some batteries can be charged quickly and others take a long time. . . . Parents should not be impatient. Parents should know how much energy their children have stored. . . . If children use more energy than they have recharged, they get hurt and exhausted. If parents could come to be aware of the limits of their children's energy, their children would be lucky indeed.

(Ishikawa *et al.* 1995: 504)

He continues:

When children go to such trouble to rest from school [*sekkaku yasunde iru*], I would like you to let them rest well. . . . Even if the child does not go to school and just rests physically, if their mind [*kokoro*] is not also able to rest, they cannot recharge their energy. I would like parents and other people around the child to understand that it is necessary for the mind of the child to be rested. . . . Only when parents accept from the bottom of their hearts the way the child lives, can their child rest at ease. Children are very sensitive, so they understand the feelings of their parents.

(Ishikawa *et al.* 1995: 506)

When parents are not able to accept the fact that their children genuinely need rest, violence may ensure. A 15 year old who calls himself Danieru Harumuzu (Daniel Halmuz) writes:

When I was in the second year of junior high school, I hardly could go out of the house. Even if I did not want to see my classmates, they came to visit me and my homeroom teacher came almost daily. In the mornings my parents would force me to go to school. How many times did I feel that I was going to die? There were times when I seriously thought about calling the police. . . . I had dreams in which I killed my father. In fact I thought of killing my father. . . . My mother cried a lot and this was hard to take. . . . Even if I said I had headache and stomach-ache, nobody believed me. So when I developed appendicitis, I thought 'I've won'.

(Ishikawa *et al.* 1993: 500)

Parents are generally reluctant to discuss domestic violence in *tōkōkyohi* situations, but Hashimoto Yukiko, who had a *tōkōkyohi* son remarks that in the meeting of the 'Kangaerukai' there were parents who would say such things as 'I was hospitalised because my ribs were broken by my child', or 'the child's grandparents had to move somewhere else for safety' (Ishikawa *et al.* 1995: 394). These violent situations seem to occur when the student's need to rest is met with increased pressure to attend school. The 14-year boy who killed his parents and grandmother, mentioned earlier, is an example of the extremity to which such pressure can lead.

Stage 3: The shift from 'I cannot go to school' to 'I do not go to school'

While taking substantial time off school and staying mostly at home in a self-imposed state of isolation, students usually go through a long and hard process of self-doubt and self-questioning. During this stage they re-evaluate who they are, what they make of school, as well as their absence from school. After spending several months in this state, troubled by anxiety and somatic symptoms, many come to feel that what used to be seen as a matter of ill-health is actually a matter of choice. Thus, in the third stage of *tōkōkyohi*, students gradually come to terms with their absence from school as well as with themselves. Oouchi Taeko (14) writes:

> It is one year since I started *tōkōkyohi*. . . . For a long time I thought that I 'cannot' go to school. This is [partly] because my physical condition had been so bad, and [partly because] I do not particularly dislike study, my classmates nor teachers. . . . But recently, I came to think that I 'do not' go to school. No, [actually] I knew one year ago that I 'choose not to go' to school. But I was afraid to admit it, and kept saying that I 'cannot' go. . . . One change I can feel in myself is that I have come to be able to have a proper rest when I am away from school. Before, even if I did not go to school, my mind was not rested. Now, I think that I can rest my whole system body and mind, although my poor health still lingers.
>
> (Ishikawa *et al.* 1993: 293)

Takeko says, however, that she has not yet found the '*jibun rashisa*' (sense of being at one with herself) which she has been searching for. She says that she has a 'big worry and impatience' in her mind. Her poor condition still troubles her, and she seems to be under pressure from her family (pp. 293–5).

Suzuki Akira, who coordinated the survey of *tōkōkyohi* children, also pondered for nearly a year about the question of self. He used to think that *tōkōkyohi* students were 'the scum of the earth'. When he himself began *tōkōkyohi*, however, he had to face up to his own perception. He writes:

But when I myself began *tōkōkyohi*, I started to wonder whether I am indeed scum, and whether *tōkōkyohi* students are [all] scum. This question, however, was not an easy one to answer. I reflected on it for about ten months, but my thoughts shifted between two ideas. One was that since so many children go to school, it should be all right that some do not. The other was that not all children who go to school want to do so, and therefore that it is simply the *wagamama* [selfishness] on the part of *tōkōkyohi* students that they do not go to school. It took me about one year to be freed from the fixed idea that one must go to school no matter what.

(*Kodomotachi* 1991: 164)

Similarly, Watanabe Madoka (13), who stopped going to school at the age of 10, recalled the commencement of her *tōkōkyohi*, writing:

I thought it was bad not to go to school. . . . It's only recently that I began to think that not going to school doesn't matter. When thinking about whether it is bad or not . . . I used to think also that I was 'no good' [*dame*] as a human being because everyone else was going to school. Now I think that it is not a bad thing not to go to school; that study is not all there is to life; and that it is not that I cannot go to school but have chosen not to go because school doesn't suit me.

(Ishikawa *et al.* 1993: 426–7)

What happened to Madoka after this is noteworthy. No sooner had she come to realise that it was not a bad thing not to go to school, then she started to 'go out of the house a little, and then to dislike school' (p. 427). In other words, by accepting herself as a person who does not go to school, she could liberate herself from the stigma which bound her and shamed her for years. This in turn 'permitted' her to dislike school, i.e. to unleash the criticisms she had suppressed for so long.

Stage 4: Discovery of selfhood and critical reappraisal of school

In the student's account, what comes in the final stage of *tōkōkyohi* is the discovery of selfhood on the one hand, and the critical reappraisal of school on the other. Not a single *tōkōkyohi* student wrote that she or he was happy with the prospect of simply adjusting again to school or society. It is not their rediscovery of an ability to fulfill their expected social role that makes them feel strong towards the end of their *tōkōkyohi* experience. On the contrary, what 'heals' them is their sense of enpowerment, based on their own will, even if it is not what is normally expected in mainstream Japanese society. What comes towards the end of *tōkōkyohi* in the student discourse is a resolution quite antithetical to the 'cured' state of *tōkōkyohi* as defined in the dominant, psychiatric and behavioural discourses.

The sense of empowerment is usually coupled with a critical reappraisal of school. A number of students come to juxtapose their selfhood and school as fundamentally incompatible. Senda Yōko (18), for instance, writes that *tōkōkyohi* is a 'natural [and inevitable] response which happens when the autonomy of children is about to be erased by heteronomy imposed by school' (Ishikawa *et al.* 1993: 633).

The following are accounts given by *tōkōkyohi* students regarding the relationship between their sense of self and school. Ishiwari Minako, quoted earlier, who used to be an 'all round super-achiever', writes how she has changed in about one year of *tōkōkyohi*.

> How did I change? Although I was a person who tried to please everyone before, I came to disagree with various things. When I don't agree with something, I [now] can say so clearly. Maybe I have gained more confidence than before. I came to be able to express my emotions fairly openly. It feels as if the tight heavy lid which used to repress my feelings began to open a little.
>
> (Ishikawa *et al.* 1993: 311)

Minako, once an 'elite' student, is now critical of Japanese education. She writes:

> I do not want 'victims of the examination war' to increase further. The fact that nobody can stop or improve a situation nobody wants suggests that the very basis of Japanese education is wrong.
>
> (Ishikawa *et al.* 1993: 312)

Arinaga Shinji (16) also talks about how he changed through his *tōkōkyohi*.

> Comparing the time when I was attending school and the time when I was doing *tōkōkyohi*, I can conclude that it is not worth going to school. . . . If I go to school, I do not think anything or feel anything, and just waste time in being passive. . . . When I think in this way, I come to forget such narrow ideas as 'study at school' or 'I am inferior to those who go to school, because I do not go to school'.
>
> (Ishikawa *et al.* 1993: 555)

In effect, Shinji is saying that 'to be oneself' and 'to go to school' are virtually incompatible; that questions such as 'Am I inferior to others who go to school?' are part of a school-centred way of thinking; and that when one understands the relationship between oneself and school, one is liberated from asking such questions. Such a view is also shared by 'Serurian' (15), who is about to resume going to school in order to realise a dream she has about the future. Despite her 'return' to school, she still identifies herself as 'a praise-worthy *tōkōkyohi* child' and writes:

> '*Kyohi*' means to be able to say 'No', and in that *tōkōkyohi* children are 'Japanese who can say 'No'[19] I see myself as a 'praiseworthy' person . . . 'proud of not going to school' but also 'having enough spirit to be able to ignore the criticisms of stupid people'. . . . Lately I no longer have trouble living. It is true that it used to be difficult. There's only one reason why it used to be difficult for me to live before. I's because I did not like myself, everything about me, including my personality. This is no longer the case . . . I have become fond of my character. It has become easy to live. I think that it is necessary to be positive about oneself to some extent in order to live.
>
> (Ishikawa *et al.* 1993: 473–4)

Serurian is fiercely critical of school, especially teachers (see Chapter 3). Nonetheless, she intends to go back to the education system, not to conform but to use it to actualise her dreams for the future. It is a completely different mindset from the one expected in the 'cured' state of *tōkōkyohi* as defined in the dominant discourse. Like Shinji, she has transcended the question of whether she 'wants to go back to school' or not. The question has become secondary to her, and returning to the education system is merely an pragmatic choice.

Nakajima Ryū (14) also points out that in his *tōkōkyohi* experience, he came gradually to realise that what was at stake in school was his sense of selfhood. In his words:

> I had a great experience this year . . . . Since the beginning of the school year I have been *tōkōkyohi*. First, I just thought 'I don't like close-cropped hair'. . . . But I came to realise that it's not just that. Things which were not clear in my mind before became clearer. The reason I don't want to go to school, in a word, is that 'it feels as if I am going to lose myself, being controlled by school'.
>
> (Ishikawa *et al.* 1993: 880)

Like Ryū, many consider *tōkōkyohi* a positive and empowering experience. Sabashi Haruna (19) writes:

> For me, the experience of *tōkōkyohi* was a great 'plus'. Had I remained a good student, I would not have noticed the problems in education and would have contributed to the side of those who control students. . . . Through *tōkōkyohi*, what I learnt was not commonsense but how to judge things on the basis of my own will; not to do something because others do, but because I want to do it. In other words, I learnt 'freedom'. Each time I introduce myself, I say 'I did *tōkōkyohi*'. The only thing I can be proud of is my *tōkōkyohi* experience. I've proved to myself that I can live properly without going to school. . . . *Tōkōkyohi* equals freedom.
>
> (Ishikawa *et al.* 1993: 651)

Similarly, Ogura Masahiro (15) wrote a verse entitled, 'Diverting from the main path', which goes as follows:

> I think that it was good that I did not go to school
> If I had, I would have become a very ordinary salaryman
>   with no dreams
> Now I have a dream of becoming
> either a kindergarten teacher or a psychologist
> I am proud of having the precious experience of
> not going to school
> of having done *tōkōkyohi*
>
> (Ishikawa *et al.* 1993: 450)

In the same vein, Hayashida Soeyuki (14) wrote a piece called 'The feelings of students who cannot go to school'. It begins as follows:

> Your individuality is something only you have,
> and my individuality is something only I have.
> School with its rules
> crushed your individuality and my individuality.
> Education is supposed to help people to live
> but actually it stifles life
> Everyone just concentrates on studying,
> and their freedom and individuality vanish. . . .
>
> (Ishikawa *et al.* 1993: 202)

Similarly, Shimada Erika (15) writes:

> I don't want teachers to smash the individuality of each student. Students are human beings and it's natural that there are differences in children. But teachers decide that this child is '*wagamama*' and that child is 'such and such'. Children who cannot follow such a way of doing things and whose academic records are not good are all called 'drop-outs'. Once you are labelled a 'drop-out', you remain a 'drop-out' no matter how hard you work. Nobody likes it, and everyone does what the teacher says, trying not to be a 'drop-out' in study even if it means joining in kicking others out of the academic competition.
>
> (Ishikawa *et al.* 1993: 479)

Not surprisingly, *tōkōkyohi* students who have the opportunity to return to school (even temporality) after a long time of absence are often astounded at various school practices which before they had considered 'normal'. Uchida Yōko (15) who returned to junior high school after some two years remarks:

> Frankly, when you go to school, you have no room to think about others. So you project your stress onto others who are weaker than yourself. This is quite obvious in school. . . . After my long absence from school, I could no longer follow this method. . . . I used sometimes to bully others . . . . But I could not do it any more. . . . I was really shocked to see the horrific way my friends bully someone. But now I suppose it's natural for them to become like that when they go to school every day. If you do not abuse others and release your stress, you yourself get squashed. . . . To resist that requires enormous physical and mental strength.
>
> (Ishikawa *et al.* 1993: 488)

Similarly, a 15-year-old boy reflects upon a friend who directly caused his *tōkōkyohi*. He writes:

> I played a lot with my friend since primary school and did not dream of being ostracised by him. But school changed my friend. It is as if he were hypnotised . . . . I now think that that kind of school environment can change anyone.
>
> (Ishikawa *et al.* 1993: 507)

This boy visited school temporarily after being absent for several months just to sit for a test. Since his uniform had become too small, he wore ordinary clothes. On seeing him, a teacher infamous for corporal punishment shouted at him saying:

> Hey you! Do you think you can come to junior high school in plain clothes! Are you really a student of [this school]! You idiot!
>
> (Ishikawa *et al.* 1993: 507)

He remarks, 'It was so sudden and because I hadn't been scolded for some time, I was taken aback and couldn't say anything'. Quoting the words of another teacher, 'Pluck up courage and come to school', he raises the question, 'Should school be a place where students can go only when they are brave enough?' (Ishikawa *et al.* 1993: 508–9).

What most impressed both this boy and Yōko was the sense of 'abnormality' of the school environment. They could now see this more clearly than before. Many *tōkōkyohi* students see school as an 'abnormal' place. J.N. (12) writes:

> As of today, I quit school.
> I am a total stranger to you people.
> If you want to glare at me, please do so.
> But from today, I become a normal person [*futsū no hito*].
>
> (Ishikawa *et al.* 1993: 401)

The notion of 'normalcy' (*futsū*), which appears in the student discourse of *tōkōkyohi*, is directly opposed to the notions of 'normalcy' presupposed in the dominant discourses of *tōkōkyohi*, i.e. normalcy meaning fulfilling the role prescribed by society. When this boy declares himself 'a normal person', he means someone who is not pushed around by 'abnormal' school demands, pressures which ultimately coerce children to renounce their very selfhood, in order to mould themselves into what is accepted as 'normal' in school and society.

The dominant notion of '*futsū*' (ordinary/normal/conventional) is deeply detested by *tōkōkyohi* children. Ishiwari Minako writes:

> Is the '*futsū*' that we hear about all the time really right?
> So many cases of '*futsū*' seem not right at all,
> And the '*futsū*' which can be evil is the one which stands out.
>
> (Ishikawa *et al.* 1993: 316)

Yamaguchi Kayo (13) ponders what it is to be 'normal'.

> What is '*futsū*'? What is '*ijō*' [abnormal]? . . . What most people call '*futsū*' is what most people do. That is, they go to school properly and

get a respectable job. People seem to see someone like myself who doesn't go to school as being not normal, as being queer. But I think that it's wrong to think that way. I think that to go to school and to get a job is the easiest way to live. . . . I do not want to run on the fixed rails but on rails created by myself. It's a difficult and painful way, but I believe that it'll be good for me.

(Ishikawa *et al.* 1993: 421)

It is not surprising that *tōkōkyohi* students hold a critical view of Japanese society in general. Although what they say about Japan is extremely general, the perception that 'something is wrong with Japan' is widely held. Shiotani Norio (16), for instance, writes that 'Japan today is wrong and therefore I want to become the kind of a person who'll be regarded as an oddball Japanese' (Ishikawa *et al.* 1993: 537). Yamada Tadataka (12) once told his parents that 'even if Japan pays out a lot of money, if it is not paid from the heart, Japan will be criticised by other countries' (Ishikawa *et al.* 1993: 286). The daughter of Aoki Fusako accused her parents, saying that their generation 'only destroys things and did not hand down a new culture' (Ishikawa *et al.* 1995: 9). Although student critiques of Japan are fragmented and have no systematic structure, there is little question that their reappraisals of school can easily be extended to critiques of the society. This they themselves see in its broader context, containing school, parents, neighbours and every other party they have to deal with.

TŌKŌKYOHI AS A MEANS TO RECOVER SUBJECTIVITY

The phases of *tōkōkyohi* do not just signify different psychological and physical conditions, nor merely a reluctance or unwillingness to go to school. *Tōkōkyohi* is a process in which students go through a major paradigm shift, at first only dimly aware of the process, but gradually sorting out what is important in their life and what is not. It is a hard process in which students are confronted with a number of questions within themselves. The most fundamental of all is the one about their own selfhood. Other things – study, school, friends, family, society, future – gradually become secondary and only have significance in relation to the central question concerning self. Nor do students reflect on these things in an abstract way. For many of them, it is virtually a matter of life or death to find an answer to such questions which will allow them to live their life. Only when they can reconstruct their own identity, contrasting it with the other identities prepared for them by society, can they resume their social life.

The adult discourse about *tōkōkyohi* confronts them with an ideology of how they should identify themselves. Students, who are commonly urged to see themselves as '*yoiko no jibun*' (myself as a good student/child) or '*futsū no seito*' (normal student) are exposed to pressures to change into one or other of the following identities.

> A school and social drop-out self (*ochikobore no jibun*)
> A mentally ill self (*kokoro no byōki no jibun*)
> A lazy self (*namakemono no jibun*)
> A school resister self (*tōkōkyohi no jibun*)
> A physically ill self (*byōki no jibun*)

The first three of these constitute the dominant view of *tōkōkyohi* as social failure. Most students spend months liberating themselves from such views and from the 'school faith' which underpins them. Even the citizens' discourse which has provided a counter-ideology and a solid support network for *tōkōkyohi* students and their parents may also be rejected by students who do not see themselves as 'school resisters'. Whether through negating them as 'social failure', 'social victim', or 'social resister', the point is that each type of adult discourse can be taken as an imposition, something which each individual students must either accept or reject.

The 'student discourse' presents a strong yet only general pattern. By the very nature of the quest, there is no 'proper' outcome, since *tōkōkyohi* is the process through which each student tries to scrutinise her or his identity against externally-defined identities presented by adults. As an extremely individualistic and personal quest, the outcome of *tōkōkyohi* varies from person to person. Yet, whatever the way each student emerges from *tōkōkyohi*, the process ends when the major task of 'de-alienation' is over or nearly over for the particular individual.

The re-construction of the sense of selfhood coincides with re-construction of the perception of school (and society). Students' accounts indicate that even if the 'triggers' of *tōkōkyohi* might be specific to each individual student, it is ultimately the entire school system that makes students unable to attend school. The reason why *tōkōkyohi* students are often unable to pinpoint what exactly it was that prevented them from going to school is probably because they are reacting to the composite effects of school, i.e. not just study, not just *ijime*, not just rules, not just corporal punishment, but the whole system constituting the social environment of school in which all of these are organically intertwined. In the survey designed by *tōkōkyohi* students, it is noteworthy that 'the atmosphere of school' is given as one of the options for 'the reason to stop going to school' and that it constituted the second-most-frequently selected answer to the question (attracting 38.8 per cent of respondents) (*Kodomotachi* 1991: 202).

Tōkōkyohi in its origins is a state in which over-socialised students burnout, experiencing almost complete discrepancy between their consciousness and their physical condition. It is an almost complete state of alienation in which social understanding is utterly at odds with the way one's body registers the experience. Physical disorder is the last resort, through which students come to be aware of what is happening to them. The fact that students cannot explain their *tōkōkyohi* is therefore not accidental, but a manifestation of the very nature of the problem. They are in a state of profound alienation. Their critical consciousness fails to grasp the conditions which threaten their existence. Even though at an early stage *tōkōkyohi* is not perceived as such by students themselves, it is still 'school refusal', initiated not at a conscious level but by fundamental physical needs. The fact that students are not aware of it indicates the seriousness of their condition and the severity of their alienation.

Tōkōkyohi, however, is not just the burnout of alienated and over-socialised students. For some, the end of the process is suicide (or murder). For some, it is recovery with a re-integrated subjectivity, which unfolds as a process of reconstruction and de-alienation of the self, involving also a critique and a resistance to school and society (like Ishiwari Minako, Serurian, Sabashi Haruna, Ogura Masahiro, Yamaguchi Kayo and many others). But the majority of cases may fall somewhere in-between.

For society at large, it is a social movement initiated by children whose lives are threatened by the existing paradigms of school and society, children who have been obliged to go through a long and painful process of self-discovery involving a paradigmatic shift in their personal lives in a constraining and stunting environment. It amounts to a legitimation crisis for the Japanese education system, and more broadly, for Japanese society.

NOTES

1 Source: Ishikawa *et al.* (1993: 302).
2 The distinction between *tōkōkyohi* and *hikō* adopted in this book parallels with the distinction between '*tōkōkyohi* with nervous syndrome' (*shinkeishō-teki tōkōkyohi*) and 'taigaku' (truancy) made by Hokkaidōritsu kyōiku kenkyū-sho (quoted in Inamura 1994: 12), and the distinction between 'introverted autistic type' and 'extroverted deviant type' made by Kikuchi (quoted in Inamura 1994: 36).
3 There are only four categories under 'long-term absence from school': 'disliking school', 'illness', 'economic reasons', and 'other'. Strictly speaking, 'disliking school', which is generally referred to as '*tōkōkyohi*', includes 'truancy'. Conversely, it is likely that some *tōkōkyohi* students are put under the category of 'illness', and

not under 'disliking school'. In any case, 'truancy' does not constitute the majority of long-term school nonattendance due to 'disliking school'. According to a survey by Monbushō, it constituted 14 per cent of all the 'long-term absentees' from school due to 'disliking school' (ME 1995b). Similarly, the proportion was 19.4 per cent for junior high school students in Tokyo in a survey conducted by Tokyo Metropolitan School Maladjustment Study Committee (quoted in Inamura 1994: 41).

4 *Tōkōkyohi* at primary school level has been substantially less than that at the secondary level. In 1997, 19,488 primary students (compared to 74,757 secondary students) were absent from school for more than 30 days for 'disliking school' according to the official statistics. This means that one in every 416 primary students (compared to one in 61 secondary students) were recognised as *tōkōkyohi* students (ME 1997a).

5 Morita uses the broader concept of '*futōkō*' (school nonattendance) rather than '*tōkōkyohi*' (school refusal).

6 Morita (1991) uses a slightly different classification from what is presented below (see pp. 23–33, 201–7).

7 This gets more confusing because Monbushō, for instance, uses the term '*tōkōkyohi*' to include 'truancy'.

8 The sample size of this data is not clear. Inamura states that it is based on a study of 564 cases he and his team examined. This, however, includes not only '*tōkōkyohi*' but also 'violence at home', 'delinquent' and 'mentally ill', and the breakdown by these categories is not shown (1988: 52).

9 Again, the sample size is not known.

10 Inamura does not make it clear which year(s) this figure refers to.

11 This is commonly called 'doctor shopping' (*dokutā shoppingu*).

12 He escaped with another 'patient' when the surveillance lessened after a ceremony in the hospital. He walked for three hours barefoot before he sought help at a private counselling place he used to go to. He had attempted to escape earlier, but was caught and received three injections which knocked him out until the following day (Kikuchi 1989).

13 They are referring to advocates of the discourse of *tōkōkyohi* as 'resistance' who take the position that *tōkōkyohi* children are not sick.

14 Miike and Tomoda consistently use '*futōkō*' instead of '*tōkōkyohi*'.

15 The other major factor is 'friendship-anxiety factor' (p. 168), which will be discussed later.

16 Morita does not claim that there is a clear causal relationship. He is very much aware that factor analysis does not detect the causality itself (p. 173).

17 The difference in their view can be attributed partly to the fact that the data in Morita's study were collected primarily from students who were still attending schools most of the time and thus included a substantial number of students who were 'fed up with school', but had a more extroverted character and were often regarded as '*hikō*' students (i.e. having peer support to spend time outside school to have fun). This student population is excluded from the category of *futōkō*, as used by Miike and Tomoda. This discrepancy is the case despite the fact that both Morita, and Miike and Tomoda use the term '*futōkō*' instead of '*tōkōkyohi*'.

18 Students could choose multiple answers for the question (p. 331).

19 Refers to the book by Morita and Ishihara (1989), '*No' to ieru nihonjin*, which was translated by Frank Baldwin (1991) as *The Japan that Can Say 'No'* (New York, Simon and Schuster).

9   Conclusion

I declare.
Tōkōkyohi is not simply the rejection of school.
It is subconscious resistance to society which
distorts the free growth of the self.

(Hanaoka Shinji, a *tōkōkyohi* student[1])

Japanese education has entered what might be called the 'post-Kobe' era. Since the murder of the primary school boy by the 14-year-old 'school killer' in Kobe in May 1997, the Japanese media has been dominated by the 'discourse on children'. Numerous special issues of journals have been published under such titles as 'children in crisis' (*kodomo ga abunai*), 'children beyond comprehension' (*kodomo ga wakaranai*), 'children gone alien' (*kodomo ga henda*) (*Sekai*, January 1998: 62). In no other time in the history of Japanese education or Japanese society in general, has so much attention been paid to children.

In the context of Japanese society, the crisis of children is above all the 'crisis' of Japanese education. According to Ishikawa Norihiko, a child psychiatrist at Tokyo University Hospital who compiled 402 accounts of *tōkōkyohi* by children, the collective message from these children is that 'school is dying' (Ishikawa *et al.* 1993: i). Ogi Naoki, a former teacher and currently a lecturer of education at Hōsei University, says that schools are 'falling apart' and 'melting down' (Ogi 1998). According to Yoshimoto Yukio, a primary school teacher, if it were a company, 'the school system would have collapsed by now' (Kobayashi 1998). The notion that the Japanese school is in a state of institutional fatigue (*seido hirō*) is widespread (Takigawa 1996). There is a general perception that Japanese education is unsustainable in its present form.

Meanwhile, the kinds of problems examined in this book persist.

• Violent 'corporal punishment' by teachers persists. In October 1997, a 17-year-old student in Fukaya Senior High School in Saitama was ordered to sit on the floor with his legs folded. Tobita Tomiyuki, his teacher, was upset because the student did not carry out his assigned duty of cleaning the blackboard. Tobita then kicked him in the face, breaking his jaw and badly twisting his neck. (*ANEN* 21 October 1997)

• *Ijime* and *ijime* suicide persist. In August 1997, a 14-year-old boy in Asahikawa, Hokkaido, killed himself after being bullied and forced to hand over money by his classmate. In the letter addressed to his friends, the boy explained that he decided to commit suicide to avoid being killed by the bully. Classmates were extremely reluctant to talk about the incident for fear of retaliation. The principal said that he did not understand what had happened. (*Mainichi shinbun* 23 August 1997)

• Atrocities unexpectedly committed by 'good students' persist. In November 1997, a 16-year-old boy killed his 83-year-old grandmother by stabbing her more than a dozen times with an ice-pick. He rang the police immediately afterwards and said that he stabbed her because she had said something about his missing school. He had no record of being a 'problem student' except that he began to miss school from time to time after entering senior high school in 1996. (Itami and Ooshige 1997)

These are merely the tip of the iceberg in the crisis of Japanese education. Student violence in 1996 at public schools (between students, against teachers, or involving objects) increased by 37 per cent in junior high, and 16 per cent in senior high schools compared to the previous year. Student violence against teachers increased by 48 per cent in junior high, and the damage done to school property increased by 56 per cent in senior high schools (*AS* 23 December 1997).

It is not only in the area of student behaviour that problems exist. Satō Manabu, professor of Education at Tokyo University, holds that Japanese students are 'running away' from study. In the growing phenomenon known as 'collapse of classes', students simply ignore their teacher and show no sign of interest in study, no matter how experienced the teacher is. The number of drop-outs (*chūtai*) from senior high schools has increased considerably, reaching almost 40 per cent in one public academic school near Tokyo (Satō 1998).

The myth of 'academic ability' is also breaking down. Satō refers to the 1995 international study which found that Japanese students' motivation to study was at the bottom of 41 countries. Although the test score in mathematics and science for Japanese students ranked third, 47 per cent of junior high school students indicated that they 'dislike' or 'hate' mathematics, only slightly less than was the case in Czechoslovakia, the bottom country. The number of Japanese students who said they 'liked' science was least of all countries, and only 48 per cent of Japanese students, compared to the world average of 78 per cent, thought that it might be useful in life. Other studies confirm, he continues, that Japanese students are weak in thinking creatively, solving problems, and expressing themselves. This is despite the 'New View of Ability' (*shin-gakuryoku-kan*) and the point-evaluation system of 1989, whereby such things as 'motivation' and 'creative thinking' were supposed to be integrated as a major part of student assessment (Satō 1998) (see Chapter 6).

What we see in Japanese education today is the end of an educational paradigm. Paradoxically, this coincides with the accomplishment of the educational agenda pursued by Monbushō since 1955. It appears, as Ogi remarks, that 'the postwar education system was programmed to self-destruct' (Kobayashi 1998), and the process would be complete by the end of the century.

What is the Japanese paradigm of education, upon which Monbushō has concentrated its energies for four decades, and which is now crumbling? What does it mean for students to go to school in Japan? It is hoped that this book opens a fresh window of understanding of these questions for those not familiar with the growing Japanese crisis literature.

While the grip of the 'faith in school' is loosening in the mid-1990s (Ogi 1998, Satō 1998), attending school is still a taken-for-granted norm for the majority of students who live in a 'super-meritocratic' society. Even small children assume that in order to be happy, it is essential to do well at school (Chapter 2). The most distinct characteristic of this 'mass-education society' is that students feel more or less the same degree of academic pressure, regardless of their future educational prospects. This is made explicit through a highly developed stratification of schools and students (Chapters 2 and 6).

The Japanese high school to which students are bound, however, is a stifling place. Its organisational structure is extremely formal, rigid, and autocratic. Not only student–teacher relationships, but relationships between teachers and between students are hierarchical. Student–teacher communication is typically teacher-centred, one-way and top-down, and the student–teacher relationship is bureaucratic, distant and impersonal. In this milieu, students largely do not expect things like understanding, respect and personal care from teachers. Paternalistic care is nothing but a myth. Students are assigned a subordinate role and expected to remain silent (Chapter 3).

The space constituted by the Japanese high school is dominated by the powerful, and it is supported by complex rules and practices. School rules codify student behaviour in an unquestionable manner, and provide the foundation for teachers to exert their power (Chapter 5). The violence used by teachers in the name of corporal punishment is mostly hidden and tacitly approved by school authorities. It reflects, in many ways, the fundamental nature of the educational system (Chapter 4). Physical violence is only one aspect of teacher power. Teachers also make comprehensive assessments of students, including their behaviour as well as academic ability. In the context of a super-meritocratic society, teachers' power to convert students' behaviour into academic opportunity is considerable, especially in junior high schools, where the report is subsequently used as part of the selection criteria for admission to senior high schools (Chapter 5). In Japanese schools, teachers are empowered *vis-à-vis* students, and students are constantly under explicit and implicit threats from teachers.

In this disempowered state, the peer relationship among classmates becomes not one of friendship and solidarity but of threat, competition and surveillance. Japanese schools have integrated conformism as the most effective method of control (Chapter 5). In this structure, students mutually watch and check each other and punish the slightest hint of non-conformity, by reproducing and emulating the ways teachers exert power over them. Students learn to use collective violence (physical, verbal and psychological) to release stress in a social environment in which their power is extremely curtailed. *Ijime* is a phenomenon firmly rooted in the social structure of school. For fear of each other, students remain silent. Teachers too remain silent because they are also locked within the same system (Chapter 7).

For students, the Japanese high school is a most uninteresting and boring place. While it is overwhelmingly focused on study, the knowledge propagated by the school has all the characteristics of alienating work. Study, regulated by Monbushō's textbook and curriculum control, is designed to suppress critical thinking and political awareness. While the world around students is highly political, global and domestic issues directly affecting their lives – environment, gender, employment, welfare – are kept as low-key as possible, and school knowledge is extremely objectivist, compartmentalised and positivistic. Students are unable to relate the content of study to their own lives, or to see the meaning of what they are studying. The teacher-centred pedagogy used in Japanese classes augments the alienating nature of school knowledge (Chapter 6).

The alienating character of school knowledge is further strengthened as 'examination knowledge', which is highly instrumental, specialised and commercialised. Yet, students are put in a position to 'benefit' if they accept 'examination knowledge' no matter how alienating, rather than questioning it. Thus, they are caught in the middle of the educational agenda tripod – Monbushō's nationalistic agenda which necessitates the suppression of critical thinking, the corporate sector's elitist agenda (i.e. the selection of supreme 'talent'), and the student agenda of maximisation of life opportunity within the existing structure (Chapter 6).

In sum, Japanese education is a super-control model in which symbolic (e.g. authoritarian), coercive (e.g. employing corporal punishment), and instrumental (e.g. super-meritocratic) controls are deployed in concert.

For most students in Japan, the school is above all the place which makes them tired (*tsukareru tokoro*). Yet, many students keep pushing themselves (*ganbaru* and *gamansuru*) in a state of chronic exhaustion until they reach the state of burnout, or until they just become unable to go to school. The pressure to attend school can persist with or without apparent symptoms. Being pushed beyond their limit, some get very sick and withdrawn, while others become violent, killing themselves or others. It is only with months to years of rest that students gradually regain the strength to live. For many, it is a process of reconstructing one's subjectivity, which is often accompanied by the emergence of a critical approach to school. *Tōkōkyohi* is a painful process of de-alienating oneself from various social understandings learned at school and in society at large. The phenomenon of *tōkōkyohi* indicates the depth of the problem of alienation among Japanese students (Chapter 8).

Super-controlled Japanese schools are the epitome of alienation, in their organisational structure, their human relationships, and the nature of work involved. The consensus among many Japanese that they produce children who are virtual automatons, therefore, is not surprising. Although the expressions differ, the message is the same. Students say so: they view themselves as 'invisible existences' (the 'school killer' and his contemporaries) or 'vegetables' (the 'school killer'). Teachers say so: our students are 'alien-like', '*shijimachi ningen*' (human beings waiting for instructions) and '*botsu-shutai*' (devoid of subjectivity) (Ashizawa 1997). Researchers and educational commentators say so: children today are 'program-driven', heartless (*kokoronashi*) human beings (Mimori 1997) or 'salaryman type with bureaucratic spirit' (Takeuchi 1995).

The crisis of Japanese children, and the crisis of Japanese education, are part of the larger context of the crisis of Japanese society which may be seen as a schooling society (*gakkō-ka shakai*) (Horio 1994), in which schools present a discrete model of society as a whole. It is enough to consider the pathological (yet structural) responses common to children and adults in their respective worlds to realise the parallel. The problem of death from overwork with chronic fatigue (*karōshi*) and company refusal (*shusshakyohi*) are the adult version of *tōkōkyohi*. *Ijime* is just as prevalent among adults as among children, especially in the world of bureaucrats (Miyamoto 1994).

Ijime and *tōkōkyohi* among children are, however, perhaps more important than similar problems among adults because children express the problem in the purest and the most acute form. Their responses to school and society are their lived responses to the social system, which are rarely based on fixed ideas, preconceived values, or abstract ideology. The Japanese paradigm of education makes it difficult for them to live, for them to maintain life, let alone to enjoy it. Whether their response is directed against others (*ijime*) or against themselves (*tōkōkyohi*), in extreme cases suicide or homicide, it is ultimately their resistance to and rejection of the dominant educational paradigm. When education becomes a question of life or death (Kamata 1995), it is nonsensical to talk about the 'high standard of education', as measured by an international test score of mathematics (which is gradually declining in any case). Even with Japan's complex system of control, it becomes increasingly difficult to maintain what is left of 'order' in the classroom.

If Japan's alienating (and alienated) education system can be changed, it is most likely that such change will come through the regenerated energy of students themselves. For the first time in history, a movement by young people to reconstruct their subjectivity and in the process their schools, seems to be emerging as a social force. The activities of some *tōkōkyohi* students, supported by their parents and various specialists, constitutes a vibrant alternative social movement in Japan. This includes publishing books containing their accounts of *tōkōkyohi* (e.g. *Kodomotachi* 1991, 1995), conducting surveys and other studies on *tōkōkyohi* (*Kodomotachi* 1991; Ishikawa 1993: 995–1028), producing newsletters and videos on *tōkōkyohi* (Okuchi 1992). Their activities are important because they can provide alternative values which allow alienated children to understand what may be happening in their lives. The most important feature of the movement is its flexibility. Individuality is accorded the highest value which means that these children have come by their own painful route to understand the fundamental principle of pluralist democracy. It is left in the hands of each student how they come to terms with *their* question of selfhood in the specific social milieu in which they live. This is an extremely radical position in that it is not proposing to do something collectively in order to achieve one fixed model of school and society. It does not fall into the trap of imposing one social model to replace another. In that sense too, the *tōkōkyohi* movement constitutes the antithesis to the fundamental way of thinking behind the bureaucracy-led educational reform.

The sad thing about the 'school killer' of Kobe was that his crimes were founded upon precisely what he learnt at school, the dominance of the weak by the powerful, ultimately to the point of depriving the victims of their existence. This is precisely what 'the school killer' himself resented most about school. He was an unwanted changeling of the Japanese education system.

Asakura Kageki, a sociologist who wrote an ethnographic study of the children of *Tokyo Shure*, regards *tōkōkyohi* children as the '*oni*' (ogres) of contemporary Japan. Just like ordinary and diligent Gregor Samsa in Kafka's *Metamorphosis* (1915) – who, one morning, finds he has become a huge, ugly insect, hated and feared by his family, but who then, in his diversion from the 'taken-for-granted' social order, re-discovers his lost subjectivity – *tōkōkyohi* students go through an unintended transformation to become contemporary '*oni*' of Japanese society. Their behaviour, too, is outside the framework of the 'ordinary' world and beyond the comprehension of 'ordinary' people (Asakura 1995). But unlike Samsa, who dies at the end of Kafka's story, many *tōkōkyohi* students successfully complete the transformation and regain the energy to live.

There are a number of similarities between *tōkōkyohi* students and the 'school killer'. Their behaviour is deeply rooted in their experiences of school. Both are ultimately resisting school, and both are unwelcome 'outsiders' threatening to society, who can be depicted as '*oni*' and changelings (*oni-go*). For both, the question of subjectivity is their existential question. The way they grapple with it determines whether they live or die. Both regain power through their resistance to school.

Their powers, however, are vastly different. The power some *tōkōkyohi* students attain after a long recuperation is positive and constructive, in clear contrast with the negative and destructive power exhibited by the 'school killer', Sakakibara. The difference is whether they can find the language to explain their indefinable unhappiness, apathy, lassitude, anxiety, and anger. The changeling Sakakibara did, but only in the closed and isolated world of his own mind. Until he had committed his crimes, he had nobody to sympathise with him. In a society where large number of children empathise with him, only the language of children, with its deep sympathy based on common experience, has the positive energy to identify and fight back against the cause of their discontent and to do so in a manner respectful of the individuality of each other. Their experience points to the way to turn the general and deep-seated malaise among children into something positive and constructive.

In the 1970s when I was in high school in Japan, we talked about 'examination war', but what we understood by 'war' was only academic competition. More than two decades on, students do not hesitate to say that 'school is a battle field' (*gakkō wa senjyō da*), and to be at school is like being at war

(Ishikawa *et al.* 1993). Japanese schools have turned into places where students feel threatened to the core of their existence.

If the movement initiated by the *tōkōkyohi* students can grow it may be that it will come to mark the beginnings of a new 'post-war' period – marking the beginning of the end to the war within schools, the war against children. The challenge involves nothing less than reversal of the 'reverse-course' of the mid-1950s, the dismantling of the legislative constraints which repealed the spirit of the 1947 Fundamental Law of Education. Students today would find much to support in the spirit of that Law.

Ogi remarks that examples of students playing a positive role in successful educational reform can be found in places like Denmark, where each school has a steering board that selects textbooks and determines budgets. Each board is composed of parent–teacher association members, students' representatives, teachers, and the school's principal and deputy principal. The votes of student representatives have the same value as those of their adult counterparts. 'In Denmark, children are considered to be partners in the operation of schools' (Ogi quoted in Kobayashi 1998).

To achieve such a model is not unrealistic in Japan, and indeed to a large extent what he describes is close to what existed in postwar 'democratic education' under the 1947 Law. This was to some extent maintained in the 1950s and 1960s (i.e. even after the 'reverse-course') in the so-called 'Citizens' Education Movement' which resisted the bureaucratic taking-over of education (Horio 1988 and 1994). Today some students who have gone through *tōkōkyohi* (or who support those who have done so) are equipped with a solid understanding of their subjectivity and a robust ability to think critically in a way, perhaps, that few students in the 1950s and 1960s were. The numerous accounts of *tōkōkyohi* examined in this book indicate that Japanese schools have confronted some students with vital questions of selfhood, and quite paradoxically, provided them with the opportunity to empower themselves in a way which otherwise might not have been possible. By going through the anguish of *tōkōkyohi*, many students have also developed a genuine sympathy for the socially weak, and a strong sense of moral and social justice. Because of their negative experience of school, some *tōkōkyohi* students develop the enthusiasm to become the kind of teacher they wanted to have but could not (Chapter 3). Such young Japanese are developing qualities such as will enable them to play a pivotal role in the reconstruction of new schools in the coming 'post-war' period.

When teachers were full of energy in the immediate postwar years of the 1940s, their slogan was 'Never again send our students to war'. In the second-round 'post-war' era, however, teachers may not have much energy left. If students today were to take a greater role in the reconstruction of Japanese schools a greater diversity might be anticipated. To the extent that such schools would operate on an uncompromising principle of democracy, they may be loosely connected to a slogan reminiscent of the past: 'Do not make *our* school a battle field'.

NOTE

1 Source: Ishikawa *et al.* (1993: 376).

Appendices

Appendix 1: The Japanese sample

	Gender				University[1] intention	Father's level of education						Rejection[2] rate
	Boys	Girls	Unknown	Total		Primary	Junior High	Senior High	Tertiary	Total		
	(n)	(n)	(n)	(n)	(%)	(%)	(%)	(%)	(%)	(n)	(%)	(%)
'Elite' schools[3]												
1	28	15		43	100.0	0.0	2.4	11.9	85.7	42	100	0.0
2	48	0		48	97.9	2.3	7.0	39.5	51.1	43	100	4.0
3	69	28		97	95.9	0.0	7.4	33.7	58.9	95	100	0.0
4	45	0		45	95.6	0.0	6.8	47.7	45.4	44	100	0.0
Subtotal	190	43		233								
Percentage of 'elite' school total	81.5%	18.5%		100%		0.0	6.3	33.5	59.8	224	100	0.9
Percentage of Japanese total	(61.7%)	(18.0%)		(42.4%)								
'Academic' schools												
5	26	21	1	48	72.9	0.0	2.1	58.3	39.6	48	100	2.1
6	23	24		47	66.0	0.0	17.0	44.7	38.3	47	100	0.0
7	33	50	1	84	54.2	5.3	39.5	42.1	13.2	76	100	1.2

	(1)	(2)	(3)	Total						N		
Subtotal	82	95	2	179		2.3	22.8	47.4	27.5	171	100	1.1
Percentage of 'academic' school total	45.8	53.1	1.1%	100%								
Percentage of Japanese total	(26.6%)	(39.7%)		(32.6%)								
Commercial schools												
8	11	33	0	44	20.5	5.3	55.3	31.6	7.9	38	100	0.0
9	25	68		93	19.4	3.3	47.3	48.4	1.1	91	100	0.0
Subtotal	36	101		137		3.9	49.6	43.4	3.1	129	100	0.0
Percentage of commercial school total	26.3	73.7		100%								
Percentage of Japanese total	(11.7%)	(42.3%)		(25.0%)								
Japanese sample total	308	239	2	549		1.9	22.3	40.5	35.3	524	100	0.7
	56.1%	43.5%	0.4%	100%								
	(100%)	(100%)		(100%)								

Notes:

1 Percentage of students in each school who intended to go to university.

2 The number of questionnaires unused in the analysis divided by the number of questionnaires returned.

3 To maintain confidentiality, only codings are shown.

Appendix 2: The Australian sample

	Gender				University intention[1]	Social benefit[2]	Main language spoken at home			Father's level of education						Rejection rate
	Boys	Girls	Unknown	Total			English	Italian/ Greek	Total	Primary	Secondary	HSC[3]	Tertiary	Total	Total	
	(n)	(n)	(n)	(n)	(%)	(%)	(%)	(%)	(%)	(%)	(%)	(%)	(%)	(n)	(%)	(%)
Private schools																
1	0	171		171	82.5	1.2	86.8	10.2	97.0	0.0	21.0	13.0	66.0	162	100	5.5
2	190	0		190	77.2	1.1	85.4	13.5	98.9	6.1	27.2	13.9	52.8	180	100	1.6
3	0	237	5	237	76.7	0.4	85.0	11.5	96.5	3.1	33.8	16.9	46.2	225	100	3.3
4	117	0	7	117	69.0	6.7	87.2	10.1	97.3	2.9	28.4	18.6	50.0	102	100	10.2
5	77	0		77	66.2	2.6	81.8	16.9	98.7	8.0	44.0	14.7	33.3	75	100	1.3
Subtotal	384	408	0	792						3.6	29.7	15.3	51.2	744	100	4.2
Percentage of private school total	48.5	51.5%	0.0%	100%												
Percentage of Australian total	(34.9%)	(44.4%)		(38.9%)												
State high schools																
6	32	33		65	68.8	34.9	18.8	81.2	100.0	70.0	20.0	1.7	8.3	60	100	0.0
7	13	27		40	65.0	22.5	20.0	80.0	100.0	68.4	28.9	0.0	2.6	38	100	0.0
8	50	52	5	107	57.0	32.7	12.9	86.1	99.0	50.0	39.4	7.4	3.2	94	100	12.8
9	37	27	7	71	50.7	33.9	9.5	87.3	96.8	35.3	52.9	2.0	9.8	51	100	20.0
10	12	11		23	47.8	31.6	50.0	50.0	100.0	0.0	38.9	50.0	11.1	18	100	0.0
11	39	44		83	54.2	12.2	57.8	42.2	100.0	24.4	51.3	11.5	12.8	78	100	0.0
12	48	51		99	45.5	8.2	68.0	29.9	97.9	11.0	50.5	12.1	26.4	91	100	13.9
13	55	81	1	137	58.4	6.6	70.8	27.7	98.5	13.3	47.4	11.1	28.1	135	100	0.0
14	11	18	1	30	63.3	0.0	100.0	0.0	100.0	3.6	57.1	7.1	32.1	28	100	3.3

Subtotal	297	344	14	655							30.5	43.8	9.3	16.4	593	100	7.0
Percentage of state high school total	45.3%	52.5%	2.1%	100%													
Percentage of Australian total	(27.0%)	(37.4%)		(32.1%)													
State technical schools																	
15	63	27	3	93	45.2	13.1		23.0	77.0		100.0	18.8	60.0	6.3	15.0	80	100	15.9
16	43	28		71	40.0	29.9		39.4	60.6		100.0	36.4	58.2	5.5	0.0	55	100	13.4
17	40	27		67	34.3	33.8		29.9	70.1		100.0	27.3	63.6	3.6	5.5	55	100	0.0
18	29	20	2	51	32.0	12.5		27.9	72.1		100.0	30.0	62.5	5.0	2.5	40	100	47.9[5]
19	39	6		45	28.9	27.3		20.5	79.5		100.0	27.5	60.0	7.5	5.0	40	100	2.2
20	97	37		134	28.4	9.9		30.3	69.7		100.0	20.5	73.5	3.8	2.3	131	100	0.7
21	108	22		130	27.9	13.4		17.8	81.4		99.2	10.9	70.6	7.6	10.9	119	100	14.5
Subtotal	419	167	5	591							21.7	66.2	5.6	6.3	520	100	14.2
Percentage of state technical school total	70.9%	28.3%	0.8%	100%													
Percentage of Australian total	(38.1%)	(18.2%)		(29.0%)													
Australian sample total	1,100	919	19	2,038						100.0							8.2
	53.9%	45.1%	0.9%	100%													
	(100%)	(100%)		(100%)													

Notes:

1 Percentage of students in each school who intended to go to university.

2 Percentage of students in each school whose family received social benefit.

3 High School Certificate.

4 The number of questionnaires unused in the analysis divided by the number of questionnaires returned.

5 This is partly because the supervising teacher left the school about the time of the distribution of the questionnaires, and also because many of the students in this school found it difficult to read and answer the questions.

Appendix 3: Scale scores of the experience of school by gender

		Australia			Japan		
Alienating aspects of school		*Elite*	*Academic*	*Voc*	*Elite*	*Academic*	*Voc*
1 Alienating student–teacher relationships	F	13.9	12.8	13.5	14.0	18.1	18.2
	M	13.0	13.0	13.4	16.3	16.9	16.9
	s	.001	n.s.	n.s.	.002	n.s.	n.s.
2 Dehumanising treatment by teachers	F	5.9	5.9	6.0	6.3	7.3	7.2
	M	5.7	6.0	6.5	6.5	7.4	7.9
	s	n.s.	n.s.	n.s.	n.s	n.s	n.s
3 Imposition of rules	F	5.9	5.3	5.7	5.0	6.0	6.1
	M	5.5	5.3	5.9	5.2	5.9	5.6
	s	.002	n.s.	n.s.	n.s.	n.s.	n.s
4 Meaninglessness of study	F	6.9	7.7	7.4	8.8	10.6	10.2
	M	7.5	7.4	7.1	9.1	9.8	10.1
	s	.000	n.s.	n.s	n.s.	n.s.	n.s.
5 Academic achievement pressure	F	9.8	7.8	6.7	5.7	6.4	6.3
	M	8.7	8.0	6.9	6.7	6.5	7.6
	s	.000	n.s.	n.s	.007	n.s.	n.s.
6 Alienation from peers	F	5.7	5.3	5.9	4.6	5.3	5.3
	M	8.9	7.3	8.4	7.0	6.3	7.4
	s	.000	.000	.000	.000	n.s.	.001
7 School-related problems at home	F	8.3	9.7	9.4	8.0	9.8	9.4
	M	7.9	8.9	8.5	8.6	8.4	9.8
	s	n.s.	n.s.	n.s.	n.s.	n.s.	n.s.

Notes:
F = mean for female students
M = mean for male students

Appendix 4: Scales and scale reliabilities

1 Alienating student–teacher relationships (r = .84)
- The teachers are easy to get along with
- The teachers treat you with respect
- My teachers care about me as a person
- We have fun with our teachers (e.g. joke and have a laugh together)
- Our teachers show they trust kids
- Teachers really understand students
- My teachers take enough time to explain what I need to understand (They give all the help I need with my work)
- My teachers are easy to talk to, should you have a personal problem

2 Dehumanising treatment by teachers (r = .62)
- Teachers are unfair
- Teachers ask you questions when you are not sure (yet) about the answer
- Teachers pick on me or put me down in front of the class
- Teachers lose their temper and yell
- My teachers are strict
- Teachers treat me as if I am not much good at things

3 Imposition of rules (r = .40)
- Our school rules are sensible and have good reasons
- Teachers let you have a say in making up classroom rules
- If teachers set rules, they explain the reasons well

4 Academic achievement pressure (r = .58)
- You have to think about tests and exams
- School work is difficult
- You must do a lot of homework at this school
- School is a competitive place
- This school pushes you to achieve high academic results

5 Meaninglessness of study (r = .65)
- At this school I can learn things that interest me
- School teaches me things that are useful in my life right now

- School prepares you well for the future
- I can have a say about what I WANT to learn at school (or what subjects to do)
- Teachers make their lessons interesting

6 Alienation from peers (r = .70)
- School is good for meeting kids
- It is easy to make friends with other kids in my class
- Other kids at school are against me because I am not from the same country or culture
- (or speak a different language) (I am bullied by other students: Japan)
- My classmates care about me as a person
- Other kids pick on me or put me down
- I get into fights with other kids from school
- I have friends at school with whom I can discuss my personal problems
- My classmates would help me with my work if I needed them to
- Kids at school treat me as if I am not much good at things

7 School-related problems at home (r = .68)
- There is pressure on me from home to do well at school
- I can find a quiet place at home when I want to study
- At home I am treated as if I am not much good at things
- I have to help with chores at home or do things for my family when I need time for study
- There are problems at home which are on my mind
- If I have problems with my schoolwork I can discuss them with someone at home
- If anything else upsets me or bothers me, I can discuss it with someone at home
- I wish I had someone else to talk to about my problems

Note: See note 7 on p. 154 about scales.

Appendix 5: Inter-school differences of students' experiences of school demonstrated by the means of scale scores: Japan

Scales	Mean	s.d.	Elite	Academic	Vocational	F = **
Academic achievement pressure	6.5	2.7	6.5	6.5	6.6	1.1
Meaninglessness of study	9.7	2.5	9.1	10.3	10.1	10.4*
Alienation in student–teacher relationships	16.9	4.3	15.9	17.6	17.8	8.4*
Dehumanising treatment by teachers	7.0	3.1	6.5	7.4	7.4	4.1
Imposition of rules	5.6	2.1	5.1	5.9	5.9	7.6

*Statistically significant differences at $p < .001$ or better.
** Anova.

Appendix 6: Inter-school differences of students' experiences of school demonstrated by the means of scale scores: Australia

Scales	Mean	s.d.	Elite	Academic	Vocational	F = **
Academic achievement pressure	8.2	2.5	9.4	7.9	6.8	183.2*
Meaninglessness of study	7.3	2.3	7.2	7.5	7.2	4.5
Alienation in student–teacher relationships	13.3	4.2	13.5	12.9	13.4	5.7
Dehumanising treatment by teachers	6.0	2.4	5.8	5.9	6.4	7.2
Imposition of rules	5.6	1.8	5.7	5.3	5.8	17.8*

* Statistically significant differences at $p < .001$ or better.
** Anova

Glossary

bukatsu	abbreviation of '*kurabu katsudō*' meaning club activities. It often refers, especially to, sports-club activities
chikuru	to inform a teacher of *ijime* (*ijime* jargon)
chūtai	drop-out
futōkō	school nonattendance
futsū	ordinary, normal (the word can be used as either a noun or an adjective)
futsūka	general academic senior high schools
gakkō	schools
gakkō-girai	disliking school
gakureki shakai	society based on academic credentials
gamansuru	to endure, persevere, put up with
ganbaru	to persist, do one's best
gyaku kōsu	'reverse-course'
han	small group
hensachi	the deviation score which shows one's academic position relative to others
Hinomaru	the 'Sun Flag' used in many settings as Japan's national flag, seen by many as symbolic of prewar militarism
hokenshitsu	school clinic or health room where a nurse-teacher is in charge
hokenshitsu tōkō	going to *hokenshitsu* instead of 'going to school' (i.e. attending classes)
ijime	bullying, more specifically, group/collective bullying in contemporary Japanese schools
jidō sōdan sho	Child Consultation Centres, which operate in each prefecture under the auspices of the Ministry of Health and Welfare

jitsugyōkōkō	vocational senior high schools
juku	private schools where students cram outside school hours
jukensei	students preparing for the entrance examination
Kangaerukai	abbreviation adopted in this book for *Tōkōkyohi o kangaeru kinkyū shūkai jikkō iinkai* (The executive committee to call for an urgent meeting to think about *tōkōyohi*)
kantenbetsu hyōka	the point evaluation system
kenshū	teacher training
kikokushijo	Japanese children returned from studying overseas
Kimigayo	'His Majesty's Reign', a hymn to the emperor used in many settings as Japan's national anthem
kireru	to lose temper and snap (student colloquialism)
karōshi	death by chronic fatigue from overwork
kokoro	heart, *kokoro-nai* (or *-nashi*), not having a heart
kōtōgakkō (or *kōkō*)	senior high schools
kyōiku iinkai	the local (prefectural/municipal) board of education
kyōiku sentā	Education Centres, under the auspices of the local boards of education, which provide psychological and counselling services to students with school-related problems
Monbushō	Ministry of Education, Science, Sports and Culture
mukatsuku	to be irritating (student colloquialism)
naishinsho	confidential academic and personal reports written by teachers on students
Nihonjinron	'theories of Japan(eseness)', the genre of literature which constructs what it means to be Japanese
Nikkyōso	Ni*h*on kyōshokuin kumiai, Japan Teachers' Union
Rinkyōshin	Rinji kyōiku shingikai, Ad Hoc Council on Education, supra-cabinet advisory council under Prime Minister Nakasone's office, established by law in 1984 and functioning until 1987 (Schoppa 1991: xi)
rōnin	students preparing for an examination for a second time or more
seikatsu shidō	life guidance

seiza	to sit on one's haunches/knees
sensei	honorific way of addressing a teacher
shidō	guidance
shikato	to ignore someone completely (*ijime* jargon)
shinbun	newspaper
shingakkō	elite schools which prepare students for university
shin gakushū shidō yōryō	New Course of Study. It is a substantially revised version of the Course of Study, an officially prescribed curriculum of Monbushō. It was launched in 1989 and fully enforced in 1993.
shōgyōkōkō	commercial senior high schools
taibatsu	physical/corporal punishment
taishū kyōiku shakai	mass education society
teihenkō	'rock bottom school'
tōkōkyohi	school phobia or school refusal (*tōkō* means going to school, and *kyohi*, refusal)
Tokyo Shure	a leading alternative school for *tōkōkyohi* children and adolescents. Established in 1985 by Okuchi Keiko. It constitutes a model for numerous similar establishments all around Japan. '*Shure*' is pronounced '*Shūre*'.
wagamama	selfish, egotistical or self-centred (the word can be used as a noun or an adjective). 'To say *wagamama*' is 'to say selfish things'
wagiri sentaku	'ham-slice' selection based on extremely narrow tracking
yōgo kyōshi	nurse-teacher
yobikō	a supplementary educational institution between senior high schools and universities, designed specifically for *rōnin* students to prepare for the next examination
zainichi	ethnic Korean and Chinese residents in Japan
Zennikkyōren	*Zenkoku nippon kyōshokuin renmei*, a teachers' union in rivalry with Nikkyōso

Bibliography

(ABS) Australian Bureau of Statistics (1984) 'National Schools Statistics Collection, Australia 1984', ABS Catalogue No.4221.0.

—— (1981, 1984, 1990, 1996a) 'Schools Australia', ABS Catalogue No.4421.0.

—— (1996b) 'Education and Training in Australia', ABS Catalogue No. 4224.0.

Akita Sumiko (1990) 'School Phobia: The Case of M-kun', in Kawai, H. (ed.) *Jirei ni manabu shinri ryōhō* [Psychotherapy learnt through case studies], Tokyo, Nihon hyōronsha: 1–13.

Akuzawa, E., Hasegawa, M. and Shiokura, Y. (1997) 'Reformatory Fear for School Dropouts', *Asahi Newspaper E-News*, 23 June.

Althusser, L. (1971) 'Ideology and Ideological State Apparatus', in Cosin, B.R. (ed.) *Education: Structure and Society*, London, Open University Press: 243–80.

Amano Ikuo (1995) *Kyōiku kaikaku no yukue* [The destination of educational reforms], Tokyo, Tokyo University Press.

Anderson, D.E. and Vervoorn, A.E. (1983) *Access to Privilege: Patterns of Participation in Australian Post-Secondary Education*, Canberra, Australian National University Press.

Apple, M.W. (1982) *Education and Power*, London, Ark Paper Books.

Arita Yoshio and Yamaoka Shunsuke (1992) '*Kodomotachi ga miete imasuka?*' [Can you see the children?], *Asahi jānaru*, 20 March: 11–6.

Asakura Kageki (1995) *Tōkōkyohi no esunogurafi* [The ethnography of *tōkōkyohi*], Tokyo, Sairyūsha.

Ashizawa Shunsuke (1997) 'Kodomo-tachi wa naze bōryoku ni hashiru noka' [Why are children driven to violence?], *Sekai* (August): 221–31.

Asō Masataka (1997) '"Kimigayo" ni konna hanashi mo' [About '*Kimigayo*' there is this story too]. Letter to the editor. *Shūkan kinyōbi*, 11 April 1997: 2, 63.

Ayukyō Machiko (1995) '"Ijime 110-ban" kara no hōkoku' [Report from the *ijime* emergency call number], *Shūkan kinyōbi*, 16 June: 44–5.

Azuma Hiroshi, Nada Inada, Ogi Naoki and Yazaki Ai (1986) 'Coming to Grips with Bullying', *Japan Echo*, 13 (2): 56–62.

Balson, Maurice (1992) *Understanding Classroom Behaviour* (third edition), Melbourne, Australian Council for Educational Research.

Beauchamp, Edward (1978) *Learning to Be Japanese*, Hamden, CT, Linnett Books.

Befu Harumi (1990) *Ideorogī to shite no nihon bunka-ron* [Theories on Japanese culture as ideology], Tokyo, Shisō no kagakusha.

Berg, I., Nichols, K. and Pritchard, C. (1969) 'School Phobia – Its Classification and Relationship to Dependency', *Journal of Child Psychology and Psychiatry*, 10: 123–41.

Besag, Valerie (1989) *Bullies and Victims in Schools*, Philadelphia, Open University Press

Bor, W., Presland, I., Lavery, B., Christie, R. and Watson, K. (1992) 'Teachers' Perceptions of Students' Adjustment Difficulties', in Elkins, J. and Izard, J. (eds) *Student Behaviour Problems*, Melbourne, Australian Council for Educational Research: 77–92.

Bourdieu, Pierre (1986) *Distinction: A Social Critique of Judgement of Taste*, London, Routledge and Kegan Paul.

—— (1976) 'The School as a Conservative Force: Scholastic and Cultural Inequalities', in Dale, R. *et al.* (eds) *Schooling and Capitalism*, London, Open University Press: 110–17. (Reprinted from Eggleston, J. (ed.) (1974) *Schooling in a Corporate Society: The Political Economy of Education*, London, Methuen: 36–46.

Bowles, S. and Gintis, H. (1976) *Schooling in Capitalist America*, London: Routledge and Kegan Paul.

Chikushi Tetsuya (1997) ' "Shōnen 14 sai" no shūhen' [The circumstances of a boy of 14-years old], *Shūkan Kinyōbi*, 11 July: 5.

Chiland, C. and Young, G. (1990) 'Introduction', in Chiland, C. and Young, G. (eds), *Why Children Reject School: Views from Seven Countries*, New Haven, CT, Yale University Press: ix.

Chōnabayashi Kaoru (1997) 'Chigai hōken' [Extraterritorial rights], *Aera*, 11 August: 6–8.

Collins, Cherry, Batten, Margaret, Ainley, John and Getty, Corinne (1996) *Gender and School Education*, Melbourne, The Australian Council for Educational Research.

Connell, R.W. (1985) *Teacher's Work*, Sydney, George Allen & Unwin.

Connell, R.W., Ashenden, D.J., Kessler, S. and Dowsett, G.W. (1982) *Making the Difference*, Sydney, George Allen & Unwin.

Connell, W.F. (1993) *Reshaping Australian Education 1960–1985*, Melbourne, Australian Council for Educational Research.

Corrigan, Paul (1979) *Schooling the Smash Street Kids*, London, Macmillan.

Creative21 (1996) *Kyōshi shakai zankoku monogatari* [Cruel stories in the society of teachers], Tokyo, Ēru shuppan.

Cummings, W.K. (1980) *Education and Equality*, Princeton, NJ, Princeton University Press.

Davies, Bronwyn (1996) *Power, Knowledge, Desire*, Canberra, Department of Employment, Education, Training and Youth Affairs.

(DEET) Department of Employment, Education and Training (1988) *Taking Part: Educational Participation in the 1980s*, Canberra, Department of Employment, Education and Training.

—— (1993) 'Telling Tales: Girls and Schools Changing their Ways', Canberra, Department of Employment, Education and Training.

Duke, Benjamin (1986) *The Japanese School*, London, Praeger.

—— (1991) *Education and Leadership for the Twenty-First Century*, New York, Praeger.

Durkheim, Emile (1956) *Education and Sociology*, Sydney, Croom Helm.

Ebimura Jun-ichirō and Watanabe Setsuko (1997) 'Tonari no seki ni iru Sakakibara yobigun' [The reserve army of Sakakibara sitting in the next seat], *Aera*, 14 July: 14–6.

Elkins, John and Izard, John (1992) *Student Behaviour Problems: Context, Initiatives and Programs*, Melbourne, Australian Council for Educational Research.

Esland, Geoffrey (1971) 'Teaching and Learning as the Organization of Knowledge', in Young, M. (ed.) *Knowledge and Control*, London, Collier Macmillan: 70–115.

Everheart, R.B. (1983) *Reading, Writing and Resistance*, London, Routlege and Kegan Paul.

Feinberg, Walter (1993) *Japan and the Pursuit of a New American Identity*, New York and London, Routledge.

Foucault, Michel (1977) *Discipline and Punish: The Birth of the Prison*, New York, Penguin.

Freire, Paulo (1972) *Pedagogy of the Oppressed*, New York, Penguin Books.

Fujii Seiji (1983) 'Kōkōsei no mita kanri kyōiku' [Regimentation in education as seen by high school students], *Sekai* (September): 175–81.

—— (1984) 'Nakama no wa hirogaru: Kanri kyōiku o tou kōkōsei tachi' [Expanding networks of friends: high school students who question regimentation in education], *Sekai* (September): 279–84.

Fujita Midori (1997) 'Tōkō shinai to shisetsu ni irerareru? Jidō fukushi-hō kaiaku' [You are sent to the reformatory for not attending school? A change for the worse in the child welfare law], *Shūkan kinyōbi*, 4 July: 26–8.

Fukaya Masashi (1983) 'Taibatsu o sodateru kyōiku fūdo' [The educational climate which cultivates corporal punishment], *Sekai* (September): 199–209.

Fukuda Hiroyuki (1997) *Ijimenai jibun-zukuri* [The making of a self that does not bully], Tokyo, Gakuyō shobō.

Fukuda Sachio and Arimoto Norifumi (1997) 'Cross-cultural Study on Bullying in School: A Case of Japan and Australia', paper presented at the Conference of Japanese Studies Association of Australia, Melbourne University, Melbourne.

Giddens, Anthony (1989) *Sociology*, Cambridge, Polity Press.

Giroux, H. (1983) *Theory and Resistance in Education*, London, Heinemann Educational Books.

Hasegawa Hiroshi (1990) 'Kyōshi no bōryoku o kabau kyōiku' [Education which supports violence by teachers], *Aera*, 18 December: 22–4.

Hata Masaharu (1983) 'Kyōiku kikai no kakusa' [Inequality in educational opportunity], *Gendai no esupuri* (no.196): 150–74.

Hayashi Kaori (1994) 'Jibun ga taisetsu dakara' [Because I care about myself], *Shūkan kinyōbi*, 8 April.

Hendry, J. (1986) *Becoming Japanese: The World of the Pre-school Child*, Honolulu, University of Hawaii Press.

Henry, Miriam, Knight, John, Lingard, Robert and Taylor, Sandra (1988) *Understanding Schooling: An Introductory Sociology of Australian Education*, London, Routledge.

Higaki Takashi (1991) 'Chūtai saseru kenri?' [The right to allow students to leave school?], *Sekai* (May): 216–32.

Hirai Tadashi (1997) 'In the Troubling Twilight between Horseplay and Bullying', *Asahi Newspaper E-News*, 2 June.

Hirano Yūji, Tomabechi Masato and Fujii Seiji (1990) *Seito jinken techō* [Notebook for students' rights], Tokyo, San'ichi shobō.

Hirayama Katsumi (1995) 'Ima, gakkō wa: ijime no shūhen de' [School now: in the periphery of *ijime*], *Shūkan kinyōbi*, 10 February: 8–14.

Hirose Makoto (1989) *Gakkō e ikitai: Hokusēyoichi no atarashii kokoromi* [I want to go to school: a new attempt by Hokusēyoichi], Sapporo, Arisu.

Horio Takehisa (1988) *Educational Thought and Ideology in Modern Japan*, Tokyo, University of Tokyo Press.

Horio Teruhisa (1992) *Kyōkasho mondai* [The textbook issue], Tokyo, Iwanami booklet.

—— (1994) *Nihon no kyōiku* [Education in modern Japan], Tokyo, Tokyo University Press.

—— (1996) 'Yuragu gakkō shinkō to saisei e no mosaku' [The declining faith in school and the search for a new way forward], in Horio, T., Sanuki, H. and Tanaka, T. (eds) *Nihon no gakkō no gojyū nen* [Fifty years of Japanese schools], Tokyo, Kashiwa shobō: 214–70.

Hosaka Nobuto (1990) 'Joshi kōkōsei o asshi saseta monko to kōsoku' [The gate and school rules which crushed a female student to death], *Asahi jānaru*, 27 July: 128.

—— (1992) 'Saraba naishinsho' [Goodbye naishinsho], *Sekai* (May): 59–72.

Hsia Heidi (1984) 'Structural and Strategic Approach to School Phobia/School Refusal', *Psychology in the Schools*, 21 (July): 360–7.

Hyde, Norm (1992) 'Discipline in Western Australian Government Schools', in Slee, R. (ed.) *Discipline in Australian Public Education*, Melbourne, Australian Council for Educational Research: 61–78.

Ichikawa Hiroshi (1989) 'Gakushū shidō yōkō o kaita no wa dare ka' [Who wrote the New Course of Study], *Sekai* (November): 42–55.

Ida Hiroyuki (1998) '"Hinomaru", "kimigayo" ni shika kanshin o shimesanai kōchō' [The principal who is interested only in '*Hinomaru*' and '*Kimigayo*'], *Shūkan kinyōbi*, 5 June: 70–1.

Ikeda Takuma, Hara Keiji, Hikosaka Yūji and Miki Hitomi (1991) 'Motto jiyūna sentakushi o' [Increasing free choices], *Sekai* (May): 254–63.

Ikeda Yūko *et al.* (1986) 'Tōkōkyohi to shakai byōri: Chūgakusei no seishin eisei chōsa kara' [The social pathology of *tōkōkyohi*: the results of the mental health survey of junior high school students], *Shakai seishin igaku* [Social psychiatry], 9 (1): 3–8.

Illich, I. (1971) *Deschooling Society*, New York, Penguin.

Imahashi Morikatsu (1995) 'Naze ijime wa hōchi sarete iruka' [Why is *ijime* left unresolved], *Sekai* (April): 134–44.

Imahashi Morikatsu, Saitō Yoshifusa, Hayashi Hideki, Tawara Moeko *et al.* (1986) 'Taibatsu ijime no gen'in to kaiketsu: symposium' [Symposium on causes and solutions of corporal punishment and *ijime*], *Sekai* (April): 70–110.

Imahashi Morikatsu, Hattori Shunzō, Higashimoto Hisako and Nakanishi Takuko

(1992) 'Fubo ga gakkō ni kaze o iretatoki' [When parents blew fresh air into school], *Sekai* (May): 81–95.

Inaizumi Megumi (1997) 'Haha no kiroku: "Musuko no kokoro, oya shirazu"' [A mother's record: 'A mother who had no idea what was in the mind of her son'], *Bungei shunjū* (October): 280–90.

Inaizumi Ren (1997) 'Ko no kiroku: Boku ga gakkō o yameru to itta hi' [A child's record: The day I said that I would quit school], *Bungei shunjū* (October): 270–8.

Inamura Hiroshi (1988) *Tōkōkyohi no kokufuku* [Overcoming *tōkōkyohi*], Tokyo, Shinyōsha.

—— (1994) *Futōkō no kenkyū* [The study of *futōkō*], Tokyo, Shinyōsha.

Ishida Hiroshi (1989) 'Gakureki to shakai keizaiteki chii no tassei' [Academic qualifications and the attainment of socioeconomic status], *Shakaigaku hyōron* [Sociological review], 159: 252–66.

Ishikawa Norihiko (1986) 'Ijime ni wa mada kibō ga aru' [There is still some hope about *ijime*], *Sekai* (April): 63–9.

Ishikawa Norihiko, Uchida Ryōko and Yamashita Eizaburō (1993) *Kodomotachi ga kataru tōkōkyohi: 402 nin no messēji* [*Tōkōkyohi* as discussed by children: 402 Accounts], Yokohama, Seori shobō.

Ishikawa Norihiko, Uchida Ryōko and Yamashita Eizaburo (1995) *Oyatachi ga kataru tōkōkyohi: 108 nin no non fikushon* [*Tōkōkyohi* as discussed by parents: 108 non-fiction accounts], Yokohama, Seori shobō.

Itami Kazuhiro and Ooshige Fumio (1997) 'Otonashii kō-2 fubo metta zashi' [Gentle 16-year-old stabs grandmother repeatedly], *Aera*, 22 December: 10–12.

Johnson, Wendy (1992) 'South Australia: From Good School Practices to Effective Policy', in Slee, R. (ed.) *Discipline in Australian Public Education*, Melbourne, Australian Council for Educational Research: 79–104.

Kamata Satoshi (1984) *Kyōiku kōjō no kodomotachi* [Children in the 'educational factory'], Tokyo, Iwanami.

—— (1995) *Ikiru tame no gakkō* [School for living], Tokyo, Iwanami.

—— (1997) 'Yume o ubawareta shōnen tachi' [Boys who are deprived of dreams], *Jidō shinri* [Child psychology], November 1997 (Special issue on the murder of a primary schoolboy in Kobe): 6–11.

(Kangaerukai) Tōkōkyohi o kangaeru kinkyū shūkai jikkō iinkai [Executive committee to organise an emergency meeting to think about tōkōkyohi] (ed.) (1989) *Tōkōkyohi to wa* [What is tōkōkyohi?], Tokyo, Yūkyū shobō.

Kariya Takehiko (1995) *Taishū kyōiku shakai no yukue* [The destination of a mass-education society], Tokyo, Chūōkōron.

Kariya, T. and Rosenbaum, J. (1987) 'Self-selection in Japanese Junior High Schools: a Longitudinal Study of Students' Educational Plans', *Sociology of Education*, 60 (July): 168–80.

Katō Jyūhachi (1990) *Nihon kyōiku no hikari to kage* [Light and shadows of Japanese education], Tokyo, Ishida pan research.

Katō Yoritoshi (1993) *Gakkō ni ikanai, ikenai kodomotachi* [Children who do not and can not go to school], Tokyo, Murata shoten.

Kawai Hayao (ed.) (1990) *Jirei ni manabu shinri ryōhō* [Psychotherapy learnt through case studies], Tokyo, Nihon hyōronsha.

—— (1996) 'Ijime to "naiteki ken-i"' [Ijime and 'internalized authority'], *Sekai* (March): 102–12.

—— (1997) 'Nihon no kyōiku no soko ni aru mono' [What is at the base of the Japanese education system], *Chūōkōron* (October): 54–67.

Kikuchi Ken'ichi (1989) 'Kōshi no mukou kara sakebi-goe ga kikoeru' [Screams heard from the other side of the lattice], *Asahi jānaru*, 15 December: 36–40.

Kim Ch'an-jong (1991) 'Fue tsuzukeru kōkō chūtai' [Increasing dropouts from senior high schools], *Sekai* (May): 233–42.

Kimura Takashi (1998) 'Sotsugyō, nyūgaku gyōji o meguru kono ichi-nen-kan no tatakai' [Fights over graduation and entrance ceremonies in the past year], *Shūkan kinyōbi*, 5 June: 67–9.

Kinoshita Ritsuko (1988) *Tsuma-tachi no kigyō sensō* [The corporate war of the wives] Tokyo, Shakai shisōsha.

Kobayashi Ginko (1998) 'Schools on Verge of Entering a New Era?', *Daily Yomiuri On-Line*, 5 January.

Kobayashi Tsuyoshi (1985) *Ijime o kokufuku suru* [Overcoming *ijime*], Tokyo, Yūhikaku.

—— (1995) 'Mazu kyōshi ga taibatsu o yameyo' [First, teachers should stop using corporal punishment], *Shūkan kinyōbi*, 10 February: 20.

(Kodomotachi) Tokyo Shure no kodomotachi (ed.) (1991) *Gakkō ni ikanai boku kara gakkō ni ikanai kimi e* [From me who does not go to school to you who do not go to school], Tokyo, Kyōiku shiryō shuppankai.

—— (1995) *Boku-rashiku, kimi-rashiku, jibun-iro: Tōkōkyohi, watashitachi no sentaku* [Just be yourself: *Tōkōkyohi*, our choice], Tokyo, Kyōiku shiryō shuppankai.

Kohama Itsuo (1985) *Gakkō no genshōgaku no tame ni* [Towards a phenomenology of school], Tokyo, Yamato shobō.

Koizumi Eiji (1990) 'School Nonattendance and Psychological and Counselling Services', in Chiland, C. and Young, G. (eds), *Why Children Reject School: Views from Seven Countries*, New Haven, CT, Yale University Press: 88–97.

Kuji Tsutomu (1997) 'Kyōikukai mo kane mamire' [Education is also smeared with corrupt money], *Shūkan kinyōbi*, 11 July: 26–9.

Kunie Kyōko (1991) 'Kōkō "say" world' [High school students have a say], *Sekai* (May): 243–53.

Kurahara Kanae (1991) 'Jibun rashiku aritai to omou kara' [Because I want to be myself], in 'Tokyo Shure' no kodomotachi (ed.) *Gakkō ni ikanai boku kara gakkō ni ikanai kimi e* [From me who does not go to school to you who do not go to school], Tokyo, Kyōiku shiryō shuppankai: 119–30.

Kuroda Kiyoshi, Ohtani Akihiro, Yano Hiroshi and Awahara Kayoko (1997) '14 sai no shōnen o hankō ni karitateta? Shakai byōri o kaibō suru' [To analyse the social malaise which drove a 14-year-old boy to crime], *Shūkan kinyōbi*, 18 July 1997: 19–23.

Kuroiwa Shitsuko (1997) '"Sakakibara"-kun ni miru kodomo-tachi no ima' [Children today as seen through the case of 'Sakakibara'-kun], *Shūkan kinyōbi*, 8 August: 65.

Lamb, S., Polesel, J. and Teese, R. (1995) '*Where do they go?*' *An Evaluation of Sources of Data used for the Monitoring of Students' Destinations and Other Educational Outcomes in Australia*, Australian Government Commissioned Report No. 40, Canberra, National Board of Employment, Education and Training.

Lansdown, R. (1990) 'Nonattendance at School and School Refusal in Britain', in Chiland, C. and Young, G. (eds), *Why Children Reject School: Views from Seven Countries*, New Haven, CT, Yale University Press: 109–22.

Last, C., Francis, G., Hersen, M., Kazdin, A. and Strauss, C. (1987) 'Separation Anxiety and School Phobia: A Comparison Using DSM-III Criteria', *American Journal of Psychiatry*, 144, 5 (May): 653–7.

LeTendre, Gerald (1996) '*Shidō*: The Concept of Guidance', in Rohlen, T. and LeTendre, G. (eds) *Teaching and Learning in Japan*, Cambridge, Cambridge University Press: 275–94.

Lewis, Catherine C. (1995) *Educating Hearts and Minds*, New York, Cambridge University Press.

Lock, Margaret (1986) 'Plea for Acceptance: School Refusal Syndrome in Japan', *Social Science and Medicine*, 23 (2): 99–112.

McCormack, Gavan (1996) *The Emptiness of Japanese Affluence*, Armonk, New York, M.E. Sharp and Sydney, Allen and Unwin.

Marshall, Byron K. (1994) *Learning to be Modern*, Boulder, CO, West View Press.

(ME) Ministry of Education (various years) *Monbu tokei yoran* [Summary of statistics of education], Catalogue no. MESO 3-8511, Tokyo, Monbushō.

Miike Teruhisa and Tomoda Akemi (1994) *Gakkō karōshi* [School *karōshi* (death by overwork)], Tokyo, Shindan to chiryōsha.

Mills, C. Wright (1959) *The Sociological Imagination*, London, Oxford University Press.

Mimori Tsukuru (1997) 'Gendai nihon no "kokoronai" wakamono-tachi' ['Heartless' youths in contemporary Japan], *Shūkan kinyōbi*, 8 August: 46–8.

Miyachi Sōshichi (1990) *Kikokushijo* [Returnee children], Tokyo, Chūōkōron.

Miyadai Shinji (1997) 'Chūmoku subeki wa chūgakusei no sutoresu' [Stress among junior high school students deserves attention], *Jidō shinri* [Child psychology] special issue '*Kobe shōgakusei satsugai jiken*' [Murders of primary school children in Kobe], November: 24–31.

—— (1998) 'Kobe Murder Shows Adults out of Touch', interview with the *Daily Yomiuri*, *Daily Yomiuri On-Line*, 22 June.

Miyadai Shinji and Terawaki Ken (1998) '"Gakkō" o dō kaete ikuka' [How to change 'school'?], *Sekai* (January): 132–44.

Miyagawa Toshihiko (1995) *Kokoro ga kowareru kodomotachi* [Children whose hearts get broken], Tokyo, Kadokawa shoten.

Miyamoto Masao (1994) *Straitjacket Society*, Tokyo, Kodansha International.

Mizusato Seiga (1997) 'Kodomotachi wa naze shi ni mukau ka' [Why are children heading towards death], *Aera Special Issue '*Kodomo ga abunai*' [Children in crisis], November: 30–5.

Monbushō (1983) *Seito no kenzen ikusei o meguru sho-mondai: Tōkōkyohi mondai o chūshin ni (Chūgakko, kōtōgakko hen)* [Issues regarding the healthy growth of students: with special focus on *tōkōkyohi* (Lower and upper secondary schools)] Monbushō seito shidō shiryō no. 18; Seito shidō kenkyū shiryō no. 12 [Monbushō guidance on how to instruct students no. 18; Research materials for the instruction of students no. 12], Catalogue no. MEJ 1-8326, Tokyo, Monbushō.

—— (Shotō-chūtō kyōiku kyoku chūgakkō ka) [Lower Secondary School Division, Elementary and Secondary Education Bureau] (1989) 'Jidō seito no mondai kōdō no jittai to Monbushō no seisaku' [The reality of student problematic behaviour and the policy of Monbushō], *Monbu jihō* [Monthly magazine of Monbusho], issue no. 1346.

—— (Shotō-chūtō kyōiku kyoku chūgakko ka) [Lower Secondary School Division, Elementary and Secondary Education Bureau] (1991, 1994, 1995a) *Seito shidō-jō no sho-mondai no genjō to Monbushō no shisaku ni tsuite* [Current situation and Monbushō's counter-measures regarding problems related to the guidance of students], Tokyo, Monbushō.

—— (1995b) '94 nendo mondai kōdō hakusho' [1994 white paper on problematic behaviour], Tokyo, Monbushō.

—— (Daijin kanbō chōsa tōkei kikaku ka) [Research and Statistics Planning Division, Minister's Secretariat] (1997a) *Gakkō kihon chōsa sokuhō* [The school basic survey] (preliminary) August, Tokyo, Monbushō.

—— (1997b) 'Program for Educational Reform (Revised on 5 August 1997)', http://www.monbu.go.jp/series-en/00000004.

Morita Akio and Ishihara Shintarō (1989) *'No' to ieru nihon* [A Japan which can say 'No'], Tokyo, Kōbunsha.

Morita Yōji (1991) *'Futōkō' no shakaigaku* [The sociology of '*futōkō*'], Tokyo, Gakubunsha.

Mouer, Ross and Sugimoto Yoshio (1986) *Images of Japanese Society*, London and New York, KPI.

Munakata Tsunetsugu (1991) *Sutoresu kaishō gaku* [A theory of stress coping], Tokyo, Shōgakkan.

Murakami Ryū (1997) 'Kodomo ni totte genki no deru koto ga nanimo nai' [There is absolutely nothing to spark healthy feelings in children], *Aera Special Issue 'Kodomo ga abunai'* [Children in crisis], November: 4–19.

Murakami Yoshio (1984) 'Kōnai bōryoku no "kanri" de inshitsuka suru sogai enerugī' [The force of alienation gets insidious due to the 'control' of school violence], *Asahi Jānaru*, 30 November: 6–10.

—— (1988) 'Kodomo no mune no uchi ni hirogaru kurai kiretsu ni kigatsuite imasuka?' [Are you aware of the dark cracks in the minds of children?], *Asahi jānaru*, 22 July: 20–1.

—— (1990) 'Taibatsu to iu biyaku ni hisomu fukusayō' [Side effects of the sweet medicine called corporal punishment], *Asahi jānaru*, 24 August: 22–4.

Nagahata Michiko (1991) 'Kōkōsei tachi e' [A message to senior high school students], *Sekai* (May): 209–15.

Nakajima Katsuyo (1995) 'Hitomi kagayaku hi o negatte: tōkōkyohi no seito to hokenshitsu' [Wishing for the day when their eyes will sparkle: *tōkōkyohi* students and *hokenshitsu*], in Takagai, C., Fujimoto, F. and Yokoyu, S. (eds) *Tōkōkyohi futōkō 3: Kōkōsei* [*Tōkōkyohi* and *futōkō*: Senior high school students], Tokyo, Rōdōjunpōsha: 68–89.

Nakane Chie (1970) *Japanese Society*, Berkeley, University of California Press.

New South Wales Teachers Federation (1984) 'Peace, Disarmament and Peace Studies. Annual Conference Decision', Sydney.

NHK yoron chōsa-bu (1991) *Gendai chūgakusei, kōkōsei no seikatsu to ishiki* [The life and consciousness of high school students today], Tokyo, Meiji tosho.

Nihon keizai shinbun (1997) *2020 nen kara no keishō* [An alarm bell from the year 2020], Tokyo, Nihon keizai shinbun.

Nihon PTA zenkoku kyōgikai [Japanese national council of PTA] (1988) *Gakkō seikatsu (tōkōkyohi-to) ni kansuru chōsa kekka hōkokusho* [A survey report on school life (including *tōkōkyohi*)], Tokyo, Nihon PTA.

Nishiyama Akira (1997) 'Shōnen jiken ga tou "yohaku no nai shakai"' ['Society without margins' question raised by an incident concerning a boy], *Sekai* (September): 22–6.

Nishizato Osamu (1989) *Aru shōgen: Kōkō chūtai* [A documentary: dropping out of high school], Tokyo, Kōbunken.

Ogi Naoki (1998) '"Kodomo shimin" no kanōsei' [The possibility of 'child citizens'], *Sekai* (January): 97–106.

Ohtorii Yūko (1995) 'Ijimerareteiru aite o mite anshin shitakatta' [I wanted to feel safe by watching someone being bullied], *Shūkan kinyōbi*, 10 February: 21.

Okano Kaori (1993) *School to Work Transition in Japan*, Clevedon, Somerset, Multilingual Matters.

Okonogi Keigo (1990) 'Comment 1 (to the report by Akita Sumiko)', in Kawai, Hayao (ed.) *Jirei ni manabu shinri ryōhō* [Psychotherapy learnt through case studies], Tokyo, Nihon hyōronsha: 13–18.

Okuchi Keiko (1992) *Gakkō wa hitsuyō ka* [Is school necessary?], Tokyo, NHK Books.

Okuchi Shigeo (1990) 'Kodomo ni oshierareta "jibun no ikikata"' ['My way to live my selfhood' taught by my children], in Ishii Shinji (ed.) *Gakkō ni ikanai shingaku gaido* [A school guide for those who do not go to school]: *Bessatsu takarajima* 111, Tokyo, Takarajima: 96–107.

Okuchi Yuiko, Komatsu, J., Kasahara, H. and Fuji, M. (1989) '"*Gakkō*"-tte nan darō [What is 'school'?]', *Sekai*, (May): 65–73.

Olweus, Dan (1993) *Bullying at School*, Oxford, Blackwell.

Oride Kenji (1996) 'Nakama kankei no yokuatsu sei to kaihō sei' [The oppressive and liberating nature of peer relationships], in Horio, T., Ohta, M. and Yokoyu, S. (eds) *Kodomo no iyashi to gakkō* [School and the healing of children], Tokyo, Kashiwa shobō: 131–55.

Otto, Rosemarie (1986) *Teachers Under Stress*, Melbourne, Hill and Content.

Parsons, Talcott (1956) 'The School Class as a Social System: Some of its Functions in American Society', *Harvard Educational Review*, (Fall): 297–318.

Peak, Lois (1989) 'Learning to Become Part of the Group: The Japanese Child's Transition to Preschool Life', *Journal of Japanese Studies*, 15 (1): 93–123.

Pilkington, C. and Piersel, W. (1991) 'School Phobia: A Critical Analysis of the Separation Anxiety Theory and an Alternative Conceptualization', *Psychology in Schools*, 28 (October): 290–303.

Reischauer, Edwin O. (1977) *The Japanese*, Tokyo, Charles E. Tuttle.

Rigby, Ken (1996) *Bullying in Schools*, Melbourne, Australian Council for Educational Research.

Rohlen, Thomas (1980) 'The *Juku* Phenomenon: An Exploratory Essay', *Journal of Japanese Studies*, 6 (2): 207–42.

—— (1983) *Japan's High Schools*, Berkeley, University of California Press.

—— (1995) *Differences That Make a Difference: Explaining Japan's Success*, Stanford, Asia Pacific Research Centre, Stanford University.

Saijō Nobumitsu (1996) 'Tsukareteiru kodomotachi' [Tired children], in Nihon kodomo o mamoru kai (Japan association to protect children) (ed.) *Kodomo hakusho* [White paper on children], Tokyo, Sōdo bunka: 72–3.

Sakamoto Hideo (1986) *Kyōshi no kenkyū* [The study of teachers], Tokyo, San'ichi shobō.

—— (1990) *Kōsoku no hanashi* [Stories about school rules], Tokyo, San'ichi shobō.

—— (1995) *Taibatsu no kenkyū* [Studies in corporal punishment], Tokyo, San'ichi shobō.

Sakamoto Tetsushi and Takahashi Junko (1997) ' "Sakakibara" ni natta shōnen' [The boy who became 'Sakakibara'], *Aera*, 14 July 1997: 6–9.

Sandē mainichi (1997) '1997 Zenkoku chomei 1380 kōkō no shuyō daigaku gōkakusha-sū' [The number of those admitted to major universities in 1997 from 1380 famous high schools in the country], *Sandē mainichi*, 20 April: 78–137.

Sanuki Hiroshi (1996) 'Kyōsō shakai no naka deno gakkō no henshitsu to aratana gakkō zukuri' [The change of schools in the competition society and the making of new schools], in Horio, T., Sanuki, H. and Tanaka, T. (eds) *Nihon no gakkō no gojyū nen* [Fifty years of Japanese schools], Tokyo, Kashiwa shobō: 123–76.

Sarup, M. (1978) *Marxism and Education*, London, Routlege and Kegan Paul.

Satō Akira (1985) ' "Inu" no yōni shinu noka: Kyōshi no satsujin ni tsuite' [To die like a 'dog': on the murder of students by teachers], *Sekai* (July): 18–21.

Satō K., Ito, I., Morita, S., *et al.* (1987) 'The Issue of 'Bullying': Neuroses and Psychosomatic Syndromes of Bullied Children' [in Japanese], *Japanese Journal of Child and Adolescent Psychiatry*, 28: 110–18.

Satō Machiko (1989) *Gōrei no nai gakkō* [Schools without commands], Tokyo, Gakuyō shobō.

Satō Manabu (1998) ' "Manabi" kara tōsō suru kodomo-tachi' [Children who run away from 'learning']', *Sekai* (January): 63–72.

Satō Takashi (1996) 'Kyōiku seisaku no "tenkan" to gakkō' [Schools and the 'change-over' in educational policies], in Horio, T., Sanuki, H. and Tanaka, T. (eds), *Nihon no gakkō no gojyū nen* [Fifty years of Japanese schools], Tokyo, Kashiwa shobō: 66–121.

Schoenheimer, H.P. (1973) *Good Australian Schools and their Communities*, Technical Teachers' Association of Victoria, Melbourne, pp. 5–6.

Schoolland, Ken (1990) *Shogun's Ghost: the Dark Side of Japanese Education*, New York and London, Bergin and Garvey.

Schoppa, Leonard (1991) *Education Reform in Japan*, London, Routledge.

Sekai (1998) 'Gakureki byōdō-do' [The degree of equality among those with different

academic qualifications], in *Nihon Yutakasa Data Book* [Databook on Japan's afflu-
ence], *Sekai* special issue, January, pp. 133–5.

Seymour, Brenda (1992) 'A Sparse Sparing of the Rod: The Changing Status of
Student Welfare and Discipline in New South Wales Schools', in Slee, R. (ed.)
Discipline in Australian Public Education, Melbourne, Australian Council for Educa-
tional Research: 44–60.

Sharp, Rachel (1980) *Knowledge, Ideology and the Politics of School*, London, Routledge
and Kegan Paul.

Shimizu Kazuhiko, Akao, K., Arai, A., Ito, M., Sato, H. and Yaosaka, O. (1996)
Kyōiku dēta lando 96–97 [Databook of educational statistics], Tokyo, Jijitsūshin.

Shimizu Yoshinori (1990) *Kokugo nyūshi mondai hisshō hō* [A sure way to pass the
contemporary Japanese language examination], Tokyo, Kōdansha.

Shimojima Tetsuo (1989) ' "Gerunika" wa naze hagasareta ka' [Why was the picture
of 'Guernica' taken away], *Sekai* (November): 56–73.

Singleton, J. (1989) *'Gambaru*: A Japanese Cultural Theory of Learning', in Shields,
J.S., Jr. (ed.) *Japanese Schooling*, University Park, Pennsylvania State University
Press: 8–15.

Slee, Roger (1992a) 'Changing Discipline Policy in Victorian Schools: a Critique of
the Policy Process', in Slee, R. (ed.) *Discipline in Australian Public Education*,
Melbourne, Australian Council of Educational Research: 12–43.

—— (1992b) 'National Trends in Discipline Policy Development', in Elkins, J. and
Izard, J. (eds) *Student Behaviour Problems: Context, Initiatives and Programs*, Melbourne,
Australian Council for Educational Research: 1–12.

South Australia Department of Education (1989) 'School Discipline: The Management of Student Behaviour. Policy and Guidelines for Practice', Adelaide, South
Australia Department of Education.

Stevenson, Harold (1989) 'The Asian Advantage: The Case of Mathematics', in
Shields, J.S., Jr. (ed.) *Japanese Schooling*, University Park, Pennsylvania State
University Press: 85–95.

Stoddart, Jim (1992) 'School-based Discipline Policies and Procedures in the
Australian Capital Territory', in Slee, R. (ed.) *Discipline in Australian Public
Education*, Melbourne, Australian Council for Educational Research: 145–62.

Sugimoto Yoshio (1983) *Chō-kanri rettō nippon* [Super-control archipelago Japan],
Tokyo, Kōbunsha.

—— (1997) *An Introduction to Japanese Society*, Cambridge, Cambridge University
Press.

Tachibanaki Toshiaki (1996) *Wage Determination and Distribution in Japan*, New York,
Oxford University Press.

Takabatake Michitoshi (1986) *Chihō no Ohkoku* [Regional kingdoms], Tokyo, Ushio
shuppan.

Takahashi Junko (1997) 'Shōnen no yuganda "jiko hyōgen" ' [The distorted 'self
expression' of a boy], *Aera*, 4 August: 13–6.

Takayama Yōji (1989) 'Kenshō Monbuso' [Examining Monbushō], *Sekai* (November): 23–41.

Takeuchi Kiyoshi (1983) 'Nichibei kōkōsei hikaku chōsa kara' [Report on a comparative study between Japanese and American senior high school students], *Gendai no esupuri* (no. 195): 152–68.

Takeuchi Tsunekazu (1993) *Nihon no gakkō no yukue* [The destination of Japanese schools], Tokyo, Tarō jirōsha.

Takeuchi Yō (1995) *Nihon no meritokarashī* [The meritocracy in Japan], Tokyo, Tokyo University Press.

Takigawa K. (1996) 'Datsu gakkō no kodomotachi' ['Deschooling' children], in Inoue, S. (ed.) *Kodomo to kyōiku no shakaigaku* [Sociology of children and education], Tokyo, Iwanami: 39–56.

Tawara Yoshifumi (1997) '"Jūgun ianfu", "sengo hoshō" wa dou shūsei saretaka [How the accounts of "comfort women" and "compensation for war" were corrected]', *Shūkan kinyōbi*, 31 October: 28–9.

Teshigahara Katsuo (1986) 'Ijime to taibatsu ni miru gakkō seikatsu no sutoresu' [School stress as manifested in *ijime* and corporal punishment] *Gendai no esupuri* (no. 227): 50–65.

Tokutake Toshio (1995) *Kyōkasho no sengo* [Postwar history of textbooks], Tokyo, Shin nihon shuppan.

Toyoda Mitsuru (1995) 'Kyōshi wa muryoku na mama ka: kurikae-sareru ijime' [Are teachers powerless?: Repeated *ijime*], *Asahi Shinbun*, 11 January.

Tsuchiya Mamoru and Shūkan shōnen Jump hensūbu (1995) *Jump Ijime Report: 1800 tsū no kokoro no sakebi* [Jump Ijime Report: the cry of 1800 children], Tokyo, Shūeisha.

Tsukada Mamoru (1991) *Yobikō Life: A Study of the Legitimation Process of Social Stratification in Japan*, Berkeley, California, Institute of East Asian Studies, University of California.

Ujioka Mayumi (1997a) 'Anti-bullying Course Uncovers a Classroom Hell', *Asahi Newspaper E-News*, 16 March.

—— (1997b) 'Stepping out from the Endless Bullying Circle', *Asahi Newspaper E-News*, 23 March.

—— (1997c) 'Ijime kō: "koko de shika katarenu" 2000 tsū' [*Ijime* considered: 2000 voices 'which can be raised only here'], *Asahi shinbun*, 2 July.

—— (1997d) 'LIFE: Classroom Talk Unlocks Teen Frustration and Sympathy for the Devil', *Asahi Newspaper E-News*, 3 August.

—— (1997e) 'Jaws Drop at Memorial Service for Bullying Suicide Victim', *Asahi Newspaper E-News*, 31 August.

van Wolferen, Karel (1989) *The Enigma of Japanese Power*, London, Macmillan.

Vogel, Ezra (1979) *Japan as Number One*, Cambridge, MA, Harvard University Press.

Washida Kiyokazu (1997) 'Ikiba o ushinatta zankokusa' [Cruelty without any outlet], *Asahi shinbun*, 8 July.

Watanabe Takashi (1992) *Futōkō no kokoro* [The sentiment of school non-attendance], Tokyo, Kyōiku shiryō shuppankai.

Watanabe Osamu (1994) 'Kigyō shakai ga umidashita kyōiku no kyōsō kōzō' [The structure of educational competition brought about by the corporate society], *Shūkan kinyōbi*, 18 November: 34–7.

Welch, Anthony (1996) *Australian Education: Reform or Crisis?*, Sydney, Allen and Unwin.

Western Australia Ministry of Education (1988) 'Guidelines for School Discipline', Perth, Western Australia Ministry of Education.

White, Merry (1987) *The Japanese Educational Challenge*, New York, Free Press.

White, Merry (1993) *The Material Child: Coming of Age in Japan and America*, New York, Free Press.

Wills, Paul (1977) *Learning to Labour*, Farnborough, Saxon House.

Yamanaka Toshiko (1997) 'Kosei yutaka na fugōkaku kyōkasho ni manabou!' [Let's learn from the textbooks which flunked the censorship, because they are full of character!], *Shūkan kinyōbi*, 31 October: 26–7.

Yamauchi Kōji and Chōnabayashi Kaoru (1997) 'Kamen chūgakusei umu ii ko kyōsō' [Good child competition which creates students with masks], *Aera*, 28 July: 10–13.

Yamazumi Masami (1986) 'Educational Democracy versus State Control', in McCormack, G. and Sugimoto, Y. (eds) *Democracy in Contemporary Japan*, Sydney, Hale and Iremonger: 90–113.

—— (1989) 'Monbushō haishi sairon' [Recommending the idea of scrapping Monbushō], *Sekai* (May): 81–90.

Yokoyu Sonoko (1992) 'Kodomo no himei to kunō kara' [From the screams and suffering of children], in Saeki, Y., Shiomi, T. and Sato, M. (eds) *Gakkō no saisei o mezashite* [Aiming at the regeneration of school], Tokyo, Tokyo daigaku shuppan-kai: 1–49.

—— (1996) 'Iyashi to anshin no ba to shite no gakkō' [School as the place for healing and security], in Horio, T., Ohta, M. and Yokoyu, S. (eds) *Kodomo no iyashi to gakkō* [School and the healing of children], Kashiwa shobō: 38–71.

Yonezawa, N., Horiguchi, H. and Sasaki, R. (1998) 'School Welcome Party Munity [*sic*] not Welcomed by Authority', *Asahi Newspaper E-News*, 25 May.

Yoshioka Shinobu (1997) 'Miyazaki, Ohmu, Sakakibara, tsugino fuan' [Miyazaki, Aum, Sakakibara and the next anxiety], *Aera*, 11 August: 61–3.

Young, G., Brasic, J., Kisnadwala, H., and Leven, L. (1990) 'Strategies for Research on School Refusal and Related Nonattendance at School', in Chiland, C. and Young, G. (eds), *Why Children Reject School: Views from Seven Countries*, New Haven, CT, Yale University Press: 199–224.

Young, G., Chiland, C., and Kaplan, D. (1990) 'Children Rejecting School and Society Rejecting Children', in Chiland, C. and Young, G. (eds), *Why Children Reject School: Views from Seven Countries*, New Haven, CT, Yale University Press: 3–13.

Young, Michael (1971a) 'An Approach to the Study of Curricula as Socially Organized Knowledge', in Young, M. (ed.) *Knowledge and Control*, London, Collier Macmillan: 19–46.

Young, Michael (1971b) *Knowledge and Control*, London, Collier Macmillan.

Subject index

academic achievement 34, 42; achievement pressure 132–3; achievement pressure and brain fatigue 216–19

academic freedom 79, 80, 82–3, 109, 148; *see also* autonomy of education

academic (high) schools 37–8, 43, 49, 133–5; Australia (state high schools) 31; Japan (general academic high schools) 35, 38, 243

Ad Hoc Council on Education 11, 18, 109, 118, 180

Aichi prefecture 11, 65, 69, 72, 105–9, 118, 124, 158, 174; *ijime* suicide in 175

alienation 24, 42, 54–5, 115, 143, 152–4, 175, 212, 240, 246–7; de-alienation 239, 246; as the hidden curriculum 146–7; paradigm (teacher-student relationships) 61–90; and school knowledge 150, 245; *see also* education paradigms

All Japan Teachers League (*Zennikkyōren* or *Zenkoku nippon kyōshokuin renmei*) 108

alternative schools 13, 83, 188, 198–9, 208, 211, 213

America 7, 13, 18, 47–8, 61, 67, 139, 142; American occupation 150; 'head-start' programmes in 51; relationship between Japanese education and 20

apathy (syndrome) (*mukiryoku-shō*) 9, 19, 193, 200–2, 219, 223, 225, 248

Asahi shinbun 4, 13, 159, 211

Association of Hope (*Kibōkai*) 214

Australia: academic achievement pressure 133–7; bullying 164, 167; comparability between Australian and Japanese data 32–44; discipline issues 114–6; educational opportunity 49–50; educational paradigms 75–9; gender issues 42–4; general trends of education 83–5; as a reference point 29–32; school rules 129–32; typology of schools 36–9

automatons 9, 53, 246

autonomy of education: local 12, 79, 82; teachers' 164, 168; *see also* academic freedom

bamboo swords (*shinai*) 92, 101–2, 104

'banking education' 63, 86

behavioural problems 6, 115; correcting 93, 122, 129, 195, 200; *tōkōkyohi* as 201–11

Board of Education 69, 106–8, 158, 180; Chiba 108; Gifu 103, 107; Hyōgo 16; Kobe 16; Osaka 180; Yamanashi 98

Board of Education Law 81

Britain 13, 25, 36, 48; compensatory education in 51

bullying: aetiological issues 24–5; methodological issues 26–7; *see also* ijime

bunking off/wagging (*zuru-yasumi*) 190, 201, 209

buraku 35

burnout 27, 29, 215–22, 246, 249; *see*

also exhaustion, fatigue, *karōshi* and tiredness

Catholic schools 36, 38, 56
censorship 68–9, 96, 108, 122; of teachers' political inclination 106, 108; of textbooks 12, 83, 148–50
changelings (*oni-go*) 10, 248; ogres (*oni*) 248
Chiba prefecture 67, 69, 98, 105–9, 118, 180
Child Consultation Centres (*Jidō sōdan sho*) 111, 188
Child Welfare Law (*jidō fukushi hō*) 111
clubs (*bukatsu*) 11, 62, 96, 101–5, 107, 117, 124, 127, 138, 140, 169, 183, 193, 212, 229
collapse of classes (*gakkyū hōkai*) 14, 243
collectivism 170; collective order 64, 165; *see also* conformity, groups, peer-management
commercial (high) schools: *see* vocational (high) schools
competition: academic 6, 18–19, 21–3, 36, 42, 46–7, 52–3, 105, 136, 146–7, 151–3, 212, 236, 245, 249; 'good child -' 12, 151; 'loyalty to teachers -' 12, 151
compulsory education 2, 12, 29, 31, 187
conformity 108, 181; and control 124–6; *ijime* as over-conformity 166–9, 182; *ijime* as policing non-conformity 169–70; *see also* collectivism, groups, peer-management
consumerism 146–8, 150, 152
corporal punishment 2, 18, 23, 73, 89–90, 91, 94, 96, 101–3, 113, 196, 212, 237, 243, 245–6; abolition of 84, 91, 114–16; child protection and 115; Japanese teachers disciplined in relation to 97; peace studies and 115; similarities between *ijime* and 174; *see also* discipline
Course of Study 80, 82; *see also* New Course of Study
creativity 84, 147, 151, 244
crimes (by students) 1–8, 15–16, 129, 218–19, 242, 248; murder by students

11, 201–2, 240; *see also* knife attacks, 'school killer'
critical thinking/awareness 79, 83, 113, 211, 249; about Japan 238; about school 232–8; and physical 'punishment' 113; students' lack of 7, 14, 86, 146–7, 151, 233; suppression of 22, 64, 68–9, 113, 127, 146–8, 150, 245–6; teachers' lack of 75, 83, 104, 106, 113; *see also naishinsho*
curriculum 16, 37, 40–1, 46, 76, 80, 82–3, 139, 142, 147, 154, 245; hidden – 10, 54, 146, 148

dehumanising treatment of students 91–118, 153–4; survey results 87–9; lack of political power of teachers and 107; methodological difficulties 89–90; students' view 95, 99, 112; school rules and 123
delinquency (*hikō*) 5, 29, 111, 113, 124, 186, 191, 201, 240–1
democratic education 12, 72–5, 79, 81–3, 100, 109, 150, 249; in Australia 30, 76, 78, 83–5, 99, 132, 167; and *ijime* 168, 175
democracy 80, 82, 168, 247, 250
diaries 62, 69–70, 102–3, 126, 196
discipline 30, 64, 73, 91–118, 125, 131–2; Australia 62, 76, 116, 130–1; self-discipline 20, 85, 126; *tōkōkyohi* as lack of 201–11
dislike of school (*gakkō-girai*) 14, 17, 27, 187, 190, 201, 240–1
'double-school' phenomenon 139, 146; *see also juku*
drop-out (*chūtai*) 11, 25–6, 29, 35, 56, 68, 236, 239, 243; difference between *tōkōkyohi* and 29

economy, the: and education 19, 108, 147–50; corporatism 152
Education Centres (*kyōiku sentā*) 27, 188
education paradigms 30, 54, 91, 99–100, 116, 132, 147, 153, 240, 247; Australia: mixed 75–7; autocratic and democratic 72–4; end of a paradigm 244; functionalist theory of education 21, 55; Japan: autocratic – 73–5, 86; democratic – 79–81, 83; functionalist

– 18–23, 65, 75–7; *see also* alienation, and pedagogy
egalitarianism: in Japanese education 51, 54
elite schools 33, 49, 133–6; in Australia 30–1, 36–7, 42–3; in Japan (*shingakkō*) 31, 34–6, 38–40, 42, 47, 50, 66
examination: entrance 20, 46–7, 127, 138, 142, 144–5, 229; industry 47, 14; international tests 18–19, 141, 247; '- war' 22, 46, 52–3, 173, 233, 249
exhaustion 102, 186, 212, 216–19, 229; chronic 246; energy depletion 226, 229–30; over- 221; *see also* burnout, fatigue, *karōshi*, and tiredness
existence (students' sense of) 1–2, 8, 16, 71, 123–4, 129, 184, 214, 240, 248–9; invisible being (*tōmei na sonzai*) 2–4, 9, 16, 246; *see also* individuality, selfhood, subjectivity

fatigue (*tsukare*, *hirō*) 186, 212, 216; apathy and weariness 219; chronic 215–21, 224–5, 246; *see also* burnout, exhaustion, *karōshi*
flag and anthem (*Hinomaru/Kimigayo*) 12, 82–3, 106, 109, 118, 150; *see also* Monbushō, nationalism
freedom 64, 151, 199, 213, 235
Fudōjuku 93–4, 110–1, 201
Fundamental Law of Education (1947) 79–80, 109, 249
futōkō 26, 188–90, 210, 215, 217, 224; difference between *tōkōkyohi* and 189–90, 241; sentiment 219; *see also* school nonattendance, and *tōkōkyohi*

gaman (*suru*) (to endure, persevere) 11, 175, 189, 221, 246
ganbaru (to persist, do one's best) 51, 175, 217, 221–2, 246
gender issues 33, 39–44; in Australia 42–4; capitalism and patriarchy and 41–2; educational opportunity 40–3; in Japan 39–42; sex difference 42, 44, 256; wage differentiation 41
'good child' 5, 12, 27; model students 68, 218, 226, 228–9, 235, 239, 243; *see also* 'problem children'
groups: emphasis on 104–5, 194–5, 197;

group values 20, 22; groupism and authoritarianism 124–6; *han* 128, 132; *ijime* as group domination 157–9, 164–6, 169–72, 174; small-group management 125; *see also* collectivism, conformity, peer-management
guidance (*shidō*): 62, 64, 66, 69, 72, 92, 95–6, 101, 103, 111, 117, 122, 126, 201; by Monbushō 82; successful instruction 61; *see also* life guidance

hair regulations: students 11, 123–5, 169; teachers 123
heart (*kokoro*) 9, 71, 108, 204; heart-to-heart interaction between a teacher and a student 103; *ijime* as the cleansing in the 183; *kokoro-nai* 9, 246; patriotic love and 109; *see also* mind
hensachi 4, 46–7
Hinomaru/Kimigayo see flag and anthem
hokenshitsu (school clinic) 14, 71, 188, *hokenshitsu tōkō* 14, 266–8; *see also* nurse-teacher
Hokusēyoichi (school) 68
homeroom 11, 62, 181–2; homeroom teacher (*tannin*) 4, 62, 69, 92, 106, 121, 157–9, 167, 176, 196, 204, 206, 230
hospitals/clinics 92–4, 96, 112, 204, 206, 210, 214; doctor shopping 241; Kōnodai Hospital 205, 213; Kōsei Hospital 200, 212; mental clinics and hospitals 198–202; 212–13; National Urawa Nervous Sanatorium (Urawa *shinkei sanatoriumu*) 213; rules in mental hospitals 199–200; Tokyo Metropolitan Umegaoka Hospital 199; Tokyo University Hospital 242; violence in mental hospitals 199–200; Youth Health Centre (*sēshōnen kenkō sentā*) 193, 195
human rights (of children) 69, 96, 98–9, 101, 103, 109, 116–17, 121, 150, 174

Ienaga Cases/Ienaga Saburō 148, 150
ijime 4–5, 14, 18–19, 22–4, 72, 101, 154, 157–85, 212, 236, 245, 247; 'anti-*ijime* course' 162–4; authoritarianism and 175; 'cannot be eliminated' 163; in comparative perspectives 161–2; extortion of

money by 98, 158, 183; hidden
functions of 169–77; hidden nature of
162–4; individual motives 176–9;
individuality and 163, 170, 184;
involvement of teachers in 163;
manifestation of 24, 81–3;
methodological problems of 26,
162–4; official definition of 180;
problems in the official data 180;
reasons behind 171–3; silence
surrounding 162–4, 177–81; students'
discourse on 166; suicide 157–60,
175–6, 243; teachers' responses to
175–6, 178
ijime as: collective bullying 164–6;
'copycat' behaviour 166–8, 174;
'erasing' of individuality 169–70,
183–4; expression of powerlessness
181–3; fun 159, 182; over-conformity
166–9, 182; over-socialisation 166–9;
policing non-conformity 169–70;
shigoki 165, 170; stress coping mode
181–3
ijime jargon: *chikuru* 160, 179; *puroresu
gokko* 5, 160; *tsukaippa* 157, 159; others
160; *see also mukatsuku*
individuality 73, 123, 147, 151, 212–14,
232–40, 247–8; *ijime* as the 'erasing'
of 169–70, 183–4; *see also* existence,
selfhood, subjectivity
interactionist approach 19, 22

Japan: comparability between Japanese
and Australian data 32–44; gender
issues 39–42 super-meritocracy in
44–55; typology of schools 34–6;
Japan Parents and Teachers Association
National Conference (*Nihon PTA
zenkoku kyōgikai*) 189
Japanese education: English discourse
on 18–22; general trends of 79–83;
legitimation crisis in 186; major
events in 11; paradigm of 72–5;
'tripod' of 151; as a super-control
model 246; as super-meritocracy
44–55; as 'war education' 150
Japaneseness 12, 22, 52, 54; Japanese
who can say 'No' 234; *see also
Nihonjinron*
juku (cram school) 6, 46, 136, 138–9,

145, 225, 229; participation in 46,
139, 145, 154; *see also* 'double school'
phenomenon
junior colleges (*tandai/tanki daigaku*) 35,
40, 139
Junior High School: Higashita (Tokyo)
4, 162; Iki (Fukuoka) 98; Nakano
Fujimi (Tokyo) 157, 177; Narashino
Nanachû (Chiba) 98; Nishio
Municipal Tōbu (Aichi) 158–9;
Tomogaoka (Kobe) 1, 3, 5

Kangaerukai (Full name: *Tōkōkyohi o
kangaeru kinkyū shūkai jikkō iinkai*)
211–12, 215, 230
karōshi (death by overwork) 107, 216,
246; *see also* burnout, exhaustion,
fatigue
Kazenoko-gakuen 93–4, 110–12, 201
knife attacks 11, 14; stabbing 94, 161,
218–19, 243; *see also* crimes, 'school
killer'
Kobe 1, 3–7, 11, 16, 92, 128–9, 242,
247; 'Association to think about
human rights and health issues of
children in Kobe' 96; earthquake 12;
Kobe shinbun 1
Kodomotachi (Full name: *Tokyo Shure no
kodomotachi*) 222
Kokugo sakubun kenkyūjo (Institute for essay
writing in Japanese) 7; *see also*
Miyagawa Toshihiko

LDP (Liberal Democratic Party) 107–8;
education clique (*Bunkyōzoku*) 108, 118
life guidance (*seikatsu shidō*) 62, 64, 128,
204; *see also* guidance
love: of education 81; patriotic – 109;
teachers' – 101, 103, 185

manhood: father as a model of 197;
'father-image' 194; fatherland 109;
'make a man' 165, 204
manpower allocation 18, 21, 147–8
'Marutō' exercise 105
Marxist perspective 22, 55, 65
'mass-education society' (*taishū kyōiku
shakai*) 45–6, 48, 133, 202, 207, 244;
see also meritocracy
meritocracy 21–9, 33, 44–55, 133, 136,

146, 153, 244; as a belief system 47–9; as the central structure of Japanese education 44–6; 'ham-slice' selection (*wagiri sentaku*) 46, 52, 136; *Nihonjinron* and 48; outcomes of 53; phenomenology of 46–7; social class and 48; *see also* 'mass-education society'

methodology 29–44; data-collection 30–2; methodological problems regarding *tōkōkyohi* and *ijime* 26–9, 162–4; question of comparability 32–44; sampling 38–9, 252–5

militarism 79–80, 95, 104–5, 108, 165; militaristic cheer group (*ōendan*) 104

mind 7–9, 13, 21, 146, 148, 221, 230–1, 234, 238; 'bureaucratisation of mind' 53, 246; a 'counselling mind' 16; education for the mind (*kokoro no kyōiku*) 16; power-docile 170–7; reinforced homogeneity in the mind 21; *see also* heart

Ministry of: Education, Science, Sports and Culture (Monbushō) 12; Finance 140; Foreign Affairs 140; Health and Welfare 111, 189; Justice 101, 174; Labour 41, 48; Transport 140

modernisation theory 18

Monbushō (Ministry of Education, Science, Sports and Culture): agenda of 12, 82, 109, 147–8, 244, 246; campaign to heighten motivation to study by 244; changes in the postwar era 79–83; control by 81, 168; educational reforms by 139, 151; *ijime* and 158, 161, 179–80; Kobe murder and 16; model prefectures (Aichi, Chiba and Gifu) 107–8; LDP and 108; surveys by 14, 46, 101, 175, 180, 191, 208; Nikkyōso and 11, 12, 51, 82–3, 107; screening of teachers and 106; *tōkōkyohi* and 187, 191, 201, 208, 223–4, 241; *see also* flag and anthem, nationalism, New Course of Study, textbooks

morals 9, 21, 62, 249; moral education 12, 109, 145, 150

mothers: care of children by 20; of *tōkōkyohi* children 194

motivation to study 11, 29, 127, 243

mukatsuku (annoying/irritating) 160, 170–2, 174, 182; *see also ijime* jargon

naishinsho (confidential reports) 126, 178, 198

National Centre for Neuropsychiatry (*Kokuritsu seishin shinkei sentā*) 189

National League of Teachers' Union 81

nationalism 109, 151–2; nationalistic education 79, 83, 113, 118, 147–8, 150, 154, 246; nationalistic values 12, 22, 82; *kamikaze* pilots 109; *shūshin* 150; ultra-nationalism 80, 105; *see also* flag and anthem, and Monbushō

New Course of Study (*Shin gakushū shidō yōryō*) 10–13, 127, 150; *see also* Course of Study, Monbushō

'new' sociologists of education 55

New View of Ability (*Shin-gakuryoku-kan*) 151, 244

Nihonjinron 19, 48, 65; Japanese education and 20, 22; *see also* Japaneseness

Nikkyōso (Japan Teachers' Union) 11–12, 81–3, 105; in Aichi and Chiba 107; egalitarianism and 51; 'normalisation' of 107; and *Zennikkyōren* 108; *see also* National League of Teachers' Union

normal (*futsū*)/abnormal 3, 6, 28, 92, 95, 99, 107, 112, 122, 128, 181, 201–2, 214, 236–9; ordinary 10, 248

normative consensus 21–2

nurse-teacher 159, 185, 226; *see also hokenshitsu*

'objectivist' knowledge 52, 143–4

orderliness 18, 61–2, 247

paternalism 65, 101, 103, 245

peace education 109; as opposed to 'war education' 150; peace studies 115

pedagogy: teacher-centred (autocratic) 61–75, 142–4, 146, 245; *see also* alienation, education paradigms

peer-management 125–6, 170; position of 'school discipline' (*fūki iin*) 125; peer surveillance 245; *see also* groups, conformity

physical education (*taiiku*) 95, 118;

teachers' violence to students and
101–5, 108
point-evaluation system (*kantenbetsu
hyōka*) 151, 244
police-school cooperation 106, 202;
Blue Sky Movement (*aoi sora undō*)
106; School-Police Contact
Association (*gakkō keisatsu renraku
kyōgikai*) 107
politicians 106; students' perceptions of
13
positivism 22, 142, 144, 146, 148–9, 245
powerlessness: among students 114, 170,
181; among teachers 100, 159, 166,
175; *ijime* as the manifestation of 24,
81–3
prefectures: Fukuoka 97; Gifu 11, 107;
Hiroshima 11, 93; Nagano 13,
Saitama 82; Yamanashi 98; *see also*
Aichi, Chiba
Primary School Law (1890) 112
principals 2–3, 31, 61, 68–9, 75, 81–2,
84, 90–1, 96, 104–7, 110–11, 122,
158–9, 164, 174, 176, 178–9, 188,
196, 227, 243, 249
private schools: in Australia 30–1, 36–7,
39, 42, 44, 76–8, 129–30, 134,
136–7; in Japan 34, 36, 57
'problem children/students/kids' 10,
68, 94, 106–7, 111, 159, 201, 243;
identifying 124; 'no-problem' students
151; *see also* 'good child'
Professional Teachers' Association (*Puro-
kyōshi no kai*) 65
program-driven (students) 9, 53, 246
psychiatrists 2, 162, 165, 190, 193–8,
200–1, 210–11, 213–14, 222, 224
punishment *see* discipline

Recruit Scandal 118
'Red Purge' 81
reformatories/detention homes 3,
111–12, 201–2
regimentation 24, 68–9, 153, 165–6,
168, 174–5; Aichi and Chiba as the
'Mecca' of 105–9; as a counter *ijime*
measure 159; minute-by-minute
instructions 108, 202; school rules as
the web of 119–32, 212; *see also*
discipline

returnee children (*kikokushijo*): *ijime*
against 169
'reverse-course' (*gyaku kōsu*) 81, 90, 150,
249
'rock-bottom' schools (*tēhenkō*) 29, 36
rōnin 53, 138

Sakakibara *see* 'school killer'
schools: 'are dying' 242; as a battle
ground 173, 248; as a life-threatening
place 220–1, 245; as a place
demanding performance 173; as
prison 86, 182; as a 'tiring' place
(*tsukareru tokoro*) 5, 246; revenge on
schools 2–4, 129
school clinics; see *hokenshitsu*
'school faith' (*gakkō shinkō*) 202, 204, 207,
239; erosion of 219 244
school gate (*kōmon*) 1–2, 16, 69, 92–3,
95–6, 102, 104, 128–9, 158, 173, 188
'school killer' 1–17, 53, 124, 129, 242,
246, 247–8; empathy with 3–4; *see also*
crimes, knife attacks
school knowledge 54, 142–54, 245–6;
alienating nature of 150; as
commodity 145–6; as examination
knowledge 144–5; for manpower
allocation 147; meaninglessness of
study 152–3; pedagogy and 142–4,
146; standardisation of 150; state
control of 148–50, *see also* textbooks
school nonattendance 27–9; *see also*
tōkōkyohi, futōkō
school phobia (*gakkō-kyōfu*) 14, 18, 24,
26–8, 190, 193, 195–6
school refusal 24–8, 90, 193, 240–1; *see
also tōkōkyohi*
school rules 6, 23, 119–32, 212;
Australian students' view on 129–32;
hidden function of 123–4; inspection
127–8; non-negotiable nature of
12–3; ; nonsensical nature of 120–3;
trusting students and 122
'school society' (*gakkō shakai*) 26, 212,
215; 'schooling society' (*gakkōka shakai*)
202, 247
school-to-work transition 139–41
school type: inter-group comparisons
133–7, 153, 259–60; typology 33–9;

see also elite schools, academic schools, vocational schools

school uniforms 36, 119, 121, 123–4, 129–30, 182, 204, 206, 236

school work 133–54; difficulty in 141–2, 147; meaninglessness of 142–3

seiza (to sit or 'kneel' erect on one's knees on the floor or ground) 92, 95–6, 98, 102, 107, 160, 174, 243

self-discipline 20, 85, 126

self-expression 69, 86, 147, 233, 244

selfhood 224, 232–40, 242, 247, 249; negation of 123; sense of 8, 53, 154; *see also* existence, individuality, subjectivity

selfishness (*wagamama*) 121, 127, 170, 194, 201, 208, 226, 232, 236

Senior High School: Fukaya (Saitama) 243; Gifu Giyō 92, 95; Kobe Takatsuka 92, 95; Nada 6; Nakatsu Commercial (Gifu) 102, 128; Surugadai (Tokyo) 171; Tōgō (Aichi) 105, 108; Tokorozawa (Saitama) 82–3

senior high schools: admission to 12, 46–7, 49, 126–7

senior-junior relationships 62, 65, 101; bullying by senior students 169

separation anxiety 27–8, 193

shijimachi ningen see automaton

Shōnen Jump Ijime Report 167, 169–71, 184

silence 3, 23–6, 56, 113–14, 214, 245; breaking 86–7; pedagogy, school knowledge and 144; structure of 55, 104; students maintaining 22, 85–7, 162–4; surrounding *ijime* 162–4, 177–81; textbook screening and 148–50

sleep and rest 13, 146, 196, 203–4, 207, 216–19, 221–2, 224, 227, 229–31, 246; *futon* 203–4, 220

social class 49, 51, 53, 133; Japan as classless society 48–9, 51, 53

socialisation 20–1, 99, 132, 148; *ijime* as over-socialisation 166–9

socioeconomic backgrounds of students 33, 35, 37, 48–51, 57

Spartan methods 11, 93–5, 110, 212

state control: of prescribed knowledge 148; of sensitivity 149; of thought 148–9

stress: among students 4, 30, 55, 171, 197, 200, 205–6, 229, 236, 245; among teachers 131; *ijime* as a stress-coping mode 181–3

student association 11, 82, 99, 125, 158, 174, 229; and labour union 108

student–teacher relationships: autocratic and democratic paradigm 72–5; competing paradigms in Australia 75–9; dominant view and theoretical issues on 61–90; emotional connection 62, 64, 66, 70; experiences of reification in 77–8; *ijime* and 179; jokes, humour and laughter 78–9; loyalty to teachers 12, 151; negatively affecting both students and teachers 14–15; paternalism (*onjō-shugi*) 64–5, 72; students' perceptions of 66–72; teachers' love 101, 103, 185; two dimensions of 87–90

students: aggressive 7; as alien 9–10, 246; being locked up 93, 199, 202, 212–3; as children 99–100; compliant 19; as consumers 146–7; diligent 19; docile/obedient 7, 53, 64, 99, 123, 146; orderliness in behaviour 18; passive 64, 143, 202, 233; and 'salaryman' 53; utilitarianism and pragmatism among 146

students' feelings: to die 218; to eat 95, 138; to have some time off 138; to hit teachers 113; to kill someone 5, 13, 208, 218, 230; to leave home 208; to live like a human being 95; to sleep 13, 204, 227; *see also* suicide

subjectivity 8, 143, 184, 214, 224, 232–40, 246–9; *botsu-shutai* (devoid of subjectivity) 9, 246; *jibun rashisa* (sense of being at one with oneself) 231; 'unable to be myself' 226; *see also* existence, individuality, selfhood

subjects (of study): English 144–5; mathematics 11, 138, 141, 144–5, 244, 247; social studies (*shakaika*) 150

suicide 10–11, 24, 87, 102, 157–60, 162, 168, 171, 174–6, 179, 182, 184,

186, 204, 206, 208–9, 218, 229, 240, 243, 247

symptoms 28, 184, 186, 189–91, 203, 209–10, 216, 222–4, 227–31, 246; anorexia 205; anxiety 16, 28, 87, 173, 190–1, 217, 220–1, 223–4, 231, 241, 248; autonomic dystonia (*jiritsu-shinkei-shicchō-shō*) 209; breathing difficulty 186; depression 186, 203, 221, 229; dizziness 186, 208, 224, 229; headache 186, 203, 206, 208–19, 215, 228–30; inability in getting up in the morning 203–4, 206, 215; nausea 186, 214–15, 229; orthostatic ataxia (*kiritsusei shicchōshō*) 203; other symptoms 215–6; stomach-ache 186, 208–9, 215, 228–30; vomiting 209; *see also* fatigue, sleep and rest

taboo 16, 51

teachers: enthusiastic (*nesshinna*) 5–6, 96, 102, 196; benevolent 61; breakdown among 14–15; disciplinary measures against 158, 168; kind 67, 92; labour management issue 12, 107; obedience/docility to authority 83, 106; powerlessness felt by 159, 166; promotion of 104; '*sensei*' and '*kyōshi*' 101; sentenced 92–4; sick leave 14

teacher–teacher relationships: subordination to the senior 74–5, 83; surveillance by supervisors 83; Teacher Evaluation System (*kinmu hyōtei*) 81

teacher training (*kenshū*) 158, 178

textbooks 181, 218, 245, 249; censorship 12, information control in 54; screening and control 81–3, 108–9, 148–50; *see also* Monbushō, school knowledge

tiredness 217, 219, 224–7; school as a 'tiring' place (*tsukareru tokoro*) 5, 246; *see also* burnout, fatigue, exhaustion

tōkōkyohi 11, 14, 17–19, 22–4, 26, 67, 72, 87, 93–4, 107, 110–13, 123, 154, 184, 186–241; among primary school children 241; definition and categorisation of 27–9; 190–2; discovery of subjectivity 232–40;

family factor 194–5; *futōkō* and 189–90; impact of psychiatric discourse upon children 198–201; 'is not an illness' 211–2; methodological problems 26; official statistics 187–8; overfatigue of the memory function 216–20; panic and avoidance response 216–20; parents' experiences of 203–7; process of 223–38; 'reserve army' of 188–90; students' view on the behavioural discourse on 208–11; and *shusshakyohi* (refusing to go to work) 247; *Tōkōkyohi as Discussed by Children* 90, 198; *tōkōkyohi* syndrome 190, 193; *see also* school nonattendance, truancy

tōkōkyohi as: behavioural problem 201–11; de-alienation 239; defence mechanism 214, 220–1; laziness 201–11, 219–20; mental illness 193–201; a paradigm shift 207, 238; a social movement 215, 240; school burnout 215–22; social maladjustment 193–201

tōkōkyohi, discourse on: adult 190–222, 224; behavioural 201–11; classification of the adult 190–2; psychiatric 193–201, 211; socio-medical 215–22; student 222–40

Tokyo Shure 188, 198, 208, 211, 213–14, 222, 226, 229, 248

totalitarianism 105, 112; and *ijime* 174

Totsuka Yacht School 11, 94–5, 110–11, 201

truancy (*taigaku*) 25–6, 28–9, 190, 201, 208–9, 240–1; difference between *tōkōkyohi* and 28–9

university: aspiration to go to 34–9; ranking of 46

University: Hitotsubashi 193; Hōsei 242; Kumamoto 215; Takushoku 109; Tokyo 6, 35–6, 94, 140; Tsukuba 213

victim-blaming 198, 212

violence: by students 14, 19, 94, 117, 160–1, 170, 178, 185, 199, 230–1, 243, 145; by male nurses 199; by teachers; 67, 91–118 (*passim*), 174, 209, 245; *see also* crime, discipline, knife attacks

vocational (high) schools 33, 134–5; commercial schools 31, 38, 41, 102–3, 116, 128; in Japan 35–6, 38, 41; state technical schools in Australia 31, 38, 43–4

yobikō 138, 144–5
youth unemployment 56, 115
yutori no jikan 139, 154

Name index

General

Akamatsu Ryōko (Education Minister 1993–4) 132
Akita Sumiko 195
Amano Ikuo 100
Araki Sumishi 16
Asakura Kageki 248

Befu Harumi 20
Bowles, S. and Gintis, H. 63

Cummings, William 61–2

Duke, Benjamin 13
Durkheim, Emile 21

Endō Toyokichi 180

Feinberg, Walter 20–1
Freire, Paulo 63–4
Fujii Seiji 113

Hirayama Katsumi 174
Horio Teruhisa 18, 79–82, 148–50
Hsia, Heidi 27

Imahashi Morikatsu 181
Inamura Hiroshi 193–5, 200, 211, 213, 241
Ishikawa Norihiko 165, 242

Kado Shin'ichirō 200
Kariya Takehiko 45–9, 51–5
Kawai Hayao 162, 183
Kim Ch'an-jong 35, 56

Kobayashi Tsuyoshi 165, 174
Kohama Itsuo 66
Koizumi Eiji 27

LeTendre, Gerald 62
Lock, Margaret 194, 198

Miike Teruhisa and Tomoda Akemi 215–22, 225, 241
Mimori Tsukuru 9
Miyadai Shinji 4
Miyagawa Toshihiko 7–8, 184
Mizusato Seiga 13
Morita Akio and Ishihara Shintarō 241
Morita Yōji 188–90, 219–20, 224, 241
Mouer, Ross and Sugimoto Yoshio 19
Murakami Ryū 13
Muta Takeo 199

Nakajima Katsuyo 226–7
Nakane Chie 65
Nakasone Yasuhiro (Prime Minister 1982–7) 11, 109

Okano Kaori 35, 57, 140–1
Ogi Naoki 4, 242, 249
Okonogi Keigo 197
Okuchi Keiko 67, 174, 188, 205, 212–4
Olweus, Dan 174

Parsons, Talcott 21

Rigby, Ken 167
Rohlen, Thomas 61–2, 99, 145

Satō Manabu 13, 243
Satō Taizō 199
Shimizu Yoshinori 145

Takaishi Kunio 107, 118
Takayama Yōji 150
Takeuchi Yō 45–9, 51–5
Tōgō Heihachirō, Admiral 150
Tomonaga Shin'ichirō 148–9

Uchida Ryōko 200, 212
Ujioka Mayumi 4, 162–4

Wakabayashi Minoru 212
Washida Kiyokazu 16
Watanabe Takashi 205, 213
White, Merry 61–2

Students, parents and teachers

Adams 225
Aoki Fusako 238
Arinaga Shinji 233–4
Asō Nobuko 168

Baba Sumiko 207

Danieru Harumuzu 230

Echizen Takehisa 217

Fukuda Hiroyuki 162–5, 176
Fukuhara Yōichirō 62, 86,128
Fukukawa Akika 202, 227

Hanaoka Shinji 242
Hashimoto Yukiko 230–1
Hayashida Akane 221
Hayashida Soeyuki 235
Hisatomi Masako 203
Honma Tami 198

Inaizumi Ren 171–2
Ishida Ryōko 11, 92, 96, 128–9
Ishii Izuko 205
Ishiwari Minako 186, 228–9, 233, 237, 240

J.N. 237

Kameyama Masami 74
Kanbe Tomoko 226
Kanewaki Tokuji 110–11
Kawai Hidekazu 174
Kitani Kentarō 112
Kobi Yoshie 206
Kubota Gen 171
Kurita Takako 182, 220

Matsushita Kazuyuki 118
Miura Tomoko 217
Miyamoto Akiko and Sakura 210–11

Nakajima Junko 96
Nakajima Ryū 234–5
Nakamura Naomi 71

Ogura Masahiro 235, 240
Ohkōchi Kiyoteru 11, 157–60, 162, 166–7, 176, 179, 184
Okuchi Shigeo 204–5
Oouchi Taeko 231

Sabashi Haruna 235, 240
Senda Yōko 233
Serurian 234, 240
Sezoko Masatomo 225
Shikagawa Hirofumi 11, 157–60, 166, 168, 176–7, 180
Shimada Erika 71, 73, 236
Shimane Jun 133
Shiotani Norio 238
Suzuki Akira 208, 231–2

Tatara Hiroshi 91
T.I. 228
Tosaka Yumi 110
Toyosato Tetsu 209–11
Tsuneno Yūjirō 209–11

Uchida Yōko 236–7

Yamada Tadataka 238
Yamaguchi Kayo 237, 240
Yoshimoto Yukio 242

Watanabe Madoka 232